SCHLEIERMACHER ON
WORKINGS OF THE KNOWING MIND

New Athenaeum/Neues Athenaeum (NANA) is an interdisciplinary journal devoted to the scholarly exploration of the life and thought of Friedrich Schleiermacher as well as to discussions of nineteenth-century European religion and culture.

Subscription Information: Subscription price: scholar softcover $29.95 (acid-free paper) per issue; Institutional hardcover $49.95 (acid-free paper, library cloth) per issue. To subscribe, write Order Fulfillment, The Edwin Mellen Press, PO Box 450, Lewiston, NY 14092-0450. To order by phone: (716) 754-2788; e-mail: mellen@ag.net. To inquire about advertising, call John Rupnow, Journals Division Manager, (716) 754-2266.

Instructions for Contributors: *New Athenaeum/Neues Athenaeum* is a bilingual journal that publishes articles both in English and in German. Articles written in other languages may be submitted as long as camera-ready copy of the original language is included along with either an English or a German language translation. Articles in this publication are juried. Manuscripts may follow either MLA or Chicago style with endnotes, not footnotes, and a bibliography of works cited. Inclusive language is required for English language articles. Since manuscripts are printed by a computer system, authors are requested to finalize their submissions on computers, if possible, utilizing software compatible with IBM. Microsoft Word and WordPerfect are the preferred systems. Articles should be double-spaced throughout and should be submitted in duplicate with SASE. Both printouts/copies must be clear, sharp, and dark, with a minimum of corrections. We are willing to include black-and-white line drawings or photographs if the author will provide glossies for the latter and secure required permissions. Please send your articles to: Dr. Edwina Lawler, *New Athenaeum/Neues Athenaeum*, Dept. of German, Drew University, Madison, NJ 07940.

Acknowledgements:
   Many thanks to Walter de Gruyter for their permission to translate F.D.E. Schleiermacher, "Rezension von Immanuel Kant: Anthropologie," *Schriften aus der Berliner Zeit, 1796-1799*, ed. Günter Meckenstock, Vol. I/2 of *Kritische Gesamtausgabe*, ed. Hans-Joachim Birkner et al. (Berlin/New York: Walter de Gruyter, 1984), 365-369; F.D.E. Schleiermacher, "Notizen zu Kant: Kritik der praktischen Vernunft," *Jugendschriften 1787-1796*, ed. Günter Meckenstock, Vol. I/1 of *Kritische Gesamtausgabe*, ed. Hans-Joachim Birkner et al. (Berlin/New York: Walter de Gruyter, 1984), 129-134; F.D.E. Schleiermacher, "Notiz zur Erkenntnis der Freiheit," *Jugendschriften 1787-1796*, ed. Günter Meckenstock, Vol. I/1 of *Kritische Gesamtausgabe*, ed. Hans-Joachim Birkner et al. (Berlin/New York: Walter de Gruyter, 1984), 215.
   Italian translations of the articles by Hoffmeyer, Klemm, and Tice have been published in *La dialettica nella cultura romantica*, ed. Sergio Sorrentino & Terrence N. Tice (Rome: La Nuova Italia Scientifica, 1996). Our thanks to La Nuova Italia Scientifica for their permission for us to publish the original English language articles here.

SCHLEIERMACHER ON
WORKINGS OF THE KNOWING MIND
New Translations, Resources, and Understandings

Edited by

Ruth Drucilla Richardson

A Publication of *New Athenaeum/Neues Athenaeum*
Volume 5

The Edwin Mellen Press
Lewiston•Queenston•Lampeter

B
3097
.S34
1998

Library of Congress Cataloging-in-Publication Data

This book has been registered with the Library of Congress.

ISBN 0-7734-8507-4

This is volume 5 in the continuing series
New Athenaeum/Neues Athenaeum
Volume 5 ISBN 0-7734-8507-4
NANA ISSN 1048-8545

A CIP catalog record for this book is available from the British Library.

The Edwin Mellen Press   The Edwin Mellen Press
Box 450   Box 67
Lewiston, New York   Queenston, Ontario
USA 14092-0450   CANADA L0S 1L0

The Edwin Mellen Press, Ltd.
Lampeter, Ceredigion, Wales
UNITED KINGDOM SA48 8LT

Printed in the United States of America

TABLE OF CONTENTS

Texts and Translations

Articles

In memory of our beloved colleague

Ernst Behler
(1928-1997)

A CRITICAL-INTERPRETIVE ANALYSIS OF SOME
EARLY WRITINGS BY SCHLEIERMACHER ON
KANT'S VIEWS OF HUMAN NATURE AND FREEDOM
(1789-1799),
WITH TRANSLATED TEXTS

Jacqueline Mariña

I. Schleiermacher's Review of Immanuel Kant's
Anthropology From a Pragmatic Point of View[1]
(1799)

Introduction

This review of Kant's *Anthropology* appeared anonymously in 1799, in the
second volume of *Athenaeum*, a journal edited by August Wilhelm Schlegel
and Friedrich Schlegel. The first edition of Kant's *Anthropology* was itself
published in 1798; Schleiermacher mentioned his review of it in his letter of
June 19, 1799, to Henriette Herz, in which he informed her that he had finished producing a clean draft of it on that day. By the time Schleiermacher
wrote the review, Kant's influence on his thinking had lessened considerably.
This was partially the result of the appearance of Kant's *Metaphysics of
Morals* in 1797, a work that had greatly disappointed Schleiermacher. More
importantly, Schleiermacher's friendship with Friedrich Schlegel had involved him with early Romantic concerns and began to move his thinking in
new directions.
The review is written in a somewhat ironic and sarcastic tone. Its frequent playful allusions to Kant's *Anthropology* make it difficult to understand,
especially when the particular passages that Schleiermacher has in mind
(supplied here in the footnotes) are not taken into consideration. Adding to
its difficulty is the fact that the review focuses on a significant issue in Kant's

1. Immanuel Kant's *Anthropologie in pragmatischer Hinsicht* appeared in Königsberg, in
    1798. Schleiermacher's essay appeared in *Athenaeum. Eine Zeitschrift von August Wil-
    helm Schlegel und Friedrich Schlegel*, Bd. 2, Zweites Stück (Berlin: Heinrich Frölich,
    1799). The text used is Friedrich Schleiermacher, *Schriften aus der Berliner Zeit 1796-
    1799*, ed. Günter Meckenstock, Kritische Gesamtausgabe I/2, ed. Hans-Joachim Birkner
    et al. (Berlin/New York: Walter de Gruyter, 1984), 365-369). I would like to thank
    Manfred Kühn, Terrence Tice, and Edwina Lawler for checking the translation and for
    helpful suggestions.

philosophy, which is here rather loosely and playfully dealt with: the problem created by Kant's distinction between a transcendental standpoint (corresponding to freedom), and an empirical one (corresponding to determinism). The former accords with the agent's view of human action: when we act, we consider ourselves as adopting ends and acting on principles that we ourselves freely chose. The latter standpoint, on the other hand, accords with the spectator's point of view. Insofar as the spectator understands the other's actions as occurring within the empirical world, these must be understood as governed by causal laws. The spectator thereby assesses the subject's actions in terms of their causal antecedents; as such, the subject is understood as passively affected by sensibility.

Respectively, these two viewpoints correspond to that of the practical anthropologist and that of the physiologist. It is Schleiermacher's contention that the preface to Kant's anthropology, in which Kant discusses the differences between an anthropology from a physiological point of view and one from a pragmatic point of view, contains the most significant claim in the whole book. To proceed pragmatically, according to Kant, is to concern oneself with what one "makes, or can and should make" of oneself. On the other hand, an anthropology from a physiological point of view investigates how *nature* determines the individual. Schleiermacher emphasizes the impossibility of affirming both points of view, one of which presupposes freedom, and the other of which presupposes determinism. The antithesis between pragmatic and physiological anthropology "makes both impossible." Nevertheless, Schleiermacher neglects Kant's remark that it is impossible to relate both the mechanism of nature and freedom to the individual at one and the same time; it is only if conceived as a noumenon, and thus from a transcendental standpoint, that one can assert that a person is free. On the other hand, only when regarded from an empirical point of view must a person be understood as determined.[2]

In the review, Schleiermacher suggests that Kant affirms *only* that "all nature in human beings is free choice," that is, because a person is free, one is what one makes of oneself. He goes on to tell us that it is well known that for Kant the "I" has no nature. He has Kant's transcendental I in mind here.

---

2. In the *Critique of Practical Reason,* Kant notes: "The union of causality as freedom with causality as the mechanism of nature, the first being given through the moral law and the latter through natural law, and both as related to the same subject, man, is impossible unless man is conceived by pure consciousness as a being in itself in relation to the former, but by empirical reason as appearance in relation to the latter. Otherwise the self contradiction of reason is unavoidable." *Critique of Practical Reason,* trans. by Lewis White Beck (New York: Macmillan Publishing, 1993), 6; Academy edition pagination: p. 6.

If by "nature" Schleiermacher means given characteristics through which the I can be affected in accordance with certain laws, he is correct in affirming that the I can have none, since it is simply the formal unity of apperception and can never be an object of intuition. It is for this reason that Kant had denied that there can be a rational psychology, one that treats the human soul independently of experience. Yet, in focusing on Kant's pure apperception, Schleiermacher ignores Kant's recognition of the legitimacy of the empirical point of view: when one considers the individual as an appearance, causal laws do apply, and one can speak of certain characteristic ways in which an individual can be affected.

Nevertheless, in his review Schleiermacher puts his finger on a potentially serious problem: if we are to proceed in accordance with a pragmatic point of view, and hence are to assume that the individual is a freely acting cause, one not as such determined in the order of causes, how can we speak of that which helps or hinders a mental faculty? Kant admits in his preface that so long as the observations respecting that which hinders or stimulates a faculty such as memory are used practically, i.e., in order to help expand it, they belong in a pragmatic anthropology. Yet, Schleiermacher asks, if we speak about that which *affects* the mind, have we not leapt over to the empirical realm, and begun to consider the mind as an appearance? In pointing to this possible inconsistency Schleiermacher has gotten to a central difficulty plaguing all anthropology: how much should be considered nature in human beings, and how much freedom? It does seem that any useful anthropology undertaken from a pragmatic point of view cannot afford to ignore nature all together, since however much one may want to affirm freedom in Kant's transcendental sense, one must still recognize that such freedom is limited by the possibilities of the human body. Yet, once these considerations are brought in as well, we begin to consider the individual as both free and determined. We thereby no longer keep the two points of view *separate*, which is what allowed us to consider the person in the two ways without contradiction. In this way, Schleiermacher reasoned, an anthropology becomes impossible.

Yet Schleiermacher affirms that "anthropology should be the unification of the two," namely of nature and free choice. No viable anthropology can afford to ignore either. It is unclear what exactly Schleiermacher has in mind when he tells us that "the physiological and the pragmatic are one and the same, only in different respects," since he does not develop the thought here. Presumably Schleiermacher is already unsatisfied with Kant's division between the empirical and the transcendental self; several of his early essays, in particular *On Freedom* (1790-1792) already contained significant critiques of

Kant in this and other respects. And in his later *Outline of a Critique of Previous Ethical Theories*, (1803) he would contend that Kant had failed to identify the "common seed" out of which both our receptivity and spontaneity arise. As a result Kant could not provide an account of how transcendental freedom and the moral law related to human embodiment.

Yet, however much Schleiermacher wanted to find a common point allowing us to relate the transcendental self to the empirical self, he was not a determinist. This we can see from his critical remarks on the old psychology. According to this psychology, what seems to us to be our freely chosen actions can be fully explained in accordance with the mechanism of nature. Schleiermacher's criticism of this view, which he mentions only in passing here, is interesting and worth analyzing at length. If all our judgments concerning the mind are themselves determined in accordance with causal processes, there is no guarantee that they are true. For let us suppose that a causal process is responsible for some affirmation or another that we make about the mind. In accordance with the idea that all freedom is at the same time nature, whatever attempt we may make to judge the truth or falsity of that affirmation will also be causally determined. Insofar as the judgment is *causally* determined, it is not determined by mind's rational ability to judge a statement as true just in case the statement agrees with the facts of the matter at hand, but is rather determined by causal processes lying outside our reason itself. Schleiermacher brings to the fore the full irony of the determinist's position: if determinism is in fact true, one cannot really claim to *know* that it is, and hence cannot guarantee one's claim. One's affirmation was not a judgment freely made, constrained only by the facts of the matter at hand, but was, instead, the inevitable outcome of mechanistic processes.

The latter part of the review criticizes Kant's attempt to be at once systematic and popular. Schleiermacher claims that Kant's adoption of a traditional framework (so that his anthropology might be accessible to the common person) prevents him from offering the reader his own observations on the human mind. Because Kant's own observations cannot easily be integrated with such a traditional framework, the subdivisions that are ordered in accordance with it do not contain material relevant to them but are, instead, filled at best with entertaining trivia.

Text

An abstract of this book that would go into its details could be almost nothing but a collection of trivia. Should such an abstract scrupulously follow an outline of the book's design and composition to the letter, it would have to appear as a clear portrayal of the most peculiar confusion.[3] This state of affairs sufficiently explains the general silence (as far as I know) of scholarly publications to date: for abstracts, set off in a dainty frame of not too well worn phrases, have long been the sole practicable crutch of embarrassed reviewers, as well as of editors embarrassed for lack of their help.

Should some, however, also have had the good will not only to repeat something from the book, but also to say something about it, these have another likewise well-grounded excuse for their silence. It is peculiar that most readers and critics, however little they also might chance to know about thoroughness, nevertheless have a certain pedantic admiration for a book's title, especially if it points to scholarly content. Yet, even when considered from this point of view, there is, to be sure, not much to say about this book either. Those who see it as an anthropology – in fact as a pragmatic one in the sense indicated by Kant[4] – and as a consequence are intent on expanding their knowledge through new or newly put together observations, and who expect a generous revelation from the treasure of a philosophical life largely spent in introspection – must find the writing insignificant. For they who know nothing more or more thoroughly about what persons as freely acting beings make of themselves, or can and should make (of themselves), than what one finds sketched here, cannot even be mediocre knowers of themselves. It would be awkward to want to prove this, until someone who expressly denies it is found.

None of this, however, is the correct standpoint from which the work must be considered. Indeed, one must often start out with the assumption that a book that has little worth when one takes it for what it professes itself

---

3. A more literal translation of the sentence would read: Should such an abstract contain an outline of the books design and composition, however, of necessity it would have to appear, under a pen that anxiously sticks to the letter, as a clear portrayal of the most peculiar confusion.

4. In the *Anthropology* Kant remarks: "A systematic treatise comprising our knowledge of man (anthropology) can adopt either a *physiological* or a *pragmatic* point of view. – Physiological knowledge of man investigates what *nature* makes of him: pragmatic, what *man* as a free agent makes, or can and should make, of himself." Immanuel Kant, *Anthropology from a Pragmatic Point of View*, translated, with Introduction and Notes, by Mary J. Gregor (The Hague: Martinus Nijhoff, 1974), 3. Pagination from Volume VII of the Berlin Academy Edition will henceforth be provided in brackets, here: [119]. All quotations from the *Anthropology* that follow are from Gregor's translation.

to be, can be of significance when one takes it for its opposite, or as something else. And in this light the book appears to be excellent, not as anthropology, but rather as the negation of all anthropology. It is at once claim and
proof that something like this, intentionally set up in the same way Kant often expressly sets forth and specially constructs empty subjects in his division
of the sciences or of their objects,[5] is impossible in accordance with the idea
set forth by Kant, whether it be carried out by him or in terms of his line of
thinking.

Anyone who reads the preface with care (which in this respect contains
the main claim), and compares it with the work, will be easily convinced that
such could have been the opinion of this worthy man alone. The antithesis
between physiological and pragmatic anthropology, grounded in Kant's way
of thinking and quite originally set up here, makes both impossible. Indeed,
at the root of this division lie two correct but opposing claims: all free choice[6]
in human beings is nature, and all nature in human beings is free choice.
However, anthropology should be just the unification of the two, and can exist only through their unification; the physiological and the pragmatic are one
and the same, only directed differently. The old psychology, which thank
God is no longer at issue now, abstracted from the latter of these two propositions, and could therefore not answer the question of how it is then possible
to reflect on the mind, if in this reflection there is no freedom, and hence no
guarantee of its truth. Kant wants to ignore the first proposition, since, as is
well known, the "I" has no nature for him. This gives rise to the question:
Where do the "observations about what hinders or promotes a mental faculty"[7] come from, and how are these observations to be used for the mind's
expansion, if there are no physical ways to consider and treat this expansion
in terms of the idea that all free choice is at the same time nature? To make
this all the more striking, everything that is to be found here about these observations stands there, paltry and completely alone, almost intentionally, so
that one might suspect nothing from such an idea, robbed as it is completely
of all that represents it, as well as of all that relates to it, not only internally
and concerning that which falls under the idea, but also in relation to the ti-

5.   Kant believed that under the guidance of philosophy anthropology could achieve a certain
      systematic form. The human faculties are classified overall into those of cognition, feel-
      ing, and appetite. This is supposed to provide the anthropologist with a complete list of
      headings into which more detailed divisions of the faculties, as well as observations as to
      how these powers are used and misused, can be fitted.
6.   *Willkühr.* The word Schleiermacher uses for "freedom" is *Freiheit.*
7.   Cf. Kant: "But when we use our observations about what has been found to hinder or
      stimulate memory in order to increase its scope of efficiency, and need knowledge of man
      for this purpose, this is part of anthropology for *pragmatic* purposes; and that is precisely
      what concerns us here." Ibid., 3; [VII, 119].

tles, under which the particular is subsumed. Art is interwoven with nature's death verdict, and never can there have been a book that would be less of a work than this one.

No one will marvel at the misunderstanding of this antithesis, united here in an anthropology, in virtue of which Kant throughout refers nature to the corporeal, to the body, and to the mysterious relation of the mind to it. Rather, one sees here more than before how that which appears to be but a pure deification of free choice is at bottom quite closely related to a hidden realism, to which Kant still pays secret and idolatrous homage after he himself had overturned and demolished it. Without doubt, in order to make quite clear this disdain for theoretical brooding over what influence the body has on the mind,[8] and to express this quite distinctly in deed, he makes the practical influence of the mind upon the body his special goal whenever possible.[9] In this way anthropology is then completely alienated from its natural tendency to be ascetic, in the highest sense of the word (a goal that must be somehow achieved in every real treatment of it), and, to the contrary, in a very meager sense, becomes "dietary".[10] In this charming circle Kant really comes back to the physiological, from which one can patently see that *what was at issue for him* was simply to make a contradiction graphic. That rest after work and the joys of a good table always recur as important moments without being noticed, and that affects and much else that comes to the mind are properly treated as means of digestion, must be explained in this way and in no other.[11] One would obviously do wrong to take this otherwise and indeed as more characteristic.

Likewise Kant required two things of an anthropology with respect to its form, the unification of which he also simply wanted to show was impossible: namely, that it should be at one and the same time systematic and popular (luckily, a word whose meaning he himself gave at this point).[12] Here what is

---

8. Cf. Kant: "If we ponder natural causes – for example, the possible natural causes behind the power of memory – we can speculate to and fro (as Descartes did) about traces, remaining in the brain, of impressions left by sensations we have experienced. But since we do not know the cerebral nerves and fibers or understand how to use them for our purposes, we still have to admit that we are mere spectators at this play of our ideas and let nature have its way. So theoretical speculation on the subject is a sheer waste of time." Ibid., 3 [VII, 119].

9. For instance, Kant interprets becoming pale and becoming flushed as the effects of different kinds of violent anger. Ibid., 126; [VII, 260].

10. Presumably, a play on words on Kant's preoccupation with a healthy "diet" for the mind, that is, with mental hygiene. Ibid., 78; [VII, 207].

11. Kant devotes a whole section to affects, such as laughing, weeping, and anger, which he discusses as aids to digestion. Ibid., 129; [VII, 262].

12. Cf. Kant: "If an anthropology written from a pragmatic point of view is systematically formulated and yet popular (because it uses examples every reader can find), it has this

systematic has been ruined by striving for what is popular, and out of an innate tendency toward what is systematic, only the empty space where the popular could be placed remains in its stead. By the ruin of what is systematic I do not mean that immediately obvious confusion as to details mentioned already. Indeed, no principle of division is carried through, the subdivisions run amazingly helter skelter, the headings and their contents often have nothing to do with each other – an arrangement by which nothing so much strikes the attentive reader as a title that noticeably appears a couple of times: "Random Remarks." These problems could easily be remedied through a revision turning the book inside out, through a few additions and several omissions of oft repeated remarks (which are superfluous even when said just once). Nevertheless it would still have nothing of the systematic in it, since it lacks a disposition for this at its very core, and as it were, it has been ripped out with force.

In order to provide the common consciousness the opportunity to put in its particular observations, neither science nor its object could be understood and presented in a peculiar way, in accordance with some original impression[13] lying at its basis, or some other inner principle, but rather only traditionally. But precisely because this deeper thinking and farther seeing author understands the mind from another perspective, and separates its different modes of action otherwise, so that his divisions do not at all agree with this traditional framework and thus his observations also cannot be integrated with it, he had to withdraw most of these observations from us, often leaving the framework standing completely empty out of ill humor, in order to entertain himself and us with completely other things. Through this reciprocal destruction he irrevocably proved that it is impossible to reflect on the particulars that are found in inner experience if one does not somehow begin the business at a higher level. In this respect, one can call the book "the newborn's cry" of this kind of philosophy, which feels its "impotence as a fetter, through which its freedom is taken" in virtue of the double demand made of it.[14] Yet, just as in the case of a physical exertion, the form of the muscles

---

advantage for the reading public: that it gives an exhaustive account of the headings under which we can bring the practical human qualities we observe, and each heading provides an occasion and invitation for the reader to add his own remarks on the subject, so as to put it in the appropriate division. In this way the devotees of anthropology find its labors naturally divided among them, while the unity of its plan gradually unites these labors into a whole – an arrangement that promotes and accelerates the development of this generally useful science." Ibid., 5; [VII, 122].

13. *Ursprünglichen Anshauung*.
14. Cf. Kant: "The cry of a newborn child is not a note of distress, but one of indignation and raging anger: he is screaming not from pain but from vexation, presumably because he

and the limit of the different extremities come to light more strongly the more nearly it approaches the limits of physical strength, so too in the case of this effort (expressly undertaken with such an intention) the form of the mind and the limitation of its individual parts was presented in manifold ways more exactly than otherwise. Right at the outset, I have made some remarks about it having to do with philosophy; much that points to personality lies even more on the surface. The contemptuous admiration of wit, of which Kant himself nonetheless has so much, and particularly of a kind that has incomparably more worth than that which he here calls a "very difficult wit"[15] – only that he has largely rid himself of it here – the hatred of puns,[16] when nevertheless his etymologies and a good part of his technical language, in particular in his later writings, turn upon mannered wordplays, the complete lack of knowledge of art, and especially of poetry, the treatment of the female as a deviation of the male, and thoroughly as a means,[17] the description of peoples, which smacks much of the joys at table, this and much else are contributions to a Kantology, one which one could further elaborate both physiologically and pragmatically – a plan of study that we would want to have recommended highly to the blind admirers of this great man.

---

wants to move about and his impotence feels to him like fetters restricting his freedom." Ibid., 188; [VII, 328].

15. *Zentnerschweren Witz.* Cf. with Kant: "This sort of wit, which uses contrast to make what is contemptible even more contemptible, is very stimulating because it surprises us with the unexpected. But it is facile wit (like Voltaire's), and never more than *play*. On the other hand, a man who asserts true and important principles in the dress of wit (like Young in his satires) can be called a very difficult wit [*zentner schwerer Witz*], because his wit is a *serious business* and gives rise to more admiration than amusement." Ibid., 91; [VII, 222].

16. Cf. Kant: "Hunting for *witty sayings (bon mots)* – as the Abbot Trublet did, and put wit on the rack to make a lavish display of them – makes for a shallow mind, or eventually disgusts a man of profound mind. . . . Wit in playing with words is *insipid."* Ibid., 90; [VII, 221].

17. See Kant's discussion "On the Character of the Sexes," where, among other things, Kant remarks that "as culture advances, each party must be superior in his own particular way: the man must be superior to the woman by his physical strength and courage; the woman to the man, by her natural talent for gaining mastery over his desire for her." Ibid., 167; [VII, 303].

II. Schleiermacher's Notes[18] on Kant's
Critique of Practical Reason[19]
(Probably from 1789)

Introduction

While the original manuscript is itself without title or date, the notes on Kant's *Critique of Practical Reason* were in all probability written in the first half of 1789. That the *Notes* are Schleiermacher's preparatory work for the *Dialogues on Freedom* (1789) on Kant's second *Critique* is evidenced by the close parallels between the contents of the *Notes* and those of the third of the *Dialogues*. While Schleiermacher's *On the Highest Good* (1789) was written in that same year and also deals with Kant's *Critique of Practical Reason*, it is likely that the *Notes* were written nearer in time to the *Dialogues* than to *On the Highest Good* (1789), since this latter essay deals with topics distinct from those treated in the *Notes* and in the third of the *Dialogues*.

The *Notes* are concerned with specific passages of the first half of Kant's *Critique of Practical Reason* and are devoted to issues of freedom; as such they are important in understanding the overall development of Schleiermacher's thought, both in regard to Christian ethics as well as in regard to the issue of the relation of God to the world. The main question explored in the *Notes* is Kant's question of how pure reason can be practical; in particular, Schleiermacher focuses upon the issue of how the moral law can be an incentive to sensuously conditioned beings such as ourselves. The problem, as Schleiermacher sees it, is how to close the gap between freedom – according to Kant a necessary condition of an unconditioned practical law – and desire.

In his first set of comments to p. 16, Schleiermacher assesses Kant's understanding of what it means for the faculty of desire to be empirically determined. Here pleasure is what *marks* an object as being worthy of desire. Schleiermacher later acutely notes that there is something wrong in thinking that it is pleasure itself, and not the realization of a desired *object*, that is the goal of nonmoral motivation. The two remarks are related, for if pleasure is that which marks an object as worthy of desire, then the pleasure gotten from

---

18. These notes were published in Friedrich Schleiermacher, *Jugendschriften 1787-1796*, ed. Günter Meckenstock, Kritische Gesamtausgabe I/1, ed. Hans-Joachim Birkner et al. (Berlin/New York: Walter de Gruyter, 1984), 129-134. I would like to thank Manfred Kühn, Terrence Tice, and Edwina Lawler for checking the translation and for some helpful suggestions.
19. Immanuel Kant's *Kritik der praktischen Vernunft* appeared in 1788.

the realization of the object, and not the object itself, is the ultimate goal of action that is nonmorally motivated.

Schleiermacher, however, believes that this critique of Kant's hedonistic theory of nonmoral motivation is going to accomplish more than in fact it does. At this point he is still in agreement with Kant that the supreme principle of practical philosophy cannot be empirically grounded. Yet he is dissatisfied with Kant's answer to the question of how a rational principle concerning the logical form of maxims can be an incentive to the will. Wherein does the *worth* of such a judgment of pure reason lie? Is not the question of a worth one that has to do with value, one that therefore concerns the subject and his or her attitudes and feelings? How can the rational principle itself be the *ground* of the absolute worth that the moral subject must assign to it? According to Kant, it must itself be such a ground, since we cannot rely on a moral sense, grounded in the *subject's* constitution, in order to answer the question. Yet in his *Lectures on Ethics,* which Kant gave from 1775 to 1780 while he was still in the process of working out his critical ethics, Kant noted the intractability of the problem: "The understanding, obviously, can judge, but to give to this judgment of the understanding a compelling force, to make it an incentive that can move the will to perform the action – this is the philosopher's stone."[20]

The *Notes* show Schleiermacher trying to work out a solution to the problem. He suggests the following: separate the ethical principle of discrimination through which an act is judged as morally right or wrong (what Kant had called the *principium diiudicationis*) from the ground of motivation, or what Kant had called the *principium executionis* of an action. The latter is closely related to the determination of the faculty of desire. Schleiermacher believes that we can still consider pleasure the ground of the determination of the faculty of desire, without this resulting in an empirically grounded principle of discrimination, so long as we do not understand by the determination of the faculty of desire the giving of rules for the will. But this is precisely what Kant does, that is, he closely links the determination of the faculty of desire with the giving of rules for the will. Schleiermacher, however, does not consider him justified in doing so: he complains that Kant has not shown that the two are either analytically or synthetically combined. It is here that Schleiermacher's analysis of the inadequacy of Kant's theory of nonmoral motivation comes in. According to Schleiermacher, Kant could only have shown that the two were synthetically combined on the presupposition that "the feeling, which is necessary in order to set the faculty of desire in motion

---

20. Immanuel Kant, *Lectures on Ethics,* trans. by Louis Infield (Indianapolis: Hackett Publishing Company, 1963), 45.

is also the only possible end to which the desire itself could be directed." But Schleiermacher reasons that if the feeling of pleasure is not the end to which an empirically given desire is directed, then feeling can motivate without at the same time determining the rules of action for the will. The Kantian analysis of the lower faculty of desire and its relation to heteronomous actions is as follows: an object is desired because its realization will bring pleasure. Reason figures out the means for the realization of the object. However, because it is desire that marks out the object to be realized in the first place, desire is the ground of the rule for the will; reason is only instrumental in providing the rule through which the object of desire can be achieved. Schleiermacher reasons that if pleasure is not the final goal of nonmoral action, the lower faculty of desire cannot be the ground of any rules for the will, and Kant's linkage between the principle of execution and that of discrimination is effectively dissolved.

What, in fact, has Schleiermacher really accomplished here? He severs the Kantian link between pleasure and the object of desire – the object is not desired in virtue of the pleasure it will bring, but rather, it is because it is desired that its realization brings satisfaction. Kant had the cart before the horse. But the question then remains: in virtue of *what* is the object desired? Once Schleiermacher makes the move he does he is faced with the problem of providing an account of how an *object* of desire relates to the emotional character of the agent, that is, of how it is that the object of desire comes to be desired. Ultimately Schleiermacher's argument is terribly confused, since his final purpose had been, in fact, to solve the problem of how the moral law can motivate by grounding the incentive to it in feeling or moral sense. On such a theory, the worth that the moral law has for us is linked to the satisfaction that is associated with acting on it, on the one hand, and the pangs of conscience linked with failing to live up to it, on the other. Yet, in arguing in the way that he did, Schleiermacher cut off the very limb of the tree on which he was sitting. If not for this satisfaction, on what other grounds could the moral law represent something of worth?

On the other hand, it can be argued that Kant's argument linking kinds of incentive for action with kinds of principles (empirical or rational) can survive Schleiermacher's onslaught virtually unscathed, since all Kant really needs to argue is that all nonmorally motivated action is grounded in causes lying outside the will. Such action is grounded in an agent's feelings, themselves determined causally in the spatio-temporal continuum. Because feelings have to do with the subject's receptivity, i.e., have to do with the subject insofar as the subject is in the body and exists in a *particular* spatio-temporal location, they cannot be the ground of universally valid rules. This is the significance of Kant's contention that the moral law cannot be empirically grounded. Even, then, if it is *not* the desire for pleasure which is the end of nonmoral action, the nonmoral ends that a person sets for herself are grounded empirically i.e., in the order of causes. It is possible that Schleiermacher was unable to appreciate the full depth of Kant's thinking here, since he concentrates so much on pleasure logically and empirically preceding a desire. For Schleiermacher, it would seem, to ground practical principles empirically means only to ground them on past experience – a way of taking Kant that does not fully appreciate the deep structure of the split between the empirical and transcendental and its significance for this issue.

The *Lectures on Ethics*, which represent Kant's semi-critical stance, embody a position very similar to the one that Schleiermacher advocates, i.e., one according to which the principle of discrimination is provided by reason, while moral motivation is supplied by feeling, in this case, the desire for happiness. As Kant later recognized, however, the two are inextricably tied. If the principle of moral discrimination is one that is provided to us by reason alone, considerations respecting happiness – or for that matter any empirically determined desires – can play no role in its derivation. But this in turn means that if this rational ethical principle is to mean anything to us, it cannot be in virtue of any considerations concerning our empirically determined desires, and this includes any moral sense grounded in our constitution. If the moral law is of worth to us, it must be because we are transcendentally free.

A different, but related topic is broached by Schleiermacher in the paragraphs which follow the heading "Moral Feeling." Schleiermacher discusses Kant's understanding of respect for the moral law, and asks whether the nature of the moral incentive has really been clarified here at all. How does this moral incentive relate to feeling – to the pathologically determinable self? Schleiermacher correctly notes that the relation of the moral law to the empirically determined desires is only a negative one, i.e., the moral law checks selfishness and strikes down self-conceit. This is, however, the *effect* that the moral law has on me when I recognize its absolute worth; it does not explain how I recognize such an absolute worth in the moral law to begin with. The explanation of how practical reason occasions an effect on feeling is left just as mysterious as before, and no real explanation is given as to how we can understand the genesis of a feeling *a priori.*

Schleiermacher is no doubt right in most of what he says here. Kant only provides us with an a priori account of what kind of effect the moral law has on the pathologically determined feelings, and provides no positive account of the positive feeling elements produced by the moral law. Yet, Kant himself had recognized that "how a law in itself can be the direct motive of the will (which is the essence of morality) is an insoluble problem for the human reason. It is identical with the problem of how a free will is possible"[21] Schleiermacher had hinted to his own solution of the problem earlier, where he had spoken of a "feeling of pleasure, which itself relates to the law and its function without any qualification." Significantly enough, Schleiermacher speaks of this precondition being "given to us in pure self-consciousness."

Text

p. 4

Transcendental freedom: Apparently a *power* of causality having no necessary connection with what precedes.[22] Thus, I have certainly not misunderstood him.

p. 10

On the one hand. In that Kant does not present this objection as a misunderstanding here, he proves to me that I understood him, but is it still not always wrong that if I can also apply the category of freedom to myself as a noumenon (which may neither be denied nor affirmed) I may on that account apply it to my actions? On the other hand: This is not my objection, but I gladly admit it. I would, however, like to know what more definite concept of freedom Kant has put forward so as to make it more plausible.[23]

---

21. *Critique of Practical Reason*, trans. by Louis White Beck (New York: Macmillan Publishing Co., 1993), 75. Pagination from volume V of the Berlin Academy Edition will henceforth be provided in brackets, here: [72]. All following quotations from the second *Critique* are taken from Beck's translation.

22. Cf. with the following: "With the pure practical faculty of reason, the reality of transcendental freedom is also confirmed. Indeed, it is substantiated in the absolute sense needed by speculative reason in its use of the concept of causality, for this freedom is required if reason is to rescue itself from the antinomy in which it is inevitably entangled when attempting to think the unconditioned in a causal series. For speculative reason, the concept of freedom was problematic but not impossible; that is to say, speculative reason could think of freedom without contradiction, but it could not assure any objective reality to it. Reason showed freedom to be conceivable only in order that its supposed impossibility might not endanger reason's very being and plunge it into an abyss of skepticism." Ibid., 3; [V,3].

23. "In this way I can understand why the most weighty criticisms of the *Critique* which have come to my attention turn about these two points: first, the reality of the categories as

p. 13

The concept of freedom (transcendental) of speculative reason is indispensable only for an otherworldly subject.[24]

p. 16

The faculty of desire: Pleasure. Indisputably, Kant has done here what he wanted to avoid, namely subjected pleasure to the determination of the faculty of desire, for if one says "the same" instead of "for the same" in accordance with his definition, pleasure means: the idea of the agreement of an object with the faculty of desire.[25] This can mean nothing other than the idea that the object belongs among those that are desired; pleasure is therefore the characteristic of desirable objects, and this means 1) pleasure logically precedes desire, for its presence is at first the very feature through which I recognize the applicability of the idea of desire to an object. 2) Pleasure empirically precedes desire, for before I can explicitly desire something, I must previously have recognized in it its mark, namely, desirability. It is also not possible in any other way: there is a subjective character of the representable, namely, consciousness; there must also be a subjective character of the desirable, namely pleasure. Only this is wrong if one afterwards attributes determinations to this expression that do not apply to the concept in its greatest generality.

---

applied to noumena, which is denied in theoretical knowledge but affirmed in practical; and, second, the paradoxical demand to regard one's self, as subject to freedom, as noumenon, and yet from the point of view of nature to think of one's self as a phenomenon in one's own empirical consciousness." Ibid., 6; [V, 6].

24. "This reminder pre-eminently concerns the concept of freedom, for it is surprising that so many boast of being able to understand it and to explain its possibility, yet see it only psychologically. But if they had carefully pondered it from a transcendental standpoint, they would have seen its indispensability as a problematic concept in the complete use of speculative reason as well as its complete incomprehensibility; and if they subsequently passed over to the practical use of this concept, they would have been brought to the same description of it in respect to its principles which they are now so unwilling to acknowledge." Ibid., 7-8; [V, 7].

25. "*Life* is the faculty of a being by which it acts according to the laws of the faculty of desire. The *faculty of desire* is the faculty such a being has of causing, through its ideas, the reality of the objects of these ideas. *Pleasure* is the idea of the agreement of an object or an action with the *subjective* conditions of life, i.e., with the faculty through which an idea causes the reality of its object (or the direction of the energies of a subject to such an action as will produce the object)." Ibid., 9-10; [V, 9].

p. 16

To what degree is it established that the principle of practical philosophy necessarily must turn out to be empirical, that is, dependent upon experience, if the feeling of pleasure is absolutely[26] made basic to the determination of the faculty of desire?[27] This proposition is true if one understands by the determination of the faculty of desire the legislation of the will. Whoever claims that no rules can be given for the will, except in relation to a certain feeling of pleasure, in order thereby to attain it, has a merely empirical practical philosophy whose imperatives are all merely hypothetical. However, if this proposition means so much as: the faculty of desire cannot be *de facto* otherwise determined to some act or other, except through a preceding feeling of pleasure, this has no influence upon the principle itself. The reason is that 1) the content of the principle is not changed in any way, because the independence of reason, in virtue of which reason need not presuppose anything except itself in order to find the principle, is in no way superseded; 2) the form of the principle, or its sanction through the idea of obligation, is not destroyed but rather made easier, in that now nothing further belongs to it except the precondition that there be a feeling of pleasure, which itself relates to the law and its function without any qualification, and this precondition is given to us in pure self-consciousness.

Thus Kant has probably either confused the two meanings of the expression "made basic to the determination of the faculty of desire," or has taken them to stand in necessary connection. In both cases he is wrong; they are clearly not identical, and they could be synthetically connected only under the presupposition that the feeling, which is necessary in order to set the faculty of desire in motion, is also the only possible end to which the desire itself could be directed. This proposition, however, neither has axiomatic worth, nor has it been proven in any way, but it has become so general because one always speaks of the realization of the object of desire in the definition of the faculty of desire. This is why one then always imagines that which is desired only as a means (because the existence of an object can never be the real

---

26. *Schlechthin.*
27. "One could also raise the objection that I have not previously explained the concept of the faculty of desire or the feeling of pleasure. This reproach would be unfair, however, because this explanation, as given in psychology, could reasonably be presupposed. But then the definition given in psychology might be so framed that the feeling of pleasure would be made basic to the determination of the faculty of desire (as this is commonly done); and, as a result, the supreme principle of practical philosophy would necessarily [*notwendig*] turn out to be empirical, a conclusion which would have to be proved first and which is, in fact completely refuted in this *Critique.*" Ibid., 9; [V, 9].

end, but only the impression) and a preconceived end as the actual object that would then, to be sure, have to be the feeling of pleasure. This, however, cannot possibly be the case here, because the feeling of pleasure in the rule is not at all heightened by the act, but on the contrary, either ceases or passes over to another object once the act has occurred.

pp. 130-132 Moral Feeling

Kant seems to have felt the inadequacy of the deduction in the previous paragraph, particularly in that no incentive emerges in this manner. Now, what is going on here in order to improve the foregoing? 1) The word "self-conceit"[28] acquires another meaning in that it now means the propensity towards self-love taken as legislative and as an unconditioned practical principle instead of as the excessive satisfaction with oneself (namely, the pathologically determinable self). Now self-conceit is a feeling underlying a maxim and is therefore certainly an incentive; however, nothing is thereby improved in the deduction. Only a negative feeling originates directly from the relation of practical reason to self-conceit,[29] and if one says everything that one possibly can about an inhibition of the causality of a pathologically driven feeling (I like that at this point the term "humiliation" is still used for it: when people humiliate someone, they inhibit the person's causality through the impression of self-contempt) it is still, however, not an incentive. (2) In order also to bring the positive part closer to the appearance of an incentive, a new determination is also added here: namely, the idea, which is the cause of that humiliation, awakens respect insofar as it is a ground of the determination of the will.[30] On the one hand, given the altered definition of self-conceit, it was no longer necessary to add this; for because this is now a maxim, it cannot be brought down through anything other than another maxim. On the other hand, nothing is thereby improved so long as we have no other definition of respect than that it is the representation of some worth.[31]

---

28. "This propensity to make the subjective motives of one's choice into an objective motive of the will in general can be called self-love; when it makes itself legislative and an unconditioned practical principle, it can be called self-conceit." Ibid., 77; [V, 74].

29. "The moral law, which alone is truly, i.e., in every respect, objective, completely excludes the influence of self-love from the highest practical principle and forever checks self-conceit, which decrees the subjective conditions of our self-love as laws. If anything checks our self-conceit in our own judgment, it humiliates." Ibid., 77; [V, 4].

30. "Now if the idea of something as the motive of the will humiliates us in our self-consciousness, it awakens respect for itself so far as it is a positive motive. The moral law, therefore, is even subjectively a cause of respect." Ibid., 78; [V, 74].

31. The definition cannot be found in Kant. Schleiermacher seems to be relying on Schmid's *Wörterbuch zum leichtem Gebrauch der Kantischen Schriften*, 2. A., (Jena, 1788), 23.

Kant also wants to make still clearer how one can understand the genesis of a feeling a priori.[32] But it seems to me that he did not achieve this either, for even if I understand that practical reason must occasion an effect on feeling, all that I can understand by this "a priori" (and in this way too the adequacy of the expression could still be debated) is first only an indirect effect in that certain ideas, which would otherwise encourage the feeling, are destroyed; second, only negative in that what was otherwise present in feeling through those ideas is annulled; third, no particular distinct feeling, for such a feeling cannot at all be thought of as the cause of that annulment even in accordance with Kantian principles, and as a consequence of the same it cannot be understood, at least not a priori. How the positive can be understood a priori is still as empty as before, as is the claim that this feeling distinguishes itself from all others.

p. 133

Some new claims. (1) The negative effect on feeling is pathological.[33] (2) In relation to the subject of practical reason (that probably means in relation to the person as noumenon?), with respect to the negative effect, this feeling is called humiliation.[34] However, I do not understand at all how the term humiliation comes to express a relation to something intelligible; it contains nothing but a designation of the new condition of the pathologically determinable self or of self-conceit. Here he again wanted to take with one hand what he had had to give with the other, namely the avowal that the feeling is pathological. 3) The same feeling is called respect for the law in

---

32. "Now everything in self-love belongs to inclination, and all inclination rests on feelings; therefore, whatever checks all inclinations in self-love necessarily has, by that fact, an influence on feeling. Thus we conceive how it is possible to understand a priori that the moral law can exercise an effect on feeling, since it blocks the inclinations and propensity to make them the supreme practical condition (i.e., self-love) in the enunciation of supreme law. This effect is on the one side merely negative; but on the other, in respect to the restrictive practical ground of pure practical reason, it is positive. And to the latter, no kind of feeling, [even] under the name of practical or moral feeling, may be assumed as prior to the moral law and as its basis." *Critique of Practical Reason*, 78; [V, 74-75].

33. "The negative effect on feeling (unpleasantness) is, like all influence on feeling and every feeling itself, pathological." Ibid., 78; [V, 75].

34. "As the effect of the consciousness of the moral law, and consequently in relation to an intelligible cause, i.e., to the subject of the pure practical reason as the supreme legislator, this feeling of a rational subject affected with inclinations is called humiliation (intellectual contempt)." Ibid., 78; [V, 75]. Schleiermacher confuses the feeling attending consciousness of the moral law with practical reason; Kant distinguishes practical reason sharply from feeling.

relation to the positive ground of humiliation, that is, the law.[35] Because this positive feeling had not yet been properly proved, he now wishes to identify it with the other. However, this is impossible. Is that feeling, which stems from a destruction of my self-estimation, identical with the idea of a worth, which is its cause? The positive cause is indeed nothing but a maxim, which however may be entirely negative and not represent any new worth to me. The positive view of the moral law (in virtue of which it represents a new worth to us) is completely distinct from the negative one, and the latter alone cannot create any feeling that relates to the former; in this latter alone, however, did I discern an a priori feeling. 4) It is not a feeling for the law (à la Hutcheson).[36] However, in the explanation of what it then amounts to in its relation to the law, a direct causality of the latter is presupposed.

---

35. "But in relation to its positive ground, the law, it [humiliation] is at the same time respect for the law; for this law there is no feeling, but, as it removes resistance, this dislodgment of an obstacle is, in the judgment of reason, equally esteemed as a positive assistance to its causality. Therefore, this feeling can also be called a feeling of respect for the moral law; on both grounds, it can be called moral feeling." Ibid., 78; [V, 75].
36. The Scottish empirical philosopher Francis Hutcheson (1694-1746) had introduced his moral philosophy in his 1725 *Inquiry into the Original of our Ideas of Beauty and Virtue*, later much revised and translated into German as *Untersuchung unserer Begriffe von Schönheit und Tugend*, 1762. Hutcheson held that apart from the five sense used to perceive physical objects there are several "internal" senses such as those involved in perceiving honor, sympathy, the ridiculous, beauty, and morality. Thus, judgments attached to morality are not based on reason alone; in fact, for Hutcheson it is the "moral sense" that basically motivates people to benevolence and against what hinders benevolence, and this sense represents desires with respect to our own and other's pleasure. Schleiermacher's teacher, Johann August Eberhard (1739-1809) mediated the British "moral sense" tradition into German philosophy.

III. Schleiermacher's Note on
The Knowledge of Freedom[37]
(1790-1792)

Introduction

The original manuscript of this piece is undated and untitled. However, in terms of its content, the *Note on the Knowledge of Freedom* is closely tied to Schleiermacher's *On Freedom* (1790-1792); the considerations that Schleiermacher brings forth here exactly parallel the three sections of the fourth part of that essay.[38] That the *Note* is a preliminary study for this larger work is an important piece of evidence for our ability to date it correctly; it must have been written shortly before or during his writing of the larger work. Given the differences of *On Freedom* from the extant third of his *Dialogues on Freedom* (1789), both in style and in content, this piece was most likely written between 1790 and 1792.

In this piece, Schleiermacher explores the different kinds of circumstances to which the concept of freedom can legitimately be applied. He begins by defining freedom in terms of the absence of law – by "law" he means a determinate regularity in accordance with which events must take place. He notes that the concept of freedom has application in three distinct areas summed up in the last sentence. The first area has to do with how the subject relates to *the outer conditions* in which the subject is situated and concerns the ways in which it is possible for the subject to exercise powers and realize objectives given these conditions. The second is the sphere of the *inner person* having to do with the "functions of the subject," i.e., a person's intellectual and psychological profile. Questions regarding the possibility or impossibility of certain actions given a person's character are what is at stake here. The third area refers to *the individual characteristics of actions* themselves and only indirectly refers to the subjects of these actions.

---

37. Manfred Kühn, Terrence Tice, and Edwina Lawler checked the translation and provided some helpful suggestions.
38. See editor Günter Meckenstock's introduction in Friedrich Schleiermacher, *Jugendschriften 1787-1796*, ed. Günter Meckenstock, Kritische Gesamtausgabe I/1, ed. Hans-Joachim Birkner et al. (Berlin/New York: Walter de Gruyter, 1984), LIII-IV. This is a translation of the text included there on p. 215. See also Albert Blackwell's introduction to his translation of the 1790-1792 essay *On Freedom* (Lewiston/Queenston/Lampeter: Edwin Mellen, 1992), i-xli, especially xvii, and Victor Froese's postscript to his translation of the 1789 essay *On the Highest Good* (Lewiston/Queenston/Lampeter: Edwin Mellen, 1992), 57-130, especially 124-125.

Text

Now, in this classification it again depends on how one achieves the knowledge of freedom. Assuming that in this connection one must always begin with the law, the absence of which is claimed for free actions, this law can be either [1] a law of the activity of the subject and thus relates (a) partly to a situation of the subject − that is, to the external conditions, standing under certain rules, of the possibility of certain acts by the subject, to those relations of the subject to other things, through which the degree and direction in the expression of certain powers of the subject are limited or promoted in accordance with a rule − and (b) partly to a faculty of the subject, to the rule of the internal condition of the possibility of certain actions insofar as they are based on functions of the subject. In both these cases one cannot remain with the individual character of actions in order to achieve application of the idea of freedom to the case at issue, rather, in order to come to know the law one must ascend to the concept referring to the kind of actions. Therefore, in these instances, one relates the concept of freedom directly to the situation and the faculty of the subject in which the kind of actions is grounded, and one transfers it only indirectly to the single individual actions insofar as they belong to the circumstances or the faculty.

Or [2] the law, whose absence is predicated, is of a kind that does not refer to any general determination of the subject of free action, but is known only through one or another concept or relation of action, insofar as it is viewed from the side extrinsic to the subject. Thus, in order to come to know this law, and through this knowledge to apply the idea of freedom, I must examine the individual character of the action, and not simply the concept of its kind, which is posited through the subject's realization of the action; that is why, in this case, freedom is directly referred only to the actions, and is transferred only indirectly to the subject insofar as the actions, with all their characteristics, belong to the subject. Hence, we have to deal with a threefold relation of our concept: namely, of freedom as a predicate of human actions, of freedom as a predicate of human situations, and of freedom as a predicate of human faculties.

ON COLOSSIANS 1:15-20
(1832)

F.D.E. Schleiermacher

Translated by Esther D. Reed and Alan Braley
with an introduction by Esther D. Reed[1]

First published in 1832,[2] Schleiermacher's "On Colossians 1:15-20" was a
well-received article that Friedrich Lücke described as demonstrating "all the
acuteness, and the almost magical force, of his exegetical argumentation and
style."[3] In it, Schleiermacher rejects the idea that Christ had a share in creation,
asserts that the reference to Christ as "the firstborn of all creation" should be
interpreted not cosmologically but ecclesially, insists that references to Christ's
being in the image of God should be understood within the domain of the
human spirit, and infers that the reconciliation mentioned in the passage as
effected in Christ relates primarily to civic and religious enmity between Jew
and gentile. He had already preached several times on these verses[4] and had
considered them in his *Christian Faith* of 1830 *à propos* New Testament

1. Esther Reed wishes to acknowledge her indebtedness to Terrence N. Tice for his kind
    encouragement, his many corrections to the text, and his pertinent observations concerning
    Schleiermacher's theology and hermeneutics. This translation project would have been
    much the poorer without his assistance. She also wishes to acknowledge the further assis-
    tance of Edwina Lawler and the substantial participation of Alan Braley, now deceased, in
    the early stages of translation.
2. "Ueber Koloss. 1, 15-20" was first published in *Theologische Studien und Kritiken*, 1832
    vol.3, and was reproduced in Friedrich Schleiermacher's *Sämmtliche Werke* I.2 (Berlin: G.
    Reimer, 1836).
3. Friedrich Lücke, "Reminiscences of Schleiermacher" in Friedrich Schleiermacher, *Brief
    Outline of the Study of Theology*, by William Farrer (Edinburgh: T. and T. Clark, 1850),
    34. Gottfried Christian Friedrich Lücke (1791-1855) was a longstanding friend of Schleier-
    macher and Professor of New Testament at Göttingen. He had worked with Schleiermacher
    at Berlin (1816-1818) before being appointed Professor of Theology at Bonn (1818-27). His
    publications included the *Grundriß der neutestamentlichen Hermeneutik und ihrer Ge-
    schichte* (Göttingen, 1817) and the four-volume *Kommentar über die Schriften des Evan-
    gelisten Johannes* (Berlin, 1820-22). It was to Lücke that Schleiermacher wrote two letters
    On the Glaubenslehre as an apology for his dogmatic theology.
4. E.g., see his 1830 sermons on Col. 1:13-18 and also sermons of 1823 in *Sämmtliche Werke*
    II.6 (1835), 232-243 and 244-255.

Christology and the efficacy of redemption.[5] Here we have his extended reflections upon one of the great Christological passages of the New Testament and
an example of his well-formed hermeneutical theory in practice.

In addition to his words of appreciation, however, Lücke also wrote when
commenting on the article that Schleiermacher "belongs to the class of those
who are far more strongly inclined towards a distinctive individuality of appre-
hension than to self-surrender; who rather draw over the author to their own
position, than allow themselves to be drawn by him."[6] He suggests that
Schleiermacher's interpretation is colored by his own particular Christology and
ideas about the spiritual kingdom of the Son, "expounding *himself*, rather than
the Apostle."[7] Lücke doubted that Schleiermacher realized in practice the self-
denial in hermeneutics that he demanded in theory, and he questioned the
effectiveness of his renunciation of individuality and concerns of the age when
expounding and appropriating the meaning of this author. He did not elaborate
upon how the prejudices of Schleiermacher's Christology determine the technology of his task. Therefore, in this brief introduction, I pursue Lücke's
comments by investigating how Schleiermacher reconstructs Paul's exposition
of the nature and dignity of Christ, his resurrection from the dead, and his
headship of the church. Given that Col. 1:15-20 is often regarded as a particularly significant passage, "declaring as it does our Lord's divine essence, pre-
existence, and creative agency,"[8] it is important to consider whether Christological pre-judgements bear upon his divination of the passage.

Schleiermacher was, of course, acutely aware of the difficulties involved in
integrating the different aspects or movements that constitute the *Kunstlehre* of
hermeneutics. Early in his career, he realized that the objective grammatical and
subjective technical sides of interpretation[9] cannot always coincide: "[T]hat

5. F.D.E. Schleiermacher, *The Christian Faith* (Edinburgh: T. and T. Clark, 1989), §§ 99 and
    164.
6. Friedrich Lücke, "Reminiscences of Schleiermacher" in Friedrich Schleiermacher, *Brief
    Outline of the Study of Theology*, trans. by William Farrer (Edinburgh: T. and T. Clark,
    MDCCCL), 33.
7. Friedrich Lücke, Ibid., 34.
8. F.F. Bruce, "The Epistle to the Colossians," in E.K. Simpson and F.F. Bruce, *The Epistles
    of Paul to the Ephesians and to the Colossians* (London and Edinburgh: Marshall, Morgan
    and Scott, 1957), 192. J.B. Lightfoot, on the assumption that Paul drew heavily on ideas of
    the Logos familiar to Philo and on ideas about wisdom in Greek and Hebrew sources, wrote
    that the passage "declares the absolute pre-existence of the Son" in *The Epistles of St. Paul
    Colossians and Philemon* (London and N.Y.: Macmillan and Co., 1892), 144.
9. After 1819, Schleiermacher tends to use the term 'psychological' in place of 'technical',
    though he does retain some use of the latter to denote an aspect of the non-grammatical side

would presuppose both a complete knowledge of and completely correct use of the language. Interpretation occurs between self-surrender to the text and appropriation of it; the 'art' lies in knowing when one side should give way to the other."[10] In order to appreciate fully the interaction that Schleiermacher sets in motion in this article, we must bear in mind that in the Academy Addresses of 1829 he supplemented the early distinction between the two aspects of hermeneutics, i.e., the grammatical and the psychological, with two additional features, namely, the comparative and the divinatory, respectively. The former is the process of setting the intentions of the author in the context of his time. The latter is that through which "the entire relationship between the production of the thoughts and its formation in language is now fully and immediately evident." It is a process of gradual discovery and reproduction through which the intentions of the author are intuited, the culmination of every aspect of the task of hermeneutics.[11] Thus, in "On Colossians 1:15-20" we are dealing with Schleiermacher's hermeneutical theory at a well-formed stage. The article provides a prime opportunity to explore how effectively he meets his own standards for the orchestration of all that is needed to reconstruct for the reader the thoughts and intentions of the author.[12]

---

of the hermeneutical task in the 1832-33 lectures. A useful definition of the terms is given in the First Academy Address of 1829: "[T]he grammatical aspect . . . aims at understanding the discourse in terms of the totality of language, and the . . . psychological aspect . . . aims at understanding the discourse in terms of a continous production of thoughts." In "The Two Academy Addresses of 1829" in Friedrich Schleiermacher, *Hermeneutics: The Handwritten Manuscripts*, ed. by Heinz Kimmerle, trans. by James Duke and Jack Forstman (Missoula: Scholars Press for the American Academy of Religion, 1977), 190.

10. F.D.E. Schleiermacher, "The Aphorisms of 1805 and 1809-10" in *Hermeneutics: The Handwritten Manuscripts*, ed. by Heinz Kimmerle, Ibid., 42. Note also: "General rule for the method: (a) Begin with a general overview of the text. (b) Comprehend it by moving in both directions simultaneously [i.e., grammatical and technical interpretation]. (c) Only when the two coincide for one passage does one proceed to another passage. (d) When the two do not agree, it is necessary to go back until the error in calculation is found." "Hermeneutics: The Compendium of 1819 and the Marginal Notes of 1828" in *Hermeneutics: The Handwritten Manuscripts*, ed. by Heinz Kimmerle, Ibid., 116.

11. "The Two Academy Addresses of 1829" in *Hermeneutics: The Handwritten Manuscripts*, ed. by Heinz Kimmerle, Ibid., 193.

12. The question likewise arises as to the extent to which he thought conditions were present that would enable a wholly effective psychological reconstruction. Clearly he did think that the passage had been lifted out of context to serve dogmatic purposes. In the translation of Schleiermacher's *Hermeneutics* by Terrence N. Tice (Atlanta: Scholars Press, 1998), see the sections from the 1832-33 lectures on the "didactic epistles."

In his study of Colossians 1:15-20, Schleiermacher concentrates heavily upon the grammatical and formal structure of the passage. Phrases such as: "the grammatical elements in this passage then require . . . " occur frequently, and the meaning of the passage is determined time and again by logical and grammatical relationships between the sentences.[13] Significantly, this leads him to distinguish between hermeneutical and dogmatic interests in the theological task: "I think it is pertinent to state here and now my belief that this endeavor proceeds not from any dogmatic interest at all but from a purely hermeneutical interest."[14] Whether or not these two interests can be so separated is open to question, especially if the effects of his hermeneutical activity are, arguably, to reinforce his peculiar dogmatic interpretations of the nature and work of Christ. His argument, however, is that "one cannot evade the demand to the extent to which the meaning of the formal elements can be detected from the logical and grammatical relationships between the sentences in which they occur."[15] For instance, he very quickly ties the "all things" (τά πάντα) of verse 20 to the "and you" (και ὑμᾶς) of verse 21.[16] This has the effect of embedding the scope of the concept of reconciliation in the life of the Christian community but is justified, he argues, because the context of verses 15-20 is the life of prayer and redemption in the Christian community. With one eye constantly on this context of prayer and redemption, he argues that the relevance of prayer intersects the flow of the passage as a whole. Experience of redemption and the kingdom of God determine his Christology. Thus, in the introductory pages he draws attention to verse 3, "In our prayers for you . . . ," verse 9, "we have not ceased praying for you . . . ," and verse 23, "so as to present you holy and blameless and irreproachable before him." There is, he suggests, with reference to the relationship between verses 20 & 21, a close connection between statements about Christ and the form and structure of the passage. The "and you" (και ὑμᾶς) of verse 21 is taken directly from the "all things" (τά πάντα) of verse 20, such that the meaning of "all things" (τά πάντα) belongs not to the universal nature-system but to the communion or association that arises from peace through the blood of the cross.

The dogmatic effect of these observations is an interpretation of the nature and work of Christ within an ecclesial rather than a cosmic context. This becomes clearer as Schleiermacher highlights what he perceives to be the most

13. "On Colossians 1:15-20," 28.
14. "On Colossians 1:15-20," 4.
15. "On Colossians 1:15-20," 4.
16. "On Colossians 1:15-20," 5.

significant structural and grammatical feature of the passage, the parallels in verses 15 and 16a, "He is the image . . . for in him all things were created" (ὅς ἐστιν εἰκὼν . . . ὅτι ἐν αὐτῷ ἐκτίσθη τὰ πάντα), and in verses 18b and 19: "He is the beginning . . . for in him all the fulness of God was pleased to dwell" (ὅς ἐστιν ἀρχὴ . . . ὅτι ἐν αὐτῷ εὐδόκησε . . .). This parallel structure is broadly supported by contemporary scholars today—for example, Andrew J.M. Wedderburn, who adopts a two-strophe outline (1:15-18a and 1:18b-20).[17] Wedderburn recognizes the possibility that verses 17-18a could form a third strophe as they do, for example, in N.T. Wright's Tyndale commentary on Colossians,[18] and warns against any overreliance on the structure of the passage, because the original form of the 'hymn' is unknown. Schleiermacher, who does not contemplate the possibility that verses 15-20 could have had a pre-Pauline origin,[19] voices no such warning and gives the form of the passage a more than contingent significance for interpretation of the nature and work of Christ. He relies upon the form of the passage in order to discern Paul's meaning. Thus, we note his observations that (a) the first part of the parallel (verses 15 & 16a) begins the statement about Christ, (b) the second part (verses 18b & 19) recalls the first by its form, (c) there is no third element of equal importance and, therefore, (d) the second must rank equally with the first and together comprise the two main clauses to which the others are subordinate. By way of confirmation he states that verse 20 is dependent upon the "for" (ὅτι) at the start of verse 19 and is therefore subordinate to the main parallel. Verse 20, "and through him to reconcile to himself all things . . . ," is regarded as a sub-clause, which stands in the same relation to the second main sentence as the clause in verse 16 from "all things" stands to the first main sentence.[20]

These observations form the basis of his argument that the verses refer to the spiritual kingdom of the Son and not to the cosmic origin of the universe.

---

17. See "The Theology of Colossians" in Andrew T. Lincoln and Andrew J.M Wedderburn, *The Theology of the Later Pauline Epistles* (Cambridge: Cambridge University Press, 1993), 14.
18. N.T. Wright, *Colossians and Philemon* (Leicester: InterVarsity Press, 1986), 65.
19. Schleiermacher assumed the Pauline authorship of the whole of Colossians, including 1:15-20. It was not until 1838 that the Pauline authorship of the letter was thrown into question by Ernst Theodore Mayerhoff who noted differences of language and style in Colossians compared to other of Paul's letters. Ernst Theodore Mayerhoff, *Der Brief an die Colosser mit vornehmlicher Berücksichtigung der drei Pastoralbriefe* (Berlin: H. Schultze, 1838). On this see Mark Kiley, *Colossians as Pseudepigraphy* (Trowbridge: Journal for the Study of the Old Testament Press, 1986), 36f.
20. "On Colossians 1:15-20," 4-5.

Other grammatical and structural arguments that he employs to the same effect include the following:

1. (v. 15) the word κτίζειν is not usually employed for "to create" from nothing but is used to translate בּרא, which refers only to the founding of something that will continue to exist in the future.

2. (v. 16) the language of 'thrones' and 'lordships' should not be assumed to refer to heavenly hierarchies, because such notions derive from Essene and Gnostic sources not Judaism and would thus be alien to Pauline thought.

3. (v. 16) there is no reason to suppose that a *Logos* doctrine makes sense of such references, not least because there is no evidence to support an argument that Paul knew anything about such a doctrine or that the Colossians would have understood such references.

4. (vs. 16f & 17a-17b&18a) the parallel formation:
"All things were created through him and for him;
he is before all things"
(τὰ πάντα δι᾽ αὐτοῦ καὶ εἰς αὐτὸν ἔκτισται, καὶ αὐτός ἐστι πρὸ πάντων)
and likewise
"And in him all things hold together;
he is the head of the body the church"
(καὶ τὰ πάντα ἐν αὐτῷ συνέστηκεν,
καὶ αὐτός ἐστιν ἡ κεφαλὴ τοῦ σώματος τῆς ἐκκλησίας)
suggests that "all things" (τὰ πάντα) again refers to the spiritual kingdom of the Son and not the cosmic origin of the world. There is, he argues, a correspondence between the two sentences such that the latter is already present in the former and Christ's headship of the church determines the sense in which "all things hold together."

5. (v. 16) the language about thrones, dominions, principalities and authorities is best interpreted in the context of earthly rather than supernatural powers:
"Principalities" (Ἀρχαί) and "authorities" (ἐξουσίαι) would have been familiar to them as
titles of superior offices and other positions held powerful persons.
"Throne" (θρόνος) was
well known as a name for kingly seats . . . "dominions" (κυριότητες) . . . could fit in equally
well with the explanation of "throne" (θρόνος) as regarding the dignity of the city government

or the regard in which the teacher was held. (p. 11)

6. (vs. 16 & 18) the prepositions "all things" (τὰ πάντα) created "*in* him" (ἐν αὐτῷ) need convey nothing more than that Christ is the foundation of the spiritual kingdom into which believers are being transferred by God:

The two particles "through him" (δι' αὐτοῦ) and "for him" (εἰς αὐτόν) together take up the

"in" (ἐν), though of course by way of analyzing and explaining it. (p. 13) This is plausible, he suggests, because the whole passage is determined by the idea of the transference of believers to the spiritual kingdom of the Son.

7. (vs. 15-20) i.e., the statements about Christ as "the image of God" and "firstborn of all creation" are interpreted within the domain of the human spirit. His interpretation of Christ's being the original likeness of God, his being "first-born" and of his being the one "in whom all things hold together," centres around the redemption that Christians have in Christ. To be created "in Christ" means to be transferred into the kingdom of the Son according to the scheme of redemption prepared by the Father, hence his resolution of uncertainties regarding the subject of the sentence in 16a and 19 in favor of God rather than Christ. God is held to be the subject, who ascribes roles to Christ: "'God was pleased . . . to dwell . . . and to reconcile . . . making peace' (εὐδόκησεν ὁ Θεὸς ... κατοικῆσαι . . . καὶ εἰρηνοποιήσας ἀποκαταλλάξαι), and so on."[21]

8. (vs. 19 & 20) refers to "enmity" and "reconciliation" and are to be understood in terms of making peace between Jew and gentile. "All the fulness" (πᾶν τὸ πλήπωμα) (v. 19) points to the "church" (ἐκκλησία) (v. 18), in which Jew and gentile are being made into one new humanity. This interpretation alone, he says, makes sense of Paul's attempts in 2:1 to indicate awareness of the situation in Colossae at the time.

In response, we could simply compare Schleiermacher's findings with those of subsequent scholars and note how they work both for and against him. For example, point 1 has been disputed since Schleiermacher, not least by J.B. Lightfoot, who wrote: "'ἐκτίσθη describes the definite historical act of creation" and cited 1 Cor. 9:22; 2 Cor. 12:17 & 1 Joh. 4:9 in his support.[22] Lightfoot also challenged point 3. He thought that Paul drew heavily on ideas of *logos* familiar to Philo, also on ideas of wisdom in Greek and Hellenic sources. Even if Paul had no developed doctrine of the *Logos*, it is possible, he thought, that the

---

21. "On Colossians 1:15-20," 24.
22. J.B. Lightfoot, *The Epistles of St. Paul Colossians and Philemon* (London and N.Y.: Macmillan and Co., 1892), 150ff.

Colossians could have had some understanding of such references (Prov. 8:22; Sir.43:26. Cf., Philo *Fug.*, 112; *Quaest. in Exod.*, 2.117-8). In contrast, with reference to point 2, we might note Andrew J.M. Wedderburn's broad agreement with Schleiermacher that the passage does not manifest Essene or Gnostic influence, based on the suggestion that explicit reference to the resurrection in verses 18b-20 renders it unlikely to be Gnostic.[23]

It is more important for our purposes, however, to view Schleiermacher's work in the context of scholarship available to him at the time. This involves asking whether Schleiermacher deals adequately with the comparative dimension of the hermeneutic task. In this article, he combines the grammatical with, to a lesser extent, the technical dimensions of the task. The language, structure and contextual meaning of terms assist him to grasp the unity of the passage as a whole. Indeed, he aims to reconstruct for the reader the meaning of Paul's Christology by investigating the logical and grammatical relationships between sentences and sub-clauses.[24] His discernment of the meaning of the passage is determined time and again by the grammatical and, to a lesser extent, technical aspects of interpretation. It is less clear, however, that he excels at the comparative task of setting Paul in the context of the thought worlds of the New Testament.[25] In an Academy Address of 1829, he described this task as discerning the intentions of the author in comparison and contrast with others: "An interpreter who does not see correctly how the stream of thinking and composing at once crashes against and recoils from the walls of its bed and is diverted into a course other than it would have taken by itself cannot correctly understand the internal movement of the composition."[26] It is arguable, however, that he could have taken more seriously the mixed history and culture of the Jewish communities to which Paul travelled and wrote. As it is, he plays down questions about the nature of the heresy at Colossae by dismissing suggestions of Essene and Gnostic influence upon Paul's apologetic as unfounded: "All these

---

23. Andrew J.M. Wedderburn, *Baptism and Resurrection: Studies in Pauline Theology against Its Graeco-Roman Background, Wissenshaftliche Untersuchungen zum Neuen Testament* 44 (Tübingen: Mohr, 1987), 18-21, 212-18) referred to in Andrew T. Lincoln and Andrew J.M Wedderburn, *The Theology of the Later Pauline Epistles* (Cambridge: Cambridge University Press, 1993), 16.
24. This reading of Schleiermacher's intention is confirmed with reference to the marginal notes of 1828 appended to the compendium on hermeneutics of 1819.
25. F.D.E. Schleiermacher, *Sämmtliche Werke* 1.7 § 1 "Vorbemerkungen. Begriff, Inhalt, Methode der Einleitung ins neue Testament," 5-6.
26. In "The Two Academy Addresses of 1829" in *Hermeneutics: The Handwritten Manuscripts*, ed. by Heinz Kimmerle, Ibid., 189.

assumptions are entirely lacking in substance and formulation."[27] This renders him vulnerable to the charge of prejudice in interpreting Paul's Christology in terms of ecclesiology and ethics. There is little doubt that Schleiermacher was, as Karl Barth admits, "a virtuoso in the field whose method hermeneutics describes."[28] Schleiermacher specified the procedure through which "the entire relationship between the production of the thoughts and its formation in language is now fully and immediately evident"[29] and was convinced that an interpreter cannot properly understand the relation between form and content of a work without sufficiently appreciating the author's relationship to the limits and rules of the literature of his/her time. It is important to ask, therefore, why he is hesitant to accept that Paul engaged in any way within the cosmological thinking that characterised the Hellenistic Judaism of the day. He believes knowledge of the Essenes and Gnostics to be insufficient for his purposes, and he finds no reason to believe that Paul absorbed their ideas. In his comments on the Epistle to the Colossians in *"Vorbemerkungen: Begriff, Inhalt, Methode der Einleitung ins neue Testament,"*[30] he simply states that Paul urged his readers not to touch, or become involved with, "traditions of men," Gnostic influences, the worship of angels or other visions, and does not countenance the possibility that Paul appropriated the language of some of these religious systems in order to correct their views by expounding the glory of Christ in cosmic terms. When he argues that, according to Paul, everything begins by being mediated through Christ and ends up by being for him, this is unpacked in the human terms of earthly conditions,

---

27. "On Colossians 1:15-20," 11.
28. Karl Barth, *The Theology of Schleiermacher* (Edinburgh: T. and T. Clark, 1982), 178.
29. "The Two Academy Addresses of 1829" in *Hermeneutics: The Handwritten Manuscripts*, ed. by Heinz Kimmerle, Ibid., 193.
30. F.D.E. Schleiermacher, *Sämmtliche Werke* I.7, § 47, 162, n.1. "The tightly interconnected part is a theoretical defence and aid against the expectation of the Jews. This is clearly to be seen in verses 2:8 and 2:20ff.; moreover, verses 15 and 18, which lie in between, have to be explained only in connection with that. Thus, if παράδοσις ἀνθρώπων (human tradition, 2:8) and μὴ ἅφη (do not handle, 2:21) come from gnostic sources and θρησκεία τῶν ἀγγέλων (worship of angels, 2:18) refers to the Essenes, nothing new may also be sought or added to ἃ μὴ ἑόρακεν ἐμβατεύων (not dwelling on visions, 2:18) in verse 18, since the angels are indeed also invisible. Through verse 16, the ἀρχαί (rulers) and ἐξουσίαι (authorities) are made known as human authorities in Judaism. Even what is theoretical in the epistle to the Colossians would, like all earlier ascriptions, refer to Christ; it would lead to the εἰρηνοποιήσας (making peace 1:20), and it is very much like the positing of equality between the Jews and gentiles in the epistle to the Romans." The author is grateful to Terrence N. Tice for this translation.

the ordering of the Christian community, and peace for those previously at enmity.[31]

It is not easy to assess whether Schleiermacher's stance was justifiable in the light of the scholarship of his day. The history of modern research into Gnosticism was at an early stage, and it is impossible to be certain what he had read on the subject. Given that August Neander qualified as a university lecturer at Berlin in 1811, it might be supposed that Schleiermacher was familiar with his 1818 publication of a *Genetische Entwicklung der vornehmsten gnostischen Systeme*, dubbed by Kurt Rudolph as the beginning of modern research into Gnosis.[32] Neander's work was followed by J. Mater's *Histoire critique du Gnosticisme* in 1828 (German edition, 1833). Ferdinand Christian Baur concluded his doctoral thesis on the Christianity of the Gnostics in 1827, but he did not publish his *Die Christliche Gnosis oder die christliche Religions-Philosophie in ihrer geschichtlichen Entwicklung* until 1835.[33] Earlier work had been done, though its conlusions were unreliable. Henry Hammond, in his *A Paraphrase and Annotations upon . . . the New Testament* (London, 1653), had thought that Paul's opponents in all his letters were Gnostics. Others, whilst criticising Hammond for his extreme position, assumed that an anti-gnostic element was present in Paul's writings.[34] Schleiermacher's passing comment in "On Colossians 1:15-20" is that nobody had yet asserted that Gnostic inferences should be drawn from Christ's teachings.[35] This, of itself, indicates that he was familiar with literature in the area, but the comment leaves one wondering whether Christological pre-judgments in favour of ecclesial and ethical terms bear upon his easy dismissal of Gnostic thought-systems that involved cosmological reference.

Similarly, with regard to the history of research about the Essenes, Schleiermacher readily rejects the possibility that Paul's Christology engaged

---

31. "On Colossians 1:15-20," 25.
32. Kurt Rudolph, *Gnosis: The Nature and History of Gnosticism* (New York: Harper and Collins, 1987; German edition, 1977), 30.
33. All this information is given in Rudolph, Ibid., 30-31.
34. E.g., J.L. von Mosheim, *Institutiones historiae ecclesiasticae Novi Testamenti* (Frankfurt/Leipzig, 1726); C.W.F. Walch, *Entwurf einer vollständigen Historie der Ketzereien . . .* (Leipzig, 1762-1785); J.D. Michaelis, *Einleitung in die göttlichen Schriften des Neuen Bundes* (Göttingen, 1750/1788). This information is given by Walter Schmithals in "The *Corpus Paulinum* and Gnosis" in *The New Testament and Gnosis: Essays in honour of Robert McLachlan Wilson*, ed. by Alastair H.B. Logan and Andrew J.M. Wedderburn (Edinburgh: T. and T. Clark, 1983), 107-124.
35. "On Colossians 1:15-20," 10-11.

with, and corrected, their theosophic speculations by speaking of Christ's cosmic status and significance. Augustus Neander's *General History of the Christian Religion and Church* records mentions of their beliefs and practices by Pliny and Josephus.[36] Their secret lore, he wrote, consisted of a peculiar "*theosophy* and pneumatology," which they surrounded by great mystery. Why else, Neander asks, should candidates for admission to the sect "bound themselves by an oath never to reveal to any one the *names of the angels*"?[37] Schleiermacher asks us to believe that Paul's discourse about the kingdom is devoid of reference to the celestial realms and concerns only the conditions on earth in which human beings are related to Christ; the terms used refer solely to earthly orders and hierarchies: "for what could the creation of the angels through the 'Word' (λόγος) now indwelling the Christ possibly have to do with our deliverance into the kingdom of the Son?"[38] This view is at least questionable, though it does not imply a belief that other scholarship of his day ignored the mingling of spiritual and earthly powers in Jewish Hellenism of the first century.[39]

A case could also be made that Schleiermacher omits to take full recognition of the apocalyptic and pseudepigraphal literature that was becoming available at the time. He wanted to link Paul's writings about Christ to the ordering of earthly conditions and therefore, it could be argued, he dismisses reference to supernatural powers and fails to take account of Pauline literature that suggests a cosmic and not solely earthly reference to Christ (Eph. 1:20-21 and 3:15; 1 Cor. 3:22, 8:5, and 15:24-28). It is difficult to know whether he had seen publications such as Silvestre de Sacy's extracts from 1 Enoch in his

---

36. Augustus Neander, *General History of the Christian Religion and Church*, trans. by Joseph Torrey, (London: George Bell and Sons, 1890, first German edit. 1825, second edit. 1842).
37. Augustus Neander, Ibid., 65.
38. "On Colossians 1:15-20," 11.
39. For 20th century investigations into apocalyptic and pseudepigraphal literature see Jack T. Sanders, *The New Testament Christological Hymns* (Cambridge: Cambridge University Press, 1971); James D.G. Dunn, *Christology in the Making* (London: SCM, 1980); *The Epistles to the Colossians and Philemon: A Commentary on the Greek Text* (Carlisle: Paternoster Press, 1996); Christopher Rowland, *Christian Origins* (London: SPCK, 1985). E.g., Dunn expands upon how Wisdom and Logos theology could have functioned effectively as an apologetic to the Jews within a wider Hellenistic milieu. The idea of Jesus as the image of God would have "chimed in with the basic Platonic distinction between the world of sense perception (κόσμος αἰσθητός/ὁρατός) and the world of ideas accessible only to the mind (κόσμος νοητός/ἀόρατος), fundamental also to Philo's religious cosmology." Dunn, *Epistles to the Colossians*, 87-88.

"Notice sur le livre d'Hénoch" in *Magazine encyclopédique*. [40] Enoch 61:10 states: "And he will summon all the forces of the heavens, and all the holy ones above, and the forces of the Lord . . . ." Wilhelm M.L. de Wette, writing in 1847, makes reference to other such relevant literature, including the Testaments of the 12 Patriarchs.[41] This suggests that access was available to such manuscripts, though there is uncertainty about which recensions were available. There are also additional complications concerning original dates, for example, de Wette mentions *The Testament of Adam*, but there can be little certainty about its provenance except that it was composed between the second and fifth centuries, A.D.[42] In summary, such material was becoming more readily available and Schleiermacher was a careful scholar who kept abreast of most issues pertinent to his areas of study. However, at this point it is impossible to know what he had or had not read and so our findings must be inconclusive.

In any case, we must ask whether Christological bias affects Schleiermacher's laying out of the grammar and structural form of the passage. Is his interpretation more understandable in the light of a predisposition to believe that the Son had no role in creation? Friedrich Lücke suggested that Schleiermacher judges the Christology of Paul too quickly, also that he follows his own instincts and preconceived opinions, and, as we have seen, our suspicions about Schleiermacher's selective use of contemporary scholarship give weight to that accusation. Full assessment of how Schleiermacher negotiates the play between the immergent and emergent aspects of interpretation[43] lies beyond the scope of this introduction. It should be noted, however, that there are many similarities between Schleiermacher's findings in this article and his previous work. Here, as in *Christian Faith*, everything concerning the nature and dignity of Jesus Christ is related to what is knowable within the physical and historical condi-

40. Silvestre de Sacy, "Notice sur le livre d'Hénoch" in *Magazine encyclopédique* 6/1, 382, 1800, (E.T. 1821, published by Lawrence). On this, see E. Isaac, "1 Enoch, a new translation and introduction" in James H. Charlesworth, ed., *The Old Testament Pseudepigrapha* vol. 1 (London: Darton, Longman & Todd, Ltd., 1983-85), 8.
41. Wilhelm M.L. de Wette, *Kurze Erklärung der Briefe an die Colosser, an Philemon, an die Ephesier und Philipper* (Leipzig: Weidemann'sche Buchhandlung, 1847), 27.
42. On this S.E. Robinson, *The Testament of Adam: An Examination of the Syriac and Greek Traditions*, 148-53, which suggests that refences in Col. 1:16 to thrones, dominions, rulers and powers, would have made sense with reference to cosmic rather than to earthly meanings. See also *Testament of Adam* ch. 4:1-8 in Charlesworth, Ibid., vol. 1, 995.
43. Friedrich Lücke uses the terms 'immergent' and 'emergent' when describing Schleiermacher's hermeneutic practice, Ibid., 32.

tions of the world. The three reasons why Christ is the image of God—that all things are created in him, he is first from the dead, and the fulness of God dwelt in him—all relate to life in the kingdom of God.[44] All references to creation in Christ concern the transference of believers into his kingdom. Thus, the two statements about Christ as the "image of God" (εἰκὼν τοῦ Θεοῦ) and "firstborn" (πρωτότοκος) of all creation are taken together; the meaning of "image" is, he says, illustrated by "firstborn". The meaning of "firstborn" is determined by the parallel structure of the passage whereby, verse 18c, "he is . . . . the firstborn from the dead" fulfils and determines the meaning of "the firstborn of all creation" in verse 15.[45] In other words, Christ is the original likeness of God only in the domain of the human spirit, to the exclusion of any reference to cosmology.

We might also note that, as in *Christian Faith*, here the perfecting of the essence of humanity is central to Schleiermacher's Christology: "he [Jesus Christ] is the head of the community whereby everything else is established in its true value, and through him the human spirit attains its full stature . . . . [T]he whole passage must refer to the progress of Christianity."[46] Jesus Christ is the archetype in whom humanity is recreated; "the appearance of the Second Adam constituted for this nature a new spiritual life."[47] Jesus Christ is the one in whom humanity attains to its perfection, therefore he is the original likeness of God in the domain of the human spirit[48] and the founder of the Christian community because its members become conscious of their redemption through him, to the exclusion of any reference to a cosmic Christ before his union with human nature.[49] For this reason, he moves quickly to establish that references to Christ's nature must be understood always in the sense of "the whole Christ" (*in dem Sinne des ganzen Christus*), that is, Jesus of Nazareth who was also the Christ.[50] At no point, he says, does Paul refer only to one part of Christ's nature; he never speaks of Christ as Son of God independent of his being Son of

---

44. "On Colossians 1:15-20," 7.
45. In this he takes issue with Chrysostom's opinion that "firstborn" (πρωτότοκος) means the same as "foundation" (θεμέλιος) in 1 Cor. 3:10. It is noteworthy, however, that in his dismissal of Chrysostom's suggestion, Schleiermacher cites only half of Chrysostom's argument and omits to mention that he interprets 'foundation' as speaking not of substance but of operation: "that all things are by Him, and in Him." "On Colossians 1:15-20," 19.
46. "On Colossians 1:15-20," 23.
47. Cf. *Christian Faith*, § 94.
48. "On Colossians 1:15-20," 23, cf. *Christian Faith*, § 11.
49. "On Colossians 1:15-20," 24-25, cf. *Christian Faith*, §§ 11,13, 97, and 106-110.
50. "On Colossians 1:15-20," 7-9, 19, 21, 22.

Man, and *vice versa*. Paul does not speak of the Redeemer from eternity before union with human nature but only of the Redeemer in whom the being of God in Christ developed within the conditions of human nature.[51] God is the subject of verses 15-20 rather than Jesus Christ; Christ acts in the scheme of redemption as the Father prepared for it.[52] As in his article of 1822, "On the Discrepancy between the Sabellian and Athanasian Method of Representing the Doctrine of the Trinity," Schleiermacher resists any suggestion that Christ had a share in creation or was hypostatically distinct from God the Father prior to God's economy of redemption in time.[53]

Thus, it can be argued that Schleiermacher's predilection that the Son had no role in creation affected his reconstruction of Paul's Christology. As was suggested by Lücke, a degree of suspicion is not misplaced when assessing the interactive synthesis that he effects between aspects of the hermeneutic task. In Schleiermacher's defence, it could be argued that there are recent commentators whose work resonates in some respects with his. James D.G. Dunn shares Schleiermacher's caution in assuming too quickly that Christ was regarded by his early followers as "God's agent in creation."[54] Primordial primacy, he argues, "is the consequence, the divinely intended outcome of his resurrection."[55] Unlike Schleiermacher, Dunn believes that cosmic claims are being made for Christ in Col. 1:15-20.[56] On the other hand, like Schleiermacher, he is suspicious of those who too quickly propound notions of Christ's pre-existence such that they impose later interpretations on to the text and wrongly suggest ideas of incarnation.[57] Dunn also shares Schleiermacher's sense that the passage falls into two strophes and that the emphasis falls on the second of these such that the cross and resurrection "provide the key to the whole." Thus he

---

51. Cf. F.D.E. Schleiermacher, *Christian Faith*, § 97.
52. "On Colossians 1:15-20," 24. Compare, for instance, Storr's recognition of ambiguity in the text: "Since huios (son) (Col. 1:13) is (n. 23) *theos* (Jn. 1:1) *ENSARKOS* [god INCARNATE] (Jn. 1:14), generally the apostle may have wanted this to mean that everything was created by God *through* the Son (Heb. 1:2). But he might also say that the universe was created *by* the Son." G.C. Storr, *Opuscula Academica ad Interpretationem Librorum Sacrorum Pertinentia* (Tübingen: Johannis Georgii Cottae, 1797), 132.
53. "Über den Gegensaz zwischen der sabellianischen und der athanasianischen Vorstellung von der Trinität," *Theologische Zeitschrift* 3 (1822) [*SW* 1.2, 485-574]. E.T.: by Moses Stuart in *The Biblical Repository and Quarterly Observer* 6 no. XIX, July 1835, 1-116.
54. Dunn, *Epistles to the Colossians*, 91.
55. Dunn, *Epistles to the Colossians*, 98.
56. Eduard Schweiter also hold this to be the case in his *The Letter to the Colossians*, trans. by Andrew Chester (London: SPCK, 1982, G.E. 1976), 63ff.
57. Dunn, *Epistles to the Colossians*, 102.

argues, in similar fashion to Schleiermacher, that the way to understand references in the passage to creation and the cosmos is first to grasp the work of reconciliation that was effected in the cross and resurrection. Similarly, like Schleiermacher, he stresses the vision of the church as the "focus and means" toward the reconciliation and redemption of the world that God intended.[58]

With this in mind, the contemporary reader might benefit from Schleiermacher's warning against the imposition of readings that are not required by the text itself. Even if one grants Lücke's perspective that Schleiermacher "imperceptibly changes the Apostle into himself,"[59] it is equally true that those of different dogmatic persuasions risk making premature assumptions about a pre-existent, cosmic Christ without effecting adequate demonstration of the interaction of each element of the hermeneutical task. To use Lücke's words, Schleiermacher might in this article have displayed the "over-might" of genius. [60] This genius, however, was such that he set new and high standards for hermeneutics. Any criticisms that might hold against him with regard to his interpretation of this particular passage are the result not of any want of genius but of an "energetic individuality" which awakened in many a faith-feeling (*Glaubensgefühl*) that inspired enthusiasm for study of the New Testament and rendered noteworthy service to the cause of hermeneutically informed dogmatics.

---

58. Dunn, *Epistles to the Colossians*, 104.
59. Friedrich Lücke, Ibid., 34.
60. Friedrich Lücke, Ibid., 33. It is, of course, possible that Lücke could himself have been prejudiced on the point of issue and unduly hesitant to accept Schleiermacher's innovative readings of scripture.

ON COLOSSIANS 1:15-20

by

Dr. Friedrich Schleiermacher

[15] He is the image of the invisible God, the first-born of all creation; [16] for in him all things were created, in heaven and on earth, visible and invisible, whether thrones or dominions or principalities or authorities—all things were created through him and for him. [17] He is before all things, and in him all things hold together. [18] He is the head of the body, the church; he is the beginning, the first-born from the dead, that in everything he might be pre-eminent. [19] For in him all the fullness of God was pleased to dwell, [20] and through him to reconcile to himself all things, whether on earth or in heaven, making peace by the blood of his cross.

Surely it can appear to be quite an odd undertaking, strictly speaking quite unfeasible, to proceed to discuss all by itself a passage that begins with a relative pronoun[61] (thus as an addendum to what has preceded it) and finishes with a comma, thus being concluded only in what follows, so that it has neither a beginning nor an ending. However, the limits indicated encompass a set of remarkable assertions about Christ that are intended to be the sole subject of the discussion that follows. Of course, in order to obtain a basis for the interpretation I shall thus have to look ahead to what follows and refer back to what came before; but I do not undertake to say more about either of these than is required by their connection with the passage we are to consider.

Plainly, the letter to the Colossians is one of those in which Paul could not proceed from one or more particular points of connection. I am still convinced that between him and this congregation no such points existed,[62] and that in all

---

61. Ed. note: the word 'pronoun' is not used by Schleiermacher but can be understood. Verse 15 of the Greek text begins with 'who is' (ὅς ἐστιν), i.e., with a relative pronoun that implies an antecedent.

62. Schleiermacher's note: "I realize that this is contrary to the view advanced by Herr D. Schulz in this periodical (1829, 535), but the text of Colossians 2:1 still persuades me to believe that Paul had not visited Colossae. Mentioned there were three kinds of people that he certainly could not otherwise have wished to distinguish. Even if he had been in Laodicea, this did not constitute a distinction between the Laodiceans and the Colossians, and there appears to be no other foundation for such a distinction, so they belonged in the

likelihood he would never have written to them if he had not made the acquaintance of Epaphras and Onesimus in Rome, and if Tychicus had not journeyed in those districts in the company of Onesimus. Hence, since every letter requires a factual basis, Paul too could base his only partly on the apparently quite general information passed on to him by Epaphras (1:7-8) and partly on his own circumstances, which Tychicus could explain to them in more detail. For this reason, all the teaching and warnings in the letter are expressed only in very

---

same class as the Colossians; were it not so, they would have had to be members of the 'all who' (ὅσοις) [ed. note: i.e., all those who had not seen Paul face to face, Col. 2:1]. However, does the sentence look as if two groups were supposed to belong together and the third was supposed to be opposed to them? Moreover, if the 'their' (αὐτῶν) [ed. note: Col. 2:2] applies only to the 'all who' (ὅσοι) and not to the Colossians as well, why does he tell the latter about his struggle for Christians who were dispersed over a variety of districts in Asia and Europe, but were of no particular concern to the Colossians at all? Further, if he wanted to speak in such sweeping terms about his struggles, had he nothing similar to say about other congregations that knew him, restricting himself to the Colossians and Laodiceans? The fact that Paul is here addressing the Colossians in the third person concerning those he does not know appears to be only a minor objection, since the congregation at Colossae was almost negligibly small compared with the vast numbers of others who found themselves in the same situation. Moreover, the discourse changes back to the second person while still on the same subject. Again, if the Colossians were not part of the 'them' (αὐτοῖς), how could Paul say to them that he was telling them this so that they should not be led astray? Hence, I still cannot believe other than that the Colossians were also one of the groups that did not know him, and I believe that most theologians have been so inescapably taken with the same idea that they could not believe that Paul had ever preached at Colossae. Moreover, once this is established, the other circumstances follow automatically. All I would say in this regard is that I also do not share Prof. Böhmer's opinion (*Isagoge in ep. ad Coloss.*, 131 ff.) that Epaphras followed the apostle to Rome expressly on account of the disquieting situations in the congregations at Colossae and Laodicea. It would be difficult for a man like the one here described to have wished to conceal this information from the congregation; and if we reject this hypothesis, Paul's good intentions would have to have found clear expression somewhere, and he would also have especially emphasized the points because of which he was making such efforts and treated them with becoming importance. Yet, I cannot find the slightest trace of this anywhere." — Ed. note: David Schultz (1779-1854) was a rationalist theologian who taught successively at the universities of Halle, Frankfurt and Breslau. Schleiermacher is referring to Schultz's article, "Sollte der Apostel Paulus wirklich nicht in Colossa und Laodicea sein?" *Theologische Studien und Kritiken* 1829, 535-538, in which he argues that Paul was twice in the province of Phrygia on the grounds, in part, that Paul's letter to Philemon suggests relations with and information about Epaphras, Onesimus and Aristarchus, best explained by personal contact in Phrygia. Georg R.W. Böhmer was Professor of Theology at Berlin. For another article to which Schleiermacher refers, see Guilielmus Boehmerus, *Isagoge in Epistolam a Paulo Apostolo ad Colossenses Datum Theologica, Historica, Critica* (Berolini: Ferdinand Duemmlert, 1829), 131-134.

general terms, and they touch only upon such failings and needs as could be
expected to occur in all mixed communities outside Palestine, though with
somewhat differing characteristics in Asia and Europe, especially since Paul
had set more constrained limits for himself and could not be implored to send
an explanation to the Colossian community like that in the letter to the Romans.
Consequently, whereas in his letter to the Corinthians the apostle was present-
ing a host of vivid details, this one appears to be quite different with respect to
composition and style. I mention this only in passing, so as not to be deflected
overmuch from my main purpose. If the letter to the Colossians had pursued the
two alternatives very far, it would be blameworthy for its restless jumping about
and for its tediously protracted argumentation. Yet, anybody comparing the two
letters would be sure to consider the development of thoughts that we find here
extremely comprehensible, all the moreso in those places where everything has
to be spun out from general information.

The whole section from verses 3-23 contains only two full stops, after verse
8 and after verse 23.[63] Viewed grammatically, the two main sentences are only:
"We always thank God, the Father of our Lord Jesus Christ, when we pray for
you . . . " (v.3)[64] and "And so, from the day we heard of it, we have not ceased
to pray for you . . . " (v.9).[65] Out of opening sentences like this, which have
almost solemn significance in Paul's letters, sentences of more substance are
developed in a way that is almost bewildering in their simplicity, by linking
relative pronouns and particles to them. Yet, along with this apparent neglect,
in which the subjects are constantly being changed, so that one has to be hidden
behind the other, a strictly cyclical feature is also prevalent. This is so, for after
the panegyrics about Christ in the verses we shall study more closely, in verse
22 Paul comes right back to the content of the prayer already adumbrated in
verse 9. Indeed, at the very end of the section he even makes a second reference
to his calling, first mentioned in his opening sentence, in an endeavor to attach
yet another train of thought to that opening one.

Both of the main sentences, verses 3 and 9, would have served equally well
to make the transition to talk of God, but Paul uses only the second one for this

---

63. Schleiermacher's note: "True, a full stop could also be inserted in v. 16, after 'authorities'
    (ἐξουσίαι); but there the 'all things' (τὰ πάντα) that follows clearly takes up the preceding
    nominatives so that, viewed logically, this punctuation is extremely subordinate."
64. Ed. note: In the Greek text this sentence begins at verse 3 and continues until the end of
    verse 8. Schleiermacher quotes only the opening few words.
65. Ed. note: In the Greek text this sentence begins at verse 9 and continues until the end of
    verse 23. Schleiermacher quotes only the opening few words.

purpose, and thus it is said of God in verse 13 that "He has delivered us from the dominion of darkness and transferred us to the kingdom of his beloved Son, in whom we have redemption, the forgiveness of sins."[66] Then in verse 15 the topic changes to Christ, and the passage we have to work on begins. It is so much concerned with the much discussed and disputed question concerning the higher nature and dignity of Christ, and concerning his relationship to God and the world that I think it is pertinent to state here and now my belief that this endeavor proceeds, not from any dogmatic interest at all but from a purely hermeneutical interest. That is to say, in all the difficult passages, the more indefinite and ambiguous and lacking in helpful parallels[67] the individual expressions are, the more the interpreter has to fall back on the form in order to overcome the difficulty. Now, undeniably this is the case here to such a degree that one cannot evade the demand to probe into the extent to which the meaning of the formal elements can be detected from the logical and grammatical relationships among the sentences in which they occur; and this is the task I have set myself here.[68]

---

66. Ed. note: Schleiermacher has: "He has transferred us into the kingdom of his Son, through whom we have obtained forgiveness."

67. Schleiermacher's note: "It might of course be thought that because this letter is so closely related to the Epistle to the Ephesians, there would be no lack of parallel passages. In fact, however, that works more in favor of the other letter than of this one. The reason is that if the plan and execution of the two letters are compared, Colossians appears by far the more orderly in its bearing and the more closely interconnected, so that if when the apostle was writing one of the letters the other one echoed in his mind, it is the letter to the Ephesians that betrays a less propitious bearing, for which such assistance would have been especially welcome, not this one. That is why I am puzzled whenever I hear it conjectured that this letter was based on the letter to the Ephesians; that would have to imply that in the present letter Paul was trying to produce an improved version of the other one." — Ed. note: The majority of New Testament scholars today agree with Schleiermacher that Colossians has chronological priority. For useful surveys of theories subsequent to his see J.B. Polhill, "The Relationship between Ephesians and Colossians," *Rev. Exp.* 70 (1975), 439-50; Eduard Lohse, *Colossians and Philemon* (Philadelphia: Fortress Press, 1971; first German edition, 1968), 4, n. 2; James D.G. Dunn, *The Epistles to the Colossians and to Philemon* (Carlisle: Paternoster Press, 1996), 34, n. 43.

68. Schleiermacher's note: "Here I would make only a general reference to Storr's well known interpretation of the letter to the Colossians (*Opusc.* II, 120-220). Yet, our methodologies for this task differ so completely that any agreement can only be coincidental and a sustained comparison appears to be quite impracticable, since we diverge from the very outset. I may nonetheless refer to Storr's work at one point or another in what follows." — Ed. note: Gottlob Christian Storr (d. 1805) was a noted historian and philologist with a wide knowledge of languages connected with criticism of the bible. He was educated at the University and the theological seminary of Tübingen, and was subsequently made Professor of

On a closer examination of this passage referring to Christ, I then perceived
that it contained what appeared to me to be two unmistakable parallels, if one
confines oneself simply to the text as the sole consideration. These were the
sentences in verses 15 and 16: "He is the image . . . for in him all things were
created" (ὅς ἐστιν εἰκὼν ί ὅτι ἐν αὐτῷ ἐκτίσθη τὰ πάντα), and in verses 18
and 19: "He is the beginning . . . For in him all the fullness of God was pleased
to dwell" (ὅς ἐστιν ἀρχὴ ί ὅτι ἐν αὐτῷ εὐδόκησε . . .). Of course, in the
second sentence the connection between "he" (ὅς) and "for " (ὅτι) appears to
be interrupted by "in order that" (ἵνα); but this "in order that" (ἵνα) is a pure
parenthesis. One has only to imagine Paul's having written "in order that he
should be the first born in all things" (εἰς τὸ γενέσθαι ἐν πᾶσιν αὐτὸν
πρωτεύοντα) instead of that. It means exactly the same thing. So we shall not
be misled by this insertion. Indeed, from the way in which the whole thing
coheres it is difficult to try to make "for" (ὅτι) relate to "in order that he may
be" (ἵνα γένηται) and not to "who is" (ὅς ἐστιν). Still, since the first sentence
begins the statement about Christ, anybody wanting to do justice to the parallel
must also concede that, as our second sentence recalls the first one by its
similarity of form, it must also rank equally with it, and consequently these are
the two main sentences on which the other clauses are dependent. The reason is
that they are not followed by a third sentence of equal importance, since verse
20 still depends on "for" (ὅτι), and the return to what was said in verses 9-11
already begins in v. 21. This alone already signifies not only that the "for" (ὅτι)
in the second main sentence stands in just the same relationship to its "who is"
(ὅς ἐστιν) as the one in the first sentence to its own, but also that verse 20
stands in the same relationship to the second main sentence as the clauses from
"all things" (τὰ πάντα) in verse 16 up to "of the church" (τῆς ἐκκλησίας) in
verse 18 stand to the first main sentence. That no such exact structural parallelism exists between these continuations or explanations is sufficiently explained
by the fact that they are only subordinate clauses, also that precisely in this way
the parallelism of the main sentences is all the more striking. However, there is
also the further reason that the last sentence had to be designed to make the
transition from this subject to the next one, which reestablishes the connection

---

Theology in that town. There, whilst also acting as Chief Chaplain to the court of the
Prince, he acquired the reputation of being a strong opponent of Semler and the hitherto
established principles of rationalism, which he attempted to show were devoid of historical
evidence. For the essay to which Schleiermacher here refers, see G.C. Storr, *Opuscula
Academica ad Interpretationem Librorum Sacrorum Pertinentia* (Tübingen: Johannis
Georgii Cottae, 1797).

with the sentences in verses 9-11. Even so, the same relationship unmistakably occurs here too. In the first addendum we find the two related verbs "have been created" (ἔκτισται) and "held together in" (συνέστηκεν), and in the second sentence we find the verbs "to reconcile" (ἀποκαταλλάξαι) and "to make peace" (εἰρηνοποιῆσαι), which are related also, and in both the things "on the earth and in the heavens" (ἐπὶ τῆς γῆς καὶ ἐν τοῖς οὐρανοῖς); and lastly, if in verse 20 we were to repeat "was pleased" (εὐδόκησε) without connection instead of "and" (καί), we would also have the same connection as that with "all things" (τὰ πάντα) in verse 16.

Let us pause for a moment at this general outline, in order to defend the decidedly biarticulate character of the passage under discussion against the interpretation of Chrysostom. I propose this for I gladly confess that I always think it worthwhile to begin by consulting what the exegetes among the Greek Fathers said about these difficult passages, because however many advantages we may enjoy compared with them, they have the supremely significant advantage of having spoken and written the language themselves, and in an idiom that had been formed from the linguistic usage of the New Testament. Now, to be sure, precisely when it comes to taking a broad conspectus they are far less authoritative, on account of the prevailing custom of treating those scriptures in a fragmented manner in their homilies and therefore tending to concentrate more on details. Thus, Chrysostom[69] distinguishes a threefold firstness (πρωτεία)[70] of Christ, which would characterize him as being the first above, the first in the church, and the first in the resurrection. The interpolated sentence "that in everything he might be preeminent" (ἵνα γένηται ἐν πᾶσιν αὐτὸς πρωτεύων) clearly reveals the apostle's intention to mention these distinctions jointly, and thus this explanation will appeal to all who are looking for triplicity everywhere. Yet, for our part we cannot find three equipollent sentences for these three members. The reason is that while Chrysostom finds the primacy above in our first sentence, and the primacy of resurrection in our second one, we find the primacy in the church only in the last subordinate

---

69. Schleiermacher's note: "Homil. III,2, concerning this letter." —Ed. note: In *S. Chrysostom's Homilies on the Epistles of St. Paul the Apostle to the Philippians, Colossians, and Thessalonians*, in *A Library of Fathers of the Holy Catholic Church, anterior to the division of the East and West* (Oxford: John Henry Parker, 1843), Homily III on Epistle to the Colossians, 212-223. Chrysostom writes: "For every where He is first; above first, in the Church first, for He is the Head; in the resurrection first. For such is the meaning of, verse 18: that He might have the preeminence." *S. Chrysostom's Homilies*, Ibid., 215-216.

70. Ed. note: This is an abstract noun formed from a Greek adverb meaning 'first' or verb meaning 'to be first' or 'to hold first place'.

clause in the first main sentence, and thus could attribute only a subordinate place to it as well. In further contrast, if we also consider that we find a common relation between Christ and things in heaven and things on earth not only under the first main sentence but under the second one as well, the traces of such a triplicity grow ever fainter, however elegantly it may trip off the tongue, for example, when we said "the primacy above, the primacy below, and primacy in the transition from earth to heaven." However, if we can detect only two main statements about Christ from the way the sentences are structured, what are those two statements?

To answer this question we must first of all look more closely at the relationships that these sentences bear to each another. The first thing that strikes me is that since in verse 13 what comes first is that we have been transferred into the kingdom of the Son, and precisely that is also referred to again in verse 21, though in a more exact reference to Gentile Christians, as the word 'estranged' (ἀπηλλοτριωμένους) shows, certainly both our main sentences must also be related to this, in that otherwise there would be no reason for the passage even as a digression, and consequently there would be no interconnection whatsoever. Then, of course, there would be nothing at all to say about such a puzzling passage; rather it would simply have to be left to the individual treatment of each scholar. However, to be sure the connection could naturally be either closer or more remote, and the two sentences might be the same, or might differ, in that respect. Suppose that we first take a look at the two main sentences without trying to get a more exact reading of their content. In general Christ is the image of God because all things are created in him, and Christ is the first from the dead because all the fullness of God was to dwell in him. The very next clarification of the first statement, then, leads us out of the moral domain which we think of with respect to the kingdom of the Son, into the domain of nature; in contrast, the latter keeps us firmly within the sphere of morals, since the "and you" (καὶ ὑμᾶς) of verse 21 is taken straight from the "all things" (τὰ πάντα) of verse 20, which phrase is in the closest connection to the phrase "all the fullness" (πᾶν τὸ πλήρωμα). This means that if there is an unlikeness here, it is at least regularly posited insofar as the closest relationship comes last. This is so because otherwise not only would the whole thing be an anticlimax, but there would be no direct route back to the point of departure. However, is the unlikeness really as great as it appears to be? If we can so easily say of Christ that all things are created through him, whether this "through him" can be found already in the "in him" (ἐν αὐτῷ) or only in the "through him" (δι' αὐτοῦ) of verse 16—in saying this we can be thinking not of the whole

Christ but only of his divine nature (to use our later terminology), or of the second person of the Trinity. If, on the other hand, we say that he is the first-born of the dead, we must expressly except precisely this divine person, which as such cannot have partaken of death and therefore also would not be the "first-born from the dead" (πρωτότοκος ἐκ νεκρῶν). Consequently, strictly speaking, the subject of our first main sentence cannot be the same as that of the second; and the parallelism of the two sentences would require this identity in the most striking way. Clearly, the first "who" (ὅς)[71] in verse 15 refers back to "Son" (υἱός), and the same must be true of the second one. Now, when Christ calls himself the Son of God or calls God his Father, he is not distinguishing one from the other within himself; rather, he totally means himself, the one who is speaking, Jesus of Nazareth, who was also the Christ. Likewise, moreover, there is no place in the New Testament where this expression would refer only to a part of Christ's nature; rather it would always refer to the whole, undivided Christ. Hence, had Paul, who could at this point refer only back to "Son" (υἱός), wanted to speak about only a part of Christ's nature in one place and about another part elsewhere, he would have had to insert a secondary definition at both places; this would have made clear the subordinated contrast between the two.

I do not know whether even at this point I must expect to hear the usual objection that this is to demand a great deal more craft than New Testament writers can be expected to display. I hope that the apostle Paul, at least, will be exempted from that particular impeachment! especially here, where it would have been so easy for him to say "who, according to the [s]pirit of holiness" (ὅς κατὰ μὲν πνεῦμα ἁγιωσύνης), or something similar, "is the image of God" (εἰκών ἐστι Θεοῦ) *etc.*, and then "according to fleshly origin" (κατὰ δὲ σάρκα ἀρχὴ) etc. However, since there is not the least trace of anything like that, we too have no right to construe the sentence "Christ is the image of the invisible God, because all were created in him" in a way that can be true only of the second person of the Trinity before he became human;[72] rather Paul can have been thinking only of the whole Christ, and we must therefore also be content to interpret the sentence in a way that can be applied to the whole Christ.[73]

---

71. Ed. note: This word is usually translated 'he' because verse 15 begins with a relative pronoun.

72. *Vor der Menschwerdung.*

73. Schleiermacher's note: "Even Storr admits this: *Ceterum Dei filius, cui liberationem referimus acceptam, est* "the god-man" (ὁ θεάνθρωπος), 131, though admittedly he subsequently says just the opposite (which Paul certainly does not bring in at this point) so as to

Moreover, we should be justified in assuming that Paul could have permitted himself such brevity of speech as to make the transition from the whole Christ to an earlier activity of the divine person that indwelt him thereafter without signalling it more clearly, only if the doctrine of the Trinity would by then have been fully developed and widely known, or if we could at least assert that Paul not only knew the doctrine of the *Logos* but also subscribed to it and, further-more, that he also knew that the Colossians and the Laodiceans were familiar with it as well. There is no evidence whatever for such an assumption, however.[74]

---

be able to refer part of the statement to Christ's divine nature and another part to his human nature, from both sentences without distinction." — Ed. note: On Storr, see note 9 above. In the article to which Schleiermacher refers, Storr writes: "Moreover, the Son of God (Col. 1:13), to whom we attribute our welcome liberation from the domain of darkness (n. 22) is ὁ θεΑΝΘΡΩΠΟΣ (Joh. 1:14; Heb. 1.2, cf. *Über den Zweck der evang. u. der Briefe Joh.*, 458), who, *seen from the prospect of the human nature*, is a *visible, created* being (v. 15, cf. *op. cit.* 507 f., 512 ff.) and connected with *our* race, for which he procured forgiveness of sins (v. 14) by his *death* (Col. 1.20-22), by an entirely unique relationship (v. 18), but, be-cause of his union (v. 19) with the divine nature (vv. 16 f.), he is the perfect image of God and entirely suitable to govern the Church and the creation in general." Storr's subsequent comments on "firstborn" are as follows: "Christ is called *protokos* (firstborn) particularly because, above all created things, he is like [†] [annotation added] God, and is therefore the pre-eminent creation (v. 18 *end* cf. Is. 14:30), dear to God above all the rest (Col. 1:13, cf. Jer. 31:9 and 31:20); rather, he is Lord of all the rest (Col. 1:18, 20; 2:10; Eph. 1:21ff., cf. *Neue Apol. der Off.*, 379 f.). Yet I would not deny that in this passage (v. 15), in a way also in v. 18 [the word *protokos*] has a *temporal* meaning, since the man Jesus is the visible likeness of God and has the sovereignty of all things (in the creation) from this same cause, because (v. 16, cf. *Über den Zwek. Joh.*, 427 f.) *the same* son of God, who is a man, is also originator of the universe and to this point is *prior to* and older [‡] than all things (v. 17), or because the man Jesus is very closely connected with the first and oldest cause of the creation of the world. Similarly, in Jn. 1:15 primacy and honour and time are linked. *Op. cit.*, 5." G.C. Storr, *Opuscula Academica ad Interpretationem Librorum Sacrorum Perti-nentia* (Tübingen: Johannis Georgii Cottae, 1797), 131-132. There is ambiguity in Storr's latin text regarding the sense in which Christ is like [†] (*similis*) God. Storr's reference to Christ being *ante omnes res creatas* could be interpreted in either a temporal sense or as a matter of degree. The subsequent reference to Christ being *prior* to and older [‡] than all things is again ambiguous in its use of the word "*prior*" but "antiquior" suggests temporality.

74.   Ed. note: There is little doubt that Paul does not use the title *Logos* as a designation for Jesus. It is possible, however, that the syncretistically influenced elements of Hellenistic Judaism, to which he wrote, would have been familiar with ideas of divine Wisdom and Logos as the image of God in Philo. See *De confusione linguarum* 97, 147; *De fuga et inventione* 101; *De somnis* 1.239, 2.45. These examples are cited by James D.G. Dunn, Ibid., 88, who also writes: "The Wisdom and Logos of God could thus function in effective Jewish apologetic within a wider Hellenistic milieu, where other similarly functioning terms

If we hold firm to this point, it inevitably entails total rejection of the usual interpretation, which deduces that Christ had a share in creation in the literal sense, and furthermore in the creation of spiritual beings, though the creation story says nothing about their origin, neither is anything of the sort passed down elsewhere in the Old Testament. In fact, there appears to be so much against this declaration that the only explanation I can find for it is a wish to find traces of the notion, and an eagerness to hit upon the sense of it as quickly as possible, without bringing the context into account. Where that seed of the lust for discovery falls on the ground of perplexity it usually produces a rank crop of hermeneutical weed. However, to begin with κτίζειν is not at all the word usually employed for "to create". It is not found in any passage treating the creation story in the Septuagint, and in his speech at Athens Paul makes use of ποιῆσαι for creation, the same word with which the writers of the Septuagint are also satisfied. In fact, wherever κτίζειν occurs in the Septuagint, whether for the Hebrew ברא or for other words, it never refers to the original production of something that had not previously existed but refers only to the founding and establishing of something that will continue to exist and develop in the future,[75] to say nothing about the places at which the usage is very much the same as the Greek. The same remark applies to all Pauline passages.[76] Thus, even supposing that the reference here were to different levels of angels, the words would signify not so much the creation of these various personal entities, their calling into existence, as their installation in these particular orders, or indeed the institution of such hierarchies among them. However, are we really entitled to entertain that supposition either? Certainly not on the sole ground that Paul can be shown to have accepted such distinctions; rather, either the impossibility of any different interpretation must be obvious or else the

---

were less suitable ('glory of God' too Jewish, 'Spirit of God' too rational)." For more on this, see the introductory essay, 7.

75. Schleiermacher's note: "I can confidently invite readers to look up all such references in Trommius and Biel; for in this regard Schleusner is very incomplete, and his numeration is marred by printing errors." — Ed. note: For Schleiermacher's reference to Schleusner's notes on ΚΤΙΖΩ, ΚΤΙΣΙΣ, ΚΤΙΣΜΑ and ΚΤΙΣΤΗΣ, see Joh. Frieder. Schleusner, *Novum Lexicon Graeco-Latinum in Novum Testamentum* (Lipsiae: Weidmannia, 1808), vol. I, 1292-1294. The editor has not been able to trace his references to Trommius and Biel.

76. Schleiermacher's note: "Where reference is made to cosmos (κόσμος), the use of this word already indicates that the main concept is the foundation of a fixed order and harmonization. Moreover, where 'the creator' (ὁ κτίσας) and 'the creature' (ἡ κτίσις) are combined it is because of this very relation, nor is creation (*erschaffen*) as such mentioned elsewhere, e.g. I Cor. 11:9; 1 Tim. 4:3; and Col. 3:10."

expositor must prove, at least through analogies, that the angelic hierarchies could be described by means of such appellations. Our knowledge of the Essenes is quite insufficient for this purpose; but even supposing, as Paul did in fact admit, the existence of such "thrones" (θρόνους) and "dominions" (κυριότητας), would he have absorbed Essene doctrines in such a manner? Both considerations likewise apply if we want to think about Gnostic teachings.[77] Now, as far as I know, nobody has yet asserted that such information should be derived from Christ's teachings, or even wished to enlarge upon Matth. 18:10 to this extent. Moreover, it is just as unlikely that the Pharisees can have imagined that some of the angels sat on thrones like co-regents or companions of the Almighty, while others were at various levels of administration and government, which could justify the use of the term "ruler" (ἀρχή).[78]

All these assumptions are entirely lacking in substance and formulation.[79] However, the other proposal that no other explanation is possible is so wide of the mark that for us it causes the utmost confusion within the context. This is so for what could the creation of the angels through the "Word" (λόγος) now indwelling the Christ possibly have to do with our deliverance into the kingdom

---

77. Ed. note: This relates to questions about the nature of the heresy at Colossae. Schnecken-burger argued in "Schrift über die Proselytentaufe," *Beit. a. Einl. ins N.T.* § 146 *Theo-logische Studien und Kritiken* 1832 that the heresy was essentially Christian. Rheinwald countered this in *de pseudodoctoribus Coloss.* (Bonn, 1834) by arguing that the main problems arose from Jewish perceptions of Christ. Böhmer, in *Isagoge in ep. ad Coloss.*, 119, detected the germ of gnostic influences, as did Meyerhofer (*der Br. und. Col.* § 157). It is unclear with how much of this type of discussion Schleiermacher was familiar, though reference is made earlier in this essay to the work of Prof. Böhmer (n. 3). For a detailed survey of early 19th century scholarship on Colossians, see Wilhelm M.L. de Wette, *Kurze Erklärung der Briefe an die Colosser, an Philemon, an die Ephesier und Philipper* (Leipzig: Weidemann'sche Buchhandlung, 1847). For more on this, see the introductory essay, 10ff.

78. Schleiermacher's note: "One need scarcely mention the unlikelihood of Paul's having presupposed the notion that developed later, that angels were in charge of the elements and of the various heavenly bodies. Cf. Origen: *in Ierem. Hom.* X,6." — Ed. note: For addi-tional comments by Schleiermacher on this, see *Christian Faith* (Edinburgh: T. and T. Clark, 1989, 1830-1831 edition), §§ 164.21.

79. Ed. note: literally, "hanging quite without form in the air." Calvin wrote in his commentary on Colossians that thrones, powers, principalities and dominions should be understood as referring to "the heavenly place of God's majesty." Paul extols the dignity of angels in order to set forth the glory of Christ. *Calvin's Commentaries, the Epistles of Paul the Apostle to the Galatians, Ephesians, Philippians and Colossians,* trans. by T.H.L. Parker, (Edinburgh: Oliver and Boyd, 1965), 309. It is likely, but not possible to establish beyond doubt, that Schleiermacher had read this.

of the Son? Indeed, it is not as if we knew anything about a doctrine of this kind held by the apostle, attributing to the angels a share in the administration of the kingdom of God:[80] rather, in order to posit such a doctrine, one would first have to deny that there was any affinity between the Letter to the Hebrews and the school of Paul.[81] Moreover, even if Paul had handed down this teaching, without our knowing about it from any other source, we should most likely hear about it in a letter to a congregation that he himself had founded, and in which he had taught for a sufficient length of time to have dealt with matters of that kind, so that his hearers could fill in for themselves any gaps in continuity from his oral teachings. However, how could he expect the Colossians to understand matters of that kind? Well, I might have swallowed that if Paul had at some point digressed into a paean of praise about Christ, in which he no longer considers the context and in which this is one element among many, but not here, where this very thought is immediately taken up again, in order to be brought into the most intimate connection with what Christ has done for us, and the gifts we have received through him.

Still, in order to become more definitely convinced that this is the case, we must take a close look at the addendum to our main sentence and the reasons for it. As I see it, this too consists of two double sentences that are unmistakably parallel. One of these is: "all things were created through him and for him. He is before all things" (τὰ πάντα δι' αὐτοῦ καὶ εἰς αὐτὸν ἔκτισται, καὶ αὐτός ἐστι πρὸ πάντων), and the other: "And in him all things hold together. He is the head of the body, the church" (καὶ τὰ πάντα ἐν αὐτῷ συνέστηκεν, καὶ αὐτός ἐστιν ἡ κεφαλὴ τοῦ σώματος τῆς ἐκκλησίας). Here the correspondence between these two sentences is so exact that the parallelism can be made with considerable accuracy. Thus, it is only through the two together that, as required by the unrestricted beginning, the sentence immediately preceding, that all things were created in him, is taken up again. Hence, "have been created" (ἔκτισται) and "hold together" (συνέστηκε) must belong together in such a way that, strictly speaking, the latter is already present in the former. The change of tense is sufficiently motivated by the fact that what is past is brought into connection with a present "is before all things, is the head" (ἐστὶ πρὸ

---

80. Schleiermacher's note: "Even Ephesians 3:10 rather speaks against this."
81. Schleiermacher's note: "'For an office of service' (διακονία) is very far from being a 'principality' (ἀρχή) or an 'authority' (ἐξουσία); and anybody who maintains that the Son is higher and more excellent than the angels in fact and in name will certainly not have the proposition that the Son is the one through whom or to whom the angels were created at one's disposal. Cf. Heb. 1:4-14."

πάντων, ἐστὶ κεφαλή), and "is the head" (ἐστὶ κεφαλή) must be in exactly the same relationship to "is before all things" (ἐστι πρὸ πάντων) as "hold together" (συνέστηκε) is to "have been created" (ἔκτισται). Now, as regards the latter, those who in reading "have been created" (ἔκτισται) unambiguously think of 'to be created'[82] will also quite naturally explain "hold together" (συνέστηκε) in the same terms. In any case, by doing this they confirm on the one hand that they understand the relationship between the two expressions in this passage in the same way as we do, and yet on the other hand they distance themselves sufficiently far from the sphere of the word if "hold together" (συνέστηκε) is to mean just the same as "to be sustained"—the intransitive forms must keep their relation to the transitive forms. However, if the guiding formula idea for the transitive forms is the well known one of bringing one thing together with another one, then I should look for the intransitive forms in such juxtapositions as "formed of milk, formed of snow" (γάλα συνέστηκε, χιὼν συνέστηκε).[83] Thus, I should look for this formula where the main concept also consists of single elements brought together, and in such a case "hold together" (συνέστηκε) follows naturally upon "have been created" (ἐκτίσθη), very correctly used of the becoming established, the being consolidated of conditions and institutional arrangements, but not at all of the continuation of existence.[84] Correctly interpreted, however, it is precisely congruent with the "have been created" (ἐκτίσθη), as was explained above.

In contrast, if "all things" (τὰ πάντα) in verse 16 refers primarily to the heavenly spirits, and thus obviously the same expression used here must also mean the same thing, this would assert an intimate connection between the statements that the orders of the heavenly spirits are held together by Christ and

---

82. *Erschaffensein*.

83. Schleiermacher's note: "II Peter 3:5 is also similar, 'earth formed out of water' (γῆ ἐξ ὕδατος συνεστῶσα)."

84. Schleiermacher's note: "Two non-biblical loci are usually adduced for this meaning: Pseudo-Aristoteles *de mundo* 6, "that all things are from God and are constituted for us by God" (ὡς ἐκ Θεοῦ τὰ πάντα, καὶ διὰ Θεοῦ ἡμῖν συνέστηκε), where usually only the preceding expression "the cause that holds the world together" (ἡ τῶν ὅλων συνεκτικὴ αἰτία) has to be recalled, in order to see the meaning I mentioned appear quite clearly. The other locus is Herodian I,9 (Bekker, 13,29) "because he was confident of his father's power" (θαρρῶν τῇ τοῦ πατρὸς ὡς ἔτι συνεστώσῃ δυνάμει); but here too the same meaning appears quite clearly, as if it had not yet been scattered and dispersed, but all its components were still firmly held in place." — Ed. note: the standard *Loeb* Classical Library translations are used here. For the texts see Aristotle, *On the Cosmos*, by D.J. Furley (London: William Heinemann, 1955), 397b, 384; *Herodian in Two Volumes*, by C.R. Whittaker (London: William Heinemann, 1969), 1.9.9, 59.

that Christ is the head of the Church. However, we have here no connecting links at all for this, and the situation is not really improved if one remembers that in any event those four heavenly orders are only a part of the "all things" (τὰ πάντα), that they belong entirely to heaven and the invisible world, but that "all things" includes both the visible heavenly world and the whole earthly one. In actuality, if we want to find this connection here, I do not see how we are to continue to keep our ecclesial teaching separate from the teaching of the New Jerusalem, and our whole ecclesiastical practice separate from the method of those who, while they direct all their prayers to Christ and trace back to his government all those earthly occurrences and all those circumstances that intervene in the lives of Christians, thrust God, whose express image Christ is here presented to be, right into the background. Nevertheless, we shall have to accept that, if that is what Paul was thinking as he wrote. However, if all this is so exactly related to Christ's position in relation to the church as it appears, how inappropriately Paul would have been writing if he had actually left out of this compass the heavenly hierarchy, the connection of which with Christ's kingdom on earth is least understandable, but he would have passed over in silence what had to be of greatest concern to the Christians to whom he was writing, namely, how all the earthly conditions relating to his kingdom are ordered and subsist!

Let us bear this concern in mind and, at the same time, how little we can assert that the expressions "thrones, dominions, principalities, authorities" (θρόνοι, κυριότητες, ἀρχαί, ἐξουσίαι), regarded as designations for super-human existence, would have been known and in current use.[85] So, we have to ask ourselves what the apostle's readers would have thought on reading these

---

85. Schleiermacher's note: "True, Theodoret in commenting on this passage says that they were in use, but it is evident from his explanation that this is not based on any tradition. He presents it only as his hypothesis 'to suppose' (ἡγοῦμαι) that the cherubim should be understood as being part of the thrones and also that the others are the angels of the nations. However, the passages in Daniel 10:13, 20 and 21 would only serve to indicate that the other nations had wicked angels, since they resist the one who is sent to Daniel, and such angels cannot be under discussion here. Moreover, it is said earlier where this notion occurs that when the Redeemer came the angels had lost this dominion (cf. Origen in *Genes. Hom.* IX.3 and in *Ioann. Tom.* XIII, 49) and furthermore there was no reason to discuss the topic here." — Ed. note: see Theodoreti, *Episc. Cyri Commentarius in omnes B. Pauli Epistolas* (Oxonii et Londini: Jacobus Parker et Soc., 1870) pars II, 74. Theodoret writes: "Θρόνους ἡγοῦμαι τὰ Χερουβὶμ αὐτὸν λέγειν. Τούτοις γὰρ εἶδε τὸν Θεῖον ἐπικείμενον θρόνον ὁ προφήτης Ἰεζεκιήλ. Κυριότητας δὲ, καὶ ἀρχὰς, καὶ ἐξουσίας, τοὺς τῶν ἐθνῶν πεπιστευμένους τὴν ἐπιμέλειαν. Καὶ γὰρ Μιχαὴλ ἦρχε τῶν Ἰουδαίων, καὶ ὁ μακάριος Δανιὴλ (Dan. x. 13) ἄρχοντα λέγει Περσῶν, καὶ ἄρχοντα Ἑλλήνων."

words. If we assume they had a taste for such lofty speculations, or that they had a theory about supernatural spirits, and that Paul also had that in mind, there are, it seems to me, only two possibilities: either these are the technical terms that were current there, but in that case, even if I wanted to concede that Paul did not find it necessary to say anything against that theory, I simply cannot believe that the apostle should have appropriated the theory in such a way as to give no hint that he was unfamiliar with these expressions; or else these expressions are not theirs, but how could he then employ expressions unfamiliar to them, whatever their source, without giving the slightest indication of how these related to their expressions? If the Colossians were cognizant of these matters then, to the extent that the apostle's expressions were to relate to these matters, they were not appropriate and therefore also could not produce any worthy, didactic or purifying effects. If, on the other hand, the Colossians were not versed in these things, these expressions would not readily suggest higher beings to them. Moreover, circumstances being what they are, we too shall be well advised to follow the question as to what the Colossians may have thought on coming across these expressions if they knew, and wanted to know, just as little about angels as we do but were curious about anything that was supposed to relate to the kingdom of the Son, wherever it might lead. "Principalities" (Ἀρχαί) and "authorities" (ἐξουσίαι) would probably have been familiar to them as titles of superior offices and other positions held by powerful persons. "Throne" (θρόνος) was well known as a name for kingly seats, but it was also used for other distinguished persons. Thus, not even this first word could give them a different clue; at most they might have been uncertain as to whether it should refer to an exclusive teaching post and office. Perhaps, on the other hand, this later locution already had its roots in that time and the thrones promised to the apostles are also to be understood in this way. Now, the "dominions" (κυριότητες) did indeed still remain, and this is completely unfamiliar to us outside the New Testament.[86] Whether it first occurred in the area of our text, or whether it was already in use, it was understandable in terms of its origin and its form, and it could fit in equally well with the explanation of "throne" (θρόνος) as regarding the dignity of the civil government or the regard in which teachers were held.

---

86. Schleiermacher's note: "As is known, it does not even occur in the Septuagint, whereas 'lords' (κυρεία) often occurs, for instance in Daniel, also in connection with king and royalty, and it is possible that the other form may have come to be substituted for this one."

Thus, these expressions would not be sufficient in themselves to cause the readers to think about things supernatural; but to what extent and in what sense was the contrast between heaven and earth, the visible and invisible worlds, bound so to do? In the first place, I see no necessity to consider these contrasts to be completely synonymous, and thus to think of one as being merely a superfluous repetition of the other. Indeed, even anywhere on earth only external things are visible, effects and deeds, whereas what is internal, the movement of the will, power, is invisible.[87] However, in order to decide whether these two contrasts do in fact overlap (as I have assumed above, though without trying to apply it to the passage under consideration), or whether only one side of one of them should be divided by the other, and if so which one, and what relation our four main terms would then have to the result, we must first reach agreement about what is in heaven and what is on earth. Meanwhile, we certainly do not want to stir up the whole investigation again at this point; rather, we only want to take it as stipulated and conceded that to say that heaven and earth constitute the universe, implying that heaven comprises everything that is not on earth, is not all that can be said. The Jews and their contemporaries had another way of looking at it. They were used to thinking of a kingdom of heaven, and it follows naturally that what belonged to that kingdom of heaven could also be called "the things in the heavens" (τὰ ἐν τοῖς οὐρανοῖς) so that in this usage everything that is outside that kingdom of heaven could just as well be called earthly, just as everything outside and above the earth was also called heaven. Now, to the Jews this kingdom of heaven meant not only the awaited Messianic kingdom; that kingdom was indeed its supreme consummation, but the Torah and the Temple worship also belonged to it already.

In their language, Christians naturally limited the expression to that narrower scope, but that does not entitle us to assert that Paul could not have used it in its wider sense as well, so that he would also have taken into account preparations for the messianic kingdom, along with the narrower meaning. Moreover, there is also something else that I wish to take as agreed, something that has more to do with the apostle's style. That is to say, he had a considerable penchant for contrasts and a particular fondness for certain ones of a solemn nature, so that when any subject matter presents itself to him as belonging to one side of such a contrast, then that which is opposed to it, in any respect, is also brought under the other side of the contrast, even if it does not

---

87. Schleiermacher's note: "The way in which Paul himself uses the words 'the invisible nature' (τὰ ἀόρατα) of God in Rom. 1:20 also leads in this direction."

fit so closely there as in some other instance where it was used. Thus, if everything belonging to the kingdom of heaven was called "the things in the heavens" (τὰ ἐν τοῖς οὐρανοῖς), then everything belonging to earthly kingdoms, civil order and legal situations, could also be designated as "the things on the earth" (τὰ ἐπὶ τῆς γῆς). It seems to follow very naturally from this contrast, moreover, that the way in which "the things in the heavens" (τὰ ἐν τοῖς οὐρανοῖς) refers to Christ was assumed to be known and not in need of further elucidation. However, it was different with the other member, and so another consequence was that the contrast "the visible and the invisible" (τὰ ὁρατὰ καὶ τὰ ἀόρατα) refers only to the last member, but that in this case, unlike the former, what is material and visible, conceived as more remote, is only hinted at, and only the invisible is severally held up to view. Consequently, the contrasts that are set up by the apostle lead us to the same meaning for our four main terms as our consideration so far has led us to; thus, Paul is not saying something inappropriate but is saying exactly what we would have had to wish him to say, namely that conditions on earth for human beings are related to Christ and how they are so related.

The only drawback is that unfortunately in this case everything is based on the meaning of the prepositions Paul uses, and these are grammatically difficult to determine. Thus, the question arises at the outset: if the first sentence "in him all things were created" (τὰ πάντα ἐν αὐτῷ ἐκτίσθη) immediately after the narrower definition which is to be added to this "all things" (πάντα) is taken up again by the following sentence "all things have been created through him and for him" (τὰ πάντα δι' αὐτοῦ καὶ εἰς αὐτὸν ἔκτισται), is this second one supposed to be just the same as the first, or is it supposed to take us further at the same time? If the two particles together correspond to the "in" (ἐν) in the first sentence, it is just the same; but if only one of them corresponds to it and the other contains something new, then it takes us further. But which one? The previous way of treating these things[88] makes "in" (ἐν) and "through" (διά) just

---

88. Schleiermacher's note: "By 'previous' I mean until Winer's New Testament grammar, which has advanced this matter so decisively that it will no longer be possible to remain in the earlier arbitrariness and indistinctness of meanings pieced together yet flying apart. I also would have no wish to deviate from his method at any point in this matter; but in some instances there are bound to be differences in its application, and this is one passage where I too differ from Winer. That is to say, in his paragraph 54.6 he chooses to make 'through him' (δι' αὐτοῦ) one and the same as 'in him' (ἐν αὐτῷ), and he defends this choice by saying that it is happening only after parenthetical statements, for at that point the passage rightly comes under the rule established in paragraph 54.3, that in parallel passages prepositions closely allied in meaning stand for each other, which he rightly would not willingly

as indefinite and indistinguishable from the genitive as it leaves "in" (ἐν) and "for" (εἰς) one and the same. Now, when I consider that the parallel sentence "in him all things hold together" (τὰ πάντα ἐν αὐτῷ συνέστηκε) again stops at "in" (ἐν), this fully compels me to assume that the first sentence did not go any further either, and that in consequence only the two particles "through him" (δι' αὐτοῦ) and "for him" (εἰς αὐτόν) together take up the "in" (ἐν), though of course by way of analyzing and explaining it.

Now, I think that Paul would have been able to say that everything was created in Christ without leaving his train of thought directed at the spiritual kingdom of the Son; he would have been able to say it of everything that stands in any relation to the spiritual world of human beings, and thus also of the corporeal world, indeed of the supernatural world of spirits as well. That is to say, he could have affirmed this providing that redemption through Christ, and one can also just as correctly say Christ himself, is the key to all the divine institutions that refer to humankind, and consequently that he is the one foundation of all; and this is the way to express this relationship, which ever remains

---

allow in one and the same context. Only here I cannot agree to any parenthetical statements, since everything that comes in between was simply defining 'all things' (πάντα) more precisely; rather, I think this would amount to both of them making 'in him' (ἐν αὐτῷ) and 'through him' (δι' αὐτοῦ) stand right next to each other and yet mean the same thing, and in this light Winer would agree to this as little as he rightly does with Rom. 11:36. However, the triplicity in the latter passage is obviously different from the triplicity in our passage. That is to say, in our passage the three prepositions are coordinated with each other in exact relation to the preceding questions, which I too regard as three and not, as Lachmann also interpunctuates, as two. This is the case, for the 'the' (ἤ) in verse 34 does not stand in the same relationship to the 'who' (τίς) in that verse as the 'and' (καί) in verse 35 does to the first sentence in that verse. Otherwise Paul would have said 'and who has been his counsellor' (καί σύμβουλος αὐτοῦ ἐγένετο) there too. The second sentence in verse 35 is also a more precise definition of the 'given' (προέδωκεν) just as if 'so that' (ὥστε) were there, so that it would have to be restored to it. Moreover, in the same way the 'from him' (ἐξ αὐτοῦ) refers to the exclusive origin of the idea, the 'through him' (δι' αὐτοῦ) refers to the exclusive origin of the method of realizing it, and the 'to him' (εἰς αὐτόν) relates to the exclusivity of the ultimate relationship." — Ed. note: J.G.B. Winer was Professor of Theology at Erlangen and subsequently at Leipzig. His particular concern was to supplement investigation of the lexicography of the New Testament, such as that pursued by Storr, with a rational method of treatment applied to its grammar. See his *Idioms of the Language of the New Testament*, by J.H. Agnew and O.G. Ebbeke (New York: Robert Carter and Brothers, 1850). Karl Lachmann (b. 1793) was primarily a philologist but had extensive interests also in theology and jurisprudence. He was Professor at Königsberg 1818-1825 and at Berlin 1825-1851. For Lachmann's recension of Col.1:15-20, see Carolus Lachmannus, *Novum Testamentum Graece et Latine* (Berolini: Georgii Reimeri, 1850), 498-502.

the same. However, in what follows, this same relationship is broken down into its temporal elements. Indeed, everything begins by being mediated through him, since things would have been ordered differently if he was not supposed to make his entrance in the fullness of time;[89] and everything ends up being for him and furthering his kingdom in one way or another. The fact that Paul then quite prominently mentions the public authorities in their various hierarchical ranks when trying to induce the Colossians to take this to heart, as he unmistakably does in verse 21, may be partly due to what he had already learned about how the congregations in Phrygia had come into being and how they had hitherto been led, and partly to the fact that he paid far too much attention to the progress of Christianity in general to be able to write to what was virtually a new province to him without being filled with thoughts of that kind. Indeed, both of these elements may be more definitely separated and brought together in our four substantives themselves than we are directly aware. The reason is that, since "throne" (θρόνος) obviously refers more to the monarchical system that prevailed then, whereas "principality" (ἀρχή) is a recognized republican expression, but at that time these forms were much less in use and were largely confined to municipal affairs, "dominion" (κυριότης) naturally comes after "throne" (θρόνος), and "authority" (ἐξουσία) comes after "principality" (ἀρχή), since the four words collapse into two pairs. It must not be overlooked, however, that the latter's being mentioned by itself anticipates the end of our passage—that is, its immediate reference is to the Colossians; but only taken together with what is contained in "all things" (τὰ πάντα) does this "created in him" (ἐν αὐτῷ ἐκτίσθη) cohere with the first main sentence as its foundation.

We must now address the question: What is the statement made about Christ in our first main sentence, then, precisely because in the meaning that is given everything that relates to the human world has its foundation in him? Now, as far as I know, it is indeed generally assumed that two kinds of things are said about Christ in our sentence, namely that "image of God" (εἰκὼν τοῦ Θεοῦ) is something special in itself, and that "firstborn" (πρωτότοκος) with its sub-definition is also something special; only I do have serious reservations about this, reservations that perhaps have not received sufficient attention. By virtue of these reservations, moreover, I think that an alternative view should at least be entertained, namely, that the statement could also be a simple one if "firstborn" (πρωτότοκος) with its sub-definition belonged to "image" (εἰκών). We ask accordingly: What should actually be the meaning of the statement that

89. Ed. note: Eph. 1:10.

he is the first-born of all creation? The facts do not support the only possible grammatical explanation, that of "all creation" (πᾶσα κτίσις)[90] being portrayed as the mother of Christ. This being so, "of all creation" (πάσης κτίσεως) can only refer to the "first" (πρῶτος), which is a component of the word "firstborn" (πρωτότοκος), but then, as he is the "firstborn" (πρωτότοκος) likewise the "creation" (κτίσις) is the "second born" (δευτορότοκος) born afterwards.

Chrysostom's attempt to escape such a conclusion, that the Son is "of the same substance of creation" (ὁμοούσιος τῶν κτισμάτων), by saying that "firstborn" (πρωτότοκος) means the same as "foundation" (θεμέλιος),[91] is too arbitrary and far-fetched. Moreover, what Theodoret says (afterwards followed by nearly everyone else), namely that "before all things in creation" (πρὸ πάσης κτίσεως) needs to be supplemented and that, in order not to appear similar to "creation" (κτίσις), Christ is not called "first of creation" (πρωτόκτιστος) but "firstborn" (πρωτότοκος), does not seem to help matters very much. This is so for even in that case anybody must think of the creature as being born afterwards, otherwise there would be no relation between the nominative and the genitive or the preposition, and that would itself mean both that he is the firstborn without anyone coming after him and that he precedes all creatures; and if the effect is no better than this, it seems hardly worth while inserting the "first" (πρό). However, that is how it is with polemical explanations! If we endeavor only to show that some thought or other is not contained in a given passage, we always run the risk of failing to find the correct meaning as well. Meanwhile, apart from all that, we could not subscribe to these explanations, because both of them refer to the eternal procreation and thus take the Son not in the sense of the whole Christ but only as the second person of the Trinity.

If at this point we then wish to remain true to the principle we have established and take "firstborn of all creation" (πρωτότοκος πάσης κτίσεως) by itself, in accordance with what has been said, we should only be able to conceive of "creation" (κτίσις) as the establishment and arrangement of things

---

90. Ed. note: πᾶσα is a feminine first declension form of πας.
91. Ed. note: See 1 Cor. 3:10. about which Chrysostom writes: "So also the word *firstborn* is said as *foundation* is. But this doth not shew the creatures to be consubstantial with Him; but that all things are by Him, and in Him. So also when he says elsewhere, *I have laid a foundation*, he is speaking not concerning substance, but operation." Ibid., 215. Theodoret writes: " Πρωτότοκος τοίνυν ἐστὶ τῆς κτίσεως, οὐχ ὡς ἀδελφὴν ἔχων τὴν κτίσιν, ἀλλ' ὡς πρὸ πάσης κτίσεως γεννηθείς. ἱ Ἄλλως τε οὐδὲ πρωτόκτιστον αὐτὸν εἶπεν ὁ Θεῖος ἀπόστολος, ἀλλὰ πρωτότοκον, τουτέστι πρῶτον οὕτω καὶ ˄πρωτότοκος ἐκ τῶν νεκρῶν'." Theodoreti, *Episc. Cyri Commentarius in omnes B. Pauli Epistolas* (Oxonii et Londini: Jacobus Parker et Soc., 1870), pars II, 73ff.

human,[92] and to be the firstborn of these would be in effect to be its first member, on which all others depend; and this is fully in accordance with the elucidations we have given so far concerning the substantiating sentence that follows. Moreover, the first statement, that Christ is the image of the invisible God, is quite comprehensible on its own, for it rightly brings back the memory of Christ's own words, that he makes the Father visible[93] and present. The only thing is that, as far as I am concerned, this statement on the one hand already goes beyond the interconnection that is wholly contained in the phrase "kingdom of the Son" (βασιλεία τοῦ υἱοῦ), and furthermore the second one, separated from this, would also be an anticlimax. This is so, for even to be the centrepiece of all institutions, including those of the spiritual world, and to have dominion over them, is much less than to be such an image of God.

Now, this dilemma is avoided if the two statements are taken together, which, I for one, conceive to be possible. To be sure, images are not literally[94] born, but in the literal sense there is also no image of God. Moreover, when Paul said that within the total compass of the spiritual world of human beings Christ was the firstborn image of God (in the most extensive meaning that this phrase can have) that was an obscure saying, but one that is illuminated by the illustration that followed it, which says that Christ is the image of God, in that in this area designated by the phrase "all creation" (πᾶσα κτίσις), as this expression is further defined subsequently, the same is true of Christ, that everything is through him and to him, that is true of God for all existing things—and this is the right place for a comparison with Rom. 11:36,[95]—so he is the image of God. On this scale one could also have said "from whom" (ἐξ οὗ) of Christ, but only for the kingdom of God in the narrowest sense, and all that came before would have had to be excluded from it. Moreover, it is indeed self-evident that the relation of the "creation" (κτίσις) to God, that it is "from God" (ἐξ αὐτοῦ) and "through God" (δι' αὐτοῦ) and "to God" (εἰς αὐτόν) is not ended by its relation to Christ,[96] since here too God is not only understood

---

92. Schleiermacher's note: "It is not to be overlooked that if κτίσις is here taken to mean 'creature', πᾶσα κτίσις must also be taken as 'every creature' whereas in the meaning adduced, since of itself it forms a collective πᾶσα κτίσις must be taken as equivalent to the whole establishment, as πᾶς οἶκος Ἰσραήλ is to the whole house of Israel."
93. Schleiermacher's note: "John 14:9."
94. *Im eigentlichen Sinn.*
95. Ed. note: Rom. 11:36 reads: "For from him and through him and to him are all things."
96. Schleiermacher's note: "Chrysostom has lost his way in a peculiar labyrinth here; it results in a real division and makes the Father responsible for creating the visible heavenly things and the Son the invisible ones."

as the creator (κτίσας)⁹⁷ of everything that was "created in the Son" (ἐν τῷ υἱῷ ἐκτίσθη) but, in addition, the deliverance into the kingdom of the Son is ascribed to God. Now as soon as we reach this view, and without forgetting that in the process we are talking about the whole Christ, it becomes readily apparent that what is elucidated by the "for" (ὅτι) that follows is the concept of the image, but not that of the firstborn Son. This is so for surely nobody can find any congruence in the statement that the one through whom and for whom something else is created will be in the same relationship to this as a firstborn to one born later, and consequently the "firstborn" (πρωτότοκος) would be left quite unnoticed as a superfluous addition, if it represented only itself.

Nevertheless, it might be objected that this is at the least no better than the explanation offered here, if what follows simply illustrates the concept of the likeness.⁹⁸ However, even in this epistle (3:10) we do see that the new man⁹⁹ is also related "after the image of its creator" (κατ᾽ εἰκόνα τοῦ κτίσαντος αὐτόν) and that all the faithful are to be built up into the image of Christ, which means that the likeness of God¹⁰⁰ must also emerge in them too. Indeed, this epistle says further that if the community of the faithful is the body of Christ, it must also be in his image and, consequently, an image of God of the second order. It is inconceivable that the Colossians should not have known these things, thus that we are the likeness of God but indirectly. Moreover, this must have occurred naturally to the apostle's readers, if Christ was presented to them as "firstborn image" (εἰκὼν πρωτότοκος). Furthermore, they must have found that he was such very well illustrated both by the fact that he is the foundation not only of everything that belongs directly to the kingdom of heaven but also of what exerts only an indirect influence on it, and by the fact that all this received its firm stature through its relation to him, just as the whole world has in God and in relation to God. For this reason, he is, and for ever remains, the head of the "church" (ἐκκλησία). The fact that superiority and privilege is intended by "before all things" (πρὸ πάντων) in the parallel preceding sentence, as elsewhere, is sufficiently indicated by its parallel with this sentence. Likewise, Chrysostom, when he asserts that "church" (ἐκκλησία) stands for the whole

---

97. Ed. note: the sense implies 'co-creator.'
98. *Ebenbild.* Ed. note: Just above, the term is simply *Bild*, just below successively *das Bild Christi, das Ebenbild Gottes*; then the church is referred to as *sein Bild* (Christ's) and *ein solchen Bild Gottes der zweiten Ordnung.*
99. *Der neue Mensch.* Ed. note: In the R.S.V.: "new nature" and in the N.R.S.V.: "new self."
100. *Das Bild Christi . . . das Ebenbild Gottes.*

human race here, is right only to the extent that it is also through Christ's mediation that the whole human race is to belong to it.

However, what finally persuades me to take "firstborn" (πρωτότοκος) and "image" (εἰκών) together is the nature of our second main sentence: "he is the beginning, the firstborn from the dead" (ὅς ἐστιν ἀρχὴ πρωτότοκος ἐκ τῶν νεκρῶν). I want in no way to corrupt the meaning by not interposing something after "beginning" (ἀρχή); all I want is to avoid pre-judgment as to whether the two words tend to converge or to diverge so that we can surrender entirely to the impression made by the discourse. To be sure, at this point the position appears to be that if the two are taken together it would have meant the same to us if Paul had written only "he is the first from the dead" (ὅς ἐστιν ἀρχὴ ἐκ τῶν νεκρῶν), or only "he is firstborn from the dead" (ὅς ἐστι πρωτότοκος ἐκ τῶν νεκρῶν), and thus insofar as there already lies in that, one of the two then already appears to be superfluous, indeed also insofar as there already lies in each of them contains the presupposition that others are also to follow the one who is the first or the first-born. Yet, what if we were to separate the two?[101] Can "first" (ἀρχή) be referred to anything other than the resurrection of the dead? Should something, nevertheless, quite new and unrelated link onto that? Furthermore, to what else is it to refer? Is it to be referred back to "church" (ἐκκλησία), so that it would better be written "of which he is also first" (ἧς ἐστι καὶ ἀρχή), compelling us to think about a difference between "first" (ἀρχή) and "head" (κεφαλή)? Alternatively, should it be understood in a general way, so that "of the cosmos" (τοῦ κόσμου) or "of the origin" (τῆς γενέσεως) would have to be supplemented and Paul would be Arianising here, since this could no longer apply to the whole Christ without making the transition noticeable? In short, even if we want to separate the two it follows inevitably that "first" (ἀρχή) will attract "from the dead" (ἐκ τῶν νεκρῶν) by force. Moreover, any separation within the sentence is limited by the fact that

---

101. Schleiermacher's note: "Surely nobody will wish to defend Storr's paraphrase of the words ὅς ἐστιν ἀρχή as 'who is ruler' *qui inquam regnat*, any longer. If we were to refer back the meaning of 'ruler' (ἀρχή), it could at most mean 'who is a person among the rulers'—not even that, however, for only 'to be in rulership' (ἐν ἀρχῇ εἶναι) can have that meaning. Indeed, nothing like that comes up anywhere in the New Testament. Even in Rev. 3:14 "the chief of creation" (ἡ ἀρχὴ τῆς κτίσεως) cannot be translated as 'ruler', and no other such passage bears this meaning. — Ed. note: Rev. 3:14 is translated in the N.R.S.V. as "the origin of God's creation." Storr draws on Rev.3:14, along with Tit.3:1, to defend his rendering of v.18, which reads: "idemque est caput corporis sui, ecclesiæ; qui inquam regnat, postquam princeps a mortuis excitatus suit, ut omnium principatum obtineret." Ibid., 133-35. Cf. footnote 9.

"firstborn" (πρωτότοκος) cannot actually be made an adjective to "beginning" (ἀρχή)[102] but, as it were, takes it up again, interrupting and explaining it. This is so, for even if "first of the dead" (ἀρχὴ ἐκ τῶν νεκπῶν) could mean exactly that, it is unlikely that Paul would have written it; but while he might have wanted to write "first from the resurrection" (ἀρχὴ τῆς ἀναστάσεως) or something similar, he was drawn to "firstborn" (πρωτότοκος) by the force of the preceding parallel sentence. Now, if that sentence had been biarticulate, he would have completed here what had been begun and would also have added "firstborn from the dead" (πρωτότοκος ἐκ νεκρῶν); but he did not actually want to make this sentence biarticulate, for the other sentence was not so. However, to ensure that his readers did not miss the relationship between this "firstborn" (πρωτότοκος) and the other one, he inserted the sentence "that in everything he might be preeminent" (ἵνα γένηται ἐν πᾶσιν αὐτὸς πρωτεύων).

Thus, within the whole domain of the human spirit, Christ is the original likeness of God.[103] This is not true of Adam, even though corporeally everything is traceable back to him; in contrast, spiritually nothing is founded in him or referred to him. Moreover, this comparison, which comes easily, indeed almost irresistibly, to mind, first makes the "firstborn" (πρωτότοκος) here truly full of meaning. Furthermore, as the "because" (ὅτι) shows, Christ is here so named because his relationship to this microcosm is exactly the same as God's relationship to the whole world; on this account, he takes precedence over everything in the world; he is the head of the community whereby everything else is first established in its true value, and through him the human spirit attains its full stature.

Thus, this explanation appears fully to satisfy the requirement indicated above, that the whole passage must refer to the progress of Christianity, and to the arrangement for gathering the gentiles into it. Now, the only question that remains is whether in terms of its content our second main sentence with its foundation stands in such a relationship to the first one, and to its foundation, that they make a second statement about Christ that, like the first, belongs here

---

102. Schleiermacher's note: "Chrysostom did not treat this sentence as biarticulate either. However, his 'firstfruits' (ἀπαρχή) does not go any more exactly with "firstborn" (πρωτότοκος) and appears to be simply an old gloss, an attempt to join the two in one, yet failing to do justice to the apostle's thought."

103. Schleiermacher's note: "'Firstborn' (Πρωτότοκος), just as if he had said 'first-type' (πρωτότυπος), if such a locution would have been in his language usage, because 'to be made into an image' (τυποῦσθαι) is the coming into being of a likeness (*Geborenwerden für ein Abbild*)."

and differs from the first one in a certain way, and yet is closely related to it. However, before we can discover this, the grammatical form must be determined as accurately as possible, for it will undoubtedly be hard to find a way through these masses of "through him" (δι' αὐτοῦ) and "to him" (εἰς αὐτόν) without stumbling upon one or another of them; the only thing is that they are strongly reminiscent of the similar though less difficult constructions in verse 16.

As always, the first question is: What is the subject about which the statement "was pleased" (εὐδόκησε) is made? The context alone makes it impossible to nominate "fullness" (πλήρωμα); also, as far as I know, no interpreter has taken this path. It is probably natural to hesitate between God and Christ as the subject. Now, I have no wish to defend Storr's remark that "was pleased" (εὐδόκησε) should be referred to "to the Father" (τῷ πατρί) in verse 12; nevertheless, I share his opinion that the subject must be God. I do so, first, because the "for" (ὅτι) here corresponds to that found in verse 16, where God continues to be the subject; for "in him all things were created" (ἐν αὐτῷ ἐκτίσθη τὰ πάντα) is only another way of saying "God created all things in him" (ὁ Θεὸς τὰ πάντα ἔκτισεν ἐν αὐτῷ). If, however, contrary to this clear indication, Christ were to be the subject, the subject would soon have to be changed again without any indication. Indeed, if the sentence in verses 21 and 22[104] is transposed into the active voice, it too can only revert to God as the One to whom the "transferred us to the kingdom of his Son" (μεταστῆσαι εἰς τὴν βασιλείαν τοῦ υἱοῦ) was ascribed above. Besides this, "to be pleased" (εὐδοκῆσαι) is so predominantly used of God in books of the New Testament[105] that scarcely a couple of instances appear to the contrary where Paul uses the words of himself and others in a somewhat different turn of phrase—instances to which I attach no special significance. Consequently, there is no reason to impugn the accuracy of the parallels. Christ is "firstborn image of God" (εἰκὼν τοῦ Θεοῦ πρωτότοκος), because God has created all things in relation to him; and Christ is "the beginning, the firstborn from the dead" (ἀρχὴ ἐκ νεκρῶν πρωτότοκος), because God has willed that the "fullness" (πλήρωμα) should dwell in him.

I see just as little need, or justification, for assuming with Storr and others that "making peace" (εἰρηνοποιήσας) is there in one case instead of "making

---

104. Ed. note: In the N.R.S.V. and other translations these verses are already in the active voice.
105. Ed. note: a literal translation here would read: "in our books."

peace" (εἰρηνοποιήσαντα) in another.[106] Certainly there are plenty of such instances, but they take a different form. Such arbitrariness is in evidence when the discourse has to drag on too long in a form made cumbersome by a series of *casus obliqui* or threatens to become entangled in some other way. However, that is not occurring here; rather, "God was pleased . . . to dwell . . . and to reconcile . . . making peace" (εὐδόκησεν ὁ Θεὸς ἱ κατοικῆσαι ἱ καὶ εἰρηνοποιήσας ἀποκαταλλάξαι), and so on, combines directly and easily. For this reason, I would not wish to cite the parallel in Ephesians 2:12-16 (exact though it be) against the contention that in this passage God, not Christ, is to be thought of as the author of peace, because the two can subsist perfectly well together. Christ has become our peace by destroying the old law, and God has established this peace by sending Christ; God wills to unite all things under God's self and has made at peace even those who were estranged and at enmity, and Christ has become the end of the law in order to reconcile them. Yet, if we now go on to ask between whom God has established peace, or whom God made peaceably disposed towards whom, it is very difficult to make the twofold "whether" (εἴτε) refer to "making peace" (εἰρηνοποιήσας). This is so for in no instance could it be understood as saying that God established peace between things on earth and things in heaven; rather, the disunity would have to have existed either among different earthly things or with a third thing, and the disunity among heavenly things too would have to have existed either with a third thing or among the things themselves. However, before proceeding further in our investigation, at this critical juncture we should look at what lies immediately outside our circle, where, according to the sense given, we must put together "you who were once set at enmity having been reconciled" (ὑμεῖς ποτὲ ὄντες ἐχθροὶ νυνὶ ἀποκατηλλάγητε), whereby "having been reconciled" is contrasted with "having been set at enmity."[107] However, since having been set at enmity[108] contrasts with the latter just as well, this shows us how in exactly the same way in our sentence "to reconcile . . . making peace" (εἰρηνοποιήσας ἀποκαταλλάξαι) are also to be conjoined and consequently

---

106. Ed. note: In the Greek, both are active aorist participles but use different cases. The former is nominative masculine singular and the latter is accusative masculine singular, agreeing with the preceding αὐτόν.

107. Ed. note: *Feindlichgewesensein* is a perfect infinite formed with *sein* and is used to indicate the present *state* of the subject of the verb as a result of a previous action.

108. Ed. note: *Feindlichgewordensein* is a passive formed with *werden* and is used to indicate a *process* which is thus more closely related to an action than is the *sein* form. Likewise, just before in the text, 'having been reconciled' translates *Zusammengebrachtwordensein*.

how "whether things" (εἴτε τά ἱ) is to be immediately referred to "to reconcile" (ἀποκαταλλάξαι), so that at most only "through the cross" (διὰ τοῦ σταυροῦ) is left for "making peace" (εἰρηνοποιήσας) in particular. Still, the latter can also be directly combined with "to reconcile" (ἀποκαταλλάξαι), just as in what follows "reconciled through his death" (ἀποκατηλλάγητε διὰ τοῦ θανάτου) belongs together, and then "making peace" (εἰρηνοποιήσας) is left without anything at all in apposition, and hence coalesces the more intimately with "to reconcile" (ἀποκαταλλάξαι), so that essentially the second "good pleasure" (εὐδοκία) consists in satisfactorily bringing all things together under itself, things on earth and things in heaven; and in the same way, continues Paul, the Colossians too were once at enmity but have now been brought together.

At this point, moreover, all that would remain to elucidate grammatically is where "through him" (δι᾿ αὐτοῦ) and "in him" (ἐν αὐτῷ) and "to him" (εἰς αὐτόν), which are repeated so often, belong. Now, if God is the subject of "was pleased" (εὐδόκησε), obviously "in him" (ἐν αὐτῷ) is to be referred to Christ, and likewise the completely parallel "through him" (δι᾿ αὐτοῦ); on the other hand, whether "to him" (εἰς αὐτόν) can then be referred to Christ as well or whether it is rather to be referred to God must depend on whether the meaning of "to reconcile" (ἀποκαταλλάξαι) allows through whom and to whom it occurs to be one and the same, or whether in any case it requires the one through whom this action occurs and the one in relation to whom it is made possible to be different. The most difficult locus is the second "through him" (δι᾿ αὐτοῦ) before "whether" (εἴτε); and the latinizing authorities that omit these words are not sufficient to proscribe them.[109] If, however, we reflect that, in any event, "through the blood" (διὰ τοῦ αἵματος) belongs more to the first element, the establishing of peace, whereas "whether" (εἴτε) is to be joined directly to "to reconcile" (ἀποκαταλλάξαι), it is indeed possible to explain this second "through him" (δι᾿ αὐτοῦ) as a repetition of the first one, though it still remains very unwelcome.

However, what do the two sentences then actually mean, considered both in and of themselves, and in their capacity as an underpinning for the second main sentence? Here we are immediately confronted by the difficult word "fullness" (πλήρωμα). Here too Chrysostom, looking at chapter 2:9, interprets it as being about the deity, and many interpreters have followed him in this. Theodoret diverges from him and takes it to mean the church; but the reason he adduces, namely that the church is filled with divine gifts of grace, is not very

---

109. Ed. note: the K.J.V. retains the second "by him"; the N.R.S.V. does not.

convincing. Of all the places where Paul uses this word, the one most closely related to this one in its entire context is Rom. 11:12 & 25.[110] This passage is most closely related in that for us too what is spoken of here is unquestionably the uniting of Jews and gentiles in the kingdom of the Son and under his lordship. Now, while the theme in Romans is first Israel's holding back and the fullness of the gentiles, and subsequently the whole of Israel too, here all the fullness of both is brought together, the fullness of the gentiles and the totality of Israel. Thus, according to the substance, Theodoret is indeed right to hold that "all the fullness" (πᾶν τὸ πλήρωμα) points back to the "church" (ἐκκλησία), mentioned just before; and there is no need to enlarge upon how the fact that the fullness dwells in Christ is connected with the fact that he is the head of the community,[111] just as no apology need be made because Paul did not prefer to write "to dwell" (κατοικίσαι) at this point, though to be sure this would have yielded a more exact parallel.

Although to my knowledge no one has objected to this, it is more puzzling that a Hellenist should have connected "in him" (ἐν αὐτῷ) with "to dwell" (κατοικῆσαι), and yet have placed it next to "was pleased" (εὐδόκησε), since this juxtaposition is a solemn way of saying: God was well pleased with him. Now, if one wants to insist on this, then "to himself" (εἰς αὐτόν) must be brought not only to "to reconcile" (ἀποκαταλλάξαι) but also to "to dwell" (κατοικῆσαι); but it then lacks a more prominent connection either through "of the" (τοῦ) or "so that" (ὥστε) and something similar, so that the two expressions turn out to be the same. We need only to consult the lexicographers on "to reconcile" (καταλλάξαι) and "to reconcile completely" (ἀποκαταλλάξαι), in the New Testament universe of discourse, and it becomes evident that the metaphor is retrospective. This is obvious, for the dwelling of this totality in Christ is the definitive, constant condition; it is the complete unification that must necessarily precede that condition and that determines it; yet, in the same way this unification is conditioned by the fact that both parts must have become peaceable.

The only thing I should not wish positively to assert here is that "to himself" (εἰς αὐτόν) is to replace the simple dative that appears with this verb in Ephesians 2:16, also the simple "to reconcile" (καταλλαγῆναι) wherever Paul makes use of this word. Even if in that passage, in which only Christ is decidedly

---

110. Ed. note: the K.J.V. has "the fullness of the Gentiles"; the N.R.S.V. has "the full number of the Gentiles."
111. *Gemeine.*

the subject, at least "and might reconcile both groups to God in one body" (καὶ ἀποκαταλλάξη τοὺς ἀμφοτέρους ἐν ἑνὶ σώματι εἰς τὸν Θεόν) were written instead of "to God" (τῷ Θεῷ), I would not understand this as "so that he might bring them both together again with God" but as "so that he might bring the two back together in relation to God," just as it is written in verse 14 "he made both groups into one," and the same in verse 17 "he proclaimed peace to you who were far off and peace to those who were near," which I take to be putting them in opposition, for here there is no "whether . . . or" (εἴτε εἴτε) to divide them—and this because they both then have the same access to God, and consequently every reason for disunity is abolished. Indeed, I would say that it would be better to explain the dative in this passage after the same manner of the "to himself" (εἰς αὐτόν) in our passage than to say on the contrary that our "to" (εἰς) stands for the dative. In fact, for clarification here I would prefer to use for "to" (εἰς) the concept of goal rather than that of direction.[112] Two who are at enmity with each other can be united by being placed into an equable relationship to a third; and that is the case here. Precisely this can also be expressed by the use of the dative. Both, Jews and gentiles, have become one new humanity, reconciled with each other, to the glory of God, when God's decree is thereby fulfilled; and the same applies to us. It pleased God to reconcile to God everything that had been divided among themselves.[113]

Now, however much all the grammatical elements in this passage then require the unifying and reconciling process characterized as "to reconcile" (ἀποκαταλλάξαι) to bear only this meaning, I am the last to deny that in verse 21, which already lies outside the actual passage under discussion, alienation from God and enmity towards God are also spoken of. Yet, this is all the less relevant to our passage in that there too precisely that occurs only in an addendum and does not affect the main statement but also refers only to gentile Christians, whereas here both kinds are under discussion. It would be natural that polytheism among the gentiles, where they were situated over against Jewish monotheism, should become enmity against the One God, just as the fact that they despised the Jews also entailed a revulsion from their monotheism.

The "all things" (τὰ πάντα) in verse 20 is necessarily the same as that in verse 16, and in just the same way it disintegrates into "things on the earth" (τὰ

---

112. Schleiermacher's note: "Cf. Winer, paragraph 53, 338." — Ed. note: see note 29 above.
113. Schleiermacher's note: "Or else 'to reconcile for Christ', as also 'through him', a play with forms that I should regard as quite characteristic of Paul were it not followed by the two 'through's (διά), which destroy it in turn."

ἐπὶ τῆς γῆς) and "things in the heavens" (τὰ ἐν τοῖς οὐρανοῖς). Hence, if the explanation we gave these in that context were to be quite unacceptable here, in turn it would have to become doubtful to us there as well. To be sure, those who conceive heaven and earth literally in both passages take it less exactly but, in the first passage, wish to understand the neuter word as applying not only to personal beings but to all other things heavenly and earthly as well, whereas here they apply it only to persons. Yet, why should Paul have used the neuter when he meant dwellers in heaven and on earth, thus misleading his readers? Moreover, what kind of reconciliation was then needed for dwellers in heaven, since the structure rules out thinking of a reconciliation between them and dwellers on earth? Again, how were we supposed to imagine that such a reconciliation is conditioned by an establishment of peace by virtue of the cross? So, there is no sufficient reason at all for understanding the neuter at this point differently from the other one. However, a literal interpretation is just as much out of place here as there. This is the case for it is unimaginable what kind of heavenly things would have fallen into such disunity among themselves as to be in need of a "reconciliation" (ἀποκατάλλαξις), to say nothing of how Paul would have come to mention such matters in this context, where "and you" (καὶ ὑμᾶς)[114] is taken so directly from "all things" (τὰ πάντα).

In contrast, if we attach these expressions to the explanation we set forth above, expressions for which the adjectives "of the earth" (τὰ ἐπίγεια) and "of the heavens" (τὰ ἐπουράνια) could also have been substituted, then even those aspects of gentile life that in terms of their subject refer to the kingdom of heaven can be designated as heavenly things. Thus, Paul could also call all their relationships in worship and the attitudes of mind and heart associated with them, in short all their "gods" (θεῖα), "heavenly" (ἐπουράνια) or "things in the heavens" (τὰ ἐν τοῖς οὐρανοῖς),[115] so that we have no need at all to refer one

---

114. Ed. note: In verse 21.
115. Schleiermacher's note: "Only the two theocratic elements, which were now no longer to be held together, are separated by the two expressions in this broader meaning. Everything belongs to the 'heavenly' (ἐπουρανίοις), the 'citizenship of heaven' (πολίτευμα ἐν οὐρανοῖς) that is to be given to God. Everything that is to be given to the Emperor belongs to the 'earthly' (ἐπιγείοις), and this includes everything that has to do with human externality. Therefore in this sense 'of the heavens' (ἐπουράνια) there may also be something false, and on the other hand expressions such as 'those enthroned over earthly things' (οἱ τὰ ἐπίγεια φρονοῦντες) or 'your members on the earth' (τὰ μέλη ὑμῶν τὰ ἐπὶ τῆς γῆς) may mean something highly praiseworthy, though nothing that relates to the kingdom of heaven. I cannot, however, accept an explanation according to which rebirth can also

member, "the things on the earth" (τὰ ἐπὶ τῆς γῆς), to the gentiles alone, and the other member, "the things in the heavens" (τὰ ἐν τοῖς οὐρανοῖς), to the Jews, as this would in turn do violence to "whether" (εἴτε). Now, Jews and gentiles were at enmity over both heavenly and earthly things, and they were to be brought together in relation to God, "to Godself" (εἰς αὐτόν), once God had established peace by the cross of the Son.[116] These then are the two elements of which the whole "fullness" (πλήρωμα) dwelling in Christ was to consist. Civic enmity was ever present among the Greeks, for the *odium generis humani* rested upon the Jews, because they separated themselves from the rest of humankind, while religious enmity was at work among the Jews because idolatry was abhorrent to them, and therefore the gentiles were unclean. Now, if the two parts were to become Christian, both earthly and heavenly things had to be reconciled. "And you too are like that," Paul continued, "you too were caught up in this enmity, and have now been drawn into this reconciliation as well, so that you can be represented as spotless, no longer defiled, and freed from any such general condemnation."[117]

It must be self-evident how easy our interpretation makes this transition to be, or rather this return to what was said earlier, compared to the interpretation that at this point confidently assumes an advantage that was entirely unknown hitherto and is not described in detail at all, or is in any way discoverable, an advantage that higher beings would possess through the reconciliation wrought by Christ. Furthermore, this is over and above the merits our exposition already possesses, because it is grammatically more correct and the content of the sentences is more appropriate to the value due to them in terms of their position. Thus, all that now remains is to make clear the connection between the sentence that Christ is the firstborn from among the dead and the two subordi-

---

belong to the 'earthly' (ἐπιγείοις), irrespective of the fact that even Lücke has accepted it." — Ed. note: for basic information about Lücke see introductory essay n. 3.

116. Ed. note: By now it may have become apparent that in this article Schleiermacher tends to omit "the blood of" in his references to the cross, as he typically does. To understand why see his account of the doctrine of reconciliation in *Christian Faith* (Edinburgh: T. and T. Clark, 1989, 1830-1831 edition), §§ 100-105, especially § 101:4 and § 104. There Christ is taken to be more the sacrificer than the sacrificed, and his suffering (thus his blood, which is not featured) is but an aspect of his overall obedience as the Redeemer. See also his 1830 sermons on Col. 1:13-18 and 18-23 in *Sämmtliche Werke* II.6 (1835), 232-243 and 244-255. The entire series of Schleiermacher's sermons on *Colossians* is forthcoming in English translation (Edwin Mellen Press).

117. Ed. note: This is a paraphrase, drawn from Col. 1:21-22.

nate clauses, that the fullness of God dwells in Christ, and that through him things on earth and things in heaven, in both elements, are reconciled.

It is true that I find it much easier to demonstrate even this than to grasp how Paul could ever have arrived at the general assumption that things in heaven were reconciled with things on earth (for that is how the matter is understood, in defiance of all grammar), and how he could ever have made a connection between this reconciliation and the resurrection of Christ! Let us not forget that before his conversion Paul himself was zealous for the law and as such was deeply involved in this enmity. However, he could also not be swayed by a vision, as Peter may have been, to frequent the company of gentiles. Rather, he had to have a theory for the purpose of self-justification and to provide a reason for the tenet that in the messianic age the law had already come to an end here on earth as well, notwithstanding that even if Jesus himself did not accept the pharisaic tradition he was still under the law. Now, this theory is headed by the proposition that the law has power over a person only as long as that person is alive.[118] Consequently, the law had ceased to have any hold over Christ, the more so since the law itself had been the cause of his death.[119] From this it follows, first, that all those who have been put in the same condition through faith in Christ have also died to the law. Second, however, it also follows that after his resurrection Christ was able to command his disciples to move among the gentiles and make disciples of them too, freed from the law.[120] Previously Christ, being himself under the law, could not have been in a position to give such a command, but now he had to give it if he was to remain the foundation stone of the church and if his disciples were not to be forced to act on their own authority, thus arbitrarily laying a different foundation. By virtue of the former situation, it could be said that through the death of Christ peace had already been concluded, but, thanks to the latter, it could be said that Christ had had to be the firstborn from the dead, in order truly to reconcile both parties whether on the earth or in the heavens, through the newly arisen relationship to God, as participants in the kingdom of heaven.

Now, no matter how clearly all the elements of this demonstration are articulated in other Pauline passages, and however naturally all the expressions that occur in this passage can be reduced to this, it may still appear necessary to defend this interpretation against the objection that I have raised against the

---

118. Schleiermacher's note: "Rom. 7:1."
119. Schleiermacher's note: "Gal. 2:19; 3:13."
120. Schleiermacher's note: "Gal. 3:14, 22."

generally accepted contention that if Paul had never been to Colossae, it was most unlikely that the Colossians would have known anything about this teaching, so that he could not reasonably have expected them to place this interpretation upon what he wrote. Nevertheless, since the apostle already made it a matter of principle not to interfere in the work of others in the first place and further, because of their own situation, it is also extremely likely that these congregations were at least indirectly of Pauline origin and thus had been founded on his type of teaching. Furthermore, he could scarcely have felt the kind of concern he describes here for all the Christian congregations in the world that had not yet seen him; rather, he would have felt it only for those that to some extent lay on his conscience, because those who founded them or first taught there had been sent out by him. Now, on this assumption, which is supported by the personal circumstances mentioned in this letter and the letter to Philemon, we can have little doubt that the Colossians could not have been so familiar with these teachings (on which in essence the relationship between Jewish and gentile Christians is based, and which Paul was endeavoring to introduce everywhere) that they could not misinterpret the expressions used. The way in which at the beginning of his letter he recalls these teachings almost only by way of suggestion before reverting to the calling of the Colossians, which follows immediately upon the passage we are discussing, is also completely natural, since the admonitions he addressed to them later on in the letter,[121] as a result of what Epaphras had told him, partly aim at warning them not to be seduced into making disadvantageous concessions, in that this peace alone could be their defence against such provocations. In contrast, everything that is to be said here about higher spirits, either that they were created or that they have been reconciled by the Son, would be equally without any influence on the remaining content of the letter, as it would necessarily have been quite incomprehensible to the readers in and of itself.

---

121. Schleiermacher's note: "Col. 2:8-3:15."

VIER PREDIGTEN ÜBER DAS GLEICHNIß VOM SÄEMANN

gehalten von
Fr. Schleiermacher
im Sommer 1826.

Transkription: Hermann Patsch

*In einer zum Buch gebundenen Handschrift unbekannter Herkunft hat sich die
Mitschrift von vier Predigten Schleiermachers aus dem Sommer 1826 – genauer
vom 28.5., 11.6., 25.6. und 9.7. – erhalten, die einem zusammengehörigen
Thema gewidmet waren. Es handelt sich dabei um die bei Wichmann von
Meding (Bibliographie der Schriften Schleiermachers nebst einer Zusammen-
stellung und Datierung seiner gedruckten Predigten. Schleiermacher-Archiv 9,
Berlin/New York: de Gruyter 1992, 262) unter der Nummer P 122-125
gebuchten und als "Literarische Predigtausarbeitung Schleiermachers" bezeich-
neten gottesdienstlichen Reden. Schleiermacher hatte diese 1827 in das von ihm
mit Röhr und Schuderoff herausgegebene 'Magazin von Fest-, Gelegenheits- und
anderen Predigten und kleineren Amtsreden', Fünfter Band, Magdeburg: Hein-
richshofen, 257-329 gegeben; von dort wurden sie in den Sämmtlichen Werken
II/4, 1835, 656-716 und erneut 1844,707-768 abgedruckt. Die hier transkri-
bierten Predigten scheinen eine wörtliche Mitschrift wiederzugeben; sie sind
knapper, weniger syntaktisch untergliedert, d.h. nicht nachträglich stilistisch
überarbeitet. Sie halten sich, was der spätere Druck getilgt hat, noch genau an
das liturgische Predigtformular. Im Druck sind auch die thematischen Über-
schriften etwas gewandelt. Insgesamt macht die Mitschrift einen frischeren,
weniger literalisierten Eindruck, wenngleich wahrscheinlich ist, daß auch sie von
dem Stenographen bei der Übertragung geglättet wurde. Sie wird hier als ein
Beispiel veröffentlicht, Schleiermachers lebendigen Predigtstil im Unterschied zu
den überarbeiteten Druckfassungen kennen und beurteilen zu lernen.*

Vom Untergang des göttlichen
Worts in der Seele

Die Gnade unseres Herrn und Heilandes Jesu Christi, die Liebe Gottes, unsers himmlischen Vaters, und die trostreiche Gemeinschaft seines Geistes sei mit uns allen! Amen.

Text: Lucas 8,12.

"Die aber an dem Wege sind, das sind, die es hören, darnach kommt der Teufel, und nimmt das Wort von ihrem Herzen, auf daß sie nicht glauben und selig werden."

Wenn wir an das zurückdenken, was wir in der zuletzt vergangnen Zeit vorzüglich in unserem gemeinsamen kirchlichen Leben betrachtet haben – wir haben mit einander gefeiert das Fest der Ausgießung des Geistes und der ersten öffentlichen Predigt des Evangelii, von wo an erst unter den verschiedenen Völkern Gemeinden der Bekenner unseres Herrn sind gesammelt worden, von wo an das Wort Gottes seinen Lauf genommen hat immer mehr über die ganze Erde; in den vorhergehenden Tagen sind überall in den verschiedenen Gemeinden unsrer Stadt, hier früher, dort später, eine Anzahl junger Christen aufgenommen worden in ihren Schooß, welche von sich bezeugt haben, daß sie das Wort Gottes empfangen haben in ihrem Herzen und daß sie es machen wollen zur Richtschnur ihres Lebens – wenn wir daran zurückdenken, sage ich, meine guten Freunde, so muß uns ganz besonders eins wichtiger gemeinschaftlicher Gegenstand sein, das Gedeihen des Wortes Gottes überall, so weit wir selbst mit der Kraft unseres Lebens reichen, zu fördern, und mit einander darüber nachzusinnen, was eben dem Gedeihen desselben im Wege steht. Dies hat mich darauf gebracht, dies Gleichniß des Herrn, aus dem die verlesenen Worte entnommen sind, theilweise zum Gegenstand unsrer nächsten Betrachtungen zu machen. Denn, meine guten Freunde, die Kraft des göttlichen Worts ist eine göttliche. Wir können nichts dazu thun und nichts davon. Alle aber freilich sind Träger desselben und, wie der Apostel sagte, wir bewahren das köstliche Kleinod in einer schwachen und gebrechlichen Schaale. Dadurch wird es an und für sich immer und überall sich selbst gleich, freilich ein schwächeres und stärkeres durch diejenigen, die es fortbewegen sollen. Aber anderer Seits müssen wir auch wieder sagen, es kommt nicht nur darauf an, mit welcher Kraft oder mit welchem Geschick wir es bewegen, sondern auch, wie es aufgenommen wird, und was es nun da, wo es aufgenommen wird, wirkt, oder nicht. Und über dies letzte ist der Gegenstand, womit sich das Gleichniß Christi beschäftigt. Ich setze es als bekannt voraus, und habe eben des wegen nur den Theil desselben gelesen, mit welchem wir es heute zu thun haben. Nun habe ich wohl nicht nöthig, bei der Veranlassung erst eine Verständigung oder Ausgleichung zu versuchen in Bezug auf die verschiedenen Meinungen, welche unter den Christen herrschen über den Teufel, wie er in den Worten des Textes, oder den Argen, wie er in anderen Erzählungen des Evangeliums vorkommt. Denn, wenn wir Alles, was Versuchung und Verleitung zum Bösen, Alles, was Hinderniß ist gegen die Mitwirkung an der göttlichen Gnade, auf einen, der eben der Versucher ist, zurückführen, so müssen wir doch gestehen, wenn unser Heiland nachher sagt, daß das Wort bei vielen unwirksam bleibt, weil, sobald Zeiten der Anfechtung kommen, sie abfallen, daß es bei Andern nicht gedeihen könne, weil die Sorgen und Lüste des Lebens es weit überwachsen und unterdrücken, so müssen wir fragen: nun! sollen wir die Anfechtungen und Verfolgungen, die das Evangelium und seine Bekenner von jeher erfahren, nicht auf denselben zurückführen, sollen dem nicht auch die Lockungen zuschreiben, die von den Freuden und Lüsten des Lebens ausgehen oder die Ängstlichkeit und den Mangel an Besinnung, der aus den Sorgen des Lebens entsteht? Dann werden wir zweifeln, der Erlöser hätte auch bei den andern Erklärungen, die er giebt, sagen können, der Teufel kommt und nimmt das Wort hinweg, indem er Anfechtungen in die Seele bringt, weil er die Seele verstrickt in die Sorgen und Lüste des Lebens. Da ist nicht das Unterscheidende und das, worauf es hierbei eigentlich und wesentlich ankommt, sondern indem Christus nachher sagt, wenn Zeiten der Anfechtung kommen, so fallen sie ab, wenn sie unter den Reichthümern und Sorgen dieses Lebens aufwachsen, so erstickt das Wort, so giebt er in dem einen und in dem anderen Fall den besondern Grund und eine eigenthümliche Quelle an von dem Verlorengehen der Fruchtbarkeit des göttlichen Worts. Hier aber giebt er keinen solchen an, sondern sagt: die am Wege gesäet sind, sind die, die das Wort hören, und dann kommt der Arge und ohne Weiteres nimmt er es hinweg. Das ist also der eigentliche Hauptpunkt, wonach zu fragen das ist, was wir uns deutlich zu machen haben, wenn wir den Erlöser verstehen wollen. So laßt uns also fragen, wie doch das eigentlich zugehen kann – und an Erfahrungen darüber wird es keinem unter uns fehlen – daß in so mancher menschlichen Seele das Wort, was schon in das Herz gesäet war, wieder verloren gehe und ohne Wirkung bleibe, ohne daß man eine bestimmte Ursache angeben kann. Laßt uns dabei zuerst fragen

1) was denn dies im Einzelnen für ein Gemüthszustand sei, bei dem das möglich ist und dann

2) wie ein solcher hervorgebracht wird.

Dann werden wir wissen, wie Jeder für sich und mit welcher Kraft der Liebe, die uns zusammen erhält und verbindet, er uns und Andere vor einem solchen Untergang des göttlichen Worts in unserem Herzen zu behüten habe. 1. Fragen wir: was ist es für ein Gemüthszustand, in welchem auf eine so leichte und unmerkliche Weise die geistige, göttliche Kraft, wenn sie einmal in die Seele gelegt ist, wenn sie, wie es in einer anderen Erklärung des Gleichnisses heißt, wirklich ins Herz gesät ist, kann hinweggenommen werden und verloren gehen? Uns diese Frage zu beantworten, laßt uns recht an das Bild uns halten, was der Erlöser uns vor Augen stellt. Da finden wir den Gegensatz zwischen dem Acker, auf welchen der Säemann das Wort säen will, und zwischen dem Wege, auf welchen einzelne Körner desselben fallen, und eben da nicht gedeihen können. Meine guten Freunde, über den Acker geht der Pflug und zieht seine breiten Furchen hinein, da wird die Oberfläche und das, was tiefer liegt, mit einander vermischt, daß eines auf das andere wirken könne, und was auf die Oberfläche gelegt wird, eindringen kann in das Innere. Nach dem Pfluge geht die Egge über den Acker, den störenden Zusammenhang, die jener noch übrig gelassen hat unter den einzelnen Theilen, hinwegzunehmen, und wenn dann so der Boden aufgelockert ist und vorbereitet, so streut der Säemann den Samen hinein, und wenn er ihn auch nur auf die Oberfläche streut, jeder Thautropfen, der darauf fällt, jede leise Bewegung der Luft bringt in den einzelnen Erdtheilchen eine Bewegung hervor, durch welche das Samenkorn immer tiefer hineindringt unter die Oberfläche, und so gelangt es dahin, wo es verborgen und ungestört den wohlthätigen Tod stirbt, durch welchen es nicht allein bleibt, sondern viele Frucht bringt. O, meine guten Freunde, was giebt uns das für ein Bild von der Seele, die einem solchen Acker gleicht. Da sehen wir die lebendige Empfänglichkeit der Seele abgebildet für die heilsamen Wirkungen von oben, da sehen wir ein Gemüth, in welchem das das Gewohnte und Leichte ist, daß die heilsamen Eindrücke sich in's Innere verlieren und versenken. Sind sie aber da, dann geht ohne Störung die Befruchtung der Seele durch das göttliche Wort von statten, da wird durch jedes Samenkorn ein neues Leben in der Seele geweckt, und wenn wir auch nicht sagen dürfen, keines geht verloren, so entsteht doch nach Maaßgabe des Übrigen eine reiche und gesegnete Erndte. Aber was ist der Weg? Da! meine guten Freunde, dringt nichts unter die Oberfläche, sondern alles bleibt auf derselben liegen. Freilich viele Bewegungen und Aufregungen erfährt der Weg; aber nur solche, wodurch er immer mehr verhärtet wird, immer fester die Oberfläche zusammen drückt, und jede Möglichkeit entfernt, daß etwas könne in die Tiefe eindringen. Da ist also auch keine Thätigkeit zu erwecken, sondern was auf denselben fällt, ist rein verloren und die Beute von jedem, der es nehmen will. Keine Fähigkeit etwas festzuhalten, zu verbergen, in sich selbst zu verarbeiten, ist vorhanden, und so, meine guten Freunde, so sind alle die, welche, wie der Erlöser sagt, wenn dahin das Wort Gottes fällt so kann es der Arge ohne Weiteres vom Herzen nehmen. Im Gegensatz gegen jene Empfänglichkeit des Gemüths für das Erkennen des göttlichen Worts sehen wir hier, ach! wovon es nur gar zu viele Beispiele unter uns giebt, den flachen Sinn, welcher unfähig ist etwas in die Tiefe des Gemüths aufzunehmen, zu verbergen und dort festzuhalten, alles bleibt auf der Oberfläche liegen, ohne daß irgend ein gedeihliches Leben daraus entsteht. Ja, meine guten Freunde, in einem Leben wie das unsrige, so zusammengesetzt, so verwickelt, wo jeder Mensch so vielfältigen Berührungen ausgesetzt ist, wie kommt uns nicht so oft diese bedauernswürdige Verfassung des Gemüths entgegen. Aber laßt uns die Sache auch von der andern Seite betrachten. Wenn wir ein Feld sehen, wohl vorbereitet und bearbeitet, und sehen entweder selbst, daß der Säemann den Samen hineinstreut, oder merken seinem ganzen Zustand an, daß das geschehen ist; müssen wir nicht alle sagen, wenn wir nicht mit anderen Dingen beschäftigt sind und also gleichgültig vorübergehen, das ist uns ein rührender, ein heiliger Anblick! Es erregt ein stilles Sinnen, und Achtung und Ehrfurcht. Wir sehen die Geheimnisse der Schöpfung walten, gedenken des göttlichen Segens, der daraus hervorgeht, und jeder ernste und besonnene Mensch wird weit entfernt sein, das geheimnißvolle Werk stören oder etwas zum Nachtheil desselben thun zu wollen. Was ist aber der Weg? Zu nichts gemacht, als daß alles sich auf demselben begegne, durch einander renne und an einander vorüber, da sehen wir nicht auf das, was er selbst ist, sondern auf das, was auf demselben geschieht. Der Weg selbst ist für uns nichts, sondern nur das Begegnen, eben diese Mittheilung, dies Hin- und Herbewegen der verschiedensten Gegenstände und zu den verschiedensten Zwecken. Je mehr dies geschieht, desto mehr erfüllt er seine Absicht, aber ohne daß er einen anderen Eindruck auf uns macht, als durch die Leichtigkeit und Schnelligkeit, mit welcher der allgemeine Verkehr auf demselben erfolgt.

Meine guten Freunde, finden wir diesen Gegensatz nicht auch in den menschlichen Gemüthern? Wenn wir einen Menschen sehen, dem es anzusehen ist, daß er mit dem Ernst seines Wesens auf etwas Bestimmtes gestellt ist, sei es uns nahe verwandt oder fremd und fern, sei es das Günstigste und Höchste, oder auch nur etwas Bedeutendes in den menschlichen Dingen, so ist er ein solcher, der uns eine Achtung und Ehrfurcht einflößt.

Da sehen wir ein inneres Schaffen und Bewegen, was wir uns scheuen zu
stören, und diese Scheu ist eine heilige und kommt davon her, daß wir dabei
an den allgemeinen Beruf aller Menschen, an das große Werk, an welchem
und für welches wir alle arbeiten sollen, und an die Weisheit und Mannigfaltigkeit denken, mit welcher Gott die Gaben ausgetheilt, und jedem seinen
Ort und seinen Beruf angewiesen hat. Sehen wir dagegen Menschen von
jener Art, ohne alle innere Tiefe, ohne Fähigkeit in dieser etwas
aufzunehmen, die auf eine flache Weise Alles über die Oberfläche der Seele
verbreiten, wie können wir etwas von der heiligen Scheu empfinden! Wozu,
das ist der Eindruck, den solche Menschen auf uns machen, wozu ist er da,
als dazu, daß jeder jede augenblickliche Bewegung des Gemüths in ihn
niederlege und ausschütte? Er nimmt alle Eindrücke auf und weist keinen
von sich, und so wie der Weg sich gefallen läßt, daß alle über ihn hingehen,
aber ohne daß etwas Gedeihliches für ihn entsteht; die Bewegungen pflanzen
sich fort, was er empfängt, giebt er wieder, ohne etwas hinzuzuthun oder zu
dem Seinigen zu machen. Da kann also das Wort Gottes nicht gedeihen und
auch niemand hat eine Aufforderung, das zu befördern oder zu denken, daß
es auch da geschehen möge. Das, meine guten Freunde, ist der Unterschied
zwischen der tiefen und stillen Empfänglichkeit eines ernsten, durch etwas
Besonderes und Würdiges bewegten Gemüths, und zwischen der Oberfläch-
lichkeit und dem Mangel an Werth eines flachen, eben deshalb auch der Unfähigkeit desselben, auch irgend eine Scheu einzuflößen, an dem wir nichts
bemerken als einen Reichthum flüchtiger leicht vorübergehender Eindrücke.

Wenn ein Samenkorn auf den Weg fällt, spricht der Herr, so kommen
die Vögel des Himmels und mehmen es mit leichter Mühe hinweg. Wenn die
Vögel des Himmels sich über den Acker verbreiten, so wandern sie hin und
her, und strengen ihr Auge an, weil sie unter die Oberfläche dringen müssen,
um etwas zu finden, und so wird ihnen wenig zu Theil. Was aber auf den
Weg fällt, sei es ein Samenkorn oder anderes, so ist es verloren und jeder
nimmt es weg und trägt es heim, wer es findet. So ist es mit solchen Menschen. Nichts ist und nichts wird zu ihrem bleibenden Eigenthum! und es ist
nicht etwa nur gegen das göttliche Wort, daß sie eine solche Un-
empfänglichkeit besitzen, es aufzunehmen, sondern je mehr sie so sind, wie
der Heiland sie beschreiben will, desto mehr gilt es von allem, alles kommt
auf die Oberfläche, aber alles wird auch wieder weggenommen, und ebenso
viele Bewegungen erfolgen, durch welche bald dies, bals jenes auf der Oberfläche liegen bleibt, als wodurch es weggenommen wird; immer sind sie leer
und niemals werden sie im wahren Sinn des Worts mit etwas erfüllt. Alles
geht nur durch sie hindurch, alles gleitet nur über sie hinweg. O meine guten
Freunde, wenn wir nun denken, wie der Mensch vom Anfang des Lebens an

ein Kind der Sorge ist und ein Kind der Liebe, wie er nur gedeihen und zu seinem selbständigen Dasein gelangen kann durch das, was an ihm geschieht, wenn wir bedenken, wie doch alle die, die an dem Menschen arbeiten, vom Anfang seines Lebens an, und wie an ihm gearbeitet wird, immer doch einen würdigen Begriff davon haben, wie der Mensch sein soll und nicht die Meinung haben, ihre Sorge und Liebe an etwas Nichtiges zu verschwenden, so müssen wir uns um so mehr noch wundern, wie der Fall so häufig eintritt, daß aus dem Menschen nichts gemacht ist, daß aus einem gedeihlichen Acker für das göttliche Wort nichts wird, als eine offne Heerstraße.

2. So laßt uns denn die zweite Frage aufwerfen: wie wird ein solcher Gemüthszustand ungedeihlich für das göttliche Wort, herabwürdigend für die Natur, unempfänglich für alles Gute, was der Mensch aufnehmen soll, wie wird er hervorgebracht? Wie entsteht er vor unsern Augen leider so häufig? Von Natur, meine guten Freunde, ist ein solcher Unterschied nicht. Wie kein Theil unsres Erdbodens von Natur ein fruchtbarer Acker ist, so auch kein Theil ein Weg, sondern jeder wird es nur durch die Bestimmung, welche die Menschen ihm geben, und wo überhaupt ein fruchtbares und gedeihliches Land ist, da gehen auch die Straßen über das fruchtbare und gedeihliche Land hinweg, und es ist nicht möglich auf eine solche Weise beides zu sondern. So auch hier. Der Unterschied liegt nicht in einer ursprünglichen Verschiedenheit der Gemüther. Wenn wir diese auch annehmen, *so* ist sie nicht beschaffen und keinesweges wollen wir auf irgend eine Weise über unseren Antheil daran, daß es so viele Menschen der Art auch unter den Geschlechtern der Christen giebt, keinesweges wollen wir uns dadurch entschuldigen, daß es in einer gewissen ursprünglichen Beschaffenheit der Seele läge. Nein, meine guten Freunde, mögen immer von der Geburt an die Gemüther der Menschen verschieden sein, so hat es Gott gewollt und geordnet. Aber es sind nur solche Verschiedenheiten, durch welche eine jede menschliche Seele ein fruchtbarer Boden werden kann. Trägt auch nicht jede hundertfältig, auch nicht jede dreißigfältig, keine ist so, daß sie nicht tragen könnte. Wollten wir das nicht glauben, so können wir auch nicht glauben, daß der Heiland der Erlöser sei für das ganze menschliche Geschlecht, so können wir auch nicht sagen mit dem Apostel, daß das Evangelium eine Kraft Gottes sei, selig zu machen alle, die daran glauben. Darauf also wollen wir uns nicht zurückziehen, sondern vielmehr fragen: wie geschieht es, durch das, was andere an dem Menschen thun und durch das, was er selbst an sich thut, daß er leider ein solcher wird? Ja, meine guten Freunde, die Antwort auf die Frage ergiebt sich von selbst aus dem, worauf ich auch vorhin habe aufmerksam gemacht. Ohne Vorbereitung und ohne Bearbeitung wird kein

Mensch ein fruchtbarer Boden. Das Alles muß an ihm geschehen, was der Landmann thut an seinem Acker, daß der Same des göttlichen Worts in die Seele fallen kann, und es muß geschehen, ehe er in dieselbe gestreut wird. Ehe dazu Zeit und Stunde gekommen ist, muß geschehen sein, wodurch das göttliche Wort in der Seele kann fruchtbar gemacht werden. Nun wohl, was geschieht am Acker? Aber, meine guten Freunde, was geschieht am Wege? Was am Acker geschehen ist, haben wir uns schon vorgehalten. Wenn am Wege gar nichts geschieht, dann ist es noch eher möglich, daß ein Samenkorn, das zufällg hinfällt, bis zum Keimen gelangt und sich über die Oberfläche erhebt, wiewohl es bald wird zerstört werden durch das, was die Bestimmung des Weges ist. Wenn aber der Weg künstlich bereitet wird, da müssen eine Menge von Bemühungen an ihn gewendet werden und eine herbe und saure Arbeit, und vieles muß aus der Tiefe bis auf die Oberfläche zusammengetragen werden, alles aber zu keinem andern Zweck und in keiner anderen Absicht, als ihn zu verhärten, daß er nichts sei als eine Oberfläche, und diese undurchdringlich für alles. Dann ist er, was er sein soll, aber auch so, daß nie ein Samenkorn auf ihm keimen und gedeihen kann. Ach, meine guten Freunde, möchte doch recht viel Mühe und Sorgfalt überall auf jede menschliche Seele gewendet werden, um dem göttlichen Wort Zugang zu derselben zu verschaffen! Was muß aber geschehen, daß das göttliche Wort, wenn es an die Seele kommt und in das Herz gesät ist, Frucht bringen kann, was muß vorhergegangen sein? Vor dem Evangelium kam das Gesetz, und wie der Apostel sagt: das Gesetz kann den Menschen weder selig machen noch gerecht, aber es bringt Erkenntniß der Sünde hervor. Diese, welch heilsames, welch nothwendiges Besitzthum! Wenn der Mensch die Erkenntniß der Sünde nicht hat, so weiß er das göttliche Wort nicht zu schätzen. Wie aber entsteht Erkenntniß der Sünde? Wenn nicht die Handlungen des Menschen auf einen bestimmten Zweck bezogen werden, wenn er nicht in den Stand gesetzt wird, sein Leben mit einer gewissen Leichtigkeit zu übersehen, wenn er nicht gewöhnt wird bei jeder bedeutenden Veranlassung auf sein Inneres zurückzugehen, so ist Erkenntniß der Sünde nicht möglich und ohne diese kein Verlangen nach Rettung, kein Durst nach dem Evangelium und keine Sehnsucht das göttliche Wort in die Tiefe des Herzens einzusaugen. Je stiller aber und je einfacher das Leben gehalten wird, desto mehr ist der Mensch bei gewöhnlichen Kräften des Geistes im Stande das Recht und Unrecht zu übersehen, ja gemessener, je weniger mannigfaltig seine Bewegungen sind, desto leichter wird es ihm in sein Inneres einzugehen, und je mehr wir uns in der Einfachheit und Ordnung eines stillen Lebens halten, desto leichter wird uns die Erkenntniß der Sünde. Denn, meine guten Freunde, die mannigfaltigen Gedanken, die sich unter einander

verklagen und entschuldigen und die zu dem Argen gehören, das aus dem
Herzen kommt, wo entstehen sie leichter als in dem vielfältigen, zusammengesetzten und verwickelten Leben. Je mehr Verhältnisse der Mensch
glaubt bei dem, was er thut berücksichtigen zu müssen, desto leichter verwirrt sich ihm Recht und Unrecht, desto mehr verschwindet ihm der Unterschied zwischen Gutem und Bösem, zwischen Sünde und dem, was Gott
wohlgefällig ist. Es ist auf einem solchen Wege nichts zu finden, als eine
kalte und träge Oberfläche, die nichts in das Innere des Grundes aufnimmt.
Daher, je zeitiger der Mensch in das bunte und verwickelte Leben hinausge-
lassen wird, je mehr man eilt ihn mit tausend Eindrücken bekannt zumachen,
je früher man glaubt, daß er mit allem Bescheid wissen müsse in der Welt,
desto mehr wird er ein solcher, vor welchem niemand eine solche heilige
Scheu und Achtung hegt, wie vor einem wohlgebauten Acker, sondern jeder
glaubt in ihm niederlegen zu können, was in seiner Seele ist und über die
Zunge gleitet, wodurch er die Eindrücke fördert, die das Leben so zerstören.
Das ist eigentlich das Geheimniß der Seele. Dadurch kommt es dahin, daß
der Mensch seine eigne Bestimmung in der Welt verfehlt, und immer un-
fähiger wird, alles Große und Herrliche, aber auch vorzüglich das Göttliche
in das Innere seiner Seele aufzunehmen. Er bietet nichts dar als einen Ort,
wo sich Alles begegnet, Gutes und Schlechtes, und was es in der menschlichen Seele Buntes und Verworrenes giebt, nimmt er auf, aber er ist auch
und wird nie etwas für sich selbst und für die Welt, für die wir alle gemacht
sind.

Was ich vorher gesagt habe, hat uns gewiß allen vorzüglich unsre Jugend
vergegenwärtigt, und jeder wird schon, was ich gesagt, von selbst auf sie
angewendet haben. O, so sei sie denn vorzüglich der Gegenstand unsrer
Sorge! O mögen wir sie bewahren, so lange wir können, vor den allzu bunten
und verwickelten Gestalten des Lebens, daß sie tiefen Grund in sich selbst
gewinnen und erst vorbereitet werden, das göttliche Wort gedeihlich
aufzunehmen, daß ihr nicht über die Mannigfaltigkeit des Angenehmen und
Unangenehmen, dessen, was sie erheitert und erfreut, und dessen, was sie
trübt und schmerzlich bewegt, daß sie nicht in dieser mannigfaltigen und
bunten, aber doch sinnlichen Fülle den heiligen Unterschied zwischen gut
und böse in sich zu erwecken unfähig werde, auf daß nicht in der ungeheuern
Mannigfaltigkeit der Eindrücke des äußerlichen Lebens das Vermögen für
die Eindrücke des Geistes zu erwecken, vergessen, und wenn es schon er-
weckt ist, desto leichter erstickt werden. Ja, wozu sie Gott mag bestimmt
haben, bewahren wir sie vor dem allzu frühen Verarbeiten alles dessen, was
die Welt darbietet, halten wir sie in der Stille und Einfachheit des Lebens,
bis der Grund des Gemüthes aufgelockert und festgemacht ist; dann werden

sie uns nie den traurigen Anblick des flachen Sinnes und leeren Wissens geben. Aber doch ist es nicht die Jugend allein, sondern wir sind es alle, die wir uns auf diese Weise hüten müssen. Es giebt eine Zeit, ehe überhaupt das Wort Gottes in die menschliche Seele gesät werden kann, in der selben muß die erste Vorbereitung gemacht werden, daß es gedeihen könne, wenn es gesät wird. Aber, meine guten Freunde, unser ganzes Leben ist nichts anders, als eine Wiederhohlung desselben, denn wir alle müssen hingehen, wenn auch nicht unter den Sorgen, doch unter den Geschäften des Lebens und den mannigfaltigen Bewegungen dieser Welt, und da ist Vieles, was uns aus der Stille des Herzens heraus reißt, was arbeitet uns in das bunte, leere Gewühl hineinzuziehen; aber dies unterbricht sich dann durch solche Zeiten, wo wir zurücktreten und auch in unsre Seelen auf's Neue der Same des göttlichen Worts gestreut wird. Jede stille Betrachtung, die wir über uns selbst anstellen, jeder häusliche Gottesdienst, jede gemeinschaftliche Erbauung, ist es etwas Anderes als eine neue Saat in die Seelen? ach! und jede muß gedeihen, jede muß Frucht bringen, wenn sich die Erndte erheben soll, und wenn wir nicht sollen leer werden an guten Werken. Aber jeder braucht eine eigene Vorbereitung und vorhergehendes Nachdenken über das Leben, daß sich, was sich in der Thätigkeit verwirrt, wieder sondern kann, daß wir die oberflächlichen Eindrücke verwandeln, und alles auf das beziehen, was heilig ist und einfach seiner Natur nach. Alles andere vergessen über dem, wie sich das, was wir gethan haben, verhält zu dem großen Berufe, der uns geworden ist; das ist die Auflockerung des Gemüths, die Vorbereitung dessen, ohne welches auch die wiederhohlte Saat des göttlichen Wortes unserm Herzen und Leben nicht gedeihlich werden kann. Je mehr wir diese unterlassen und fälschlich glauben, es sei ein Geschäft der Jugend, wenn aber das Leben gereift ist, sei es nicht mehr nöthig, und in jedem Augenblick wären wir im Stande das Gute zu finden, o je mehr wir uns dem Wahn überlassen, desto mehr werden wir Gelegenheit haben wahrzunehmen, wie wir dadurch dem Vorschub thun, was das Wort, was in das Herz gesät ist, wegnehmen will, desto mehr werden wir wahrnehmen, wie die Zerstreuungen des Lebens sich eindrängen in die heiligen Stunden, die dem Geschäft der Sammlung geweiht sind und das gottgefällige Werk derselben stören. Ja, meine guten Freunde, so ist es mit dem Menschen, und je mehr sein Leben verbreitet und verwickelt ist, desto mehr muß er sich bemühen ein fruchtbares Feld zu werden und dem Herrn zu zeigen, was ihm wohlgefällt, sei es viel oder wenig; daran arbeitet der Geist Gottes, daran arbeiten alle heiligen und gesegneten Einrichtungen der christlichen Kirche, daran arbeitet der ernste Sinn eines jeden selbst, daran arbeitet das christliche Leben, das ihn immer hebt und trägt. Aber es ist auch vieles um uns her andrer Seits, was jede Seele machen

mögte zu einer offnen Heerstraße; daran arbeiten alle Zerstreuungen des
Lebens, alles leere Treiben um uns her, dem wir uns nicht ganz entziehen
können, daran arbeitet alles in unserm Neben-Menschen, was der Eitelkeit
hingegeben auch andere hinziehen mögte in das Gebiet der Eitelkeit; immer
wieder müssen wir uns zurückziehen, immer zu diesen uns hinwenden, immer von vorn, als ob nichts geschehen wäre, die Arbeit des Pflügens und
Eggens anfangen, daß die Saat des göttlichen Worts aufgehe. Denn nur so
gelangen wir dazu, daß die Saat zur gedeihlichen Erndte aufgehe, so erheben
wir uns zur heiligen Würde, die jeden mit Scheu erfüllt, jedem ein Gegenstand der Achtung wird, und so nur kann die Einträglichkeit des Bodens
wachsen und Früchte gesammlet werden zum Preise dessen, der ausgeht zu
säen, seitdem er auf Erden erschienen ist, und zuerst es selbst gethan hat,
dann durch den Mund seiner Jünger und durch die Stimme des Worts, und
noch immer aussäen läßt überall, so weit das menschliche Geschlecht verbreitet ist, den heiligen Samen des göttlichen Worts. O! daß wir überall
Frucht schaffen mögten und bald ganz erledigt werden mögten aus unsrer
Mitte des traurigen Anblicks solcher Menschen, in deren Herz das Wort
gesät wird, aber kaum, nachdem es gesät, auch schon wieder hinweggenommen wird und verschwindet. Amen.

Von dem Abfall in der Zeit
der Anfechtung.

Die Gnade unsers Herrn und Heilandes Jesu Christi, die Liebe Gottes, unseres himmlischen Vaters, und die trostreiche Gemeinschaft seines Geistes
sei mit uns! Amen.

Text Lucas 8,13.

"Die aber auf dem Fels, sind die, wenn sie es hören, nehmen sie
das Wort mit Freuden an; und die haben nicht Wurzel, eine Zeit
lang glauben sie, und zu der Zeit der Anfechtung fallen sie ab."

Ein trauriges Bild, meine alten Freunde, welches uns der Erlöser hier auf-
stellt aus der Fülle seiner Erfahrung über das menschliche Herz und das
menschliche Leben! – Eine hoffnungsvolle Saat ist aufgegangen, das geistige
Leben keimt und grünt, aber wenn die Sonne nun höher heraufsteigt am
Himmel, die alles andere nährt und zur Reife bringt, dann welkt dies, und wo
die schönsten Hoffnungen blühten, ist nichts als ein Bild der Oede und des
Todes. Freilich diese Hoffnung war nicht so wohl gegründet wie andere,
denn in einem andern Bericht dieses Gleichnisses sagt der Erlöser, weil der
Same nur wenig fruchtbares Erdreich hatte, deswegen ging er schnell und
freudig auf. So ist es, meine guten Freunde, sie haben nicht Wurzel und zur
Zeit der Anfechtung fallen sie ab. Fröhlich ist in ihnen und zeitig der Same
des göttlichen Wortes aufgegangen, weil nicht fruchtbarer Boden genug da
war, damit er lange in die Tiefe seine Wurzeln senken könne. Gemüther, in
welchen es eine solche Tiefe giebt, welche wenn sie einen belebenden Eindruck von oben empfangen haben, vermögen, ihn in die Tiefe zu verschließen, daß er allen äußeren Eindrücken verborgen bleibt, bei denen
senken sich die Wurzeln des geistigen Lebens in die Tiefe, langsam geht er
auf; der ungeduldige Landmann verliert oft bei diesem Anblick die Hoffnung
einer Erndte, wenn er aber aufgegangen ist, so bleibt er.
    Andere giebt es, denen diese Tiefe nicht zu Gebote steht, was sie
aufgenommen haben, drängt sich bald ans Licht, aber wenn dann die stärk-
eren Einwirkungen kommen, die jenen förderlich sind, dann zeigt sich die
geringere Lebenskraft, und das schon begonnene Leben hört wieder auf.

Laßt uns diesen Worten des Erlösers näher nachgehen, und nun reden:
    Von dem Abfall in der Zeit der Anfechtung, und zwar,

1) indem wir das Gleichniß Christi beziehen auf die Wirkungen des göttlichen Wortes im Allgemeinen, und
2) auch so, daß wir dabei auf das Einzelne im menschlichen Leben sehen.

1. Der erste Theil unserer Betrachtung ist mehr nur für unser christliches Mitgefühl gemacht. Betrachten wir unsere Lage in der Kirche des Herrn, so können wir nicht sagen, daß wenn im Großen der Same ausgestreuet wird, irgend eine Zeit der Anfechtung uns bevorstehe, er erfreut sich des allgemeinen Schutzes, alles Nachtheilige wird abgehalten, eine Menge belebender, fördernder Einwirkungen stehen jedem zu Gebote, und kaum sollten wir glauben, daß es eine andere Art gebe, wie der Same wieder könne untergehen, als die, von der der Erlöser redet in einem folgenden Theile des Gleichnisses, den wir für eine künftige Betrachtung vorbehalten.

Aber freilich dem Erlöser lag die Zeit am nächsten, welche der Wirksamkeit seiner Jünger nach ihm aufbehalten war. Da war die Art, wie der Same des göttlichen Wortes sollte ausgestreut werden, etwas Fremdes und Unbekanntes, im Streit mit der Ueberzeugung, die Wurzel gefaßt hatte, durch die Gewalt der Erziehung und Sitte in allen denen, denen das Wort Gottes sollte verkündigt werden, da war es natürlich, daß sich Anfechtungen erheben.

Worin aber, meine guten Freunde, bestehen diese? – Der Erlöser sagt: als aber die Zeit kam, wo die Sonne mächtig ihre Strahlen herabsenkte, nachdem sie höher gestiegen war, da konnte das dürftige Gewächs ihre Gewalt nicht ertragen, und ging wieder unter: das sagt er, sind die Trübsale und Verfolgungen, mit Recht vergleicht er sie der Nähe der belebenden Kraft der Sonne. Allen ist gesagt: "ohne Trübsal geht niemand ins Reich Gottes ein, die Widerwärtigkeiten sind ein Segen von oben, und wenn der Herr ihn zurückhielte, es würde nicht besser stehen um unser geistiges Leben, es würde viel mehr geben, bei welchen das Gute unter den üppigen Dornen der Gemüther erstickte. Ja den kräftigen Gemüthern offenbart sich diese reinigende, läuternde, stärkende Kraft der Trübsal. Je heftiger die Verfolgung war gegen die ersten Bekenner in unserem Glauben, desto lebendiger und heftiger sprachen sie: wir werden verfolgt, aber wir gehen nicht unter – immer mehr ward alles fester gewurzelte Kraft der Ueberzeugung.

Was ist es denn nun, wodurch dies herrliche Mittel der göttlichen Gnade in andern Gemüthern einen entgegengesetzten Erfolg hervorbringt? Freilich hängt dies mit der irdischen Natur der menschlichen Seele zusammen: der Mensch will sich wohl befinden. Wenn er seine Kräfte anstrengen muß, nur um das Sinnliche zu genießen, so bleibt ihm wenig Kraft übrig für das

Höhere, wenn er alle Kräfte daran wendet, um das entfernt zu halten, was
dem irdischen Leben droht, so wird seine Aufmerksamkeit von dem Ewigen
abgelöst, wird dann nur Trübsal herbeigeführt, sieht er, das Wort Gottes
drohe ihm nur zu werden eine Quelle von Trübsal, gegen die er sich stets mit
aller Kraft wenden müßte, und keine Kraft hätte, um in der Stille dies zu
nähren – o dann ist es die natürliche Verzagtheit des menschlichen Herzens,
daß in den Zeiten der Anfechtung die erwachte Liebe zum ewigen, geistigen
Leben verloren geht. So hat die rohe Gewalt gewirkt in den Zeiten der Verfolgung, drohend allen Genuß zu hemmen, zeigend, daß nichts denen übrig
blieb, die den neuen Weg des Evangelii wandelten, da fielen viele ab, in denen schon das Wort des geistigen Lebens freudig aufzugehen begann, aber ist
es nur die rohe Gewalt, die Kraft der Drohungen, der Strafen und Martern?
– Das ist ein wahres Wort, welches irgendwo ausgesprochen ist: Verführung
ist die wahre Gewalt, und das war die heftigste Anfechtung, wenn man mit
Schmeichelworten zu den neuen Bekennern herantrat, ihnen vorstellte die
Herrlichkeit der Welt, die Lieblichkeit des Lebens, den sichren Frieden, die
Achtung, die sie genießen würden, wenn sie umkehrten, und die alte Lehre
bekenneten. Diese schmeichlerische Gewalt ist eine noch schlimmere Hitze,
die viel junges Leben des Glaubens und der ewigen Liebe getödtet hat.
Doch, es ist nicht nur die rohe und drohende That, nicht nur das schreckende
und schmeichelnde Wort, es giebt noch eine andere Anfechtung, scheinbar
weniger zu vergleichen der Hitze, als dem schneidenden, kalten Winde, der
jedes Leben zerstört. Das ist die Anfechtung des Spottes; wie viel junge
Leben hat diese schon zerstört! Wie geschäftig waren da die Vertheidiger des
alten Glaubens, denen mehr die Gewalt der Rede als äußere Gewalt zu
Gebote stand, denen das Kreuz des Erlösers eine Thorheit war, und Thoren,
die es bekannten. Und zu allen Zeiten kehrt diese verwüstende Wirkung
wieder. Selbst ein treuer Jünger des Herrn unterlag ja dieser Gewalt. Waren
die Worte: "Du bist ja wohl auch ein Galiläer, deine Sprache verrät dich" –
etwas anders als Spott der Menge, die bald herbei eilen würde, denn die
Gewalt war ja vorüber, was ihn antrieb, vorübergehend seinen Herrn zu ver-
läugnen? Und so, meine guten Freunde, haben wir es auch erfahren, beides
in den Zeiten, als nach langer Verdunklung des göttlichen Worts das erneute
Licht des Evangelii aufging. Die kräftigen Helden des Glaubens, wie sind sie
fester geworden durch die Trübsal; die sich selbst innerlich von ihrer
Wahrheit Rechenschaft geben konnten, wie wenig hat die mächtige Waffe
des Spottes auf sie gewirkt; aber wie viele Gemüther hat es gegeben, die
dieser Anfechtung nicht widerstehen konnten. Denken wir nur von den ersten Zeiten der Kirche bis heut: – welche zerstörende Kriege, welche
Greuel der alten heidnischen Verfolgungen, wie viel Leben ist auf diese

Weise untergegangen, wie viel hoffnungsvolle Saat ist verwelkt, wie ist in ganzen Gegenden die alte Finsterniß zurückgekehrt, wo die Saat sank unter dem Schwert der Verfolgung, unter dem Stachel des Spottes! Nun, meine guten Freunde, nun ist die Ruhe wiedergekehret; mit herzlichem Mitgefühl können wir der vergangenen Zeiten gedenken, und schweigend können wir die Wege des Höchsten erkennen, der allein sich Rechenschaft geben kann, warum so viel junges Leben zerstört worden.

Aber doch ist es uns nicht etwas ganz Fremdes, meine guten Freunde, und ehe wir zum zweiten Theile unserer Betrachtung gehen, heben wir noch das hervor, was auch wir uns anzueignen haben.

Wir stehen jetzt in einer besonderen Gemeinschaft in Beziehung auf die, welche die Nachkommen derer sind, die zur Zeit der Reformation dem erneuten Licht des Evangelii nicht folgten, wir erkennen jene für unsere Brüder in Christo, aber unsere äußerlichen Gemeinschaften sind getrennt, jeder Theil eifert für die Art, wie bei ihm das göttliche Wort aufgefaßt wird, wie sich da das christliche Leben gestaltet. Löblich ist dieser rege Eifer, löblich ist der Wunsch, daß eben deshalb, weil wir uns bewußt sind, daß die Anbetung Gottes im Geist und in der Wahrheit reiner unter uns erbaut ist, daß die Freiheit der Kinder Gottes sich edler unter uns gestaltet hat – löblich ist der Wunsch, daß recht viel Seelen auf jener Seite sich mit uns freuen möchten des größeren Lichtes und der reineren Wahrheit; aber daß doch dieser Eifer immer rein bleibe! Daß nie von unserer Seite weder Gewalt, noch Verführung, weder drohende That, noch höhnendes Wort angewandt werde, um neue Brüder zu gewinnen! – Zerstören können wir so das Leben, aber neues schaffen, das geht nicht; und dies Wort ist nicht nur an die zu richten, in deren Händen Gesetz und Recht ist, denen Gott das obrigkeitliche Schwert verliehen; nein, meine guten Freunde, überall, wo menschliche Gemeinschaft ist, da ist auch eine Macht; sie wird auch im häuslichen und geselligen Leben geübt, auch ohne äußere Gestalt. Wenn wir Brüder auf jener Seite das fühlen lassen, daß die allgemeine Liebe sich wirksamer beweisen werde, wenn sie auf unserer Seite ständen, wenn wir sie fühlen lassen, daß sie dann größere Theilnahme haben würden, – ist das nicht eine Gewalt, die ihre nachtheilige Wirkung nicht verfehlen wird? Wenn wir sie locken wollen, daß wir ihnen zeigen, wie schwerere Lasten sie dort zu tragen haben, wie die hemmenden Banden hier freier würden, o eine gefährliche Verführung, durch die wir das locken, was nicht dem Himmel, sondern der Erde zugewendet ist. Wenn wir unseres Lichtes uns so über sie erheben, daß wir demüthigend auf sie herabschauen, als solche, welchen nicht gleiche Freiheit zu Theil geworden, wenn unser Mitleid den Ton der Geringschätzung annimmt, das ist der verletzende Stachel des Spottes, und jeder unter uns hat sich zu hüten, daß er nicht eine Anfechtung für seine Brüder herbeiführe. Sind wir uns doch alle einer Kraft des Lebens und Geistes bewußt, jeder hat beides in einem gewissen Grade zu seinem Besitz; aber darum wollen wir uns hüten, daß wir die zarte Linie nicht überschreiten, wo die Sonne eine zerstörende Gewalt wird, für das unbefestigte Leben.

2. Doch dies führt uns zum zweiten Theile, wo wir das Bild des Erlösers anzuwenden haben auf unser eigenes Gebiet, und auf das Einzelne des menschlichen Lebens.

Wenn wir als Glieder der evangelischen Kirche der älteren Gemeinschaft gegenüber stehen, sind wir deshalb unter uns alle Eins, ist hier keine Zerstreuung der Geister, stehen wir alle in brüderlicher Liebe einander gleich? – Es ist nicht so, auch unter uns giebt es Mannigfaltigkeit der Ansichten und Ueberzeugungen, ein engeres Anschließen der Gleichgesinnten, aber es darf nicht anders sein, als daß auch beide auf einander zu wirken suchen, und so soll es auch sein, wenn unsere Ueberzeugung in uns festen Grund und Wurzel gefaßt hat, so daß sie nicht zerstört werden kann.

Verschiedenes können wir uns nicht denken, ohne daß das Eine besser sei und das Andere minder gut, und wie kann ein Mensch bei dem bleiben, was er nicht für besser erkennt? Die Liebe will, daß alle überall des Besseren theilhaftig seien. O daß es immer nur die reine Kraft der Liebe wäre, wodurch wir wirken! Aber laßt uns das menschliche Leben recht betrachten, wie es sich gestaltet, daß wir uns nicht täuschen, und uns das nicht verbergen, was uns obliegt. –

So wie gleichgesinnte Gemüther, welche auf dieselbe Weise das Wort Gottes aufgefaßt haben, dieselbe Ansicht theilen über das, was das Leitende und Beseligende ist, im Glauben der Christen, wenn sie sich so zusammenhalten, daß es äußerlich wahrgenommen wird in der Welt, so bilden sie eine äußere Macht, – o daß sie ja nicht gewaltsam suchten diese zu mehren, daß sie sie nicht brauchen möchten, um auf unrechte Weise die entgegengesetzte Meinung zu stören; so wie wir Unterschiede machen zwischen Wertschätzung und Geringschätzung gegen solche, die uns gleich sind, so wird nichts anders entstehen, als daß immer die einen und die anderen unter einander zusammenhalten. Aber solche Gleichheit giebt es nicht, und oft steht die Kraft mehrer einem Einzelnen gegenüber. Da giebt es verderbliche, zerstörende Gewalt, die unbefestigten Gemüthern zur Anfechtung dient. Fallen sie dann deshalb ab, weil sie nicht wollen von uns zerstört sein, drängen wir ihre Mittheilung zurück, und berauben sie der natürlichen Nahrung, des inneren geistigen Lebens, so wird es bald ersterben, aber schließen sie sich an unsere Weise an, ahmen sie unsere Sprache nach, o daß es nur nicht leerer Schein, nicht Trug und Heuchelei sei, was wir erzeugt haben, und nicht frohe und freudige Uebereinstimmung; und jede harte Rede gegen andre Ueberzeugung, jedes schneidende Absprechen über alles, was nicht unser ist, das ist eine harte, schneidende Waffe, und wo wir nur die Fehler und Mängel, die sich am meisten in der entgegengesetzten Art, das Christenthum zu üben, erzeugen, hervorheben; wo wir, wie die Liebe nicht thun soll, das Wort geltend machen: "an ihren Früchten sollt ihr sie erkennen!" indem wir nur die schwachen Gemüther aus ihnen hervorheben – o das ist immer wieder der schneidende Stachel des Hohns und Spottes, und wir tödten, wo wir Leben erwecken sollen. Eins nur ist das Rechte. Die Liebe schützt und pflegt, und die Wahrheit erleuchtet und beseeligt; dadurch nur wollen wir wirken! Dies beides laßt uns festhalten, und nimmt die Wahrheit die schneidende Gestalt des Rechthabenwollens an, erscheint die Liebe nicht mild und weich und jedes Leben befruchtend, so laßt es uns selbst mißtrauen, und dann erforschen, ob wir nicht Werkzeuge der Versuchung werden, wenn wir schwache Gemüther zerstören, und sie doch nicht umbilden können: denn das kann nur auf dem Wege der Liebe und Wahrheit geschehen. Darum, wo es Verschiedenheit giebt, so laßt uns bedenken, überall im großen Acker Gottes giebt es neben dem guten Boden auch schlechtes steiniges Land, welches, wenn es Früchte bringen soll, gehegt und gepflegt werden muß. Darum, wo es solche giebt, laßt uns jede fremde Waffe meiden, laßt uns vor Gewalt, Verführung und Spott uns immer hüten, damit wir uns nicht verschulden an unseren Brüdern, denn keiner kann sich von Schuld freisprechen, der Gewalt, Schmeichelei und Hohn übt; und besonders der, der vorgiebt, daß er das wahre, geistige Leben in sich trägt, wenn er auch zu den starken, festen Gemüthern gehört, die den Harnisch der Wahrheit in der Brust tragen, an dem die Pfeile des Hohnes und Spottes abgleiten – o er sehe zurück auf seine frühere Lebenszeit, wo das geistige Leben noch schwach war, ob er denn hätte dem widerstehen können, was er jetzt seinen Brüdern giebt! – Eins nur giebt es in der Trennung der Geister: Wahrheit suchen in Liebe. Je näher wir uns einander stehen, desto mehr prüfen wir, ob wir in Liebe beharren, ob wir reine Diener der Wahrheit sind, ob wir keine andere Waffe kennen, mit der gekämpft werden soll, als Wahrheit.

Aber nun laßt uns noch einen Augenblick auf das Einzelne des menschlichen Lebens in Beziehung auf jedes einzelne Gemüth sehen.

Der Säemann geht aus zu säen, und streut eine reichliche Fülle aus. Das sehen wir beständig, das erfuhren wir nicht nur als wir die Milch des Evangelii erhielten, sondern auch jetzt noch, wo die Menge der Christen zusammenkommt, um sich aus dem göttlichen Worte zu erbauen, und wo zwei oder

drei zusammen sind im häuslichen Kreise, um einander das Göttliche
mitzutheilen; und jeden solchen Samen erwartet der Wechsel der Witterung.
Da giebt es noch ein geheimnißvolles Ausstreuen des göttlichen Wortes,
wie in der Natur; eine weiche Saamenkapsel öffnet sich, der Wind wirft die
Saamenkörner auf die Erde, sie graben sich ein, und giebt es eine milde Luft
und Wärme, werden die Stürme abgehalten – manch schöner Kern keimt
empor, und wird zur Pflanze: so auch wir in jedem Augenblicke; giebt es irgend etwas, was unser Gemüth bergen kann, das von außen in uns eingeht,
was nicht im Zusammenhange stände mit der Förderung unseres geistigen
Lebens? Wenn wir das bedenken, wie reich müßte dann die Erndte sein,
wenn alles gehörig gehegt und gepflegt würde, welche Christliche Tugenden,
welche reine Einsichten in die Wahrheit, wenn nicht so manches, was schon
gekeimt, wieder unterginge! Was aber untergeht, es geht alles auf dieselbe
Weise unter. Aber es giebt nur ein Verderben der guten Saat: darum überall,
wo Gewalt geübt wird, wo wir irgend etwas Fremdes dem Gemüth auf-
drängen wollen, und es nicht schonen in den Geheimnissen seiner Bewegungen, wo wir verführerisch lockend wirken, nicht ahnend, welche
gefährliche Augenblicke gerade eingetreten, wo der verderbliche Hauch des
Spottes unseren Lippen entfährt, gewiß überall zerstören wir wenigstens ein
schwaches Leben des göttlichen Wortes, das doch hätte gedeihen können. Zu
dieser Weisheit fordert uns das Bild des Erlösers auf.
     Wohl den festen Gemüthern, die allem Aeußeren trotzen können, aber
wir wissen nicht, wer ein solcher ist – viele meinen es zu sein, und sind es
nicht! Darum giebt es keine andere Weisheit für uns in unserem Leben, als
die schonende Liebe, zarteste Sorgniß, nicht zerstörend zu wirken auf das
geistige Leben.
     Seid ihr durch Gegenden gereist, wo es fast nur felsigen Boden giebt, wo
nur wenig fruchtbares Erdreich auf dem nackten Felsen liegt, habt ihr nie
gesehen, wie mit Mühe der gute Boden hinauf getragen wird von Menschen-
händen, und wie sie pflanzen und pflegen, – da ist keine Anfechtung, da ist
kein Abfall.
     So sollte das Leben unter euch sein! so solltet ihr überall das geistige
Leben pflegen. Das Licht unter uns soll kein tödtender Sonnenstrahl werden,
in der Gemeinde der Christen.
     Diese Warnung giebt der Erlöser, und jeder sehe zu, nicht nur, daß er
selbst nicht abfalle, sondern daß er keinem zur Versuchung gereiche und
zum Aergerniß! Amen.

Vom Untergang des göttlichen
Worts in der Seele.

Die Gande unseres Herrn und Heilandes Jesu Chrisiti, die Liebe Gottes unseres himmlischen Vaters und die trostreiche Gemeinschaft seines Geistes
sei mit uns allen! Amen. –

Text: Matth. 13,22.

"Der aber unter die Dornen gesäet ist, der ist es, wenn jemand das
Wort hört, und die Sorge dieser Welt und Betrug des Reichthums,
versinkt das Wort und bringet nicht Frucht."

Meine geliebten Freunde, wenn wir uns in einer Gegend befinden, wo die
Hand des Menschen ihr Werk noch nicht begonnen hat, und wir sehen aus
dem Boden eine große Fülle von Gewächsen aller Art hervorsprießen,
möchten dann auch die widrigen und stachlichten darunter sein, so würden
wir uns doch freuen an der Fülle der Lebenskraft, wovon dies ein Zeugniß
gäbe; wo aber der Mensch gewaltet hat, und den Schweiß seines Angesichts
daran gewendet, um einen guten und fruchtbaren Samen zu streuen, da sehen wir dies alles nur mit Bedauern und Mißfallen, da möchten wir kein
freiwilliges Gewächs sehen, selbst wenn es das schönste zu sein schiene, sondern nur, was aus gestreutem Samen hervorgesprossen; aber – wenn gar die
Dornen alles ersinken, das ist der traurigste Anblick, der uns werden kann;
und zu dem führt uns unser Text, welcher ein solch unglückliches Geschick
der menschlichen Seele darstellt; nämlich: den Untergang des göttlichen
Worts in der Seele, wie dasselbe in einem unglücklichen Kampf mit den Sorgen der Welt und dem Betruge des Reichthums begriffen ist, das ist

   1) wie es damit zugeht, und wie dies unglückliche Ereigniß herbeigeführt
wird, und
   2) was geschehen kann um es zu verhindern, damit es immer seltner
werde und am Ende gar verschwinde aus der christlichen Kirche?

   1. Wenn wir uns zuerst fragen: wie es denn zugeht, so dürfen wir uns auf
eine für uns alle nicht seltne Erfahrung berufen. Wer sollte es nicht erfahren
haben, daß junge Gemüther die beste Hoffnung gaben zu gedeihen, daß sie
gern den eingestreuten Samen des göttlichen Wortes in das Innere des
Herzens aufnahmen; aber – später geht dann dieses Unkraut und diese
Dornen auf, und wenn wir sie dann in der Mitte der irdischen Laufbahn

erblicken, o gewiß! nicht selten sehen wir dann das traurige Schauspiel, das der Erlöser uns hier vor die Augen stellt. Wenn wir nun aber fragen, woher diese Sorge der Welt, und dieser Betrug des Reichthums, und die üppige Kraft mit der sie hervorschießen, und das göttliche Wort überwachsen, so laßt uns nun zuerst eine Vorstellung beseitigen, zu der die Worte in unserm Text und manche Aussprüche des Erlösers einige Veranlassung geben.

Wenn wir hören von Sorgen der Welt, denken wir gar zu leicht an die Brüder, die von der Last des Lebens gedrückt sind, und wie es ihnen schwer wird, den Bedürfnissen desselben zu genügen, und wie sie nun nichts mehr thun können, um den Samen des göttlichen Wortes in der Seele zu pflegen, wenn wir hören vom Betrug des Reichthums, so denken wir an die traurigen Bethörungen, denen die ausgesetzt sind, welche sich im Besitz des Reichthums befinden. Aber, meine Guten, so ist es nicht!

Freilich, die Sorgen der Nahrung, das sind die, die eigenthümlich sind einer großen Zahl der Brüder auf dieser Erde, die in einem zusammengesetzten und verwickelten Verhältniß stehen, daß es ihnen schwer wird, den nothwendigen Bedürfnissen des irdischen Daseins zu genügen. Aber die die sich in der Fülle des Lebens befinden, sind die etwa frei von den Sorgen dieser Welt, von denen der Herr redet? – o die Sorgen des Ehrgeizes, immer weiter emporzustreben in der menschlichen Gesellschaft, immer weiter zu reichen mit seinen Kräften, immer mehr seinem eigenen Willen zu unterwerfen, sie können nicht eher entstehen in der Seele, als bis eine gewisse Fülle des Lebens da ist; o die Menschenfurcht, die Furcht und Sorge, die Gunst derer zu verlieren, von deren Wohlwollen am meisten der angenehme Zustand und das irdische Glück abzuhängen scheint, diese so sehr drückende, die menschliche Seele so erniedrigende Sorge – wo finden wir sie anders, als bei denen die durch ihre Geburt oder ihre Anstrengungen so viel gewonnen haben, daß sie das kosten und genießen, was eine Frucht der Gunst ist, und des Reichthums!

Ja, meine guten Freunde, die Sorgen der Welt, wir finden sie überall unter einer andern Gestalt, hier unter einer andern und dort unter einer andern, aber sie sind gleich vertheilt, so wohl unter die, die beneiden, als unter die, die beneidet werden. Aber der Betrug des Reichthunms, ja, der traurige Betrug, dessen Wirkungen wir so oft im Leben vor unsern Augen entstehen sehen, wenn diejenigen, die im Besitz desselben sind, glauben, daß sie daran etwas sicheres und festes haben, und dann plötzlich verschwindet, was auf solche Weise gehalten wurde, was an so vielen Fäden hing, daß alles menschliche Geschick und alle menschliche Klugheit sie am Ende nicht mehr festhalten konnte, in der sonst so geübten Hand – das freilich ist der Betrug, dem blos die Wohlhabenden ausgesetzt sind.

Aber, meine guten Freunde, *der* Betrug des Reichthums, daß wir alles für wahres Gold, für Gold der Seele halten, was gleißt und glänzt, das für eine wahre Freude des Lebens zu achten, was auf irgendeine Weise feil ist für die Schätze dieser Welt, *der* Betrug des Reichthums, als ob wir die Freiheit fühlen und das Leben genießen könnten, erst wenn wir eine Menge äußerer Güter besäßen, das ist der Betrug des Reichthums, dem die Dürftigen eben so sehr ausgesetzt sind, als die Reichen, und wenn er die letzten verlockt, so ist er für die ersten eine Quelle von ungestillter Sehnsucht, unter der das Leben vergeht; er ist derselbe für die, die den Reichthum besitzen, als für die, die sich, freilich oft ohne ihn zu erreichen, darnach sehnen.

Dem ohnerachtet können wir uns das nicht ableugnen: es würde keine Sorge in der Welt, keinen Betrug des Reichthums geben, wenn nicht in der menschlichen Gesellschaft diese große Ungleichheit wäre, vermöge deren die einen reich sind, die andern arm. Sehen wir zurück auf die ersten und einfachen Zustände der menschlichen Gesellschaft, da finden wir weder jene Sorge, noch diesen Betrug, sondern, weil sie ziemlich gleich sind und einen und denselben Kampf zu kämpfen haben, auf derselben Stufe der Befriedigung stehen, so erscheinen sie alle unter einem und demselben Gesetz der Nothwendigkeit, darin es nichts giebt, was sie täuschen kann, aber auch nicht solche Gegenstände, auf die sie ihr Verlangen und ihre Sehnsucht heften könnten. Denken wir uns einen Zustand, wie er vielleicht einmals gewesen, der aber doch möglich wäre, wo die Menschen auf einer solchen Stufe mannigfaltiger Thätigkeit, wie wir, ständen, in eben solchem Grade Herren der natürlichen Kräfte, und ebenso getheilt in verschiedene Beschäftigungen, aber doch in einem solchen Verhältniß, daß der Unterschied zwischen dem einen und andern geringer wäre: gewiß unser gemeinsamer Zustand würde dann jenem ersten und ursprünglichen weit näher kommen; alles läge klarer vor Augen, und indem nun die Gleichheit eine gewisse Sicherheit gewährt, so gäbe es weniger, was den Menschen trügerisch überlisten könnte, so wäre weniger Grund, die Sorge im Gemüth aufgehen zu lassen. Ja, wenn dem so wäre, möchte nun einer sagen, so wäre die Sorge und Betrug des Reichthums nicht; aber die Lust, die Lust – diese gefährliche Gefährtin des Lebens – würde diese auch nicht sein? Ja freilich, meine guten Freunde, und in einer anderen Erklärung fügt der Herr auch zwischen die Sorge der Welt und den Betrug des Reichthums auch die Wollust ein; aber weil dies nicht alle auffaßten, so haben wir vollkommen Grund zu schließen, daß er es am wenigsten hervorgehoben, und gewiß, um diese Angelegenheit recht zu verstehen, so folgt, daß diese nothwendig mit eingeschlossen sein muß.

Freilich, wir können es nicht leugnen, daß so manches Gemüth untergeht in der Lust des Lebens, zu zeitig gefangen von der Sinnlichkeit die Fähigkeit verliert sich zu höheren Stufen des Daseins zu erheben, sich los zu machen vom Vergänglichen und an dem Ewigen zu hangen; aber wenn wir vergleichen wollen, die Zahl derer, die wirklich untergehen durch den Genuß des Lebens, mit denen, wo das Wort erstickt wird durch die aufs Aeußere sich richtenden Thätigkeiten, die aus der Sorge der Welt und dem traurigen Betrug des Reichthums entstehen, die, in denen es durch Übersäftigung untergeht; mit denen, in denen es dadurch untergeht, daß sie beständig für den Genuß des Lebens arbeiten, ohne je etwas zusammen zu bringen: o gewiß eine geringe Anzahl müßten uns die ersten erscheinen, kaum der Mühe werth, sie neben jene zu stellen; aber in dieser unseligen irdischen Geschäftigkeit, darin, darin geht das göttliche Wort unter, da, wo die Richtung aufs Göttliche nicht mehr zu finden ist. Jemehr sich der Mensch in den Thätigkeiten der Sorge und dem Betrug des Reichthums an die sinnliche Welt heftet, desto mehr wird er abgeführt von seinem Innern, er verliert sich und seinen Schöpfer, indem er sich nur dem hingiebt, was in der Welt für ihn zu thun ist und zu schaffen.

Und so, meine guten Freunde, ist auch der Ausspruch des Erlösers zu verstehen, da er sagt "der gute Same erstickt unter den Dornen" – nemlich, diese sind auch im Leben, es ist die selbe Thätigkeit der Erde, der Luft, des Lichtes, der Sonne, die auch das Gute zur Reife bringt, aber diese Thätigkeit – sie nimmt den Menschen so hin, daß er keine Zeit findet für etwas anderes, weil er, wenn dies oder jenes noch abzuwenden ist, hier eine Belohnung oder Strafe droht, er sich immer hiermit beschäftigt; und indem er sich mit allen verbindet, die ihn unterstützen können in der Sorge der Welt und im Betrug des Reichthums, so versäumt und vernachläßigt er die Verbindung nit denen, die, weil sie im Reich Gottes leben und mit allen Kräften dem Göttlichen dienen, im Stande sein würden, den Samen des göttlichen Worts in ihm zu erhalten und zu fördern; und so sehen wir den ganzen Hergang des menschlichen Lebens und den traurigen Weg des Verderbens, den so viele Seelen einschlagen, so sehen wir, wie die guten Regungen ersterben, und wie sie nicht mehr hervorgerufen werden können, weil das Tichten und Trachten ganz und gar hingenommen ist von den Dingen dieser Welt, von den Gegenständen der Sorge, von den Täuschungen des Betrugs.

Ja, meine guten Freunde, wenn wir auch dies vielleicht nicht mehr als so alltäglich zu bedauern Ursach haben, wie zu andern Zeiten, wenn wir sagen müssen, es giebt wohl nicht mehr irgend eine bestimmte Klasse der Gesellschaft, die dem Betrug des Reichthums den sie haben, so ausgesetzt sind, oder die von der Dürftigkeit so niedergedrückt werden, daß sie sich ausschließen von dem, wodurch der Same des göttlichen Worts begossen wird und gepflegt; wir finden die gemeinschaftlichen kirchlichen Zusammenkünfte nicht mehr verödet von irgend einer gewissen Klasse, das Interesse an religiösen Dingen hat zugenommen, in der Gesellschaft hört man die Rede sich wenden auf die ewigen und höchsten Angelegenheiten – und ist die Rede von dem, was unser wahres Heil befördern kann und sicher stellt; aber wenn wir fragen: wie groß ist die Zahl derer, von denen wir sagen können, der Same sei sicher gestellt und die Dornen allmählig verringert, wie groß ist die Anzahl dieser im Vergleich mit denen, wo uns das Schicksal des Feldes noch zweifelhaft erscheint, wo wir noch fürchten müssen, die Dornen werden siegen über den göttlichen Samen, ja, wenn wir uns diese Frage aufwerfen, so werden wir sagen müssen: auch unter uns ist die Gemeine des Herrn noch nicht, was sie sein sollte; es ist noch viel zweideutiges und verdächtiges Feld, viel Mischung von gutem Samen und Unkraut, daß eine größere Weisheit als die unsrige dazu gehört, den Ausgang zu bestimmen.

Eben deswegen muß es unsere Sorge sein, und das ist keine Sorge für die Welt, sondern für das Reich Gottes: wie wir noch weiter kommen könnten im Gedeihen des Worts, um noch mehr Mittel in Händen zu haben, das Unkraut und die Dornen zu hindern; und das ist der 2te Theil.

2. Wenn es einmal geschehen ist, wenn das Unkraut und die Dornen so empor gewachsen sind, daß sie den guten Samen erstickt haben, und der Herr des Feldes geht vorüber und betrachtet es, was wird er für einen Entschluß fassen? O dann ist die Zeit gekommen, von der der Erlöser sagt, daß er seinen Dienern befehlen wird zu erndten; aber von dem guten Samen ist keine Erndte zu hoffen; – aber auch die Dornen sollen sie abschneiden und im Feuer verbrennen. Aber doch ist dies Gericht nicht das letzte, sondern wenn die Dornen verbrannt sind, o dann kann die Asche mit untergepflügt die wohlthätigste Wirkung haben auf die Fruchtbarkeit des Bodens und der gute Säemann sagt dann, daß auch diese traurige Zeit nicht vergeblich war, und das Feld, das sonst nur dreißigfältige Frucht trug, bringt jetzt sechszigfältig oder hundertfältig. Das aber, meine guten Freunde, ist die Hülfe die nur der Herr der Erndte selbst geben kann, die wir nicht herbeiführen können und dürfen, weil wir sonst in sein Amt eingreifen würden. Das vermag nur der Herr, daß er die Seele führe in das Feuer der Trübsal und der Prüfung, in welcher der Same des göttlichen Wortes erstickt zu sein scheint, daß er die Seele in einem Feuer, was alles zu zerstören droht, was ihr den Schein des Wohlbefindens gab, läutern und sie dann durch die Erfahrung von einem großen Theil eines in vergeblichen und unnützen Bestrebungen hingebrachten Lebens zu einem höheren hinwende: das ist das Werk Gottes allein! und wohl denen, seien es blos Einzelne, denen es begegnet,

oder ein großer Theil der menschlichen Gesellschaft, zu Folge allgemeiner Trübsal – wohl denen, die so aus dem Feuer gerettet sind. Was wir aber thun können, kann nicht anders geschehen, als durch richtige Einrichtung des ganzen Lebens, durch solche Gottgefällige Ordnung, durch die der Einzelne gehalten wird, und durch die eine solche Regel des Lebens entsteht, die dem Aufwachsen der Dornen ungünstig und hinderlich, dem göttlichen Samen aber förderlich ist. – Der Herr läßt es zweifelhaft in seiner Erklärung, ob der Same des göttlichen Worts schon aufgegangen sei in der Seele, oder nicht, – deswegen wohl, weil der eine Fall so gut statt finden kann, als der andere; aber – was uns obliegt, das ist, daß wir zuerst dafür sorgen, daß der Same des göttlichen Worts zeitig aufgehe, zeitiger als die Dornen, die aus der Sorge der Welt und dem Betruge des Reichthums entstehen, in der Seele aufgehen können, und *das* haben wir, meine guten Freunde, in unserer Gewalt.

Die menschliche Seele, der Hauch aus Gott streckt sich zeitig genug dem Göttlichen entgegen; und das können wir, wenn wir es nicht versäumen, den göttlichen Samen in die zarten Seelen der Kinder zu streuen, wenn sie noch in jener Unbefangenheit des Lebens sind, wo, wenn die Sorge des Lebens noch nicht erwacht ist, der Betrug des Reichthums ihre Augen noch nicht irre leitet; wenn wir das nicht versäumen und sie in der Stille des häuslichen Lebens halten, bis wir hoffen dürfen, daß der Same nach unten Wurzel schlage und in die Höhe keime in den ersten kindlichen Aeußerungen eines frommen Gemüths, dann haben wir doch etwas den Dornen entgegengestellt, einen Kampf gegründet, daß, wenn die Dornen kommen, was wir nie ganz verhüten können, sie einen Kampf zu kämpfen haben und das ganze Erdreich nicht allein beherrschen; – aber wenn wir das auch haben, was ist die traurige Erfahrung?

Wenn auch der göttliche Same aufgegangen, so wächst er langsam, wie alles Große und Herrliche langsam gedeiht, sind aber die Dornen aufgegangen, dann wachsen sie schnell, wie alles Vergängliche zu eilen hat, um zum Ziele zu gelangen: dann überwachsen sie den göttlichen Samen und berauben ihn der Luft und Sonne. Was nun, meine guten Freunde, haben wir dagegen zu thun? – Das ist wahr, wenn die Lust gar nicht wäre, so würde weder die Sorge der Welt, noch der Betrug des Reichthums sein; – wenn es wahr ist, daß mehr Seelen in der Thätigkeit der Sorge untergehen, als in der Lust des Lebens; wie, meine guten Freunde, wie sollen wir es machen, daß nicht die Lust empfangen werde im Gemüthe und dann die Sünde gebäre? Der Mensch kann nicht sein ohne Wohlbefinden, das ist das Verlangen alles Lebendigen; aber ist der Same des Göttlichen in der Seele aufgegangen, giebt es dann nicht eine Lust, die daraus hervorgeht? Ja, meine guten Freunde, freuet euch in dem Herrn alle Wege und abermal, sage ich, freuet euch, spricht der Apostel, oder wenn der Apostel sagt, wie er hätte sagen können, freuet euch in dem Herrn alle Wege, so ist ja das eine Freude, an der wir die Seele leiten können, damit sie an dieser Genüge finde und nicht erst abweiche auf andere Pfade, sondern, daß das Göttliche erreicht werden könne. Sorgen wir dafür, daß die Freude eines Gott zugewendeten Gemüthes, die Freudigkeit eines ganz dem Dienst des Herrn geweihten Lebens, daß diese in der Seele aufgehe, daß ihre Empfänglichkeit dafür wachse, o dann wird weniger Gefahr sein, daß auch später die Dornen den göttlichen Samen unterdrücken können. Und das kann geschehen durch rechte Ordnung und christliche Art des häuslichen und geselligen Lebens. Es ist nicht so, daß alles, was die Welt darbietet in Wiederspruch steht mit der Freude im Herrn; wer dies anerkennt, der legt den Grund zu einer schweren Schuld, denn wahr ist es, daß die Seele sich grade nach dem Verbotenen sehne, aber wir sollen dieser Sehnsucht nicht verwehren, nicht untersagen, wohl aber im ersten Keim sie reinigen und läutern, alles was Gott gegeben zum Guten anwenden, mit dem verbinden, was das Tichten und Trachten des christlichen Lebens ist. Das ist es, was den Samen des göttlichen Wortes stärkt und den Dornen die Lebenskraft nimmt. Dadurch können wir die jungen Gemüther schützen vor Verführung. Haben sie einmal das Bessere gekostet, ist ihnen das Ewige zum Genuß, zum Bilde und zur Freude des Herzens geworden, dann werden sie sich schwer zu dem unschmackhaften Trüben des sinnlichen Genusses wenden. Aber dann zweitens das große Wort unseres Herrn: "niemand kann zween Herren dienen", das muß das Wort unseres Lebens werden, ehe giebt es keine Sicherheit für's göttliche Wort, sondern bis das geschieht, sind wir noch dem Mißhelligen ausgesetzt, das durch das Überwachsen der Dornen entsteht. Der Herr ist damit in die innersten Tiefen der menschlichen Seele eingedrungen; die Seele kann keine Spaltung vertragen. Lassen wir der Welt einmal ein besonderes Recht, glauben wir, daß außer dem Tichten nach dem Ewigen es noch etwas anderes gäbe, nach dem wir trachten sollen, nicht folgend dem Wort des Erlösers: "Trachtet am ersten nach dem Reich Gottes und nach seiner Gerechtigkeit, so wird euch alles andere zufallen", kommen wir dahin, daß nicht eine solche Einheit des Lebens hervorgebracht werden könnte, daß alles bezogen werden sollte auf das Reich Gottes, und gäbe es wohl einen Genuß, dessen sich der Mensch zu schämen brauchte, der nicht in Verbindung damit gebracht werden könnte, dann wäre das Wort des Herrn nicht wahr, dann hieße es besser: trachtet nach den Dingen dieser Welt! und ob ein Gottesreich daneben ist, bliebe Gottes Sorge; ein *drittes* giebt es nicht, als die Unsicherheit, der traurige Wiederspruch des Gemüths.

So aber soll ja wohl die christliche Welt sich gestalten, daß allem soviel Werth beigelegt wird, daß es blos so geachtet wird, als es beiträgt zum Reich Gottes; und wenn dies wäre, wo sollten wohl die Sorgen der Welt, die Täuschungen des Reichthums in eine Seele kommen, die von Jugend auf so erzogen wäre, die unter keiner andern Bedingung in alle irdischen und weltlichen Thätigkeiten träte; hätten wir es dahin gebracht, dann würden wir solche sein, die haben, als hätten sie nicht; die keiner Täuschung des Reichthums ausgesetzt sind, mögen sie haben oder nicht, dann würden wir solche sein, die sagen können, "wir werden verfolgt aber wir gehen nicht unter, wir weinen aber wir sind fröhlich dabei." Wie könnte uns dann die Sorge von dem Pfade des Herrn abbringen? Darum bleibt das Wort des Herrn wahr und der einzige Schatz, die einzige richtige Leitung für alle Seelen, die noch nicht zur Selbstständigkeit gelangt sind.

So lange aber das Leben so gestaltet ist, daß der Zwiespalt sich zeigt und daß auch die Jugend glaubt sich theilen zu müssen im Tichten nach dem Gottesreich und nach der Welt, so lange bleibt auch der unsichere Kampf zwischen beiderlei Samen in den menschlichen Gemüthern, so lange schwanken die Grundfesten des Reichs des Herrn auf der Welt.

Dazu laßt uns Muth fassen und das Übel an der Wurzel angreifen, und jemehr jeder Einzelne davon überzeugt wird, daß dieser Zwiespalt nicht sein darf, daß das Tichten nach dem Gottesreich für nichts unempfindlich macht, was würdig ist seiner Seele, und zu dem großen Beruf, den der Herr den Menschen gegeben hat; jemehr jeder davon ein Beispiel wird, desto mehr werden wir solche sein, die den jüngeren Gemüthern zur Stütze dienen, an denen sie sich hinaufranken und zeitig wachsen –

Und nur an dieser Kraft des Beispiels, und wenn es weiter gedeiht, eines allgemeinen wohlgeordneten christlichen Lebens, ist die Erndte des göttlichen Wortes gesichert. Dazu führe uns der Herr immer mehr. Denn überall sind wir umgeben von denen, wo der Samen noch Schutz bedarf. Behalten wir dies im Auge, so sehen wir, daß wir alle nicht vergeblich da sind, sondern wie wir haushalten müssen mit dem Anvertrauten, und daß wir nicht erfreulicher beitragen können zu dem, woran wir alle immer mehr die Freude unsers Herzens haben sollen und wollen. Amen!

Von der Fruchtbarkeit des göttlichen
Wortes in der menschlichen Natur.

Die Gnade unseres Herrn und Heilandes Jesu Christi, die Liebe Gottes unsers himmlischen Vaters, und die trostreiche Gemeinschaft seines Geistes sei
mit uns allen! Amen.

Text: Matth 13,23.

"Der aber in das gute Land gesäet ist, der ist es, wenn jemand das
Wort höret, und verstehet es, und dann auch Frucht bringet, und
etlicher trägt hundertfältig, etlicher aber sechzigfältig, etlicher
dreißigfältig."

Meine alten Freunde, die früheren Theile dieser Gleichnißrede unsers Herrn
zeigen uns, was dem göttlichen Wort Nachtheiliges in der menschlichen
Seele begegnet, so daß es die Absicht, in welcher es gesäet worden, nicht erreichen kann. Hier nun schließt der Herr die Erklärung seiner Rede mit
dem, was sich auf das Gedeihen des göttlichen Wortes bezieht. Da er nun
aber dieses in den Worten, die er an seine Jünger richtet, das Geheimniß des
Himmelreiches oder des Reiches Gottes nennt, so müssen wir auch sagen:
dies Gedeihen des göttlichen Wortes schließt alles in sich, was in der That
und Wahrheit zum Reich Gottes auf Erden gehört.

Die Kirche des Herrn in allen ihren verschiedenen Gestaltungen, die sie
in den verschiedenen Geschlechtern und Zeiten angenommen hat, alles in
jeder einzelnen, dieser heiligen Gemeinschaft angehörigen Seele, was in der
That von oben her ist, und nicht von der Welt, das alles vom Größten bis
zum Kleinsten, wird hier beschrieben, als die Frucht, die das göttliche Wort
in einem guten Lande trägt.

Wenn es nun so ist, so wollen wir unsere Aufmerksamkeit richten auf
diesen Inbegriff aller göttlichen Segnungen über das menschliche
Geschlecht, auf diese Fruchtbarkeit des göttlichen Wortes in der menschlichen Natur, und zwar auf zweierlei weisen uns die Worte des Herrn hin

1) das eine ist das Land
2) das andere ist die Erndte.

1. Einiges, so sagt er zuerst, fiel auf ein gutes Land, und das, was auf das
gute Land gesäet ist, sagt er in unserem Texte, das ist, wenn jemand das Wort
hört und verstehet es, und der Evangelist Lucas fügt noch hinzu: "und be-

wahret es in einem feinen und guten Herzen, und es gelangt dann zu seiner
Frucht". So sehen wir also wohl, was der Herr unter diesem guten Lande ver-
steht; wenn in der menschlichen Seele das Verständniß unverdorben ist,
wenn es empfänglich ist um das göttliche Wort aufzunehmen, wenn ein
Gemüth da ist, im Stande es zu behalten, es zu bewahren und zu bewegen,
dann entsteht jener gedeihliche Wachsthum, welcher den Herrn der Erndte
lohnt mit seiner Frucht. Was aber die Worte des Herrn nach der einen und
nach der andern Erzählung besagen, es ist genau genommen gar nicht verschieden, sondern einerlei; das unverdorbene Verständniß, und das unverdorbene Gemüth, beides werden wir immer vereinigt finden. Es kann dem
Menschen allerdings bei einem Herzen, welches geeinigt ist das Gute in sich
zu bewahren, zu hegen und zu pflegen, es kann dem Menschen an einer
gewissen Gewandheit des Verstandes fehlen, in Bezug auf die weltlichen
Dinge, gehörig zu sondern, an einer Schnelligkeit, das was bunt und mannigfaltig ist, sich auf eine verständige Weise zu ordnen, aber das Verständniß
des Guten ist von der Neigung es aufzunehmen und zu bewahren unz-
ertrennlich. Und wenn wir sehen auf das Traurige in den früheren Theilen
des Gleichnisses, so finden wir auch beides vereint, diejenigen, die er dem
Wege vergleicht, wo der Saame auf der Oberfläche bleibt, das sind solche
von denen man nie wird sagen können, wenn sie äußerlich das göttliche Wort
annehmen, daß sie es innerlich verstehen, weil ihr Gemüth verhärtet ist, und
ihnen die Offenheit fehlt, es in sich zu verschließen und zu bewahren, und zu
hegen. Und wiederum, die das göttliche Wort so wenig hegen, daß Unkraut
unbd Dornen es überwachsen, ja von denen werden wir sagen müssen, sie
haben es nicht so bewegt in ihrem Gemüthe, wie es sich gebührt hätte für
den göttlichen Samen, weil sie es nicht unterschieden haben von dem, was,
einmal aufgegangen, nichts werden kann, als verderbliches und erstickendes
Unkraut.

So fördert eines das andere gegenseitig, so wird eines von dem anderen
gehindert, und beides hat seinen Grund in einer und derselben Quelle.

Geheimnißvoll ist uns, was der Erlöser hier darstellt, auch in der Natur,
wie in einem fruchtbaren Lande der Samen bewegt wird, wie er Kraft entwickelt, wie daraus an dem Lichte der Sonne das gedeihende Wachsthum
entsteht, wie sich Blüthen und reife Frucht entfaltet: täglich sehen wir es vor
unsern Augen, aber es bleibt uns immer ein Wunder. So, meine guten Freunde, ist es auch mit dem menschlichen Gemüth, täglich sehen wir wie das
göttliche Wort gesäet wird, sehen den Unterschied hier und da, beklagen die
Verhärtung der Gleichgültigkeit, bejammern den Fortgang auf einem Lande,
das von Dornen und Disteln verschlungen wird, wir bemerken auch das stille
Wirken und Weben eines auf das Göttliche gerichteten Gemüthes, aber wie

nun beides sich verhält, Land und Samen, wie Fruchtbarkeit entsteht, es ist und bleibt ein Geheimniß, und eben weil der Erlöser es in einem Gleichniß erklärt, so hat er das Geheimniß des himmlischen Reiches uns zwar eröffnen wollen, aber doch so, daß die innersten Tiefen uns immer verborgen bleiben.

Darum wenn diese Betrachtung verschiedene Fragen erregt, und die Aufmerksamkeit derer spannt, die nach dem Reiche Gottes streben, so laßt uns wohl unterscheiden, was der Herr wirklich hat erklären wollen, und was uns unbegreiflich bleibt und bleiben soll. Das hat er erklären wollen, daß ohne das Verständniß des Wortes, daß ohne ein solches Bewahren und Bewegtwerden in der Tiefe des Gemüthes keine Frucht hervorgehen kann, aber die Frage, die am nächsten liegt in Beziehung auf das Land, wo hinein gesäet wird, da wollen wir uns nicht begnügen mit der Ueberzeugung, daß in einem Gemüth, wo es bewegt wird, es auch Frucht bringen wird, sondern wir möchten auch wissen, welche Menschen sind es denn, die so geartet sind, daß dies entsteht? – und welche sind die, in denen immer nur eines von jenen traurigen Begebnissen entsteht?

Meine guten Freunde, der Erlöser hat uns darüber nichts gesagt, was können, was müssen wir daraus schließen? Daß es einen ursprünglichen Unterschied in dieser Beziehung unter den Menschen gar nicht giebt, denn, meine guten Freunde, wir müssen aus seiner Rede schließen, alles ist gutes und fruchtbares Land, was nicht so verhärtet wird, wie die Straße, die durch das immerwährende Hin- und Hergehen und Fahren immer verhärteter wird; alles ist gutes Land, aber es kann sein, daß manches so dürftig ausgestattet ist, daß nicht Kraft genug da ist, den Samen zur Reife zu bringen; alles ist gutes Land, aber manchmal überwiegt die Erndte der Dornen und Disteln den guten Samen. Aber wie von Natur das Land wieder das göttliche Wort in sich hat, so hat es auch nicht die Dornen in sich.

Was der Herr uns darstellt als das dem Mißrathen zum Grunde liegende Verderben, es ist alles solches, was aus dem Zusammenwirken der Menschen entsteht, aber in der innersten Natur desselben den Grund hat.

Verhärtet muß der Boden erst werden, auf dem immer hin und her gefahren wird, ehe sich der Weg vom Acker scheiden kann, irgendwie muß die Saat der Dornen und Disteln hineinkommen, so wie das göttliche Wort. Der einzige Unterschied, der als natürlich erscheint, ist der, daß an einigen Stellen der gute Boden tief genug ist, um den Samen zu wahren, an andern das unfruchtbare Gestein zu nahe darunter liegt. Das ist der einzige natürliche Unterschied, den der Herr uns angiebt; aber ist der so, daß darum das eine Land ein gutes, das andere ein schlechtes ist? Nein, es ist nur des Guten zu wenig da. Sollten wir sagen, soll aber dieser Zustand so bleiben? Nein, wir fragen: wo ist denn eine solche Dürftigkeit der menschlichen Natur auf eine

solche ursprüngliche Weise? An den äußersten Enden der Erde, wo die
Menschen nur gleichsam hin verschlagen zu sein scheinen, da drängt jeden
Augenblick den Menschen die Noth der Natur, denn es ist nicht Kraft genug,
um den göttlichen Samen zu fördern. Immer aber geht der Verkünmdigung
des göttlichen Wortes voran, daß eine Gemeinschaft eröffnet werde mit denen, in welchen das geistige Leben schon entwickelt ist. Dies muß geschehen,
ehe der Samen ausgestreut wird. Ursprünglich soll er überall gutes Land
finden, die menschliche Natur ist es, für die er bestimmt ist. Wie aber, meine
guten Freunde, stimmt da der Erlöser mit sich selbst über ein, oder mit denen, die da sagen: es ist kein Glaube in der menschlichen Seele, ehe nicht
der Glaube an ein ursprüngliches Verderben gegründet ist, der nur durch Ihn
kann aufgehoben werden. Wenn er hier nur die menschliche Natur, wie sie
ist, nur als gutes Land beschreibt, stimmt er mit jenen überein? O, meine
guten Freunde, diese Worte sind nicht geeignet die vielen Vorstellungen von
dem wichtigen Theile unseres Glaubens zu beseitigen, und natürlich werden
wir auf die Frage geführt, worin besteht das Verderben der menschlichen
Natur? – Es besteht in der Unfruchtbarkeit, daß sie nicht vermag die Frucht
des göttlichen Wortes hervorzubringen. Dieses spricht er auch dem guten
Boden nicht ab, denn er sagt: der göttliche Same muß erst hineingestreut
werden, aber daß jenes Vermögen da ist, es aufzunehmen, zu verstehen, zu
bewahren und zu beleben, dieses ist es, was er uns will zu erkennen geben,
und soweit sollen wir uns nicht verirren, irgend einem dies Vermögen abzus-
prechen; denn wäre dies nicht der Fall, so würde der Samen vergeblich ausgestreut, und nirgends könnte etwas anderes gefunden werden, als die traurige Form der Disteln. Dabei also bleibt es: die menschliche Natur ist un-
fruchtbar, aber der Erlöser hat sie befruchtet, und es kann gefordert werden,
daß das gute Land Frucht trage, und wenn nicht überall in der menschlichen
Natur dies gute Land wäre, dann hätten wir nicht Kraft zu sagen, der Erlöser
sei gekommen, um alle zu erlösen, dann müßte ein ursprünglicher Unterschied sein, daß einige geschickt wären, um, wenn der Samen gestreut würde,
das Wort aufzunehmen und gerettet zu werden, andere wären nur Dornen
und Disteln, die verbrannt werden müßten am Tage der Erndte. Glauben wir
also an die allgemeine Gnade Gottes in Christo, so müssen wir auch glauben,
gutes Land für das göttliche Wort ist die menschliche Natur, und dieses gute
Land laßt uns pflegen, damit die Kraft des Bodens nicht ungenutzt verloren
gehe, und des allgemeinen Lebens Gedeihen entstehe und Wachsthum und
Frucht.

Wohl, meine guten Freunde, so ist es also, und immer werden wir sagen
müssen, wo das nicht geschieht, da sind es menschliche verderbliche Wirkungen, die vorangegangen sind; das ursprüngliche Verhältniß zwischen dem

Erlöser und der menschlichen Natur ist das, daß der Samen gestreut werde, in ein Land, welches fähig ist, ihn zur Fruchtbarkeit zu bringen. Aber nun laßt uns unsere Aufmerksamkeit richten auf die Erndte.

2. Er bringt dann Frucht der eingestreute Samen, sagt der Herr, einiger hundertfältig, einiger sechzigfältig und einiger dreißigfältig.

Große und bedeutende Unterschiede, aber überall, meine guten Freunde, welch ein herrlicher Reichthum tritt uns entgegen, in den Zahlen, die der Herr angiebt! Welche freudige Zuversicht zu dem Wachsthum des göttlichen Samens muß uns erfüllen, nicht daß es kein lohnendes Geschäft sei, dieselben zu säen, zu pflegen und zu begießen, sondern daß überall eine reiche und herrliche Erndte lohne.

Auch hier also haben wir auf zweierlei unsere Aufmerksamkeit zu richten, auf die herrliche Fülle, die in den Worten des Erlösers liegt, und auf die Ungleichheit, die er uns auch nicht verbirgt.

Meine guten Freunde, wenn also das ganze Reich Gottes auf Erden diese Erndte ist, wenn wir denken an die jetzige und künftige Verbreitung desselben, mit wie viel guten und fröhlichen Hoffnungen dürfen wir dann sehen auf die Gegenden des menschlichen Geschlechtes, wo der göttliche Same noch nicht ausgestreut ist! Wie viel ist schon vorbereitet, auf öde Gegenden solch fruchtbares Land zu bringen, daß der Same wird Wurzel fassen, und Frucht bringen können; ach und welche heilsamen Feuer der Läuterung und Prüfung sind schon ergangen über die Theile unsers Geschlechts, wo auf einem an sich fruchtbaren Boden nichts als Dornen und Disteln sind, und wie wird dies Feuer den Boden reinigen, daß er Frucht bringe, wenn der göttliche Samen hineingestreut wird. Und alles, meine guten Freunde, diese ganze reiche und unübersehliche Erndte von einem einzigen Korn, das edle Weizenkorn, daß in die Erde gesenkt worden und ersterben mußte, damit es nicht allein bliebe, sondern Frucht bringe, diese unübersehliche Erndte hat es hervorgebracht.

O meine theuren Freunde, wenn wir das sehen und dann finden, wie es immer fort geht, daß der Samen des göttlichen Wortes, der die Frucht ist von so vielen Geschlechtern, seit das erste Korn ist gesäet worden, daß der immer Frucht bringt, daß die, welche berufen sind, zu säen überall sich ansiedeln auf der Erde, was soll uns dann wohl die Ungleichheit kümmern, ob einiges nur dreißigfältig trägt, während anderes hundertfältig.

Aber, meine guten Freunde, so ist die menschliche Natur, daß wir von dieser Ungleichheit unsere Aufmerksamkeit nicht ablenken können. Der Herr verbirgt sie nicht, und so wollen wir sie uns auch nicht verbergen, aber sie nur so ansehen, wie er sie lehrt; und zuerst laßt uns das festhalten: der

Ruhm und Preis der dreißig- und sechzig- und hunderfältigen Erndte gebührt
nur dem Einen. Wir alle sind das Land, in das aufs neue der Same des göttlichen Wortes
immer muß ausgestreut werden, wir bedürfen es und mit verlangendem
Herzen nehmen wir den Samen auf, um ihn zu bewegen, und wenn wir eine
solche Ungleichheit finden, die auf Ungleichheit der Erndte schließen läßt,
es ist keine andere, als daß einige mehr geneigt sind, sich durch die Dinge
dieser Welt zu verhärten, andere die Neigung haben, daß die Dornen
schneller bei ihnen wachsen, als der gute Samen aufgeht. Andere Gründe der
Ungleichheit entdeckt der Herr nicht.

Wir sind aber nicht nur das Land, in welches der Samen gesäet wird,
aber so, wie er sich das Weizenkorn nennt, welches versenkt wird und er-
stirbt, und wie er sich unter dem Bilde des Säemannes darstellt, so sind wir
alle das Land, in welches er ausgestreut hat, aber wir sind es auch, zu denen
er sagt, gleichwie mich mein Vater gesandt hat in die Welt, so sende ich
euch.

Wir sollen ihn auch ausstreuen den göttlichen Samen, und so haben wir
auch zwiefachen Theil an der Ungleichheit. Wir wissen, jeder von uns hat
seine eigene Art, wie die Fruchtbarkeit des guten Samens in ihm gehemmt
wird, und jeder weiß also, woran er sich zu hüten hat, jeder findet eine Ungleichheit der Augenblicke, wie er das Göttliche aufnimmt.

Oft ist das Land so durstig und aufgelockert, daß man die beste Hoffnung einer reichlichen Erndte hat, oft so verhärtet, daß manches Korn vor
der Erndte verloren geht. Diese Ungleichheit kennen wir, und so mögen wir
sagen, es ist unsere Schuld diese Ungleichheit der Erndte. Wir sind auf der
andern Seite auch die, die da säen; ja ich darf es hoffen, es ist keiner unter
uns, der, wenn er hört, wie diejenigen die den Herrn nicht gesehen haben,
nach jener bekannten Erzählung zu ihm sagen, Herr, wann haben wir dich
Hungrigen gespeiset, dich Durstigen getränkt und, wie du nackend warst,
gekleidet? – so einer von uns sagen würde: Herr, wann habe ich den Samen
des göttlichen Wortes empfangen, so daß ich ihn hätte ausstreuen können?

O wir streuen ihn aus, bewußt und unbewußt im Leben, überall, wo irgend etwas aus uns redet, das da spricht: wie sollte ich ein so großes Uebel
thun, und wider Gott meinen Herrn sündigen? – überall, wo der Geist
Gottes uns bewegt, streuen wir aus den göttlichen Samen. Aber wie auch im
Reiche der Natur viel mehr Samen ausgetreut wird, durch die Bewegungen
in den Lüften, welche die Hüllen öffnen und den Samen herab fallen lassen
in das Erdreich, durch die Ströme vom Himmel herab, die ihn herun-
ternehmen und in den Boden versenken, so, meine guten Freunde, mehr als
von Menschen absichtlich ausgestreut wird, ist des unsichtbaren Lebens in

der Kirche, mehr als des absichtlichen Wirkens durch Lehre und Ermahnung im Öffentlichen als im Häuslichen.

So können wir das Bewußtsein haben, daß wir alle beitragen zur Erndte, mag nun der Boden tragen dreißig- oder hundertfältig; ist in uns das göttliche Leben, so haben wir alle Theil als Diener des Herrn, als lebendige Glieder seines Leibes. Aber betrachten wir uns als Theile der Erndte, so finden wir auch diese Ungleichheit, etliche tragen nur dreißig- andere hundertfältig.

Aber, wenn, meine guten Freunde, aller Schmerz verbannt sein soll, überall nichts als Freude an dem Herrn, so sehen wir wohl, hier muß es anfangen, fern von uns muß sein aller Neid, wenn ein anderer mehr trägt, noch mehr aller Hochmuth, wenn unser Acker reichlicher zu tragen scheint, denn der Hochmuth würde dann nur kommen vor dem Fall. Aber was ist das auch für eine Unterscheidung? Wird denn bei der Erndte Rechnung gehalten werden von jedem Einzelnen? ist denn jeder Einzelne etwas für uns?

Freilich wenn der Herr vor der Erndte am Acker vorüber geht, so zeichnet er sich wohl einen großen viele Körner tragenden Halm aus und freut des Reichthums, aber in der Erndte selbst verschwindet dies, jeder sieht da nur auf den Reichthum des Ganzen, und jeder Einzelne ist zu gering um besonders betrachtet zu werden. So auch wir. Wenn wir das Leben betrachten in dem Augenblick der Ruhe und Besinnung, ist es recht und billig, daß wir uns des Einzelnen freuen; wenn wir im Werke des Herrn begriffen sind, wenn wir das Feld des göttlichen Wortes begießen, dann verschwindet das Einzelne, und wir haben Freude am Ganzen. Weil wir nun alle sind, die da säen, und dann auch das Land, in welches gesäet wird, jeder giebt und empfängt, so würde es unrecht sein wenn ein Einzelner etwas besonderes sagen und sich zuschreiben wollte. Trägt einer hundertfältig, es ist die Frucht aller durch den göttlichen Beistand, ohne welchen nichts gedeiht; trägt einer dreißigfältig, so mahnt uns dies, daß auf Erden Wechsel und Ungleichheit ist. Auch dies ist ein Theil der Erndte, und nur mit innigem Dank soll er betrachtet und eingesammelt werden.

O darum, ohne uns durch solche Unterscheidungen aufzuhalten, und zu verunreinigen, laßt uns nur uns selbst und andern rathen, daß immer weniger der Augenblicke in unserem Leben sein mögen, wo irgend ein Samen vergebens ausgestreut wird, laßt uns uns ermuntern, daß wir treu und fleißig seien im Säen, Pflegen und Begießen, damit der Herr von jedem Geschlecht welches auf Erden lebt und blüht eine reiche Erndte zu sammeln habe, und wenn wir mit ihm sitzen und beschauen das Feld und sehen die unfruchtbaren Theile, wo wenig gedeiht, wohlan! so laßt uns auf das Wort des Herren hören: bittet den Herrn der Erndte, daß er Arbeiter sende. Amen.

TRANSLATION AS A PHILOSOPHICAL ART:
EXAMPLES FROM SCHLEIERMACHER'S TEXTS

Terrence N. Tice

Introduction

At base, translation requires getting an author's thoughts accurately from one language into another. There is more. For example, it may be necessary to find a word, phrase, syntactical order or idiom in the second language that comes close to rendering the original thought but cannot do so exactly. In scholarly contexts, where this might nonetheless make some significant difference as to whether the reader can truly understand what was said, a footnote may be necessary, one that at the very least offers the original text. In any case, a supposedly "literal" transcription is almost bound to be among the worst strategies possible, for it almost inevitably renders the text wooden, confusing or even meaningless. Thus, the ploy of simply "getting the words down" in a "first draft" is never very fruitful, in my view, and can lead to mistakes, or infelicities at the very least, that are retained through all drafts. It is better to slow down and try to follow the thought, marking places that are not clear, than to rush ahead. This I have learned through years of working on others' draft translations.

Now, the picture is still incomplete, even for the more strictly reflective texts such as we find in all of Schleiermacher's work, including his sermons. There are always a certain dignity of sound and distinctiveness of style that should be honored, if at all possible, in appropriately good English. Occasionally, some slight awkwardness will remain—better that than a smooth but false rendition.

This essay will focus on the first, basic task, which beyond what may be termed a philological effort (involving close attention to grammar and other linguistic tradition) amounts to being the practice of a philosophical art. Here I shall outline what I take to be the chief elements of such an art—by which I chiefly mean craft, as traditionally, reserving a much richer meaning for other, more modern uses. I use as examples material from Schleiermacher's work. Fortunately, we also have available a great store of evidence of his own translative practice to draw upon, most notably his fine translations of English sermons early in his career (1795-1802) and the classic translations of almost the entire Platonic corpus over the entire period of his academic life, a translation still widely used. In an 1813 essay given at the Berlin Academy of Sciences he has also contributed a general philosophical theory of translation reflective of his own practice. Although in large part I agree with this theory, itself consonant with his larger, famous, if much embattled hermeneutical theory, my aim here is to go more into some details regarding the particular kind of translative work just mentioned.

The Nature of Reflective Discourse

From early on, Schleiermacher's discourse was almost exclusively of a highly reflective sort, even when he added more fully metaphorical material and offered self-styled works of a "rhapsodic" sort. The latter include some early philosophical essays, *On Religion* (1799), *Soliloquies* (1800) and *Christmas Eve* (1806). They tend to be more free wheeling than what he took to be proper "scientific" discourse, which (in its presentation, not in its initial modes of inquiry) would begin with quite general considerations then, in a rigorously principled and empirically based manner, descend to the particulars. They also typically contain rather poetic reports from his personal life story, sometimes regarding friends, whose identity is always veiled, and they occasionally employ rather florid imagery. Yet, even they tend to display a strictly logical form throughout. This practice is especially evident both in the details of syntax and in the succession of mostly very long paragraphs, which are mostly sectional in function, and of unindented subparagraphs. It is mainly because of these consistent features of Schleiermacher's reflective discourse that I choose them here, though I am also especially in touch with them as a translator.

Naturally, reflective discourse comes in many shapes and forms. Over a forty-year period, each of Schleiermacher's sermons, for example, was presented as a "reflection" (*Betrachtung*), carrying all the general features just outlined but adding the connotations of carefully, reverently attending to the biblical text, in preparation exactly exegeted and then interpreted in the light of its original context, also of thinking out its primary meanings with special regard for current experience within the Christian community and in a given cultural setting. I have now worked translatively with so many of these sermons that certain regular characteristics to be found in them are quite clear to me, all indicating the distinctive, yet in general terms replicable, reflectiveness that Schleiermacher brought to them. This was true even during the decade before he was an academic but in heightened, mature form from 1804 to 1834, the year of his death at age 65.

First of all, in the sermons closely interlocking themes drawn from the text determine its overall structure, sometimes painstakingly so. From beginning to end, this structure is conveyed on the wings of thought, free, creative and yet highly disciplined, logical, leading sensibly—I do not say deductively—to its final conclusions. The listener is invited to think on these themes, is helped to understand why and is led by reference to recognizable experience to grasp its benefits. All the while, as a reader one can scarcely help but enter into the deeply religious feelings that animated preacher and listener alike, that in their implicit dialogue connected them in one community—diverse, faithful and free. One not only understands the themes, as he has very thoughtfully laid them out; one is also grasped by them, feels their impact—this, moreover, despite any wondering, doubt or disagreement as to various of the sermon's contents. One has been led to reflect at both levels of processing simultaneously and, always, to reflect on practical alternatives and their consequences. Thus, the process is that of thought, feeling and proposed action rolled into one. Although Schleiermacher never strays even a short distance from the text and only points toward, does not actually give, concrete examples or real-life stories, one is unfailingly refreshed by these hugely reflective presentations, as if one had been stimulated precisely in these ways. One wishes to continue by meditating upon them and applying them on one's own, and I am sure that these are the very results that Schleiermacher intended and hoped for. "The truth shall make you free."

Now, in, as it were, the fine print of these discourses, all these same processes are going on—phrase by phrase, sentence by sentence. The discourse is not scientific in the general way indicated above, but it is indeed reflective, and this means several more things that are to be found in most other kinds of reflective discourse. (1) First, each thought is in some way logically connected with every other thought. Thus, for readers and listeners alike (most of his 1,089 extant sermons, sermon outlines and talks were simply transcribed from extemporaneous speech and not specially prepared for readers), the text is peppered with and's and but's, thus's and then's and therefore's—and much else, as will be indicated later.

(2) Second, each segment is part of an argument, geared not so much to prove or convince as to lead and to aid understanding. It is all a "presentation" (*Darstellung*), or exposition as may be, not a strictly deductive or rhetorical

argument; nonetheless, premises are formed and conclusions are drawn, not loosely or haphazardly gathered, from them.

(3) Third, the content and texture of the discourse is derived from critical study and thought, which to the knowledgeable person is evident in every paragraph. In a given sermon, for example, an incorrect or misleading translation in the German bible is gently, covertly replaced, or a series of other words or phrases is introduced to bring out the original meaning in context. Further, I have discovered that in a remarkable way a sermon on, say, a passage in Hebrews is full of accurate, exactly reinforcing material from other parts of the book, as if a part of his brain that had stored finely detailed information from study of that book had been switched on. Then, as in this case, exactly pertinent material from the apostle Paul might be brought in to extend and deepen the meaning being conveyed. None of this, moreover, is in the nature of proof-texting, and the quotes simply appear as part of the texture of the discourse, not laid out for discussion on their own. They are simply woven in, without citation of verses. As the years go by, this teacher of New Testament exegesis, term after term, brings the increasing presence of higher-critical work to this extraordinary preaching, though he never re-performs it in front of his audience.

Besides careful historical-critical effort, "criticism" meant probing reexamination: taking nothing for granted, reopening old issues and raising new ones based on available, publicly verifiable evidence. For the purpose of preaching it especially meant letting no traditional dogma intervene, not at least without the same prior, relentless re-examination, not letting any mere letter spoil what is a matter of spirit, of faith and the search to understand at this time and place what is experienced in faith. Faith itself is no mere belief, else this critically reflective discourse would simply be a scholastic exercise. Faith is a mode of relationship carried above all in feeling; it becomes an immediate consciousness borne out of the depths of one's self and is given there though also to some extent shared within a community of faith. As such, all the documents pertaining to faith are completely open to critical scrutiny, so that the message of faith that they had variously begun to convey will come through, albeit in new forms of speech and proposed action.

Every other kind of "text" of any importance, whether spoken or written, long known through customary practice or newly arising, was to be subjected to these same processes of critical reflection, and this complex of procedures was seen to lay the groundwork for all science.

(4) Another, closely allied characteristic, contributed especially by philosophy, was what Schleiermacher called "dialectic," a highly developed art of

thinking derived from a period in which the Greeks were discovering both philosophy and science without yet being able to distinguish much between the two. For him dialectic was a dense mixture of examinations into the nature of reason and reality, knowing and being, both members of these pairs being viewed within a continually clarified, somewhat altered matrix comprised of all the functions of mind and including all the possibilities of existence, human and otherwise. In his sermons, as everywhere else, we see strong but gently, easily appearing evidence of this prior work too, of this thoroughgoing examination of nature and culture. Though mostly indirect, never intrusive upon the domain of faith yet illumining it, as could be expected from any part of God's creation, such an approach no doubt also lends to these products their unusual power. More particularly, Schleiermacher took very seriously the capacity of mind helpfully to reveal the "dia" in both "dialectic" and "dialogue." By this he meant, and I mean, the presence of counterpoint among objects of thought and of experience generally. Usually the counterpoint, which he was hearing brilliantly introduced into music by the Baroque and Romantic masters of his period every year, was twofold in nature. It came, however, far, far less in true oppositions than in contrasts, each reciprocally affecting the tone and message of the other. Sometimes it came in three's or more. The important things were, first, to eschew any claim to absolute truth, as if it could ever be wholly attainable thus stopping history, or, for that matter, any claim to absolute, unmitigated error and then, second, by carefully, critically reflecting one would see how counterposed thoughts do address and complement each other. Almost to a fault, the main structure of Schleiermacher's sermons, as of his more scientific work, bears this characteristic, whereas today the more likely tendency—not always the better one, perhaps—would be to try to look at an identified object from all sides, however many there may be.

The Little Words: Borrowed from the Greek

I have become very much aware that for any of us to understand Schleiermacher's typical mode of discourse fully some studies must be done showing, how he—and no doubt many of his contemporaries, though perhaps none more than he—drew from the habits of Greek discourse. Plato would be the special source but also the rest of classical philosophical discourse and, no less, the *koiné* as found in the New Testament. From his school days onward through his entire career, there would not have been many weeks in a year when he was not working with Greek texts. Further still, the volumes of sermons by the noted Edinburgh rhetorician Hugh Blair and by the great London preacher Joseph Fawcett that he early translated bore much of the same classical influences. These influences were, of course, in part from Latin as well as from Greek, as was true in Enlightenment Germany, where scholars wishing to create a more viable modern German were then catching up to the English in that respect. Now, my point, which I raise for further testing, is this: that especially in Schleiermacher's case the Greek models were ever before him and served mightily to form his own distinctive style. This was true, moreover, right down to the placement of the little words, as I call them, to the logical operators that string together the meaning units of that discourse.

To illustrate what I mean, I shall take a select number of examples from both Plato and the New Testament. Fortunately for my purpose, since 1977 an edition of Plato's Greek texts with Schleiermacher's translation on facing pages has been available from the Wissenschaftliche Buchgesellschaft in Darmstadt. Of no little consequence, of course, was the influence of Luther's New Testament translation, as of later variants upon it, on the German language itself. Schleiermacher preached from some text of that bible every Sunday, and he used it alongside the Greek for exegesis courses nearly every term from 1805 to 1833. The latter instructional practice, however, he pursued in years after his style was already well established.

What I have just said gives rise to an important side observation about translation as a philosophical art—namely, that one need not learn this art from reading philosophical texts alone, nor, in fact, need one learn to do philosophy itself only in this way. Alas, a great deficiency in reflective, critical skills is generally evident among supposedly educated people everywhere, dependent as education is largely on rhetorical, not philosophical traditions. This lack shows how much is to be missed if students will not at least have gained from what philosophical texts would contribute, even if, as may be, rarely from these texts themselves. Certainly Schleiermacher did not derive or hone his reflective, critical skills only from studying philosophical texts, though these are without a doubt predominant among his sources.

Schleiermacher sprinkles his discourse with such little words as *denn, aber, und, ja, zwar, doch, auch*—and I shall name many more that serve similar functions. To show how prevalent such terms already were in Greek discourse, I take a few notable examples from the initial exchanges of Plato's *Ion*—which comes first in the 1977 edition of Schleiermacher's German translation—and, as is usually possible in these particular cases, from the New Testament as well.

This procedure will get us well underway toward a full analysis of such terms, which cannot be supplied here. I register these examples as they appear, within four pages of text.

(1) αλλα – Ion 530a: Ουδαμῶς . . . αλλη: *Mitnichten Sokrates, sondern von Epidauros* . . . This first one, meaning "but" or "rather," is fairly straightforward. A variation in German usage, as in ours, would be *nicht nur . . . sondern auch* ("not only . . . but also"). In Mt. 4:4: "Man shall not live by bread alone *but* by every word." It can also mean "nevertheless," as in Jn 16:7: "sorrow has filled your hearts, nevertheless I tell you the truth." In German this could be rendered *doch.* — An allied word is πλην, used in Lk. 6:24: "But woe to you." This word has a meaning closely allied to *sondern* (rather) or *allein* (only) but also *doch* or *aber* (nevertheless, however). Thus, Lk. 11:41: "But give for alms"— KJV: "But rather"; Lk. 12:31: "Instead, seek his kingdom"— KJV: "But rather"; then Eph. 5:33: "however, let each one of you love his wife"—KJV: "nevertheless." Two more allied words appear below, but it is already clear that it is not always sensible to use only one word to translate them. As logical operators they function slightly differently in different contexts, though serving the same emphasis on a contrasting thought. In fact, in Schleiermacher's discourse *aber* is sometimes to be translated "in contrast." I recall series of four *aber*'s," which in English must come out something like this: "In contrast . . . however . . . but (as the strongest contrast in the series) . . . yet."

(2) δη – Ion 530b: αγε δη: *Wohlan denn, mache, daß* . . . Ordinarily, in Schleiermacher's usage *denn* means "for" or "then," as here. In I Cor. 6:20: "you were bought with a price. *So* glorify God"—KJV: "therefore." More about this in the section to follow.

(3) γε – Ion: 530a: Πανυ γι και τηζ αλληζ γε μουσικης : *Jawohl, so wie ja auch in den übrigen Musenkünsten.* Here πανυ means very much, quite (*jawohl*), and here γε means indeed, too, truly (*so wie ja auch*). In the New Testament it ordinarily means "yet" and is used in various compound connective words. — Also Ion 530b: και μην πολλακις γε εζηλωσα: *Wahrlich, oft habe ich schon . . . beneidet.*" Here *oft* = πολλακις, *schon* = μην, and γε = *wahrlich*; although each has a function, their meaning is formed in combination, as is often true in Schleiermacher's discourse where like combinations are used.

(4) γαρ . . . μεν – Ion 530b: το γαρ αμα μεν το σῶμα . . . δε : *Denn* (γαρ) *sowohl daß auch* (αμα) *am Leibe . . . als.* Here is another combination. We find *denn,* frequently appearing at the beginning of a sentence in Schleiermacher's discourse as in Greek, *auch* (for which a choice must be made among "also,"

"too" and "even"), then the pairing of *sowohl* (which in Schleiermacher would usually be *wie* or *sowie*) and *als*. The *denn* is of particular interest when we compare New Testament usage of γαρ. (a) Lk. 20:26: "for they cannot die anymore." (b) Lk. 23:22: "Why, what evil has he done?" (c) Jn 3:19: "because their deeds were evil." Jn 16:37: "No!" — KJV: "nay verily." (d) as και γαρ = yet (*aber*), as in Mt. 15:27: "yet even the dogs eat the crumbs." (e) Rom. 8:7: "indeed it cannot." This comparison shows that one cannot reasonably carry the same word over from one linguistic context to another, and yet they do perform similar though not identical functions. The German word *gar* is also used for emphasis as in *gar kein* (none whatsoever, at all).

(5) ουν – Ion 530b: Τατα ουν παντα: *Dies alles also*. In English, *also* is usually translated "thus" in Schleiermacher's discourse but sometimes "therefore." Mt. 3:10: "every tree therefore that does not bear good fruit." It would be of interest to see whether Schleiermacher regularly translates ουν as *also* and so with connectives of a similar kind.

(6) μην . . . δε – Ion 530d: και μην εγω . . . δε: *Gewiss, ich werde mir*. Here μην = indeed, truly; ordinarily και μην means "and yet," but not here, for it is accompanied by δε (but, however). So, in Ion 530d just above: νυν δε: *Jetzt aber*. In the New Testament μην is not to be found, but δε appears numerous times in an adversive sense over against a μεν clause, as in Lk. 2:19: "But Mary kept all these things" and Lk. 1:13: "But the angel said to him" and Mt. 5:33: "But I say to you."

The logical operators noted thus far are all in constant use within Schleiermacher's discourse as well, fit in according to normal rules of German grammar and syntax. Here I add but a few more locutions.

(7) In Ion 531b-d: τι δι: *Und wie*; then τι ουν: *Wie also?* then τι μην: *Wie doch?* We may simply note how discriminating Schleiermacher is here, as was Plato.

(8) ουκουν – Ion 531d: *Wenn nun . . . einer am besten spricht, so wird . . .* The "*so*" is silent in this Greek passage but is quite often present in Schleiermacher's sentences within a *wie . . . so* construction. In Ion 531e ουκουν is translated *nichtwahr*, then *nun nicht*, then *nun . . . doch*, then in 531a *also wenn*, then again in 531b followed by *so*, and finally simply *also*, followed by *so*. The only instance of ουκουν in the New Testament is in Jn 18:37: "So you are a king?"

To reach something nearer completeness, I simply add to these the two words that most often appear as logical operators in both Plato's and Schleiermacher's discourse and in the New Testament writers' discourse, as in almost any: "and" and "but." In both Plato and the New Testament, κα⍳ can mean *und*, *auch* (meaning either also or even), or *doch*, as is true in Schleiermacher's discourse, though when he wants *doch* he adds it in. The word ουκ is almost always *aber*, as in Lk. 1:7: "But they had no child." The word δε, already noted above in another connection, also means "but," as in Lk. 1:13: "But the angel said to him" and Mt. 5:22: "But I say to you," as does ηδε in Lk. 2:19: "But Mary kept all these things." Sometimes δε can mean also now, further, and even *doch*. Also, μεν, noted above in one use of the μεν . . . δε combination, ordinarily means something like *zwar* (indeed, in truth) when accompanying the first of two contrasting words or clauses. The equivalent of this word too is often found in Schleiermacher's discourse.

Except for the frequent and direct carryovers of Greek usage into Schleiermacher's German, at a time when the language itself was in rapid flux and others were also attempting to enrich it through translation particularly from Greek and English, what I have demonstrated here all fits under the rubric of drawing from the classics. This is much less true of the distinctions among words for logical use that are to be presented next.

Words of Implication, Consequences or Entailment

Finally, we may note that eventually Schleiermacher developed sets of distinctions among logical operators to which he could refer in establishing direct connections among or between successive statements. Among these, especially important to attend to are the following, for which the attached translations are almost always the most appropriate ones in his texts.

(1) *Da* – since. Often this choice seems to represent a looser or more complexly indicated connection than do *weil* or *darum*. I have not determined to what degree this would be the case.

(2) *Weil* – because. Ordinarily, one ground, reason or occasion is given, or a set of them is given, each introduced by *weil*.

(3) *Denn* – for. At the beginning of sentences other locutions work, such as "This is true because" or "The reason is that," and occasionally "Actually" or "In actuality," pointing to the way things go in the natural course of events, or "It [does X] in that" or "[A given practice X] is called for because" as explaining or illustrating what was said before. Only the context can tell us which of these different meanings is intended, so to that extent Schleiermacher's usage is inexact.

(4) *So* – so, hence, accordingly, then, in this way. Sometimes there is no word but "so" is simply implied when it is preceded by "if" (*wenn*).

(5) *Alsdann* – then (adv.), accordingly (*als so* = *also*).

(6) *Und so* – and so, accordingly, consequently.

(7) *Mithin* – consequently. However, this word sometimes presents a difficulty and so must be rendered "as a result" or even somehow carry the meaning "along with that."

(8) *Also* – thus, then; or, rarely, so. This is by far the most frequently used word in the set, ordinarily expressing simple implication but occasionally of a very weak sort so that it almost sounds gratuitous, and sometimes expressing nearly full entailment. Here too, the right counterpart in English can usually be discovered, but this too is a somewhat inexact term for that reason.

(9) *Darum* – for that reason, this means (implies) that, therefore.

(10) *Dafür* – therefore, for that reason—a word that rarely appears.

(11) *Daher* – almost always hence, and sometimes therefore, for that reason, accordingly.

(12) *Deswegen* – on account of which, on that account.

(13) *Deshalb* – on that account, sometimes consequently or accordingly.

(14) *Demnach* – accordingly, or according to—a word or phrase also sometimes used in other constructions where *nach* appears.

(15) *Demgemäß* – accordingly, by that measure.

(16) *Zufolge, infolgedessen, heraus ergiebt sich* – consequently, it follows that.

Schleiermacher did not invent these distinctions among sometimes overlapping usages, though various writers of his time used them differently. They represent developments in the logic of language, particularly among philosophers of the eighteenth century. Yet, he does tend to display his own careful and characteristic use of them in his writings.

Schleiermacher has several ways of expressing more nearly strict entailment, which bears the connotation of identity or equivalence. In a brief statement he may use *das heißt*—that is, which means—or some locution meaning utter sameness, but even here the meaning is restricted to "which is the same thing as saying," or "that is to say" (*nämlich*), which does not necessitate anything approaching full entailment because it may loosely refer simply to certain elements that are similar or alike. Similar references to sameness are also used in linking larger structures of thought, as is the identitative (as compared with the predicative) *ist* – is. He also uses *also* and *infolgedessen* for entailment. Rarely, however, does he employ entailment outside philosophical discourse and even there infrequently—more obviously in the *Dialektik* than elsewhere it would seem.

This matter needs to be explored further, but because of his historical sensibility, his feel for context and his refined sense for the nuances of language it is unlikely that he would normally, if ever, use strict, identitative entailment, except to identify two statements or concepts that are meant formally to mean exactly, or virtually, the same thing. The supposition that he does could lead to some serious misunderstandings. For example, in *Christian Faith* § 4 he refers to "the consciousness of being absolutely dependent" (A) as meaning "the same thing" as that of "being in relation with God" (B). These two statements must not be seen as transposable, as has occurred in innumerable interpretations. For one thing, within the development of religious consciousness A itself has undergone development, in his view, and is still developing, so it could not be true that every instance of A means B. In fact, he clearly shows this in his exposition of A. For another thing, B has many meanings, thus only a select range of meanings of B could be identified with A, and in this context primarily Judaic, Islamic and Christian conceptions of God are in mind (and certainly not all of them or in every respect). More, outside normal practice within the Christian setting Schleiermacher can readily conceive and support thinking of "deity" or "Supreme Being" in a non-theistic way. Finally, even where he establishes an area in which A can truly mean "the same thing" as B, it does not follow that each implies the other such that each phrase can simply be replaced by the other in any and all sentences within that area, which would be possible if full entailment were present.

In short, we must be very cautious in our interpretation of these little words.

Some Further Aspects

I conclude by briefly indicating several features necessary to appropriate translation of reflective discourse, including Schleiermacher's. First, it will surely be apparent that by "reflective" I do not mean simply musing or introspective or reactive or uncritically minded. It is far more rigorous than any of these things, though it too is subject to sloppiness, inattention, lack of information, mistakes in reasoning and the like. The point is to be able to see what is being said both with and despite any error and to render what is seen accurately. The next step of interpretative effort beyond translation (or at least only in the footnotes) is to engage the text synoptically and critically and to open up or advance inquiry.

For the present purpose, I restrict myself to four general features that directly come into play in translative work. These may serve as a complement to what was indicated in the first section of this essay.

(1) Getting clear about the author's definitions of terms (concepts and phrases) or any lack of clear and consistent definition, including any synonyms or near synonyms, and of typical relations between given terms.

(2) Ascertaining, as much as possible in the author's own language, what issues are being addressed and what problems are raised for solution through inquiry.

(3) Grasping how the author goes about making assertions and what the author's understanding of these assertions is (i.e. their status among statements that can be made). For example, are they doctrinal propositions (and, if so, what limitations are variously attached to these)? Are they truth claims, observations, descriptions, explanations, presuppositions, provisional assertions, statements to be entertained, or assumptions within an argument? Finally, are these actually held by the author or are they only represented within an argument? Regarding the status of assertions, one must be particularly watchful as to what is meant in clauses beginning with "if" or "when" (Schleiermacher follows ordinary usage in employing *wenn* for both). The same considerations apply to clauses within questions.

(4) Detecting from available evidence what is being affirmed (or pointed out in one of the ways just indicated) and what specifically is, explicitly or implicitly, being denied or is not being included. — Schleiermacher, for one, will often give quite definite indications of precisely what is meant in these respects. It is very important not to take one for another, for example to suppose that not including something means denying it or that stating a general negation applies across the board to every element within what is being denied, opposed or not affirmed. These are all matters of logic, and I find that they are frequently honored only in the breach by Schleiermacher interpreters, not to say more broadly. More's the shame, for he tried very hard to be exact and clear, even in extemporaneous discourse.

Now, philosophical art may certainly include more than these procedures, but if these are not followed there is not much else to go on. Particularly in a thinker like Schleiermacher, where riding on metaphors and allusions or hovering over only associatively connected pieces is very little done, it is essential to use them. Ultimately, the translator has got to have the sentence read in English the way it was meant in the original, as exactly so as is possible. One must closely follow the author's lead. It is this quality in the work of translation that makes it an exquisitely craftful endeavor, a philosophical art.

Within the cultural outlook of the Early Romantics arose a major new interest in translation. Whether on philological or on philosophical grounds, this interest included a sharp awareness of cultural and linguistic context and of individual style. To this extent, Schleiermacher's own work and the theory that accompanied it are indeed representations of Romantic culture. On the other hand, his efforts to understand and produce reflective discourse of the sort discussed here amount to a critique of much Romantic discourse, then or later. The key to this critique lies in the precise dialectical demands that he placed on his own use of reflective discourse, whether in more strictly philosophical works, in philosophically oriented rhapsodies or in sermons. Moreover, these demands chiefly reside not in his setting up contrasting observations or concepts, though this process was certainly important, in his view, for both philosophical and scientific discourse, but in his use of logical operators to order thought.

THE DESIRE TO KNOW GOD
IN SCHLEIERMACHER'S *DIALEKTIK*

David E. Klemm

In his "Nachwort" to a selection of texts by Schleiermacher, Karl Barth acknowledges that Schleiermacher determined the nineteenth century in the field of theology, and that, in many ways, the caliber and stature of Schleiermacher's thought far surpasses that of his subsequent critics.[1] Moreover, Barth admits that where he has serious reservations about Schleiermacher's theology, he may not sufficiently understand Schleiermacher to make an accurate judgment. Hence, for the sake of understanding Schleiermacher, Barth poses a two-part question to Schleiermacher. Barth's question is:

In Schleiermacher's theology or philosophy, do persons feel, think, and speak (a) in relationship to an indispensable [*unaufhebbar*] Other, in accordance with an *object* which is superior to their own being, feeling, perceiving, willing, and acting, an object toward which adoration, gratitude, repentance, and supplication are concretely possible and even imperative? . . . Or, for Schleiermacher, do persons feel, think, and speak (b) in and from a sovereign consciousness that their own beings are conjoined, and are indeed essentially *united*, with everything which might possibly come into question as something or even someone distinct from them?[2]

In this paper, I will not reflect on what Barth himself may have meant by God as *ein unaufhebbares Andere* or as "wholly other" [*ganz anders*]. I will, however, attempt to think how Schleiermacher would understand Barth's question, a question that cuts right to the core of theology.

A proper understanding of Barth's question rests on grasping two implied epistemological issues: 1) the nature of an object in general (so that one can understand the sense in which God could be conceived as an object), and 2) the nature of the relationship between consciousness and an object (so that one can understand the sense in which consciousness is essentially united

---

1. Karl Barth, "Nachwort," in Heinz Bolli (ed.), *Schleiermacher – Auswahl* (Gütersloh: Gütersloher Verlagshaus Mohn, 1968). This essay was translated by George Hunsinger and reprinted in the English edition of Barth's *Die Theologie Schleiermachers*: Karl Barth, *The Theology of Schleiermacher*, ed. Dietrich Ritschl, trans. Geoffrey W. Bromily (Grand Rapids, Michigan: William B. Eerdmans, 1982), 261-79. The English translation first appeared in *Studies in Religion/Sciences Religieuses* 7/2 (1978), 117-35.

2. Barth puts the same two-part question in four ways. I am focusing on the second of the four. See page 275 of the above reference.

with or distinguished from God in its acts of thinking, perceiving, and feeling). In his lectures on dialectic, Schleiermacher presents and defends an answer to Barth's question, an answer that Barth did not consider in his own lectures on Schleiermacher's theology.[3] Schleiermacher's *Dialektik* is a thinking about thinking, and in the nature of the case the two epistemological problems implied in Barth's theological question arise in that context: 1) What is an object? and 2) What is the relationship between consciousness and objects? Nonetheless, the theological question about God's otherness is the driving question of Schleiermacher's *Dialektik*. Schleiermacher's *Dialektik* expresses the desire to know God, and it articulates what we can and cannot know about God. Yet Schleiermacher claims that anyone who wishes to speak about the otherness of God must engage in thinking about thinking. Why is that the case? To speak about anything as something, such as to say that God is Wholly Other, is to think about that thing. Thinking is a rule-governed, purposive activity. To think about a thing is to think with a purpose in mind, according to the rules of thinking. So to think requires that we know the purpose and the rules of thinking. To know the purpose and the rules of thinking requires thinking about thinking. The task of Schleiermacher's *Dialektik* is precisely to think about the structure, limits, and absolutely first principle of any and all thinking that intends to become knowing. Any cogent reflection on the otherness of God must do the same.

In this paper, I attempt to reconstruct Schleiermacher's argument that to think about the absolutely first principle of thinking, a principle that is essentially united with every thinking that desires to know, ultimately is to think about God as the uncancellable Other.

I. The Task of Thinking the Otherness of God

A. Step 1: Otherness Means Essence

I begin by considering the general task of thinking about God according to Schleiermacher. What does it mean to think the otherness of God according to Schleiermacher? I proceed in three steps, beginning with this

---

3.   I shall be using primarily the Odebrecht edition of the 1822 lectures, although I am aware of and have consulted the Arndt edition of the 1811 lectures, the Jonas edition of the 1818 lectures, and the Halpern edition of the 1831 edition. Subsequently, the reference of "Odebrecht" is to Friedrich Schleiermacher's *Dialektik*, ed. Rudolf Odebrecht (Darmstadt: Wissenschaftliche Buchgesellschaft, 1988, reprinting the original Leipzig edition of 1942).

question: What does it mean to think the otherness of anything at all? The answer is that to think the otherness of something is to think its essence. Here is the argument:

In the *Dialektik*, the activity of thinking is the combining of otherness and sameness in a unified thought. When we speak of the otherness of some- thing, we denote that quality or property that makes it distinct or different from other things. Primarily we make this distinction in two ways: 1) we distinguish the concept of one kind of thing from other kinds of things; 2) we distinguish one empirical instance that falls under a concept from other instances that fall under the same concept. In both kinds of distinction, it is possible to denote the distinguishing characteristics only by referring to a common concept. For example, if I am to think how cats are other than dogs, then I must think the specific difference distinguishing cats from other mammals, such as dogs. Clearly, however, in doing so, I simultaneously speak of the sameness of cats and dogs, for it is possible to distinguish them only with reference to the higher genus "mammal," a concept contained in the concepts of both cat and dog that makes possible recognition of their specific difference.[4] Likewise, when I say "Here is a cat," and then, "Here is another," I distinguish two individual and sensibly appearing cats from each other. It is possible to do so only by subsuming the two appearances under the common concept "cat."[5]

According to Schleiermacher's analyses, otherness and sameness, difference and identity, are mutually co-implying logical terms that are irreducible to one another in the general logic of concepts. Concepts of real or ideal beings include both the otherness of specific difference and the sameness of generic identity. Likewise, judgments, which are combinations of concepts, necessarily combine sameness and otherness in the logical structure of ascribing universal predicates (e.g., the color tan) to particular subjects (e.g., my cat Scooter). Even tautologies such as "A cat is a cat" combine sameness and otherness when repeating the same concept in the different logical positions of subject and predicate. Therefore, when we are thinking the otherness of something, we are also thinking the sameness or identity of that thing; and when we are thinking the otherness proper to something, we are thinking a content that is a conjunction of sameness and otherness. Consequently, nothing can be thought that is absolutely self-same or wholly other. Other-

---

4. A concept includes both a formal and a material component, that is, genus and specific difference include the idea of possible empirical appearance. The concepts of cat and dog are both formally and materially distinct, yet formally and materially identical with regard to the concept of animal.

5. The concept cat remains formally and materially the same in subsuming both sensible appearances, but the two cats are different as actual appearing individuals.

ness and sameness are reversible terms in the sense that although they are distinct, they are nonetheless co-dependent; think one and you think the other.

Thinking broadly after the tradition, we should say that the co-dependence of the terms sameness and otherness refers thinking to the essence of the thing. When thinking combines the sameness and otherness proper to something, it thinks the essence of that thing, the combination of both a formal possibility of intelligibility and a material possibility of actual appearance in time and space. Essence is the principle through which a thing can be determined as 1) the same as all other things (the thing is a being like other beings; 2) the same as itself (the appearing thing is the same as its concept); 3) different from all other things (the thing is specifically different from all other things); and 4) different from itself (the appearing thing is in certain regards different from its concept).

Now, because the essence of a thing is what is signified through its definition,[6] to speak of the otherness proper to something is to define it, so that we know what it is and what it is not. That is, to speak of the otherness of anything is to determine the essence in question through the thinking activity of combining and distinguishing. We have now come to the end of the first step: thinking the otherness of something means thinking the essence of that thing. In the next step, we must ask: How is thinking the essence of a thing possible?

B. Step 2: Thinking the Principle of Thinking Essence

According to Schleiermacher's analysis of the structure of thinking, it is only possible to relate the elements of sameness and otherness within concepts and judgments, if the relatable elements are in principle originally the same. In other words, to think the essence of something it is necessary to posit a primordial common ground, an absolute sameness of sameness and otherness that makes possible the acts of combining and distinguishing sameness and otherness in concepts and judgments.

Moreover, according to Schleiermacher, the common ground must be formulable as an absolutely first principle of thinking. How so? If in every particular instance of thinking, otherness is logically related to sameness, and if this relation can and must be reduced to an original sameness of otherness and sameness, then for there to be actual instances of thinking, the absolute identity of sameness and otherness must function as the universal and neces-

---

6. Thomas Aquinas, *On Being and Essence*, trans. Armand Maurer, C.S.B. (Toronto, Canada: The Pontifical Institute of Mediaeval Studies, 1968), 34.

sary principle or rule of all thinking. This principle accounts for our capacity to relate elements of sameness and otherness in forming actual concepts and judgments. What status does this principle have?

According to Schleiermacher, the first principle of thinking has a transcendental-logical status as the formal condition of the possibility of actual instances of thinking about being. But in addition, the first principle of thinking must also be a transcendental-ontological principle, in order to prevent the collapse of the otherness of being from thinking into non-dialectical sameness with the concepts by which thinking thinks real beings. In other words, the absolutely first epistemological principle of thinking must be the absolutely first principle of being as well as the absolutely first principle of knowing, i.e., an original knowing that is. The first principle must be the absolute identity of the sameness and otherness of thinking and of being, the absolute ground of ideality and reality in their identity and difference. We have now followed Schleiermacher's deduction of a necessary absolutely first principle. How does the task of thinking the absolutely first principle relate to the task of thinking the otherness of God? The short answer for Schleiermacher is that they are the same, as the next step shows.

C. Step 3: Thinking the Otherness of God as Divine Essence

What are we thinking when we think the otherness of God? If otherness ultimately denotes essence, then the task of conceiving the otherness of God is identical to the task of thinking God's essence – the divine essence. However, the word God, the object of theology, denotes the essence of no particular being, either real or ideal, to which the general logic of sameness and difference applies. Let us use the word God to name that than which none greater can be conceived. According to the rules of thinking in the *Dialektik*, when we think that than which none greater can be conceived, we think the essence of the thinking of essence. We think the essence of essence when we think the absolutely first principle of thinking essence as the absolute identity of thinking and being, the only God imaginable for us. If we try to think something greater than the absolutely first principle, we purport to refer altogether outside or beyond the principle and structure of thinking itself, which is quite impossible for thinking. We have now completed the third step of determining the task of thinking the otherness of God. Having attempted to grasp what the task is as Schleiermacher himself would conceive it, I propose now to elucidate how Schleiermacher executes the task in his *Dialektik*.

II. Schleiermacher's Conceiving of the Otherness of God

The thesis of my elucidation of Schleiermacher's lectures on dialectic is that although Schleiermacher does not put it so, the dialectic expresses the desire to know the essence of God as just defined, namely, as the Other whose essence is unique, the essence of essence rather than the essence of any particular thing.[7] Moreover, to know God includes both a positive knowing as well as a knowing of what cannot be known, a knowing and a not-knowing that unite with and make possible the knowing and not-knowing of anything at all. In other words, for Schleiermacher we think the otherness of God in thinking anything at all. There are three steps to my elucidation. First, Schleiermacher thinks the structure and limits of thinking and being. Second, he thinks the limits of those limits. Third, Schleiermacher thinks the essence of God.

A. Step 1: The Structure and Limits of Thinking and Being

I focus initially on the dual structure of thinking and being. Thinking is the temporally- and spatially-located mental act of combining and dividing formal and material elements with respect to being, the "about which" of thinking. In other words, thinking is always thinking about something that is given to thinking, or being. This dual structure clearly emerges when thinking thinks about thinking and thereby posits itself as being. In thinking about thinking, the activity and content of thinking, that is, thinking and being, show themselves from themselves in their identity and difference. There is no thinking without the positing of being as the "about which" of thinking, and there is no being that is not posited by thinking. The distinction between thinking and being is an original and fundamental ontological distinction. Neither can be reduced to the other; each implies the other. In the dialectical activity of thinking about thinking, as well as in the presupposed structure of immediate self-consciousness that is the condition of the possibility of any thinking ascribable to a thinker, the subject of thinking is conscious of itself as an identity in the difference of being and of thinking: in thinking, the thinking I is at one and the same time a thinking being and a being thinking.[8]

---

7. Schleiermacher does not put it that way himself in the *Dialectic*. Rather, he claims that the task of dialectic is (quote him: knowing about knowing for the sake of resolving dispute = knowing about the first principle of knowing. But what else could this be than a knowing about the otherness of God so defined?

8. "Wenn wir uns selbst als die Identität des Seins und des Denkens bewußt sind und uns gegeneinander ein denkendes Sein und ein seiendes Denken sind, so repräsentiert hier das ideale das Denken und das Reale das Sein." Odebrecht, 181.

Schleiermacher derives the related distinction between ideal being and real being accordingly: Real being is the being in the thinking that is (exists); ideal being is the thinking in the being that thinks.

From the dual ontological structure of thinking and being, Schleiermacher derives the epistemological distinction between the intellectual function and the organic function of thinking. That thinking is a being occurs through the organic function of thinking; that there is a being that thinks occurs through the intellectual function of thinking. The intellectual and organic functions are the two poles of thinking; the former is the relatively active or formative pole of thinking, and the latter is the relatively passive or receptive pole of thinking. The intellectual function provides the forms of thinking, and the organic function provides the material that is formed.

In any actual instance of thinking, both the intellectual function and organic function are involved in different quantities. When we abstract the activity of thinking in the narrow sense, which produces the logical forms of possible objects, we isolate a thought-activity in which the intellectual function exercises predominance over the organic function. When we abstract the activity of perceiving, which produces images of material objects, we isolate a thought-activity in which the organic function predominates over the intellectual function. The term intuition denotes the form of thinking in which the organic and intellectual functions reach equilibrium, concept and image merge into a unified thought-thing, which is the essence of language as the embodiment of a thinking that is a being and a being that is a thinking. All thinking strives to become intuition, the ideal of perfect knowing. Actual thinking under conditions of time and space, however, inevitably falls short of perfect knowing in completed intuition and takes the form of temporal oscillation between the intellectual function and the organic function. By "oscillation" Schleiermacher signifies the activity of combining and distinguishing formal and material elements of thinking to which correspond the ideal and real elements of being.

All actual thinking proceeds by way of concept-formation and judgment-formation. In forming concepts, thinking formally determines material that is sensibly perceived through the organic function. The concept itself is a combination and distinction of "characteristic marks" into the more inclusive genus and the less inclusive specific difference. In forming judgments, and here Schleiermacher has synthetic or "proper" judgments in mind, thinking combines concepts with reference to a given object. The judgment is a combination and distinction of the subject-concept denoting an independent being and a predicate-concept denoting a determination of being that is not already contained in the subject-concept. Concept-formation and judgment-formation are interrelated and irreducible to each other. Concepts, as combinations of genus and specific difference, can only be defined through judgments. Judgments are themselves combinations of concepts. All actual thinking involves both concept-formation and judgment-formation in their identity and difference.

As forms of actual thinking, concept-formation and judgment-formation are derived from analysis of the intellectual function. When considered as objects of thought, these forms have ideal being. Both forms of thinking, concept-formation and judgment-formation, have correlates in real being, however, derived from analysis of the organic function. Corresponding in being to the relation between genus and species in the concept is the relation between force and appearance in the image of actual objects, for force is defined as the relatively universal ground of the more particular and subordinate manifestation of that ground. Corresponding in being to the relation between subject-concept and predicate-concept in the judgment is the relation between cause and effect in the actual object of judgment, for the subject-concept posits an independent being that contains the possibility of receiving the determination denoted by the predicate-concept.

At this point, we have followed Schleiermacher's analysis of the structure of thinking and being. In order to determine the single principle making possible combining and distinguishing of the various elements of sameness and otherness within this structure,[9] I turn now to Schleiermacher's analysis of the limits of the dual structure of thinking and being. His analysis begins with the intellectual and organic functions and their respective noematic correlates – concept and image. According to Schleiermacher, the intellectual function or activity provides formal determination of given material content through the concept. The organic function or activity receives sensible impressions through the image. There are three substeps to Schleiermacher's determination of limits.

In the first substep, Schleiermacher isolates the common upper and lower limits of all thinking by analyzing the intellectual function and abstracting from the differences between concept-formation and judgment-formation. Schleiermacher argues that in abstracting from all given content and ascending from less inclusive to more inclusive concepts, one arrives at the absolute limit-concept of the coherent structure of being as a whole. This is the idea of pure form, pure ideal being, the limit-concept of sheer sameness.

---

9.   These elements are: thinking and being, the intellectual function and the organic function, thinking in the narrow sense and perceiving, genus and species within the concept, force and appearance within the image, subject and predicate within the judgment, cause and effect withn the object of judgment.

Similarly, in abstracting from all form and descending to all-inclusive content, one arrives at the absolute limit-concept of the infinite chaos of possible stimulations. This is the idea of pure content, pure real being, the limit-concept of utter otherness. Pure form, i.e., pure sameness, marks the unity of the upper limit-concepts; pure content, i.e., pure difference, marks the unity of the lower limit-concepts.

In the second substep, Schleiermacher analyzes the organic function: In abstracting all content from the form of the image, product of the organic function, and ascending to the most inclusive sensible form that is empty of content, one arrives at the pure image of time. In descending to the most inclusive sensible form that is full of content, one arrives at the pure image of space. To posit time is the same on the organic side as the positing of ideal being on the intellectual side, and to posit space is the same on the organic side as the positing of real being on the intellectual side.[10]

Ideal-being and real-being on the side of the intellectual function, and time and space on the side of the organic function: these pairs constitute the highest formal relative limits for the products of each function respectively. In other words, actual thinking oscillates among these limits in formally determining any given material content. The relative limits of ideal-being and real-being, time and space, mediate the thinking activities within the absolute limits of the idea of being in general (pure form) and the idea of a chaos of sensible impressions (pure content).

In the third substep, Schleiermacher removes the brackets around the specific activities of concept-formation and judgment-formation in order to determine the limits of thinking and being with regard to these activities of concept-formation and judgment-formation. The following structure emerges: In concept-formation, in which the intellectual function predominates, the upper limit is 1) the purely formal idea of absolute being without oppositions, the most inclusive ideal determination. The lower limit of concept-formation is 2) the infinite manifold of perceivable characteristics, the most inclusive determination of possible real content. In judgment-formation, in which the organic function predominates the upper limit is 3) the idea of the absolute subject of judgment, the most inclusive real logical subject. The lower limit of judgment-formation is 4) the infinite manifold of possible predicates, the most inclusive ideal set of predicates.

Because all thinking oscillates between these limits, they represent the limits of sameness and difference as they are conjoined in actual concepts and judgments. Because the four limit-concepts converge when actual thinking determines a single real object, the limit-concepts must be identical

---

10. Odebrecht, 182.

in their identity and difference.[11] How may we think the absolute identity of the identity and difference of the limit concepts? The task at hand becomes to discover the identity of the limit concepts, the limit of the limits. In other words, the aim is to determine the sameness of sameness and otherness, the identity or essence that as final ground both is other than the whole structure of thinking and yet which makes its appearance within the whole structure of thinking. How does Schleiermacher proceed?

B. Step 2: The Limit of the Limits

There are two substeps in Schleiermacher's determination of the limit of the limits. First, Schleiermacher reduces the fourfold structure of sameness and difference to a twofold structure that he calls the structure of primary presupposition and final presupposition of actual thinking.[12] The steps of the argument are as follows:

1) He argues first that the two upper thought-limits of absolute being without opposition and the absolute subject must in principle be the same, because the highest concept of absolute being without oppositions can only be characterized through the judgment in which that concept is the absolute subject, of which nothing more can be predicated.[13]

2) He argues that the two lower thought-limits of the infinite manifold of possible predicates and the infinite manifold of perceivable characteristics must in principle be the same, because knowledge would not be possible unless the concept of the infinite manifold of possible predicates refers to the infinite manifold of perceivable characteristics.

3) Taken in their identity, the first pair of limit-concepts (absolute being and absolute subject) refer to the originating principle of the structure itself, the principle of the intellectual function in its purity, the principle of concept-formation. This principle of identity between the highest genus and all particular genera or specific differentia makes possible the combining of form with empty content. This principle is the primary presupposition of actual thinking. Schleiermacher names this principle "God," meaning primary unity exclusive of all oppositions. The term "God" in this usage is to be carefully distinguished from the sense in which the *Dialektik* may be said to express a desire to know God, for in the latter usage "God" means that than which none greater can be conceived, or the absolute principle of thinking and be-

---

11. Odebrecht, 215.
12. Odebrecht, 222.
13. Odebrecht, 219.

ing, the absolute unity of primary and final presuppositions and not merely the primary presupposition.

4) Taken in their identity, the second pair of limit-concepts (the absolute manifold of possible predicates and absolute manifold of perceivable characteristics) refer to the culminating principle of the structure, the principle of the organic function in its purity, the principle of judgment-formation. This principle of identity bctwccn absolute subject or highest being and the divisible infinite manifold of predicates makes possible the combining of pure form with full content. This principle is the final presupposition of actual thinking. Schleiermacher names this principle "world," the culminating unity inclusive of all oppositions.

In a second substep, Schleiermacher reduces the twofold structure of limits to identity in principle: the limit of limits, the absolute identity of the first and final presuppositions.[14] Why must the first and final pre-suppositions be absolutely identical? Unless the idea of pure form empty of content through which the infinite manifold of possible judgments is determined (i.e., the intellectual function in its purity) is absolutely the same as the idea of pure form filled with all possible content out of which all oppositions can emerge (i.e., the organic function in its purity), there could never be a thinking which could also be a knowing. The idea of ideal being as presupposed by the intellectual function must be the same as the real being that is given to the senses through the organic function. Concepts and images of objects must be identical in their identity and difference for there to be knowledge at all. The fact of knowledge implies some necessary relations between our forms of thought and our sensible representations, else sensory stimulations could never be ordered and thinking would sink back into chaos.[15]

Schleiermacher has now deduced the necessity of an absolutely first principle of identity between the pure possibility of intellection and the pure possibility of perception as the transcendental condition of the possibility of thinking about being. But how is it possible to think the unity of the limits? We turn to the third and final step.

C. Step 3: Conceiving The Essence of God

In the third step, Schleiermacher confronts the problem of determining the limit of the limits. This is a difficult task, because the absolutely first

---

14. The formula of being without opposition in its relation to the absolute subject is to be equated with the formula of the manifold of possible judgments in its relation to the absolute manifold of predicates. Ibid., 219.
15. Odebrecht, 219.

principle of knowing itself can never be made into an object of knowing precisely because it is the unconditioned principle that makes knowing of conditioned objects possible. In this sense, the first principle is other than anything else. Nonetheless the task cannot be altogether impossible, because we
use the first principle in knowing any particular thing, hence we must have
some knowledge of it, and we can deduce its universal necessity for all
knowing. In this sense, the first principle is essentially united with any and all
knowing. We know that we both know and do not know the absolutely first
principle. Moreover, to think anything greater than the absolutely first principle is itself inconceivable for thinking. To think the first principle is to
think God's essence.

According to Schleiermacher, all attempts to name or to determine the
limit of the limits, the absolute identity of the primary and the final identities
of thinking and being, encounter the same intrinsic problem. The names for
God, by which we attempt to think God's essence, fail to name God precisely
because of the interior doubling of the unconditioned identity into conditioned primary and final forms.[16] The primary and final forms further divide
into a quaternity, because each refers to an intellectual and organic element.
Thus the limit of the limits inherently divides into the four limit-concepts
through the thinking activity itself. Consequently, according to Schleiermacher, we should understand the traditional names of God as referring to possible relations among the limit-concepts.

For example, in the pantheistic construction, the name of God is deduced from concept-formation by abstracting the activity of perceiving material content from thinking in the narrow sense of formally determining that
content. In this construction, one begins with the image of a particular being
and traces it back to the final condition of its possibility in being. The ground
of such a particular being is the unity of the world as a whole, the totality of
all that is, of which any particular being is an appearance. One can ascribe a
divine name to this unity as natura naturans. But, according to Schleiermacher, the name natura naturans cannot adequately name the first principle,
for natura naturans as the unity of the whole of being presupposes natura
naturata as the parts through which the unity of the whole is expressed as a
formative force. The divine name is arbitrarily assigned to one side of a necessary duality when it should name the ground of the duality.

The second way of deriving the highest being from concept-formation
would be to abstract the form of thinking in the narrow sense from perceiving. Here we begin with the idea of pure form, absolute being without differentiation, and we think God as Creator. But clearly God as Creator cre-

---

16. "Eine Einheit suchend haben wir eine zweifache Duplizität gefunden." Odebrecht, 269.

ates the world out of matter, and so in thinking the name we enjoin the limit-concept of pure matter, the chaos of sensible stimulations. Thus the name God divides into a reciprocal duality and cannot be contained on one side of the duality.

The effort to name God fares no better if we deduce the idea of the highest being from the elements of judgment-formation. One can reduce from the finite connection between subject and predicate, which in being is a connection of cause and effect, to the generative ground of that temporal connection conceived as the final principle of cause and effect. Then one can name that final ground "God." But when we think the ground of causal connections, do we think freedom or necessity? The name God must encompass both, yet we assign it to one or the other because we cannot think both.

The other possibility for deriving the name of God from judgment-formation is to reduce from the relata of subject and predicate as forms to the totality of substantial forms in its relation to the unified system of cause and effect. What is the final identity of the totality of substantial forms brought about in time? We could name that identity "God," but do we think thereby Fate or Providence? Once again, duality emerges from the attempt to conceive God's essence. Seeking unity, pure thinking uncovers a thorough-going difference.[17] Proceeding on the basis of the relation between thought and being, thinking necessarily remains within the domain of the opposites and cannot transcend it as thinking.[18] The desire to know God appears to take the form of a pure seeking that cannot be satisfied.[19]

Schleiermacher is undaunted by the apparent impasse and seeks out a point where the opposition is sublated in a primary or secondary way, and we are able to find as a unity what we hitherto had found as plurality. Schleiermacher seeks his clue by returning to the same starting point from which he deduced the structure of thinking and being in the first place: "Die Identität des Seins und Denkens tragen wir in uns selbst; wir selbst sind Sein und Denken, das denkende Sein und das seiende Denken."[20] Schleiermacher proposes to proceed by reflecting on the identity of being and thinking in us and from there to think the first principle, or, as he also calls it, the transcendent-transcendental ground. Where and how does it appear?

Schleiermacher claims that we have so to speak the ultimate ground in us both as the originating principle of our conscious strivings and as the culminating goal of consciousness, a perfect intuition of the unity of all real and

17. Ibid.
18. Ibid., 270.
19. Ibid., 293.
20. Ibid., 270.

ideal being.[21] As such, the absolute principle is both the ground of our own impulse to think and the ground of the totality of being that affects us.[22] The absolute principle is in us as the unconditioned ground of any thinking about being. To think this transcendent-transcendental ground, however, one must reckon with the fact that thinking divides between the thinking that posits being through its own activity (or reason in its practical function as willing) and the thinking that reflects being given to it (or reason in its theoretical function as knowing). Is it possible to think the unified ground of the opposition between thinking as knowing and thinking as willing?

Schleiermacher's answer is that willing and knowing represent the same relation of sameness and otherness with which we have been working all along. As forms of thinking, they are identical. But they are distinct forms nonetheless: knowing reflects given being; willing brings forth new being. He argues that the temporal human experience of thinking is determined by alternations back and forth between discrete acts of knowing and willing, and that such alternations are only possible if there is a point of identity between the beginning of the one and the ceasing of the other.

According to Schleiermacher, in positing the alternation between willing and reflecting, we co-posit pure immediate self-consciousness or "feeling" as the point of identity between them. Immediate self-consciousness must be thought both transcendentally and empirically. Posited in itself as a transcendental condition of the temporal life thinking of thinking in alternation, immediate self-consciousness is timeless; it is the essence of the subject, the "I," not as reflected, hence mediated self-consciousness, but as originating ground and principle of all thinking. Posited in its empirical appearance as actual "feeling," immediate self-consciousness is a filled moment of time on which one can reflect after the fact.[23] Schleiermacher is careful to distinguish feeling, as the empirical appearance in real intentional consciousness of the presupposed immediate self-consciousness, from sensation, which is pure passivity. Empirical feeling is not pure passivity, but is the determinate form of self-consciousness, the general form of the self's having itself.[24]

Schleiermacher claims that feeling best expresses the way that the subject has and knows its own being as unity. Feeling is always a self-mediated immediate consciousness in which the "I" recovers the given awareness of its own being as thinking. Contained in this awareness is the fact that the "I" as "I," or the originating principle of thinking, is not the "world" nor anything in

21. Ibid. 272.
22. Ibid., 275.
23. Ibid., 286 and 287.
24. Ibid., 288.

it. Otherwise immediate self-consciousness would not be self-consciousness in contrast to worldly consciousness. Without this subjective certainty, objective knowledge would not be possible. In addition, Schleiermacher claims that immediate self-consciousness carries a conviction that the unified being of the "I" as positing, indeed self-positing, is not itself self-posited. As a thinking that is a being and a being that is a thinking, the being of the "I" is thinking and its thinking posits itself as being: in thinking, "I am," agrees Schleiermacher. Yet, he adds, ingredient in the idea of the "I" as immediate self-positing is a distinction as well between "I" and "God." How so?

To think that the being of the "I" as immediate self-positing is itself posited by the "I" leads thinking into a logical contradiction. Any theory that the "I" is absolutely self-positing must presuppose what it purports to explain – the emergence of the "I." The being of the "I" as self-positing, claims Schleiermacher, cannot itself be thought to be self-posited, but must be thought to be posited by another, that is, by the absolutely first principle. This formal point of analysis is corroborated by the fact that my being as positing is not itself produced by my thinking any more than I can negate my being as thinking simply by thinking. Thinking receives its being from a transcendent ground outside itself that we name "God."

The necessity of thinking the absolute dependence of the being of thinking on the transcendent-transcendental ground or absolutely first principle, is corroborated by the empirical feeling of religious consciousness that "I" am absolutely dependent on the transcendent-transcendental ground. The religious feeling is the empirical correlate to the intellectual necessity of striving to know God and the failure adequately to do so. The feeling of absolute dependence, a complex empirical feeling of "holy sadness" or religious awe,[25] is, then, a universal and necessary feeling whether actualized in an individual or not. Religious consciousness is always potential in a finite think-

---

25. *Reden*, 166.

ing being, if not actual, precisely because it is the empirical analogue to the thinkable-unthinkability of the first principle.[26]

III. Conclusion

This paper began with a theological question put to Schleiermacher by Karl Barth:

In Schleiermacher's theology or philosophy, do persons feel, think, and speak (a) in relationship to an indispensable [*unaufhebbar*] Other, in accordance with an *object* which is superior to their own being, feeling, perceiving, willing, and acting, an object toward which adoration, gratitude, repentance, and supplication are concretely possible and even imperative? . . . Or, for Schleiermacher, do persons feel, think, and speak (b) in and from a sovereign consciousness that their own beings are conjoined, and are indeed essentially *united*, with everything which might possibly come into question as something or even someone distinct from them?[27]

Barth's theological question implies two epistemological questions: 1) What is an object?; 2) What is the relationship between consciousness and an object? Schleiermacher answers the theological question by way of answering the implied epistemological questions in the *Dialektik*. There he argues that the concept of object as such – any being or thing, including God – is that toward which an act of thinking is directed. The definition of an object therefore necessarily includes a necessary relation to consciousness: an object is an object of and for consciousness. How does Schleiermacher conceive God and how is consciousness related to God?

---

26. Taken together, the formal thinking of the unthinkability of God, the knowing of the unknowability of the divine essence, on one side, along with the religious feeling that is the positive appearance of the necessary and universal dependence of the "I" on God, on the other side, we have a non-arbitrary symbol or representation of the divine essence. In thinking the necessary connection between the absolutely first principle, as the universal and necessary ground of all thinking and being, and the real feeling of religious consciousness, we both have and have not the transcendent ground. The lack we experience in thinking the unthinkability of the absolute ground, and the surplus we experience in actual religious feeling of holy sadness, awe, absolute dependence, correspond to each other. The lack on the one side is reciprocally joined to the surplus on the other; taken together as the ideal and real, formal and material sides of the essence of God, the too little and the too much manifest all that can be manifest of the otherness of God.

27. Barth puts the same two-part question in four ways. I am focusing on the second of the four. See page 275 of the above reference.

In thinking about thinking, one conceives the formal essence of God as the absolute combining of ideality and reality, of form and matter. The material essence of God can be derived from the analogue of pure combining found in finite self-consciousness. The finite subjective condition of the possibility of thinking anything at all is immediate self-consciousness. Immediate self-consciousness is the finite appearance of the pure activity of combining form and matter. If we combine the formal essence of God with the material essence found in finite self-consciousness, we think the essence of God as pure being, an object of consciousness that is the first principle of thinking and being. That is the definition of God, conceived as that than which none greater can be conceived. The definition provides the highest rule by which one thinks – namely, when thinking always combine form and matter – and it denotes the highest being – namely, pure being as the pure activity of the absolute combining of ideality and reality. In other words, the essence of God is not merely a regulative principle for thinking; it is.

The definition of God, like that of any other object, includes a necessary relationship to consciousness. God is only in relation to consciousness. Whatever God is apart from human consciousness cannot be a concern for human consciousness, for any attempt to think God apart from human consciousness necessarily brings God into relationship with consciousness.

How, then, would Schleiermacher answer Barth's question? First, Schleiermacher would answer affirmatively to the question: Do persons feel, think, and speak in relationship to an indispensable [*unaufhebbar*] Other, in accordance with an object which is superior to their own being, feeling, perceiving? God, for Schleiermacher, can be rightly called an objective and uncancellable other in the sense that the absolutely first principle is an object of consciousness that is radically unlike any other object – it is the principle of any possible knowing (consciousness) of objects. This God is properly conceived by Schleiermacher as an object in a strong sense: the first principle is not merely a subjective principle of thinking but also an objective principle of being.

Second, Schleiermacher would answer both negatively and positively to the question: Do persons feel, think, and speak in and from a sovereign consciousness that their own beings are conjoined, and are indeed essentially united, with everything which might possibly come into question as something or even someone distinct from them? Schleiermacher would dispute the claim that human consciousness is sovereign: Finite consciousness is self-positing, but its being as self-positing must be conceived as posited by another, that is, as absolutely dependent on God. Yet at the same time, Schleiermacher would affirm the idea that God is essentially united with human consciousness: the first principle appears as the primary and final pre-supposition of any act of consciousness.

Finally, there is no doubt that adoration, gratitude, repentance, and sup-plication are not only concretely possible in view of this God, but indeed im-perative. These empirical feelings are manifestations of religious conscious-ness as a consciousness that is both directed toward God as an other and is united with God as its ground.

WORLD SPIRIT AND THE APPEARANCE OF THE GOD: PHILOSOPHY OF RELIGION AND CHRISTIAN APOLOGETIC IN THE EARLY SCHLEIERMACHER

Roger A. Badham

Und wecket der dunklen Gefühle Gewalt
Die im Herzen wunderbar schliefen.
(Schiller: Der Graf von Habsburg).[1]

It is hardly to be doubted that the young Schleiermacher's assurance of the possibility of religious experience, the manner in which it may be apprehended and the particular limits of what religion may be said to be, were formulated following considered reflection upon his own entry into the Eleusinian mysteries, when he had, to use his own early Romantic imagery, laid "upon the bosom of the infinite world," at that moment becoming its soul, and the world becoming his body.[2] His interpretation of religious experience opened up a new horizon for understanding the nature of religion that was destined to awaken bold, new possibilities for nineteenth and twentieth century theology. His interpretation led to three particulars. (i) He was able to refute the reductionist claims of eighteenth-century rationalism, wherein religion was devoured whole by an omnivorous moral law, which, for Fichte, had taken the place of the substance of God. Following Kant, Fichte argued that the moral experience of the categorical imperative was tantamount to being in relationship with God, subsuming religion under ethics. (ii) Schleiermacher was able to differentiate between religion and supernaturalism without resorting to rationalist claims. Thus he can define religion as an active and continually vital force in and of the universe over against the metaphysical abstractions of supernaturalism which had been discredited primarily by Kant, the resultant being (iii) that he was able to spread the canopy of the religious beyond the confines of exclusivist systems, and cover his own cultured readers, or indeed any persons at all, who can intuit the action of the

---

1. "It waketh the power of feelings obscure, that in the heart wondrously slumbered," quoted in Rudolf Otto, *The Idea of the Holy* (Oxford: O.U.P., 1958), 148.
2. Friedrich Schleiermacher, *On Religion: Speeches to its Cultured Despisers*, trans. and ed. R. Crouter (Cambridge: Cambridge University Press, 1988), 113 [Henceforth, *Speeches*]. Karl Barth, while appreciating the poetry, fails to appreciate the possibility of such union with the infinite! (*The Theology of Schleiermacher: Lectures at Göttingen*. ed. Dietrich Ritschl [Grand Rapids: Wm. B. Eerdmans, 1982], 249.)

universe revealed to them every moment, that "spills forth from its ever-fruit-ful womb."[3]

George Lindbeck suggests that by "demolishing the metaphysical and epistemological foundations of the earlier cognitive-propositional views," Kant had, unwittingly, "helped clear the ground" for the experiential-expres-sivist tradition which was to spring out of the fertile ground seeded by Schleiermacher, which has been the dominant paradigm until the present.[4] Contrary to Kant's concept of mediated knowledge, the unknowability of the thing-in-itself, and the resultant separation of spirit and nature, in terms of noumena and phenomena, the Romantic movement built a theory of prere-flective feeling which promised an immediate knowledge of God through na-ture. Jacobi had sought to counter Kant's claims as foundering upon the un-substantiated presupposition of the thing-in-itself. Schleiermacher insisted upon the immediate consciousness of reality, and through the exploration of intuition and feeling launched a frontal attack upon the Kantian system with something of the spirit of a Reformer. It was no coincidence that the En-lightenment had broken forth in countries bathed in the doctrines of the Protestant Reformation, yet nevertheless unmoved by the revelatory experi-ence that for Luther went far beyond the limits of his own reason. Reforma-tion thought was never likely to be satisfactory to those schooled in the hy-brid world of an unexperienced-but-assumed revelation with its necessary correlate of the inadequacy of human reason. Michael D. Ryan has written in reference to Schleiermacher's essay, *Über das Höchste Gut*, that Kant "too closely identified the human will with the subjective grounds for determining the will which are derived from the law of pure reason," making happiness "into an inevitable requirement of reason itself."[5] Schleiermacher is alert to this enthronement of reason and sets out to discover the possibility of imme-diacy through the activity of religion at the level of consciousness rather than at the levels of intellect or morality. So in the *Speeches* he asks the question of most import to the Romantic movement: What is the self's relation to the universe? Richard R. Niebuhr suggests that consequently he "broke the stalemate of rationalism and orthodoxy and set the mind of the Protestant church free once more."[6] For Schleiermacher, piety is independent of

---

3. Ibid., 105.
4. George Lindbeck, *The Nature of Doctrine: Religion and Theology in a Post-Liberal Age* (Philadelphia: The Westminster Press, 1984), 20.
5. Michael D. Ryan, "The Young Friedrich Schleiermacher's Act of Religious Identifica-tion: His Phenomenology of Finite Spirit," *New Athenaeum / Neues Athenaeum* 1 (1989), 148-165.
6. Richard R. Niebuhr, *Schleiermacher on Christ and Religion* (New York: Charles Scrib-ners' Sons, 1964), 6.

systems of doctrine, whether rationalist, orthodox or romantic. He scandalizes the builders of systems, who through vain speculations, but without inner experience, think they have apprehended religion. Brilliantly he mocks them: "You have memory and imitation, but no religion. You have not produced the intuitions for which you know the formulas," and so they are caricatures, dead and decayed fragments.[7]

Schleiermacher's Phenomenology of Religion

The immediate consciousness is the foundation upon which all else either stands or falls. Schleiermacher is aware of it as such and speaks of the 'intuition of the universe,' as the 'hinge' of his whole speech, as a result of which "you may determine [religion's] essence and limits."[8] The concept of intuition was not foreign to Kant's work, but Schleiermacher brought it together into intimate association with religion, arguing that intuition was the means, by which and through which, the senses are able to perceive the uninterrupted activity of the universe. With such perception, one may "accept everything individual as a part of the whole and everything limited as a representation of the infinite." The polarity between the self and the universe, and the ability of the self to perceive the essential unity of the whole, lies at the core of Schleiermacher's understanding of the possibilities of religion to act within the human consciousness. "Beyond that is mythology."[9]

In the *Speeches*, the term religion is a rich and fertile complex of ideas which shares something of the ambiguity of the classical Muse. It is, on the one hand, "the sensibility and taste for the infinite," within the individual.[10] "It springs necessarily and by itself from the interior of every better soul."[11] Thus it is the ground, the possibility, of intuition within the person. It can give rise to powerful and disturbing feelings within (for which reason, it is not, for Schleiermacher the immediate impetus for determining moral actions). Yet he speaks of it sometimes as if it has its own volitional activity within the individual: "In everything that belongs to human activity . . . religion knows how to discover and pursue the actions of the world spirit."[12] But further, religion is also infinite, and "it must organize itself in manifestations that are rather different from one another . . . Each infinite force, once it di-

7. *Speeches*, 114.
8. Ibid., 104.
9. Ibid., 105.
10. Ibid., 103.
11. Ibid., 95.
12. Ibid., 128.

vides and separates itself in its manifestations, also reveals itself in unique and varied form." It is in these terms that he explains the various characteristics of the plurality of religions, which are individually rooted in the essence of religion.[13] So he can speak boldly of these manifestations of religion being revealed within the contingencies of nature and receiving varieties of names and structures. The recipients of the illumination "comprehended an act of the universe and thus denoted its individuality and its character."[14] Religion is something infinite and immeasurable, nevertheless containing within itself "a principle of individualization, for otherwise it could not exist at all and be perceived."[15] Just as there is no language-in-general, but only particular languages that may be spoken, so too, there is no such thing as the experience of religion-in-general, but particular religions. Thus religion reveals itself in an infinite number of finite and specific forms as "a work of the world spirit progressing into infinity."[16] Religion is the subjective means by which the world spirit is intuited by the individual. So Schleiermacher urges that we "freely surrender ourselves so that we may be intuited as a work of the eternal and all-fashioning world spirit."[17]

There is more of the pietist here than Schleiermacher would wish his readers to detect. Although he had given up speaking of immortality and the supernatural, there is nevertheless a Christian pneumatology at work. His system cannot, for this reason, correctly be described as only a form of subjectivism. Religion is rather a principle at work both within the universe and the self, which therefore makes possible an ontological perception of the infinite by the self.

So, to return to the hinge: It would be inaccurate to assume that the one who intuits were the only actor. Schleiermacher speaks of the "original and

---

13. Ibid., 191.
14. Ibid., 105.
15. Ibid., 192.
16. Ibid., 192. That Schleiermacher saw himself as a mediator of an original intuition within Christianity is discussed in my essay "Performative Hermeneutics: Interpreting the Speeches with Reflections upon Schleiermacher's Hermeneutical Theory," in Schleiermacher and Contemporary Theology, Proceedings of the International Schleiermacher Society, Chicago, 1994, ed., T. N. Tice, C. J. Kinlaw & J. C. Pugh.
17. Ibid., 190. The idea of surrender that is later to become central in his theology. Only once in the 1799 edition of *Speeches* does he use the word "Abhängigkeit" [dependence].

independent action" of the intuited "on the one who intuits."[18] He likens the action to emanations of light affecting the body; the emanations happen completely without the efforts of the subject, and can only be intuited by the senses. With richly-woven language he describes the ways in which the universe reveals itself to us every moment: "Every form that it brings forth, every being to which it gives a separate existence according to the fullness of life . . . is an action of the same upon us."[19] In order to inspire the imaginations of his most immediate audience, he uses panentheistic (world spirit, universe, world), classically pantheistic (the gods, the father of the gods), and theistic or deistic (the deity, God, spirit of God) linguistic imagery; imagery purposely chosen because it lay agreeably within their *Sprachgebiet.* So Rudolf Otto wrote in the preface to his edition of the *Speeches*: "One is . . . enthralled by [Schleiermacher's] original and daring attempt to lead an age weary with . . . religion back to its very mainspring."[20] Schleiermacher's purpose was to draw his peers to consider the religious possibilities of experiencing the ultimate unity of the universe, possibilities offered neither by morality nor metaphysics, nor by the aesthetics of the Romantic Revival. This last was particularly antithetical to the aims of his friend Friedrich Schlegel, who had hoped Schleiermacher would help him establish a 'religion of art'.

Schleiermacher must now define for these cultured despisers, his meaning of intuition and its relation to feeling. Feeling, for him, is the means by which anything can subsequently be known, thus it precedes knowing and doing; it is immediate and pre-reflective at its moment of origin. The senses mediate the connection between subject and object, producing a change in

---

18. Ibid., 104. Schleiermacher's later omission of the term intuition has been considered a movement away from this balance toward the purely subjective. "With the disappearance of intuition," one writer has noted, "the one window is shut, through which the subject comes in touch with the objective world." Hugh Mackintosh (*Types of Modern Religion* [London: Nisbet & Co., 1949], 47) considered the change a result of Schleiermacher's desire to take the experience of religion further from the rationalist claims of knowledge into the subjective realm. He adds: "It was a change which, from every point of view, proved singularly unfortunate." By the time of the writing of *Die Glaubenslehre*, Schleiermacher uses the terms feeling and self-consciousness and posits them over against an Other, which is God, the Whence of our receptive and active existence. For a discussion of the implications in the revisions see Crouter's excellent comparison, op cit., 59-63.

19. Ibid., 105.

20. "Wie man auch zuseiner Methode und seinen Ausführungen über die Religion selber sich stelle, immer wieder fesselt zunächst dieser kühne und originelle Versuch, ein religions-müdes und -fremdes Zeitalter zur Religion zurückzurufen." The opening of the Preface; *Über die Religion – Reden an die Gebildeten unter ihren Verächtern* (Göttingen: Vanderhoeck und Ruprecht, 1920), ed. R. Otto, 5, [henceforth *Reden*].

the inner consciousness. Intuition and feeling are always connected, but to speak of them can only be as a result of reflection upon them, and it is, ironically, the very nature of reflection that causes the split between them. The pre-reflective undifferentiated moment, when the two are one is "as fleeting and transparent as the first scent with which the dew caresses the waking flowers." He describes it as a manifestation, an event which "develops quickly and magically into an image of the universe." Rudolf Otto attempts to capture this in *The Idea of the Holy*:

> Their import [intuition and feeling] is the glimpse of the Eternal, in and beyond the temporal and penetrating it, the apprehension of a ground and meaning of things in and beyond the empirical and transcending it. They are surmises or inklings of a Reality fraught with mystery and momentousness.[21]

Following the undifferentiated moment, comes, what Schleiermacher calls the 'unavoidable separation' when "the simplest matter separates itself into two opposing elements, the one group combining into an image of an object, the other penetrating to the very center of our being."[22] Once this moment has taken place, the intuition cannot be re-experienced, only reflected upon. Thus, the religious act begins by opening one's consciousness in expectation of what Otto later described as the experience of the numinous.

Schleiermacher recognizes that different persons have different degrees of subjective desire or innate sensitivity: "The sounder the sense the more sharply will it apprehend every impression. The more ardent the thirst and the more persistent the drive to grasp the infinite, the more manifoldly will the mind itself be seized by it everywhere and uninterruptedly . . . ."[23] So those, to whom he refers as mediators, are described, with lush, erotic imagery, as "ambassadors of God," who "possess so much of the spiritual penetration drive, which strives for the infinite and impregnates all spirit and life."[24] How is this communicated from one to the other? This remains a central problem for Schleiermacher, if catechesis and praxis are no longer the means of leading the way into the courts of the Almighty. He does not think it possible that religion can be communicated, only intuited, for "words are only shadows . . . ."[25] Even his own words have returned to him void, to his disappointment! The Third Speech, therefore, is where his project is at its most vulnerable. The appeal to the subject's personal sensibility comes so

21. Rudolf Otto, op cit., 147.
22. *Speeches*, 112.
23. Ibid., 110.
24. Ibid., 82.
25. Ibid., 144.

close to the realm of aesthetics, that Schleiermacher is hard pressed to differentiate between them. Schlegel's proposal that aesthetics, in the form of a religion of art, was the deepest means for transforming human consciousness was irresistible to many. Schleiermacher is unwilling to go that far, but admits that it is his most perplexing dilemma. He finds he is better able to explain what will suppress the religious capacity than what will ignite it.

So, he asks, what are the phenomena, the finite objects, that are able to bring about this consummation of intuition and feelings? Awe and beauty in nature are not the means to give this intuition, he warns, surprising the reader with sudden dogmatism. It is not within natural religion that true intuitions of the infinite are to be had. Aesthetics and the natural religion of which they are a lure, bring the observer only to speculate on particularly wondrous discontinuities of nature. Thus Schleiermacher reveals himself as only a partial adherent to the Romantic movement. His opposition to natural religion is too profound to carry him from his deeper foundations in pietism. "What actually appeals to the religious sense in the external world is not its masses but its laws. Raise yourselves to the view of how these laws embrace everything, the largest and the smallest, the world systems and the small mote of dust . . . ."[26] It is nature's "chemical powers, the eternal laws according to which bodies themselves are formed and destroyed, these are the phenomena in which we intuit the universe most clearly . . . ."[27] The differentiation he makes is between the natural sciences and the humanities, and he takes his stand with the sciences. It is in these natural laws that he believes the unity of the eternal can be glimpsed. It is here that can be discovered the wonder and mystery of our continuity with all the particulars of nature and thereby, the infinite. But it must be said that he remains unconvincing. A stronger argument might be one that he is not ready to make: That it is only in turning away from the artifice of human culture, to that which humans did not create (that is, nature) that humans can intuit the universe. But the cultural optimism characteristic of the day remained too strong to avoid some degree of human triumphalism in viewing the human's place in the universe, and nature in itself remained too threatening a force to be linked with religion without the cultural mediation of the natural sciences.

Yet nature religion hovers on the margins of any religious doctrine of immanence, and the young virtuoso is keenly aware of the problem. At the heart of his rejection of metaphysics was his strong belief in the immanence of the ultimate, and the resultant ability to perceive it through the finite; thus he is forced to sail between the Romantic scylla of natural religion and the

---

26. Ibid., 117.
27. Ibid., 118.

rationalist charybdis of abstract speculation of the infinite. In so doing, and having separated religious consciousness from the doctrinal demands of any particular theological system, Schleiermacher is able to make his most original and far-reaching step. He can now boldly interpret the meaning of religions not propositionally but from their phenomenological point of origin.

As soon as the holy spark flares up in a soul, it expands into a free and living flame that draws its sustenance from its own atmosphere . . . and by its own choice this soul can settle even far away from the point at which it first beheld itself . . . it chooses every climate that pleases it best . . . .[28]

This vivid poetic prose is surely autobiographical. Schleiermacher had settled far from his point of religious awakening within the Moravian church, yet his choice of climate in proximity to the Romantic movement was, for his soul, the place of most fecundity. With this understanding of the nature of the religious experience, Schleiermacher was able to release religion from the confines of any religion's doctrine, and so he can speak of the relative worth of all historical religions insofar as they have emerged from, and expedite, original intuitions. Thus, each individual's perception or interpretation of the religious experience is subjective and relative, "bound to the place on which by chance one may be standing."[29] It is therefore a 'wretched limitedness' to universalize one's perception and claim it as the one, true perception. It is for this reason that the term 'world spirit' is absolutely appropriate, for it reflects most profoundly Schleiermacher's phenomenology.

The ubiquitous and immanent work of the world spirit which may be intuited by any or all, which Schleiermacher expresses, is a vast and impressive teaching of what would be described theologically as common grace, a category relatively abjected by the Reformers and their followers. Thus, it may be, that the energy which gave rise to Schleiermacher's insights emerged as much from the negative polarity of that which was lacking in the Reformation as from the two closer poles of rationalism and the Romantic movement.

Method and Purpose

In the *Speeches*, Schleiermacher uses the language of the Romantic movement to which he was attached. Nevertheless it is language that he was to jettison (though not disown) after this work. He argues on behalf of religion and its experience, regardless of outward form. At first, he gives his

28. Ibid., 145.
29. Ibid., 150.

avant garde readers the opportunity to believe that he has left behind the content and form of the Christianity they despise, drawing them on to consider the unique possibility afforded by religious experience, regardless of institutional implications. As one writer has put it, Schleiermacher's audience possesses "that enlightened and scornful temper which scarcely regards Christianity as worth the trouble of disproof."[30] It is a particularly effective style of apologetics, a purposeful accommodation to the tastes of the Romantics, whereby he adopts a rhapsodic rhetorical language calculated to arouse the sensitivity of his audience. It is precisely for this reason that he so dramatically alters the work in later editions (1806 and 1821). Terrence Tice's edition of the *Speeches* contains the letter that Schleiermacher sent to Gustaf von Brinkmann in 1806, accompanying his second edition. Schleiermacher writes: "Their themes and exposition [of the first edition of the *Speeches*] were forced upon me by the time and circumstances. Consequently they were also very tied to the specific audience intended."[31] Later, in 1821, writing to the same publisher, Schleiermacher makes the same point in a more characteristic and colourful manner, "the people to whom these addresses were specifically directed are no longer on the scene. . . . Present circumstances would rather seem to demand that one address himself to the hypocrites, to those in bondage to the dead letter, to the hard hearted dupes and fanatics!"[32] Throughout his life, Schleiermacher the rhetoritician reworked his language carefully, thoughtfully, taking old signs and making them new, that they might live again in a new generation. So he was constantly creating fresh language to connect with his audience. So Barth admits of his nemesis that "he was not one among many others, with his theology and philosophy of religion. . . . One thing is certain, that this [19th.] century could and did hear from Schleiermacher a liberating word, in some ways an answering word."[33]

Barth considers that Schleiermacher, as a philosopher of religion, and an apologist, suspends his attitude towards Christianity and his judgement of the truth or absoluteness of the Christian revelation. "Together with the other educated people he looks upon Christianity as being on the same level as the other 'pious communities', as being subject to the points of view from which

30. H. R. Mackintosh, *Types of Modern Theology: Schleiermacher to Barth* (London: Nisbet & Co., 1949), 43.
31. Schleiermacher, *On Religion: Addresses to its Cultured Critics*, trans. Terrence N. Tice (Richmond: John Knox Press 1969, henceforth Tice), 32.
32. Ibid., 36.
33. Barth, *From Rousseau To Ritschl* (*Die protestantische Theologie im 19. Jahrhundert*, ed. Macintyre & McIntyre, trans. B. Cozens, London: SCM Press, 1959), 308-9.

'pious communities' are to be regarded here."[34] Certainly Schleiermacher considered himself to be engaged in the philosophy of religion in his introduction to *Die Glaubenslehre*, and we may deduce from the similarity of subject matter that this is also what he considered himself to be doing in the *Speeches*.[35] He is describing the religious experience per se and not initially the Christian formulation of it. Nevertheless, it is perplexing, at least to his modern readers, that he appears to abandon this strategy in his Fifth Speech when he begins to defend the particular excellence of Christianity. Richard Crouter expresses the difficulty thus: "Schleiermacher's appeal to his own tradition of Christianity, especially in the Fifth Speech assumes a stance in the comparative study of religion, which is made as much on 'confessional' as on purely scholarly or philosophical grounds." So the concern arises, has Schleiermacher betrayed the integrity of his own methodology? Crouter attempts to justify the apparent shift by pointing out that to this day, the problem of relating comparative religious insights remains vexing. He points to Geerhardus van der Leeuw's resolve to engage upon his 'survey of religious phenomena from the Christian viewpoint', for van der Leeuw must own his particularity prior to purveying other particularities. Van der Leeuw was influenced directly by Schleiermacher.[36] But Crouter is only partially convinced by his own argument and remains puzzled. He writes: "But whether he [Schleiermacher] has himself resolved the dilemma may be doubted by an observer." Crouter, as that observer, is made uneasy by the privileged position granted Christianity in the Fifth Speech, for it must distort the vision "of the very thing one is searching for, namely the essential nature of religion as it is humanly embodied."[37] But this is to assume a purpose that is Crouter's and van der Leeuw's but not Schleiermacher's. For the work is not so much a philosophical treatise on the nature of religion, but a symphony in five movements, progressing inevitably towards its apotheosis (in its most literal sense). It is not so much a treatise as a tract: "I wish to lead you, as it were, to the God who has become flesh; I want to show you religion as it has divested itself of its infinity . . . ; in the religions you are to discover religion."[38] This is the watershed. It is either a particularistic distortion or the clue to his purpose. It is my conviction that the latter is true: Schleiermacher has adopted the language and concepts of the Romantic movement to seduce his listeners; firstly he seeks to lead them to consider religious

---

34. Ibid., 325.
35. See Michael D. Ryan, op cit.
36. Geerhardus van der Leeuw, *Religion in Essence and Manifestation: A Study in Phenomenology*, Vol. II (Harper and Row: New York, 1963), 645.
37. *Speeches.*, Introduction, 49-51.
38. Ibid., 190.

experience in a new and attractive light, one meaningful to their frame of reference (which does indeed afford hope for a comparative philosophy of religion, and van der Leeuw is right to attribute this discovery to Schleiermacher[39]), but secondly, he seeks to lead his sophisticated readers away from their inclination towards natural religion and pantheism back towards a newly-charged Romantic form of Christianity. He has no interest in an impartial philosophy of religion that is merely descriptive. His is a Christian philosophy of religion, that seeks to lure his readers to the religious experience and necessarily to Christianity. This second purpose he saves until the Fifth Speech, yet it is his ultimate purpose, and the climax of the work, quite different from consequent comparative studies of religion, and quite at odds with many of his interpreters' assumptions. His purpose is "to snatch at least a few souls from deadening indifference, and, by God's will, to open their eyes to true and pure piety."[40] This true and pure piety emerges ever stronger through the Fifth Speech as only fully realized in Christianity. He reveals an attitude of privilege for Christianity, that is far from amenable to a dispassionate 'neutral' philosophy of religion, the forms of which grew up only after him.

Schleiermacher wrote that "religion rises out of a definite faculty of the human spirit and must be a real element in sound and whole mankind," and Hugh Mackintosh comments, "Let him only make this point and he regards the argument as complete."[41] No. This is rather his starting point, hardly its completion, otherwise one can make no sense whatever of a Christocentric Fifth Speech, nor his attitudes to other religions in both the *Speeches* and *Die Glaubenslehre*.

Yet, it must be said that he is still writing philosophy, not theology, as only a glance at any of his later theological works will demonstrate. But it is the philosophy of religion as written by a devoted and pious Christian thinker. He is, after all, according to his own description, a Moravian of a higher order. This is not to be taken lightly. His linguistic methodology is to use the concepts of his culture, to draw his audience along, to step behind their prejudices, to disarm them. He begins at the outermost circles of religious inquiry, and reveals the way in, the moment when intuition and feeling experience the infinite. This entrance to experience is of paramount importance to comparative methodology, but as soon as he is within, he seeks to attach the experience to the fullest expression of it, which is, for him, the in-

---

39. G. van der Leeuw, op cit., 591.
40. Friedrich Schleiermacher, *On the Glaubenslehre: Two Letters to Dr. Lücke*, trans. James Duke & Francis Fiorenza (Atlanta: Scholars, 1981), 51.
41. Mackintosh, op cit., 45.

carnation of the deity in the person of Jesus. So it is that he seduces his cultured audience to desire and yearn for his religion, which, in their sophistication, they have despised and ignored, led astray by the rational morality of Fichte and Kant and 'dead orthodoxy'. So it is that the work retains such abiding, energetic passion.

Religion and Religions

But what, given his purposes, is the precise relationship between religion in general and Christianity in particular for Schleiermacher? He writes that, "I have presupposed the multiplicity of religions, and I likewise find them rooted in the essence of religion."[42] We may, with modern ears, attuned as they are to the voices of pluralism, hear him welcoming the world's religions under his canopy, Christianity being but one among equals, but we would be mistaken, not because he does not see some religions as genuine expressions of religion. He clearly does. But rather because he establishes a strict and limiting hierarchy that emerges from his own well-developed Christian triumphalism. His method of limiting and organizing the religions is a central part of his methodology.

Firstly, his polemic against natural religion is scathing. What does it offer its communicants, he asks. It offers "the freedom to remain unformed, the freedom from every compulsion to be, to see and to feel something even remotely specific. . . . It is as if religion had no pulse of its own."[43] The empty speculation of nature religion is rejected. It remains within the general boundaries of philosophy. It does not become religion. By contrast a "truly positive religion" as opposed to pantheism and naturalism, offers "determinate forms," and "only the person who settles down in such a form with his own religion really establishes a firm abode and, might I say, an active citizenship in the religious world."[44] What is essential for Schleiermacher is that the originating intuition be allowed to stand as the formative principle upon which all else within a religious system hangs. Thus he even writes, "a person who does not fit into one of those [forms] that are readily available, I might say . . . [will] make a new one. If he remains alone in it and without disciples, it does no harm."[45] Natural religion, by contrast, he considers the negation of religion, for it denies the intuitions of positive religion,

---

42. *Speeches*, 191.
43. Ibid., 205. See also Hinze, op cit., 23-25.
44. Ibid., 200. There is no citizenship-in-general, only membership of a particular nation, in the same way as there is no religion-in-general.
45. Ibid., 200. See my essay cited above, n.16.

and here Fichte and Kant (and perhaps Lessing) are very much in the foreground.[46] Rationalists had pitted natural against positive religions during the eighteenth century, employing the latter term pejoratively.

When Schleiermacher uses the term positive religion, does he refer to the world's great religions? In his 1821 supplementary notes that accompanied his third edition of the *Speeches*, he disassociates himself from the idea that "the less developed religions, especially the polytheistic religions, have no similarity at all with the Christian religion. . . . By their very nature all forms of religion have similarity – even the least developed forms."[47] So he can enthusiastically speak of the spirit of piety that infused Spinoza "even though it was not Christian piety."[48] He sees the single principle of religion at work in various religions, and seeks to describe how this is possible at a time when the exclusiveness of the truth claims of Christianity were all but assumed within the church.

On the other hand, he considers the Egyptian and Indian systems to be genuinely pantheist, having no personality underneath the symbols of their pantheons. He considers that their gods do not possess consciousness, which causes him to conclude that they represent subordinate forms of religion. In a similar vein, he considers geographically 'distant peoples' to have only "crude and undeveloped religions." He says no more about them, but we are safe in assuming that the reference is to religions of Asia, including Hinduism. He would certainly have rejected their ahistorical elements as contrary to positive religion, which always has, for Schleiermacher, a historical foundation and development.[49] He nevertheless appreciates, as one might expect of an educated Prussian of his day, the "beautiful mythology of the Greeks and Romans," but contrasts them against the approach to "the most holy, where the universe is intuited in its highest unity," by which he means "the different forms of systematic religions."[50] He is gradually introducing us to his taxonomy of religions. It is clear that he perceives that there is a plurality of 'systematic religions', and they form the highest place, yet he refers to Judaism, as one that was once alive, but that has now withered on the vine, failing to fulfil its destiny by becoming universal. Crouter attempts to excuse Schleiermacher's poor gift of prophesy by saying that many Jews at

---

46. For a brief comparison of Kant's use of the term 'intuition' and Schleiermacher's see *Speeches*, 104 n13.
47. Tice, op cit., 157.
48. Ibid., 160.
49. W. A. Johnson, *On Religion: A Study of Theological Method in Schleiermacher and Nygren* (Leiden: E. J. Brill, 1964), 36.
50. Ibid., 211.

that time believed the same thing. But this is to miss the point that Schleiermacher holds a steeply hierarchical view of religions.[51]

In *Die Glaubenslehre* Schleiermacher distinguishes monotheism as the highest plane of religious expression, and names Judaism, Islam and Christianity as those three religions at that level. Yet immediately he attributes to Judaism "a lingering affinity with Fetishism," which he regards as the animal level of consciousness. Equally unfortunate is his commentary upon Islam, which he says, "betrays . . . religious emotions which elsewhere keeps men on the level of Polytheism," which he places on the middle level of human consciousness. Thus Christianity "because it remains free from both these weaknesses, stands higher than either of those two other forms, and takes its place as the highest form of Monotheism which has appeared in history."[52] Barth simply says: "I need hardly refer to the historical dilettantism of the expositions of this paragraph. [It has] no support in modern scholarship."[53]

At least some of Schleiermacher's references to the variety of determinate religions speak of various movements within Christianity. So, for example, in the supplementary notes, he says: "France and England were almost the only countries in which we were much interested then and which alone exercised any great influence on Germany."[54] This is important to bear in mind, for it is primarily the religions as found in these three countries that we might expect Schleiermacher to discuss most. But, in 1821, he suggests he would also want to expand and include the Greek church in his considerations. (i.e., by their inclusion, he is now considering the three major

51. In his 1821 supplementary notes to the *Speeches*, he somewhat dissembles on the issue of Spinoza urging that he had not meant to suggest that the philosopher had received the Holy Spirit, in the distinctively Christian sense of the word. We would have expected the Holy Spirit to be the power at work in all those forms of religion which display true piety. It is difficult to say, with reference to the 1821 notes, whether Schleiermacher is sidestepping criticism or frankly stating his views. Certainly they were meant to clear up misunderstandings and to "deal with the contradictions some thought they discovered between what is written here and what one expects from a teacher of Christianity," but they too often wear the appearance of clever foot-work. He complains that the rhetorical form of the *Speeches*, "extravagantly indicated in the subtitle" had been almost universally ignored. But his appeals to youthful overstatement are unconvincing. We cannot help but apply a hermeneutics of suspicion with regards to his later method, for it appears in places to be revisionist. It would certainly be going too far to conclude that the *Speeches* had become an albatross, one that he could neither disown nor revise satisfactorily, for the simultaneously published dogmatics shows no sign of retreating from constructing theology of the most controversial kind. Yet neither should we assume that his 1821 notes are not an attempt to smooth over many trouble spots for the Berlin professor.

52. Friedrich Schleiermacher, *The Christian Faith* (Edinburgh: T & T Clark, 1989, referred to in the text as *Die Glaubenslehre*), 37.

53. Barth, *The Theology of Schleiermacher*, op cit., 226.

54. Tice, op cit., 63.

forms of the Christian Church). Yet what he says of the Greek Orthodox Church is far from encouraging: "all that is of profound importance seems to be stultified there through the mechanism of antiquated practices and liturgical formulas . . . it still seems to stand far behind the Roman Catholic Church."[55] So Schleiermacher not only maintains the superiority of Christianity but still differentiates within it, in fairly predictable ways. Speaking of the multiplicity of 'religions' and the unity of the church, Schleiermacher writes in the 1821 notes: "in every mode of faith . . . they [the narrow minded] refuse to take part in the religious exercises of other modes of faith thus remaining completely ignorant of the nature and spirit of these modes of faith."[56] He offers the merging of the Lutherans and Calvinists in Prussia into the Evangelical church as an example to be followed – two modes of faith joining into one. He declares that he would also like to see Catholics in Germany come under the Evangelical Church!

Schleiermacher's view of Christ is triumphalist. Christianity is gradually filling the world. Schleiermacher maintains the possibility that Christianity might finally extend over the whole human race, although it would have to undergo important changes in many places to do so. He speaks of Christianity as the greatest of all religions. His scheme is a complete taxonomy with Christ as its head. Below Christ stands the Protestant Evangelical Church, and the historic Calvinist, Lutheran and (presumably) Anglican communions. Lower again comes the Roman Catholic Church, and below that Eastern Orthodoxy. It is not clear where the Protestant 'sectarians' would stand in relation to these others, except that they belong lower than the other Protestant churches. Only then would he place Islam and lower still Judaism, followed by the 'subordinate' forms of polytheist pantheism (Hinduism et al). His desire is to see these forms evolve into the highest form. The vast majority of the comparisons he draws are between Christianity (in its Protestant form) and other current Western religious forms, namely, pantheism, naturalism, and Judaism. His concerns are thoroughly European. We may not claim, much as we might like, a voice of appreciation for Buddhism or Hinduism or other 'distant' and different religions. They are beyond his purview, even though they fall fully within the purview of those like van der Leeuw and Crouter, who seek to understand the essential nature of religion as it is universally embodied. Our danger is to read *Speeches* through their lenses. Bradford Hinze, in his monograph *Narrating History, Developing Doctrine*, has warned that too many interpreters "have sought to deduce all issues (regarding Schleiermacher's concept of the

---

55. Ibid., 64.
56. Tice, 323.

kingdom of God) from the introduction to the *Glaubenslehre* and the second speech."[57] I would like to suggest that the same is true of his use of the term 'religion'. W. A. Johnson seems to move in this direction when he writes, in his subsection 'Religion and the Religions in the *Reden*': "The essence of Religion . . . in the [*Speeches*] . . . was not identified with any particular concrete historical Religion. . . . Schleiermacher had, instead, attempted to present the religious a priori, which was to be the presupposition for all of the particular historical Religions."[58] This is, of course, true of the Second Speech, but not of the Fifth.

What we usually mean today by the historical religions of the world and what Schleiermacher means by positive religion appear to be quite different, standing as they are on opposite sides of an explosion of knowledge about the religions of the world quite undreamt of by the European Christianity of the close of the eighteenth century, divided as it was between deistic reason, which Schleiermacher opposed, and evangelical mission, which he demanded. His use of the term for religion when focussed only upon Christianity is fairly common, for example:

> When you cast a glance at the present condition of things, where churches and religions encounter one another nearly everywhere in their plurality . . . and where there are as many doctrinal edifices and confessions of faith as churches and religious communities, you might easily be misled to believe that in my judgement about the plurality of churches I have simultaneously expressed my judgement concerning the plurality of religions. . . . I have at all times presupposed the plurality of religions and their most distinct diversity as something necessary and unavoidable. For why should the inner, true church be one? . . . Thus I have presupposed the multiplicity of religions, and I likewise find them rooted in the essence of religion.[59]

Otto is correct in his footnote at this point, by placing 'Religionen' in quotation marks to stress that these are different forms of Christianity of which Schleiermacher speaks: "Zwar nur eine Kirche, aber viele verschiedene Gestaltungen der Religion, viele 'Religionen', muß es geben."[60] Thus we find that Calvinism, Lutheranism, the Moravian Anabaptist communities are

---

57. Bradford E. Hinze, *Narrating History, Developing Doctrine: Friedrich Schleiermacher and Johann Sebastian Drey* (Atlanta: Scholars Press, 1993), 18.
58. W.A. Johnson, *On Religion*, op cit.
59. *Speeches*, op cit., 190-91.
60. *Reden*, 163 note 1a.

the forms of religion most in Schleiermacher's mind, "these determinate forms in which infinite religion manifests itself in the finite."[61]

Schleiermacher nevertheless opened a door onto the comparative study of religion by providing an alternative to the true-false dualism of propositional orthodoxy. Despite his privileging of Christianity, he demonstrates the principle of religion at work in all, each religion being an expression of the world spirit. Within his privileging of Christianity, he refuses to privilege any one doctrinal expression of it exclusively. This was also a most significant and daring move, one that was truly ecumenical. Each denomination that stands faithful to its originating principle is an authentic expression of religion. While Luther had drawn a circle, and excluded the other Protestant views as in error, Schleiermacher argues for the coexistence of many circles.

So we must ask once again, why is he so unclear as to be so easily misunderstood? For his rhetorical style is often ambiguous. We conclude that to speak too plainly would be to lose the power of seduction, and fail to draw his cultured friends towards the final goal. It is a seduction which still manifests itself for those of us drawn into his luxuriant world with the task of interpretation. We discover that the linguistic web (Derrida's labyrinth?) that Schleiermacher weaves is surprisingly postmodern, for it subverts those readers who would not otherwise be lured. It is for that reason that the later editions of *Speeches* disappoint us by comparison; for the visionary no longer finds his audiences able to comprehend the wider hermeneutical horizons of his original vision, and his former audience excites us more. He has to trim his sails and speak to more orthodox readers, for the Berlin professor of theology has no desire to lose his chair, nor the preacher his pulpit. Schleiermacher, with the moderating wisdom of maturity, seems, at least to a limited degree in his later editions of *Speeches*, to feel compelled to beat his linguistic sword into a shield, but continues to wound from behind.

---

61. "diese bestimmten Gestalten sind, unter denen die unendliche Religion sich im Endlichen darstellt" (Ibid., 169).

THE POSITION OF OPPOSITION
IN HEGEL AND SCHLEIERMACHER

John Hoffmeyer

Both Hegel and Schleiermacher frequently use oppositional pairs in articulating their thought. With both Hegel and Schleiermacher, however, opposition is by no means "the" basic figure that structures their entire thought. Neither Hegel nor Schleiermacher fits the theoretical model whereby one basic figure is omnipresent throughout the entire theoretical structure. Such omnipresence invariably turns out to mean that the one basic figure is vaguely everywhere and determinately nowhere.

By contrast, Hegel and Schleiermacher give opposition a determinate theoretical position within their thought. In this paper, I shall explore two main senses in which this is true. First, Hegel and Schleiermacher reflect upon the place of opposition in relation to other theoretical figures they employ. Second, they recognize that the oppositions that they do use are not absolute, but instead have their function within a particular interpretive perspective. In seeking to demonstrate these two points, I shall proceed in three steps, considering first Schleiermacher, then Hegel, then discussing commonalities between the two.

1. Schleiermacher's Theory of the Relativity of Opposition

Schleiermacher explicitly rejects the idea of an absolute opposition. All oppositions are relative. "The first negative canon of procedure is thus the following: no opposition is absolute, but rather is only relative."[1] Again and again when Schleiermacher is referring to a particular opposition, he points out that it is only relative. To take but two examples from the *Ethics*: "the opposition between universal and individual is only a relative one and in reality the two are never fully separated"; "the act of entering into community and the act of appropriation is also only a relative one."[2]

---

1. "Der erste negative Kanon des Verfahrens ist also der daß kein Gegensaz absolut ist sondern nur relativ" (F.D.E. Schleiermacher, *Dialektik [1811]*, ed. Andreas Arndt, Philosophische Bibliothek 386 [Hamburg: Felix Meiner, 1986], 36.

2. ". . . der Gegensaz zwischen universell und individuell nur ein relativer und in der Realität nie beides völlig getrennt ist"; ". . . der Gegensaz zwischen in-Gemeinschaft-Treten und Aneignen auch nur ein relativer ist" (Schleiermacher, *Ethik [1812/13], mit späteren*

Oppositions are relative rather than absolute in Schleiermacher's thought in at least three senses. First, poles of an opposition, at the same time that they are opposed, also stand in a relation of identity. Second, a multiplicity of oppositions, each with its relative role, is required to determine any particular being. Third, all oppositions are hermeneutically constituted. They are relative to the interpretive perspective from which they are constituted.

First, when Schleiermacher calls an opposition "relative" he means that the same item of reality can be identified with both poles of the opposition. For example, "the fact that what has been found as 'doing' can in the course of the process [of deduction] be treated as 'being' is justified because the opposition is only a relative one."[3] Since oppositions are never strict but always relative, there is no hard and fast boundary between opposition and difference. "When we term the relation of the 'thingly' and the spiritual 'opposition,' and that of the universal and the particular 'difference,' this happens because the former is more rigid and the latter more fluid. But the distinction itself is fluid. Opposition is merely rigidified difference; difference merely a fluid opposition."[4]

Just how fluid this distinction is becomes clear when one turns to the 1814/15 *Dialectic*. In the *Ethics* of 1812/13, the relation of universal and particular serves as a model of difference as distinguished from opposition. In the *Dialectic* two years later, Schleiermacher speaks of "the relative opposition of the universal and the particular."[5]

Schleiermacher's insistence that all oppositions are relative stems from his conviction that any two poles that stand in a relation of opposition also stand in a relation of relative unity. He qualifies as an "empty abstraction" the supposedly strict opposition that excludes any identity of the two poles. "No opposition may be constructed in such a way that it has a [merely] posi-

---

Fassungen der Einleitung, Güterlehre und Pflichtenlehre, ed. Hans-Joachim Birkner, Philosophische Bibliothek 335 [Hamburg: Felix Meiner, 1981], 174, 173).

3. "Daß man das als Thun gefundene im Verfolg des Prozesses wieder als Sein betrachtet, dazu ist man berechtigt weil der Gegensaz nur ein relativer ist" (*Dialektik [1811]*, 54).

4. "Wenn wir das Verhältniß des Dinglichen und Geistigen Gegensaz nennen, und das des Allgemeinen und Besonderen Verschiedenheit, so geschieht dies, weil jenes gleichsam starrer ist, dieses fließender. Aber der Unterschied fließt selbst; der Gegensaz ist nur eine erstarrte Verschiedenheit, die Verschiedenheit nur ein flüssiger Gegensaz" (Schleiermacher, "Einleitung: Letzte Bearbeitung," in *Ethik [1812/13]*, 201).

5. "der relative Gegensaz des Allgemeinen und Besonderen" (Schleiermacher, *Dialektik [1814/15], Einleitung zur Dialektik [1833]*, ed. Andreas Arndt, Philosophische Bibliothek 387 [Hamburg: Felix Meiner, 1988], 46).

tive and a [merely] negative side. One is then outside the realm of life and no relative unification is possible. This results in empty abstraction."[6]

Schleiermacher's emphasis on the relative character of any particular opposition protects him from the danger of oppositions degenerating into dualisms. Michael Nealeigh has rightly written that for Schleiermacher, "polar aspects of a given reality can best be described in terms of the conjunction of the two. Together they constitute that reality. In popular language this relationship is one of 'both/and' in contrast to 'either/or'."[7]

For instance, in that process which Schleiermacher calls both "deduction" and "construction," the oppositional pairs of 'being' and 'doing' and of ideal and real are present on every level of the process. The same element in the deductive process can be either 'being' or 'doing,' ideal or real, depending on the relation in which it is being viewed. If a given element is being viewed in relation to a level below it, "the higher appears as 'being,' the lower as 'doing'."[8] But the same element that is 'being' in relation to the 'doing' of a lower level, is itself 'doing' in relation to the 'being' of a higher level. Likewise, what is 'doing' when viewed in relation to a higher level is 'being' when viewed in relation to a lower level. The same thing is true for the relation of ideal to real. A given element is ideal when viewed in relation to a lower level, but real when viewed in relation to a higher level.

The second sense in which oppositions are relative rather than absolute lies in Schleiermacher's understanding that every being is determined by a *multiplicity* of oppositions. No one opposition exercises absolute determination of any being. "No being is to be posited that would be determined by only one opposition. Rather, the identities of all other chief oppositions must also be in it."[9] As proof of this Schleiermacher points in the *Dialectics* of 1811 to the place of 'being' and 'doing,' ideal and real as "equally original" oppositions that determine all being.[10]

Schleiermacher seems to shift position in the *Dialectics* of 1814/15 when he calls the opposition of the ideal and the real the "highest opposition."[11]

6. "Kein Gegensaz darf so construirt sein daß er eine positive und eine negative Seite hat. Man ist dann aus dem Gebiete des Lebens heraus und keine relative Vereinigung ist möglich. Dies wird leere Abstraction" (*Dialektik [1811]*, 54).
7. Michael Nealeigh, "The Epistemology of Friedrich Schleiermacher from a Dipolar Perspective," in Ruth Drucilla Richardson, ed., *Schleiermacher in Context: Papers from the 1988 International Symposium on Schleiermacher at Herrnhut, the German Democratic Republic* (Lewiston/Queenston/Lampeter: Edwin Mellen, 1991), 177.
8. "Das Höhere erscheint als Sein, das niedere als Thun" (*Dialektik [1811]*, 53).
9. "Es ist kein Sein zu sezen welches nur durch Einen Gegensaz bestimmt wäre, vielmehr müssen die Identitäten aller anderen Hauptgegensäze mit darin sein" (ibid., 54).
10. "gleich ursprünglich" (ibid.).
11. "höchsten Gegensazes" (*Dialektik [1814/15]*, 27).

Schleiermacher asserts that "ideal and real run parallel to each other as modes of being."[12] They are not synthesized in any higher category accessible to human knowing. The opposition of ideal and real "can be encompassed . . . only by the *one* being."[13] But "the one being" is "that which is transcendental,"[14] inaccessible to human knowing. We can not know a higher category that synthesizes the opposition between the ideal and the real. This opposition, as the highest opposition, can not be deduced, but can only be assumed. Schleiermacher speaks of "the assumption of this highest opposition" and insists that "the opposition itself always remains . . . behind the veil."[15]

However, the fact that this "highest opposition" is not synthesized in a higher category does not mean that it has escaped from the relativity common to all oppositions. In the *Dialectics* of 1814/15, Schleiermacher deploys the opposition of ideal and real as part of a double opposition with reason and nature. As we shall see, double oppositions are in Schleiermacher's view particularly suited to demonstrating the relativity of all oppositions.

But before the present analysis moves to Schleiermacher's concept of double opposition, it must first consider his distinction between negative and positive oppositions. For example, the relation between animal and non-animal is one of negative opposition. Schleiermacher says that negative opposition has no place in the deductive process, because it does not lead to any further developments in the deductive chain. "One must not use any negative opposition for deduction, but only a positive opposition. Negative opposition completely inhibits the further elaboration of the other side."[16]

An example of positive opposition, by contrast, is the relation between reason and nature, or between the ideal and the real.[17] But simple positive

---

12. "Ideales and Reales laufen parallel neben einander fort als modi des Seins" (ibid.).
13. "kann . . . nur . . . von dem Einen Sein befaßt werden" (ibid., 28).
14. "das transcendentale" (ibid.).
15. "die Annahme dieses höchsten Gegensazes"; "der Gegensaz selbst bleibt . . . immer hinter dem Vorhang" (ibid., 27).
16. "Man darf zur Ableitung keinen negativen Gegensaz gebrauchen, sondern nur einen positiven. Der negative hemmt gänzlich die weitere Bearbeitung der anderen Seite" (*Dialektik 1814/15*, 103).
17. In Falk Wagner's reading, Schleiermacher makes the opposition of the ideal and the real a simple negative opposition. "The ideal is thus what it is only by virtue of its negative relation to the real, and this latter is what it is only by virtue of its negative relation to the ideal" ("Das Ideale ist daher das, was es ist, nur vermöge seiner negativen Beziehung auf das Reale, und dieses ist das, was es ist, nur vermöge seiner negativen Beziehung auf das Ideale") (Falk Wagner, *Schleiermachers Dialektik: Eine kritische Interpretation* [Gütersloh: Gerd Mohn, 1974], 87). If Wagner were right, then Schleiermacher would be failing to heed his own insight into the barrenness of negative opposition. But there is a positive element of identity between the ideal and the real (see p. 3). It is also the case that the

opposition is still an inadequate tool for the deductive process: "Nor must one proceed with a positive simple opposition, but only with a composite opposition."[18] The only form of composite opposition that Schleiermacher names to my knowledge is "double opposition." In the *Dialectics*, Schleiermacher talks about "the double opposition of the ideal and real in reason and nature."[19] But, in the *Ethics*, he defines reason and nature in the following way. "The mutual interpenetration of all 'thingly' and spiritual being as 'thingly' – that is, as known – is *nature*. And the mutual interpenetration of all that is 'thingly' and all that is spiritual as spiritual – that is, as knowing – is *reason*."[20] In the passage from the *Ethics* the language of "'thingly' and spiritual" replaces the language of "ideal and real." But the *Ethics* passage introduces a third oppositional pair: known and knowing. Although Schleiermacher himself does not use the term, there seems to be no reason not to call the relation described in the *Ethics* a "triple opposition."

Double opposition – which, as we have just seen, may turn out to have a still more complex form – is the required form of opposition for fruitful deductive work because double opposition, unlike negative opposition and simple positive opposition, articulates the relativity common to all oppositions that have a place in human knowing. "Only double opposition is simultaneously posited with its relativity, as must be the case."[21] Schleiermacher characterizes double opposition as "fluid."[22] For an understanding of what Schleiermacher means by "fluid," let us return to the definition of reason and nature from the *Ethics* considered above: "The mutual interpenetration of all thingly and spiritual being as thingly – that is, as known – is *nature*. And the mutual interpenetration of all that is thingly and all that is spiritual as spiritual – that is, as knowing – is *reason*." The opposition between nature and reason is fluid because the question of whether to place "the mutual interpenetration of all thingly and spiritual being" under the pole of reason or under the pole of nature is not an either-or question. The opposition between

opposition between reason and nature plays an essential role in determining the identity of the ideal and the real (see the discussion of double opposition, specifically the double opposition between ideal and real and between reason and nature, on p. 5).
18. "Man darf auch nicht mit einem positiven einfachen verfahren, sondern nur mit einem zusammengesetzten" (*Dialektik 1814/15*, 104).
19. "der doppelte Gegensaz des idealen und realen in Vernunft und Natur" (*Dialektik 1814/15*, 115).
20. "Das Ineinander alles dinglichen und geistigen Seins als Dingliches d. h. Bewußtes ist die *Natur*. Und das Ineinander alles Dinglichen und Geistigen als Geistiges d. h. Wissendes ist die *Vernunft*" ("Einleitung: Letzte Bearbeitung," *Ethik 1812/13*, 200).
21. "Nur der doppelte Gegensaz ist mit seiner Relativität zugleich gesezt, wie es sein muß" (ibid.).
22. "fließenden" (ibid., 115).

reason and nature depends on the possibility of taking the interpenetration of thingly and spiritual being in not just one way. The opposed identities of reason and nature are constituted by hermeneutical acts. "Taken as" known, the interpenetration of thingly and spiritual being is nature. Taken as knowing, that interpenetration is reason. The opposition of reason and nature does not exist prior to or apart from this interpretive "taking as." The interpretive act *posits* the opposition between reason and nature. Other oppositions are posited by the correlative interpretive acts. An opposition is relative to its interpretive position, the interpretive perspective from which it is posited. This is the third sense in which all oppositions are relative in Schleiermacher's view.

Double opposition shows this relativity with particular clarity. In the example above, the opposition of reason and nature is relative in the sense that the differentiation between reason and nature depends on interpretive acts. But *what* is taken as either reason or nature is the mutual interpenetration of the poles of another opposition: the opposition between thingly and spiritual being or, in the language preferred by Schleiermacher in the 1814/15 *Dialectics*, the opposition between the real and the ideal. If the identity of this mutual interpenetration is hermeneutically constituted, then so is the opposition whose poles mutually interpenetrate. The opposition of thingly and spiritual, or of ideal and real, is not given prior to interpretation, providing a nonrelative basis for the relative opposition of reason and nature. For the Schleiermacher who eschews abstract oppositions, oppositions that purportedly do not have an element of unity, an opposition does not exist prior to or apart from the mutual interpenetration of its poles. If the mutual interpenetration of the poles is relative, the opposition is relative. As shown above,[23] Schleiermacher's discussion of the opposition of ideal and real in the context of the deductive process bears this out. There Schleiermacher argues that what is real and what is ideal is relative to the relation within which it is being viewed.

2. The Position of Opposition in Hegel's *Science of Logic*

Opposition is part of the section entitled "Difference," which is the second section of the chapter entitled "The Essentialities or the Determinations of Reflection." This chapter is in turn the second chapter of the major sec-

---

23. See p. 167.

tion "Essence as Reflection in It-self."[24] One of the basic rhythms in the unfolding of the *Logic* is that externality generally comes to the fore in the second moment of any particular logical grouping. This point is best illustrated by Hegel's analysis of reflection. Indeed, the logic of reflection does more than just illustrate this point, for the movement of reflection is that "movement of essence where the ontological structure of all that is expresses itself in its negative universality."[25]

Hegel's analysis of reflection,[26] entitled simply "Reflection," occurs in the third section of the chapter on "Show" [*Schein*]. The second subsection of "Reflection" bears the title "External Reflection." In the first subsection of "Reflection," entitled "Positing Reflection," Hegel presents reflection as "self-movement – movement that comes out of itself only insofar as *positing* reflection is *presupposing*, but as *presupposing* reflection is purely *positing*."[27] Hegel's play on the German verbs *setzen* and *voraussetzen* would come across more clearly in English if one translated: "movement that comes out of itself only insofar as *positing* reflection is *pre-positing*, but as *pre-positing* reflection is purely *positing*."

What makes external reflection external is that it masks the fact that every *Voraussetzen* is also a *Setzen*, that every pre-positing or presupposing is also a positing. External reflection obscures the fact that it posits its own presuppositions. Instead, external reflection simply "*has* a presupposition."[28] External reflection "*finds*" its presupposition "before" it.[29] This "external" relation to its own presupposition is the hallmark of this moment of reflection.

---

24. I use the contrived form "in it-self" to translate *in ihm selbst*, as opposed to *in sich selbst*, which I would render as "in itself." Both *ihm* and *sich* are third-person pronouns, but *sich* is reflexive, while *ihm* becomes reflexive only in the compound construction with *selbst*.

25. "mouvement de l'essence, où s'exprime, en son universalité négative, la structure ontologique de tout ce qui est" (P.-J. Labarrière and G. Jarczyk, "Introduction" to G. W. F. Hegel, *Science de la logique*, vol. 1:2, *La doctrine de l'essence*, translation, introduction and notes by P.-J. Labarrière and G. Jarczyk, Bibliothèque Philosophique [Paris: Aubier Montaigne, 1976], xiv).

26. For a careful and insightful reading of Hegel's treatment of reflection, see D. Henrich, "Hegels Logik der Reflexion: Neue Fassung," in D. Henrich, ed., *Die Wissenschaft der Logik und die Logik der Reflexion*, Hegel-Studien (Bonn: Bouvier Verlag Herbert Grundmann, 1978), 203-324.

27. "Selbstbewegung – Bewegung, die aus sich kommt, insofern die *setzende* Reflexion *voraussetzende*, aber als *voraussetzende* Reflexion schlechthin *setzende* ist" (G. W. F. Hegel, *Werke in zwanzig Bänden*, vol. 6, *Wissenschaft der Logik* 2, Theorie Werkausgabe [Frankfurt am Main: Suhrkamp, 1969], 28).

28. "eine Voraussetzung *hat*" (ibid.).

29. "*findet* . . . *vor*" (ibid., 29).

Since Hegel places his treatment of opposition in the second section of a second chapter, we would expect externality to play a dominant role in the logic of opposition. First, the logic of opposition is marked by the externality characteristic of the whole chapter on "The Essentialities or the Determinations of Reflection." Hegel describes "determining reflection," which gives rise to the determinations of reflection, as "reflection that has come outside of itself."[30] Reflection has come outside of itself in the sense that the determinations of reflection mask the fact that they are *moments* in the *process* of reflection.[31] As moments of this process the determinations of reflection are interrelated. But by masking their processual character they appear "as free essentialities, hovering in the void without attraction or repulsion in relation to each other."[32] This supposed freedom – freedom from relatedness – is in Hegel's eyes not freedom, but domination: "the likeness of essence with itself has been lost in negation, which is what is dominant."[33]

Second, the logic of opposition is marked by the externality characteristic of the section on "Difference," of which "Opposition" is the third subsection.[34] This externality is not a second externality alongside that of the determinations of reflection in general. Rather it is that same externality manifesting itself in its most concentrated form in the logic of diversity. As one would expect, diversity is the second moment of the logic of difference. In diversity, externality is dominant in the sense that the diverse moments are simply indifferent or "like-valued"[35] to each other. "In diversity as the like-valuedness of difference *reflection* has become *external* to itself in general."[36]

---

30. "bestimmende Reflexion"; "die außer sich gekommene Reflexion" (ibid., 34).
31. Cf. J. Biard, D. Buvat, J.-F. Kervegan, J.-F. Kling, A. Lacroix, A. Lécrivain, M. Slubicki, *Introduction à la lecture de la "Science de la logique" de Hegel*, vol. 2, *La doctrine de l'essence*, Collection Philosophie de l'Esprit (Paris: Aubier Montaigne, 1983), 46-47.
32. "als freie, im Leeren ohne Anziehung oder Abstoßung gegeneinander schwebende *Wesenheiten*" (*Wissenschaft der Logik* 2, 34).
33. "die Gleichheit des Wesens mit sich selbst ist in die Negation verloren, die das Herrschende ist" (ibid.).
34. Stanislas Opiela calls opposition "interiorized external difference." Although "its terms are in themselves negative or oppositional unity . . . the movement that places the opposed sides in relation is still affected by a certain externality" ("la différence extérieure intériorisée"; "ses termes sont en eux-mêmes l'unité négative ou oppositionnelle . . . le mouvement qui met en relation les côtés opposés est encore affecté d'une certaine extériorité") (S. Opiela, *Le réel dans la Logique de Hegel: développement et auto-détermination*, Bibliothèque des Archives de Philosophie, n.s. 41 [Paris: Beauchesne, 1983], 162).
35. This translation of *gleichgültig*, which I take from Oliva Blanchette, has two advantages over "indifferent." First, it makes apparent the root word *gleich*, "like." Second, it avoids confusion with "difference" as the translation of *Unterschied* – a key term in this part of the *Logic*.
36. "In der Verschiedenheit als der Gleichgültigkeit des Unterschieds ist sich überhaupt die *Reflexion äußerlich* geworden" (*Wissenschaft der Logik* 2, 48.).

Even to say that diverse moments are external to each other is saying too much from the viewpoint of diversity. Diversity does not place its moments in an external relation. The diverse moments relate to each other "only as *diverse* [moments] in general that are like-valued/indifferent to each other and to their determinacy."[37]

Opposition overcomes the externality of this merely indifferent diversity. Hegel describes opposition as "the unity of identity and diversity."[38] Opposition does not deny the diversity of its constituent moments, but neither does it deny that those moments stand in a relationship that gives them a common identity: they are "diverse in *one* identity."[39]

Opposition is not the final determination of reflection in the *Science of Logic*. That role falls to contradiction. The movement from opposition to contradiction turns on the verb *exclude [ausschließen]*. Hegel uses the terms "the positive" and "the negative" to describe the sides or moments of both opposition and contradiction. "The positive and the negative are ... the sides of the opposition that have come to stand on their own."[40] In opposition, the focus is primarily on the *result* of a process. The sides of opposition *have come* to stand on their own. Hegel uses the German noun *Gegensatz*, suggesting not so much an action or process of 'op-posing' or 'op-positing' [*entgegen-setzen*], as the result of that process.

But when in the concluding paragraphs of the treatment of opposition Hegel signals the movement from opposition to contradiction he turns to the verb *ausschließen*. The negative's "negative relation to it [i.e., the positive] is thus to exclude it from itself [i.e., from the negative]."[41] It is the action of mutual exclusion that makes the difference between being, in Hegelian vocabulary, positive and negative merely '*an sich*,' and being positive and negative '*an und für sich*.' "The positive and negative is hereby positive and negative not merely *in themselves*, but *in and for themselves*. They are it [i.e., positive and negative] *in themselves* insofar as abstraction [is] made from their excluding relation to other."[42]

When Hegel moves on to the discussion of contradiction *per se*, he continues to give a central role to the verb *exclude*. The positive and the nega-

37. "nur als *Verschiedene* überhaupt, die gleichgültig gegeneinander und gegen ihre Bestimmtheit sind" (ibid., 48).
38. "die Einheit der Identität und der Verschiedenheit" (ibid., 55).
39. "in *einer* Identität verschiedene" (ibid.).
40. "Das Positive und das Negative sind . . . die selbständig gewordenen Seiten des Gegensatzes" (ibid., 57).
41. "negative Beziehung darauf ist daher, es aus sich auszuschließen" (ibid., 59).
42. "Das Positive und Negative ist hiermit nicht nur *an sich* positiv und negativ, sondern an und für sich. *An sich* sind sie es, insofern von ihrer ausschließenden Beziehung auf Anderes abstrahiert [wird]" (ibid.).

tive "make up determining reflection as *excluding*."[43] Hegel couples his repeated use of the verb *exclude* with a second verb: *differ*. The logic of opposition concludes the entire section devoted to difference [*Unterschied*]. In the
ensuing section devoted to contradiction, Hegel turns to the verbal form *differentiate* [*unterscheiden*]: ". . . because the act of excluding is *one* act of differentiating and each of the differentiated [moments] is, as excluding, itself
the whole act of excluding."[44]

The logic of contradiction brings to the fore the process of differentiating
and excluding. Opposition, as the culminating form of difference, results
from this process. The difference between opposition and contradiction is
subtle. Both opposition and contradiction are composed of the positive and
the negative. Contradiction makes plain the process that gives rise to the
positive and the negative, while this process remains unexplicated until the
transition from opposition to contradiction. But this transition is itself part of
the logic of opposition. Hegel already begins talking about the act of excluding, and about the positive and the negative in and for themselves, in the
final paragraphs of his treatment of opposition. The boundary between opposition and contradiction is fluid.

Hegel also refuses to draw any strict separation between difference and
opposition. In the structure of the *Science of Logic*, opposition appears as a
particular form of difference. The fluid boundaries between opposition and
difference, and between opposition and contradiction, are particular aspects
of one of the main points of Hegel's analysis of the determinations of reflection. That point is that the autonomous, self-enclosed status of the determinations of reflection – identity, difference, diversity, opposition and contradiction – as supposedly free essentialities is an illusion. The determinations
of reflection are interrelated because they all spring from the process of determining reflection, as explicated in the logic of contradiction and more fully
developed in the ensuing chapter on "Ground."

3. Commonalities of the Positions of Opposition in Hegel
   and Schleiermacher

Hegel's view that the determinations of reflection are interrelated and
marked by fluid boundaries finds strong echoes in Schleiermacher's thought.
As we have seen, Schleiermacher insists that opposition does not exclude a

43. "machen die bestimmende Reflexion als *ausschließende* aus" (ibid., 65.).
44. " . . . weil das Ausschließen *ein* Unterscheiden und jedes der Unterschiedenen als Aus-
schließendes selbst das ganze Ausschließen ist" (ibid.).

measure of identity. He also rejects a strict separation between opposition and difference: "Opposition is merely rigidified difference; difference merely a fluid opposition."[45] Schleiermacher likewise does not strictly separate opposition from contradiction. He seems to make contradiction a form of opposition when he says that "free and necessary are not opposed to each other in a contradictory way, but rather the shared contradictory opposite of both is the contingent."[46] Hegel and Schleiermacher both share the conviction that opposition is, to use Schleiermacher's word, "relative" in the sense that opposition is interrelated with other categories such as difference, contradiction and, of particular importance, identity.

Hegel's conclusion that the *determinations* of reflection are all moments of the process of *determining* reflection expresses more broadly and systematically the movement from the noun "opposition" to the verb "exclude," from the noun "difference" to the verb "differentiate." Opposition [*Gegensatz*] is one of the determinations of reflection. The act of opposing or 'oppositing' [*entgegensetzen*] is the correlative moment of the process of determining reflection.

Every opposition is posited – op-posited. Hegel denies the possibility of an opposition given prior to or outside of the movement of reflection. Reflection "determines" oppositions by a process that is simultaneously positing and presupposing/'pre-positing.' Every opposition is posited by the movement of reflection. That movement determines the "position" of every opposition in a way that is marked by presuppositions. The positing of oppositions never occurs in a vacuum. Presuppositions are always already at work, shaping the concrete position of each opposition.

This is Hegel's way of advancing a position that has become a widespread theme of contemporary philosophy: there is no foundational, presuppositionless view of reality. Yet even a thinker as astute as Gilles Deleuze misses the antifoundational character of Hegel's logic, and misses it precisely because of a misinterpretation of the cluster difference – opposition – contradiction. Deleuze takes contradiction to be the "resolution" of difference, because he thinks that contradiction "resolves" itself as it moves

---

45. "Der Gegensaz ist nur eine erstarrte Verschiedenheit, die Verschiedenheit nur ein flüssiger Gegensaz" (Schleiermacher, "Einleitung: Lezte Bearbeitung," in *Ethik [1812/13]*, 201). Although I have translated *Verschiedenheit* as "diversity" in the Hegel passages, "difference" seems the more accurate rendering in this passage from Schleiermacher. He is using the term to describe the relation between the universal and the particular (see p. 2).

46. "Frei und nothwendig sind einander nicht contradictorisch entgegengesezt sondern das gemeinschaftliche contradictorische Gegentheil beider ist das zufällige" (Schleiermacher, *Dialektik [1814/15]*, 56).

to its "ground." "Contradiction resolves itself and, resolving itself, resolves difference by relating it to a ground."[47]   But Hegel writes not that "contradiction *resolves* itself," but that "contradiction *dissolves* itself."[48] Playing on the German words *Grund* and *zugrunde* and, implicitly, *Abgrund*, Hegel says that in the dissolution of contradiction "opposition has not only plunged into the *abyss*, but has returned *into its ground*."[49] The dissolution of contradiction introduces a ground or foundation of a strange sort – one that is a foundationless abyss.

Hegel's placement of opposition within the movement of reflection means that he agrees with a basic aspect of Schleiermacher's analysis of the hermeneutical constitution of opposition: opposition as an abstract theoretical figure is useless on its own. In reality we confront a plurality of concrete oppositions, which have their specific identities only in the context of a given set of presuppositions (Hegel) or from a particular interpretive perspective (Schleiermacher). If we follow the lead of Schleiermacher and Hegel, the theoretical use of the category of opposition need not lead us into reductionistic dualisms. Instead it can open out into an exploration of a plurality of contextualized perspectives. Our task is not to take the oppositions constituted by these differing perspectives and "resolve" them by discovering their foundation in "reality" in the singular (*"die" Wirklichkeit*). Our task rather is to discover the manifold relations in which these oppositions – always relative – are embedded and which determine them as the concrete oppositions that they are.

---

47. "La contradiction se résout et, se résolvant, résout la différence en la rapportant à un fondement" (G. Deleuze, *Différence et répétition*, Bibliothèque de Philosophie Contemporaine [Paris: Presses Universitaires de France, 1968], 64).

48. "Der Widerspruch löst sich auf" (Hegel, *Wissenschaft der Logik* 2, 67).

49. ". . . ist der Gegensatz nicht nur *zugrunde*, sondern *in seinen Grund* zurückgegangen (ibid., 68). In translating *zugrunde gehen* in a way that brings out the overtones of *Abgrund*, I follow the French translation of Labarrière and Jarczyk (Hegel, *La doctrine de l'essence*, 74).

SCHLEIERMACHER'S "RECIPROCAL RELATIONALITY": THE UNDERLYING REGULATIVE PRINCIPLE OF HIS THEOLOGICAL METHOD

F. LeRon Shults

Introduction

The pious self-consciousness plays a central role for Schleiermacher's theology in the *Glaubenslehre*; recognizing the exact nature of its role is crucial for understanding his method. My thesis is that central to his view of this self-consciousness is the concept of "reciprocal relationality" and, further, that this principle serves as a heuristic lens (providing constructive insights) and a hermeneutical horizon (providing epistemic limits) for his whole dogmatics. In other words, the relational structure that is constitutive for Schleiermacher's theological anthropology is regulative for the rest of his theology. While this might initially appear surprising, such a conclusion would be consistent with his earlier lectures on Dialektik where, as Terrence Tice has expressed it, "constitutive and regulative principles are seen by Schleiermacher to be one and the same."[1]

A failure to recognize the principle or rule of reciprocal relationality has led many scholars to argue that Schleiermacher was inconsistent in adhering to his methodological intentions stated in the Introduction of the second edition (1830/31) of the *Glaubenslehre*. For example, he has recently been charged with methodological discrepancies in his psychology,[2] in his doctrine of God,[3] and in his christology.[4] On the contrary, I assert that Schleiermacher's allegedly ambiguous epistemic, ontic and soteric statements can be defended as wholly congruous with his method by interpreting them in light

---

1. Terrence N. Tice,"Editor's Postscript" in Friedrich Schleiermacher, *Brief Outline of Theology as a Field of Study*, trans. with notes by Terrence N. Tice (Lewiston/Queenston/Lampeter: Edwin Mellen Press, 1990), 198.
2. Wolfhart Pannenberg, *Anthropology in Theological Perspective* (Philadelphia: Westminster, 1985); Wolfhart Pannenberg, *Systematic Theology*, Vol. 2 (Grand Rapids, MI: Eerdmans, 1994).
3. Robert R. Williams, *Schleiermacher the Theologian: The Construction of the Doctrine of God* (Philadelphia: Fortress Press, 1978); Robert R. Williams, "Schleiermacher, Hegel and the Problem of Concrete Universality," *Journal of the American Academy of Religion* 56 (1988), 473-96.
4. Maureen Junker-Kenny, "Schleiermacher's Transcendental Turn: Shifts in Argumentation between the First and Second Editions of the *Glaubenslehre*," *New Atheneum/ Neues Athenaeum* 3 (1992), 21-41.

178 F. LeRon Shults

of "reciprocal relationality," a principle that is embedded in his theological anthropology.

My main goal is two-fold: to show that reciprocal relationality is *constitutive* for the pious self-consciousness and *regulative* for theological anthropology. These are the tasks of sections one and two respectively; the first involves careful exposition of the early paragraphs of the *Glaubenslehre*, the second responds to the recent objections of Wolfhart Pannenberg to Schleiermacher's psychology. In the third section I will briefly pursue a secondary goal, providing the outline of an argument that suggests that reciprocal relationality has a regulative function beyond the domain of theological anthropology; indeed, that it ramifies throughout his entire dogmatics.[5]

To thematize this deeper rationality that shapes Schleiermacher's dogmatic propositions will require a figure-ground reversal of relationality and doctrine. That is, I intend to draw out into the foreground Schleiermacher's use of relationality *qua* relationality. Now, the importance of relationality in Schleiermacher's theology has been recognized by many authors; they speak of his use of "polar dialectical reciprocity,"[6] "co-inhering polarity,"[7] "Relationalität,"[8] "polar duality in knowledge as well as being,"[9] "dipolar dynamics,"[10] and "synoptic, mediated, polar relationship."[11] However, most treatments of Schleiermacher's relationality view it merely as one element of his system, as a *result* of his method, as something that appears *after* dealing with doctrinal issues. I hope to show that relationality is for Schleiermacher not just a conclusion but also the starting point of his dogmatic method, and that it functions as a fundamental regulative principle.

---

5. In another article, I have traced the regulative function of anthropological structural relationality in the theological methods of Karl Barth and Wolfhart Pannenberg. See "Constitutive Relationality in Anthropology and Trinity: The Shaping of the *Imago Dei* Doctrine in Barth and Pannenberg," *Neue Zeitschrift für systematiche Theologie und Religionsphilosophie* (in press).
6. Robert L. Vance, "Sin and Consciousness of Sin in Schleiermacher," *Perspectives in Religious Studies* 13/3 (1986), 241-262.
7. Richard R. Niebuhr, *Schleiermacher on Christ and Religion* (New York: Scribners, 1964).
8. Christian Albrecht, *Schleiermachers Theorie der Frömmigkeit: Ihr wissenschaftlicher Ort und ihr systematischer Gehalt in den Reden, in der Glaubenslehre und in der Dialektik*, Schleiermacher-Archiv, vol. 15, ed. Hermann Fischer, et al. (Berlin/New York: Walter de Gruyter, 1994).
9. Gerhard Spiegler, "Theological Tensions in Schleiermacher's *Dialektik*" in *Schleiermacher as Contemporary*, ed. R.W. Funk (New York: Herder and Herder, 1970).
10. Michael Nealeigh, "The Epistemology of Friedrich Schleiermacher from a Dipolar Perspective" in *Schleiermacher in Context*, ed. Ruth Drucilla Richardson (Lewiston/Queenston/Lampeter: Edwin Mellen Press, 1991), 174-202.
11. Karl Barth, *Protestant Thought: From Rousseau to Ritschl*, trans. B. Cozens (New York: Harper, 1959).

1. "Reciprocal Relationality" and the Pious Self-Consciousness

The most important section for understanding the structure of the pious self-conscious is paragraphs 3-5 of the Introduction in the *Glaubenslehre* where Schleiermacher offers a description of the reciprocal relationality that holds together the unity of self-consciousness. There he argues that the self-consciousness has a "double constitution."[12] It is a co-existence of the "highest" self-consciousness and the "sensible" self-consciousness in the same moment, "involving a *reciprocal relation* of the two."[13] Life is "conceived as an alternation between an abiding-in-self [*Insichbleiben*] and a passing-beyond-self [*Aussichheraustreten*] on the part of the subject."[14] Schleiermacher viewed self-consciousness as constituted by the relational unity of reciprocal elements or "poles." Schleiermacher expresses this in various ways, placing several other pairs of terms into this kind of relation.

> Thus in every self-consciousness there are two elements, which we might call respectively a self-caused element [*ein Sichselbstsetzen*] and a non-self-caused element [*ein Sichselbstnichtsogesetzthaben*]; or a Being and a Having-by-some-means-come-to-be [*ein Sein und ein Irgendwiegenwordensein*]. . . . In self-consciousness there are only two elements: the one expresses the existence of the subject for itself, the other its co-existence with an Other.[15]

These relations, and other pairs that are similarly related throughout the System of Doctrine, are represented graphically in *Chart 1.* I recognize that any attempt to develop a graphic representation or topology of the psyche can easily lead to oversimplification or reductionism. The chart is intended only as a pedagogical tool, designed to illustrate the importance of the relationality in Schleiermacher's view of the self-consciousness. The point is to stress the fact that the two elements are "combined" [*verbindung*][16] or "conjoined" [*Zugleichgesetztsein*],[17] but never "fused" [*verschmelzen*].[18] This chart should not be taken as a "picture" of the self-consciousness, but only as a "model" for thinking about its structure. With these caveats, let me now attempt to put the model to work.

---

12. Friedrich Schleiermacher, *The Christian Faith*, ed. H.R. Mackintosh & J.S. Stewart (Edinburgh: T&T Clark, 1989), 13. Hereafter cited as CF.
13. CF, 21.
14. CF, 8.
15. CF, 13.
16. CF, 124.
17. CF, 21.
18. CF, 23.

Think of the arrows in *Chart 1* as the "figure," and the box itself (the whole self-consciousness) as the "ground"; this is what I mean by a figure-ground reversal. The arrows represent the conjoining of the two potencies of higher self-consciousness and sensible self-consciousness, which are related to each other "in the unity of the moment." These elements are inseparable, but they are never "fused."[19] The dotted line to the left of the reciprocity arrows demarcates the area in which antitheses may occur; this indicates that the relationality itself is included in what he will later call spheres of "more or less." In other words, the quantitative antitheses in experience also encompass the *manner* in which the elements are related.[20] The element to the left of the dotted line is untouched by any antithesis. There are several different German expressions that are translated by the English word "reciprocal" (the most common is *Wechselwirkung,* but one also finds *gegenseitigen Einwirkungen, Bezogensein, Verhaltnisse zueinander*), but they all refer generally to the same idea of reciprocity, or mutual interaction between elements, *without fusion.*

For Schleiermacher, self-consciousness *is* the reciprocal relational unity of the two elements. The terms in the left column represent the "constant" element in self-consciousness, while the terms in the right column refer to the "variable" element. The "essence of the subject itself" is not a third thing, but the relational unity of the two elements.[21] Though the "potency" of one element may be stronger than the other, the relationality between them cannot be eradicated. And that relationality is "reciprocal," for

the total self-consciousness made up of both together is one of *Reciprocity* between subject and corresponding Other . . . that term "reciprocity" is the right one for our self-consciousness in general, inasmuch as it expresses our connexion with everything which either appeals to our receptivity or is subjected to our activity.[22]

It should be noted that the last pair in the chart are terms that describe only the "pious" self-consciousness (which is a modification of the immediate self-consciousness). This pair is therefore described in the System of Doctrine proper, while the others are outlined in the early paragraphs of the Introduction. Prior to regeneration, the sensible self-consciousness dominates the feeling of absolute dependence. After Christ's redemptive assumption of the individual into the fellowship of grace, the feeling of absolute dependence dominates the sensible self-consciousness. The immediate self-con-

---

19. CF, 23.
20. CF, 23.
21. CF, 8,21,124.
22. CF, 14.

sciousness is then modified or determined as "pious" self-consciousness. This modification does not negate the relationality between the two potencies; it simply removes the "constraint" from the already present God-consciousness so that it dominates the relational unity.

The main sub-headings of the System of Doctrine in the *Glaubenslehre* are: 1) "The development of that pious self-consciousness which is always both presupposed by and contained in every Christian pious affection," and 2) "Development of the facts of the pious self-consciousness, as they are determined by the antithesis of sin and grace." This division makes it clear that the pious self-consciousness is central to Schleiermacher's method. In fact, he explicitly affirms that "we shall exhaust the whole compass of Christian doctrine if we consider the facts of the pious self-consciousness."[23] But this self-consciousness itself is constituted by the relationality between the "presupposed" element (the feeling of absolute dependence) and the "determined" element (antithesis of sin and grace). This means, I believe, that these two major parts of the System of Doctrine may themselves be in a reciprocal relational unity; the first describing the self-identical element, the second explicating the determined element.

Chart 1 also illustrates why "Feeling" is so important to Schleiermacher. Of course, he is not referring with this term to affect, mood, or sensation. Feeling is "the immediate presence of whole undivided being."[24] As immediate self-consciousness, Feeling is the "mediating link" in the transition between moments in which Knowing and Doing predominate.[25] This has led some process theologians to say that Schleiermacher has a dipolar view with Feeling in the center as a merging of Doing and Knowing.[26] But this misinterpretation is based on a failure to see that Feeling is able to serve as a "mediating link" not because it is in the middle, but because it is the *constant, self-identical* element of self-consciousness (on the left side of Chart 1). While Doing is wholly a "passing-beyond-self," and Knowing is a form of consciousness but only becomes real by a "passing-beyond-self," Feeling alone belongs "altogether to the realm of receptivity, it is entirely an abiding-in-self."[27]

It is important to ask *why* Schleiermacher took the approach he did in developing a reciprocal relational understanding of self-consciousness as the basis of his theological anthropology. According to Thandeka, Schleier-

---

23. CF, 123.
24. CF, 7.
25. CF, 8.
26. See, for example, the article by Michael Nealeigh, "The Epistemology of Friedrich Schleiermacher from a Dipolar Perspective."
27. CF, 8.

macher's goal, especially in the 1822 lectures on *Dialektik*, was to "find" the self that Kant "lost."[28] Arguing that Kant's division of pure and practical reason failed to ground transcendental consciousness (because it was still enclosed in "thinking"), Schleiermacher wanted to find the "common seed" of both types of reason.[29] Thandeka explains that Schleiermacher "believed that the self he discovered by means of his *Dialektik* can only be disclosed in an actual act of self-consciousness. This actual act is beyond the purview of thinking."[30] We have seen that Schleiermacher makes this clear also in the Introduction to the *Glaubenslehre* where he argues that Feeling (the *self-identical* element) is always the "mediating link" between moments in the sphere of "more or less" (the *determined* element) in which Doing and Knowing vacillate in predominance. He recognized that the gap left by Kant cannot be repaired or filled by "thought." It must be *felt* in the deeper relational unity that is the "essence of the subject itself."[31]

The evolution of Schleiermacher's view of self-consciousness has been traced in a helpful way by Junker-Kenny, who suggests that there is a noticeable shift between the first and second editions of the *Glaubenslehre*, with a distinct "transcendental turn" in the latter edition.[32] She argues that the first edition described only a feeling of dependence (not absolute) and showed its relation to his view of God, which he developed separately in *Dialektik*. In the second edition, however, the name "God" is posited as the "Whence"[33] of the feeling of absolute dependence, which Schleiermacher develops out of his transcendental analysis of the constitutive elements of human subjectivity. Junker-Kenny observes:

> In the original draft both the consciousness of ourselves as "always remaining the same" and the consciousness of ourselves as "variable" were considered "only elements of each determined self-consciousness, because each of them is the human person's immediate consciousness of herself as changed" (§ 9,1). In the corrected version the human person's consciousness of herself as "remaining the same" is not just counted as one element of determined self-con-

28. Thandeka, "Schleiermacher's Dialektik: The Discovery of the Self that Kant Lost," *Harvard Theological Review* 85 (1992), 433-52.
29. Thandeka, "Schleiermacher's Dialektik: The Discovery of the Self that Kant Lost, " 439; Cf. Wilhelm Anz, "Schleiermacher und Kierkegaard: Übereinstimmung und Differenz," *Zeitschrift für Theologie und Kirche* 82/4 (1985), 409-429.
30. Thandeka, "Schleiermacher's Dialektik: The Discovery of the Self that Kant Lost," 443.
31. CF, 8.
32. Maureen Junker-Kenny, "Schleiermacher's Transcendental Turn: Shifts in Argumentation between the First and Second Editions of the *Glaubenslehre*."
33. CF, 16.

sciousness, but as the condition of the possibility of identifying the changing conditions of consciousness as her own.[34] In the final edition, then, it is precisely the *double constitution* of the self (and not only the determined element) that provides the basis for his view of self-consciousness. Although either element may "almost disappear," both are always present. This double constitution finds its form or structure in what I have been calling reciprocal relationality. This principle is regulative for all human knowing because the self cannot escape the limits of its relational constitution, which determines all experience as "reciprocal." Thereby it confines all scientific (i.e., positive) theological statements about apparent antitheses in the sphere of reciprocity to descriptions of "more or less." Only by rejecting any real qualitative polarity of opposites can we be faithful to what is presupposed in self-consciousness: that every part of the world (nature-system) exists in *equivalently* absolute dependence upon God.

In this first section, I have attempted to demonstrate the way in which Schleiermacher's reciprocal relationality functions constitutively for pious self-consciousness. In the second section I hope to show that it also serves as a heuristic lens (providing constructive insights) and as a hermeneutical horizon (providing epistemic limits) for his theological anthropology.

2. The Regulative Function of Reciprocal Relationality in Theological Anthropology

To reiterate, my goal is to effect a figure-ground reversal, drawing out the relationality *qua* relationality which is tacit in Schleiermacher's method in order to dispel the putative ambiguity of some of his dogmatic propositions. By interpreting these doctrines through the lenses of reciprocal relationality, I hope to respond to his critics' charges that he has inconsistently carried out his method.[35] On this issue, Wolfhart Pannenberg has been particularly critical, and I will focus here on his concerns.

I will use his view of the identity of the self as a point of entry, as we follow through the logic of his transcendental description of the reciprocal rela-

---

34. Maureen Junker-Kenny, "Schleiermacher's Transcendental Turn: Shifts in Argumentation between the First and Second Editions of the *Glaubenslehre*," 25.

35. For example, Thomas Pröpper, "Schleiermachers Bestimmung des Christentums und der Erlösung: Zur Problematik der transzendental-anthropologischen Hermeneutik des Glaubens," *Theologische Quartalschrift*, 168/3 (1988), 193-214; Jan Rohls, "Frömmigkeit als Gefühl schlechthinniger Abhängigkeit: Zu Schleiermachers Religionstheorie in der Glaubenslehre," in *Internationaler Schleiermacher-Kongreß Berlin 1984*, ed. Kurt-Victor Selge, Schleiermacher-Archiv, vol. 1,1 (Berlin: Walter de Gruyter, 1985), 221-252.

tionality that constitutes the self, to show that he works out the psychological implications of his anthropology in a way consistent with his method. Even if one follows Pannenberg's material critique of Schleiermacher in light of modern psychological and anthropological research, I believe that where Pannenberg sees *internal* inconsistencies, it is due to the fact that he has not perceived the reciprocal relationality that grounds the former's view of the self. We will examine three alleged inconsistencies.

The first two are related to the use of the term "immediate self-consciousness." In his *Anthropology in Theological Perspective*, Pannenberg argues that Schleiermacher's interpretation of the feeling of absolute dependence is an "entry of finite relations into the book of 'immediate consciousness'; when the latter is also conceived as consciousness of God it can hardly be called 'immediate' any longer in view of the extensive effort of reflection required for this."[36]   What Pannenberg has missed here is the fact that Schleiermacher is talking about a specific modification of immediate self-consciousness, namely, *pious* self-consciousness, in which a person recognizes that the feeling of absolute dependence *is* God-consciousness. In this "state of grace," the redeemed person now looks back and sees that he or she has been unaware that the self-identical element of self-consciousness, in which we have the feeling of absolute dependence, was in fact a relation to God all along.[37]   For Schleiermacher, however, that feeling is still "immediately" present in self-consciousness.

Pannenberg is also concerned with Schleiermacher's use of the term "self-consciousness" to describe feeling generally. He argues in his *Anthropology* book that "we should not follow Schleiermacher in giving the name 'self-consciousness' to this phenomenon, especially since even according to Schleiermacher it includes more than simply the ego or self as distinct from the world."[38]   Pannenberg thinks his reliance on this key concept of transcendental idealism (i.e., the term "self-consciousness") has led him into an inconsistent description of feeling, which fails to recognize the priority of the distinction between I and object in the self. He makes a similar point in volume II of his *Systematic Theology*.

In § 5,1, Schleiermacher shows interest in the fact that in feeling we do not stand opposed to others, but he relates this only to the element of dependence, which in his view is contained already in the immediate self-consciousness (§ 4), whereas in fact, as his own ar-

---

36. Wolfhart Pannenberg, *Anthropology in Theological Perspective* (Philadelphia: Westminster, 1985), 253.
37. CF, 18.
38. Wolfhart Pannenberg, *Anthropology in Theological Perspective*, 250.

gument shows in § 4,2 (interaction with others), the distinction of the self and the object is presupposed already in sensory awareness.[39] Pannenberg sees this as a contradiction. However, our analysis of Schleiermacher's reciprocal relationality suggests that he can consistently say both that "in *feeling* we do not stand opposed to others" and that the distinction of the self and the object is "presupposed already in *sensory awareness*." He can do this because "Feeling" refers to the *self-identical* element (i.e., "abiding-in-self") and "sensory awareness" refers to the *determined* element (i.e., "passing-beyond-self") in self-consciousness. The former represents the "highest" grade of self-consciousness and the latter represents the "sensible" grade. These two grades cannot be abstracted from their reciprocal relational unity in the self-consciousness. However, Schleiermacher is careful to emphasize that the two elements are never "fused."[40] Pannenberg's charge of inconsistency, it seems to me, assumes a relationship of *fusion*.

A third alleged inconsistency has to do with the contrast between dependence and freedom. Pannenberg argues that Schleiermacher

> all too quickly interpreted the element of receptivity and stateness as dependence in contrast to freedom. . . . I say "all too quickly," because the concept of dependence has its proper place in the area of "reciprocity between the subject and the corresponding Other" (§ 4,2) and therefore in the relation of the person to the world. . . . The definition of freedom as spontaneous activity in contrast to receptivity, which lies behind the thesis that the denial of absolute freedom forms the meaning-content of immediate self-consciousness, must likewise be judged inadequate, because it does not do justice . . . to the concept of freedom as the expression of achieved identity with one's own being.[41]

Here too our disagreement with Pannenberg is based on an analysis of Schleiermacher's reciprocal relationality. He still seems to be assuming that Schleiermacher has a "fusion" model of self-consciousness. For Schleiermacher, however, dependence and freedom can both be found in the "reciprocity between the subject and corresponding Other," because they both occur on the right side of *Chart 1*, i.e., are determined by the "more or less" relationality which is a consequence of the relational tension between the sphere of the sensible self-consciousness and the highest self-conscious-

---

39. Wolfhart Pannenberg, *Systematic Theology*, Vol. 2 (Grand Rapids, MI: Eerdmans, 1994), 192.
40. CF, 21, 23.
41. Wolfhart Pannenberg, *Anthropology in Theological Perspective*, 252-3.

ness. Only the feeling of *absolute* dependence is found *only* in the latter self-identical element of the relational unity.

I believe these examples show the importance of examining the role of constitutive relationality itself in Schleiermacher's theological anthropology. As a conjoining without confusion, it protects the feeling of absolute dependence from any possible corruption. This function is critical for without it, Schleiermacher says, the whole edifice "falls to the ground."[42] I will argue now in the third section that a correct understanding of reciprocal relationality in self-consciousness illustrates his methodological consistency in "all religious expressions" (to use Schleiermacher's phrase), even in his highly controversial treatment of the divine attributes and the doctrine of redemption where he has been most rigorously attacked.

3. The Regulative Function of Reciprocal Relationality in all "Religious Expressions"

In describing the facts of the pious self-consciousness, Schleiermacher insists one must never contradict the feeling of absolute dependence, which is "presupposed." To avoid this contradiction, he must affirm that all apparent antitheses or "relative oppositions" are only expressions of a "more or less" [*mehr oder weniger*] within the sphere of the sensible self-consciousness. The importance of this "more or less" relationality for Schleiermacher cannot be overemphasized. It serves to "bracket" all antitheses so they do not corrupt the feeling of absolute dependence. In the crucial First Section of the First Part of the System of Doctrine (§ 36), he deals with Creation and Preservation, which together are "the original expression" of the relation between the world and God expressed in the pious self-consciousness.[43] These doctrines describe the immediate feeling that the world exists only in absolute dependence upon God. Each of his propositions, he explains, "puts forward *a greatest and a least* and, showing that the feeling of [absolute] dependence holds good in an equivalent way for both limiting cases, establishes this *equivalence as the rule for all religious expression*."[44] So, for example, the antithesis of good and evil is based on "the greatest and the least in the harmony of universal reciprocal activity with the independent being of the individual."

---

42. CF, 193.
43. CF, 142.
44. CF, 193, emphasis added.

The insistence that all propositions conform to this feeling (that all things in every sphere are *equivalently* absolutely dependent on God) is rooted in the twin doctrines of Creation and Preservation, but consistently maintained beyond them. In fact, this quantitative (more/less) relationality is found throughout the *Glaubenslehre*. For example, it is applied (using the phrase "more or less") to the relation of the sensible and higher self-consciousness in "redemption,"[45] to the receptivity of the Christian and the activity of Christ,[46] to Christ's "humiliation and exaltation,"[47] to the measured degree of the potencies in sanctification,[48] to the negative and positive qualities of race-consciousness,[49] and to the multiplicity of forms of underlying disposition.[50] The more/less rule of equivalence implicitly informs his propositions elsewhere as, for example, in describing sin as a "vanishing quantity" in the regenerate.[51] My point in listing these examples is to illustrate that this relational thought-form permeates his dogmatics. Further, this rule of "more or less" relationality cannot be understood by examining either one or both elements of the pious self-consciousness (or the parts of the System of Doctrine); rather it must be grasped intuitively out of the relationality itself that constitutes their unity.

At the beginning of the First Part of the System of Doctrine, he makes it clear that "great discrimination" should be used in discussing attributes of God and the constitution of the world, even as they appear in pious self-consciousness. This is due to the danger that they may allow in some statement in excess of the "immediate content of that [pious] self-consciousness."[52] For this reason,

> we must declare the description of *human states of mind* to be the *fundamental dogmatic form;* while propositions of the second and third forms [statements about God or the world as they appear in the self-consciousness] are permissible only in so far as they can be developed out of propositions of the first form; for only on this condition can they be really authenticated as expressions of religious emotions.[53]

---

45. CF, 55.
46, CF, 371.
47. CF, 105.
48. CF, 478.
49. CF, 559.
50. CF, 726.
51. CF, 508.
52. CF, 140.
53. CF, 125-126, emphasis added.

Because of the double constitution of self-consciousness, all descriptions of human states of mind must account for both elements (constant and variable) in the self-consciousness, as well as their relational unity. This relationality defines the horizon of theological knowledge.

In this sense, the principle of reciprocal relationality functions regulatively for Schleiermacher's theology. I would like to point briefly to two key examples: the doctrine of God and christology. In reference to the former, it will be helpful to begin with the debate between Schleiermacher and Hegel. There is general agreement among scholars that the core issue of their debate centered on the problem of immediate knowledge.[54] This bears on the metaphysical question because, as Schleiermacher argues in his Dialektik, all speculative questions can be reduced to the question of the relationship between God and the world.[55] Although "God" and "world" were equivalent terms in the 1811 edition of the Dialektik, Schleiermacher's theological concern led him to reject this identification in the 1814 draft. But this, according to Spiegler, led him to the "assertion of a relationship between in principle, unrelatable terms. Schleiermacher had returned to the conception of a duplex division of reality."[56] For Vance, the problem in his view of Feeling is due to the fact that "it must be located in a relative realm of continuous dialectical existence, but that it must exposit a non-dialectical conjunction of relative world and absolute God which together constitute its essential determination."[57]

Robert Williams, who describes Schleiermacher's conception of the relation of God and world as "non-reciprocal"[58] has written extensively on Schleiermacher's doctrine of God[59] and provides us with a detailed description of an alleged methodological inconsistency in his treatment of the divine attributes of love and wisdom. Williams starts with the distinction between Hegel and Schleiermacher. For him, the central difference is the way they dealt with "the problem of mediation between formal universal structures

---

54. See Richard Crouter, "Hegel and Schleiermacher at Berlin: A Many-Sided Debate," *Journal of the American Academy of Religion* 48 (1980), 19-43; Herbert Dembrowski, "Schleiermacher und Hegel: Ein Gegensatz," in *Neues Testament und christliche Existenz*, ed. H. Betz (Tübingen: J.C.B. Mohr, 1973), 115-141.
55. Gerhard Spiegler, "Theological Tensions in Schleiermacher's *Dialektik*," 15.
56. Gerhard Spiegler, "Theological Tensions in Schleiermacher's *Dialektik*," 21.
57. Robert L. Vance, "Sin and Consciousness of Sin in Schleiermacher," 261.
58. Robert R. Williams, "Schleiermacher, Hegel and the Problem of Concrete Universality," 488.
59. Robert R. Williams, *Schleiermacher the Theologian: The Construction of the Doctrine of God* (Philadelphia: Fortress Press, 1978); Robert R. Williams, "Schleiermacher, Hegel and the Problem of Concrete Universality," *Journal of the American Academy of Religion* 56 (1988), 473-96.

and particular Christian fact."[60] Hegel saw Schleiermacher's retreat into feeling as no better than Kant's critical formalism. The reliance on "immediate self-consciousness" empties theological statements of all substance and content, according to Hegel. Williams interprets Hegel's own response to the collapse of onto-theology as the development of an "ontology of positivity," which allowed him to formulate concrete universals, involving change in the universal.

However, Williams argues that Schleiermacher too had a "hidden" principle of positivity, though he never made it thematic and did not follow it consistently. In fact, according to Williams, Schleiermacher *only* followed this principle in the cases of the divine attributes of *love and wisdom*. On Williams' hypothesis, "the argument of the *Glaubenslehre* is incomplete on its own terms because Schleiermacher fails to show the modification and transformation of the generic universals into concrete universals. He does this only in the case of divine wisdom and love."[61] Williams notes the tension in his own interpretation. He quotes Schleiermacher's explicit statement that the divine attributes "refer to nothing special in God,"[62] but believes that this proposition does not reflect his actual method. According to Williams, Schleiermacher "did himself considerable injustice in the above proposition."[63]

More than "doing himself considerable injustice," if Williams is right we would have to say Schleiermacher is blatantly contradicting himself, for he explicitly says that we must not "subject God to the antithesis of *abstract and concrete*, or *universal and particular*"[64] and that "we have no formula for the being of God in Himself as distinct from the being of God in the world."[65] Given the powerful coherence evinced throughout Schleiermacher's writings, and his own warning that statements about the divine attributes are "based proximately on the poetical"[66] and more dangerous than the *fundamental form* of dogmatic propositions (i.e., human states of mind),[67] I believe we should at least try to understand the divine attributes in light of his broader methodological program rather than vice versa.

---

60. Robert R. Williams, "Schleiermacher, Hegel and the Problem of Concrete Universality," 481.
61. Robert R. Williams, "Schleiermacher, Hegel and the Problem of Concrete Universality," 480.
62. CF, 194.
63. Robert R. Williams, *Schleiermacher the Theologian*, 81.
64. CF, 501.
65. CF, 748.
66. CF, 141.
67. CF, 140.

My argument is that interpreting the attributes of love and wisdom as facts of the pious self-consciousness which are reciprocally related reveals that there is no inconsistency. Note carefully how the vocabulary of reciprocal relationality (terms like "more/less," "sphere," etc.) pervades Schleiermacher's language in paragraphs 164-169 on love and wisdom. First, it is critical to recognize that these attributes are treated in the overall context of "divine causality"; we are dealing with the "*sphere* of the divine self-impartation."[68] Love and wisdom are "conceived on the lines of a human distinction. . . . Now in all human causality we distinguish between the underlying temper or disposition and the *more or less* corresponding form in which it is given effect to."[69] Here we see again the *self-identical* element (underlying disposition) and the *determined* element (more or less). Love, which is the "impulse to unite," represents the underlying disposition; Wisdom represents the "more or less" element in the "*sphere* of redemption," regarded in its "manifold characteristics and in the whole round of their *reciprocal relations.*"[70]

"Love" is attributed to God because of the feeling in the pious self-consciousness of "the union of the Divine Essence with human nature." But this is nothing new to the *Glaubenslehre*. Schleiermacher already explained this to us in the Introduction, § 4: "the self-identical essence of piety, is this: the consciousness of being absolutely dependent, or, which is the same thing, of being in relation with God."[71] The essence of the divine love is that the Supreme Being "imparts himself."[72] But what is this impartation? It is the causality "whereby the God-consciousness is renewed and made perfect."[73] § 166 tells us that "the divine love . . . is seen in the work of redemption." But redemption for Schleiermacher, as we will see below, is nothing more than the completion of creation, which involves the increase of God-consciousness. Referring to God as "Love" is another way of saying "Whence" or "Determinant," i.e., of referring to the causality of the feeling of absolute dependence.

"Love" and "Wisdom" are two terms that can also be charted as reciprocal relations, i.e., facts of the pious self-consciousness. As such, they are analogous to the two doctrines that are the original expression of that self-consciousness: Creation and Preservation [*see Chart 2*]. Love alone, how-

---

68. CF, 728.
69. CF, 726.
70. CF, 727.
71. CF, 12.
72. CF, 727.
73. CF, 728.

ever, "is made the equivalent of the divine being or essence of God."[74] This makes perfect sense when we recognize that "love" is in the left column, representing the *self-identical* element of pious self-consciousness. It alone enters our consciousness directly as "feeling," while Wisdom represents the *determined* element.

If we look at the way in which we become aware of the two attributes respectively, it turns out that we have the *sense* of divine love directly in the consciousness of redemption, and as this is the *basis* on which all the rest of our God-consciousness is built up, it of course *represents to us* the essence of God.[75]

With the phrase "divine love" Schleiermacher points to the causality of the feeling of absolute dependence. This is exactly what he told us he was going to do on p. 198: ". . . all the *divine attributes* to be dealt with in Christian Dogmatics must somehow go back to the divine *causality*, since they are *only meant to explain the feeling of absolute dependence*."

Like Pannenberg, Williams seems to interpret the two elements of Schleiermacher's pious self-consciousness as united through a *fusion*; e.g., Williams speaks of a *synthesis* of two elements.[76] But I am arguing that the attributes of love and wisdom are an expression of two reciprocally related elements in the pious self-consciousness. This is completely consistent with Schleiermacher's methodological insistence that divine attributes can only be described as they appear in the pious self-consciousness, and should not be taken as referring to "something special in God." I do not think it is necessary to call in Husserl, Hartshorne or Hegel (as several scholars have done) to rescue Schleiermacher. Nor should we follow other scholars who try to save Schleiermacher from his alleged inconsistency by calling in the cavalry or structuralism,[77] phenomenology[78] or transcendental philosophy.[79] The extent to which he influenced or was influenced by these forces is not the issue; the key to understanding him is laid out in his own Introduction, and

74. CF, 730.
75. CF, 732.
76. Robert R. Williams, "Schleiermacher, Hegel and the Problem of Concrete Universality," 476.
77. Jean-Pierre Wils, *Sittlichkeit und Subjektivität: Zur Ortsbestimmung der Ethik im Strukturalismus, in der Subjektivitätsphilosophie und bei Schleiermacher* (Freiburg: Herder, 1987).
78. Eduardo Mendieta, "Metaphysics of Subjectivity and the Theology of Subjectivity: Schleiermacher's Anthropological Theology," *Philosophy and Theology: Marquette University Quarterly* 6/3 (1992), 276-290.
79. Sergio Sorrentino, "Schleiermachers Philosophie und der Ansatz der transzendentalen Philosophie," in *Schleiermacher in Context*, ed. Ruth Drucilla Richardson (Lewiston/Queenston/Lampeter: Edwin Mellen Press, 1991), 227-241.

consistently followed throughout the *Glaubenslehre*; viz., reciprocal relationality in the pious self-consciousness.

Finally, it will be helpful to examine christology as a final example of our thesis on the regulative principle of relationality in Schleiermacher's theology. This is an appropriate doctrine to explore, because of the centrality of "redemption" in his dogmatics. Several scholars have argued that his christology is inconsistent with or divorced from his Introduction.[80] But I would like to focus on the work of Maureen Junker-Kenny[81] because she explicitly treats the connection between redemption, the divine attributes, and the completion of creation. She recognizes the transcendental turn in the second edition of the *Glaubenslehre*, but thinks that this makes his christology inconsistent with the method of the new Introduction.

> [The second edition] made the whole Introduction more scholarly. But the result, *unforeseen by Schleiermacher*, was also to change its relationship to the dogmatics. . . . For if the relationship with God is not only demonstrated to be a feeling which in fact exists but rather is grounded transcendentally, then the Introduction acquires a foundational significance that any *christology can scarcely counterbalance*.[82]

Junker-Kenny later argues (rightly) that redemption is reduced to creation/preservation in Schleiermacher, but I believe that he *did* foresee the impact of his new Introduction on dogmatics. Christology is not intended to counterbalance the transcendent ground of the feeling of absolute dependence. Rather, it is the central test case for the regulative function of reciprocal relationality: statements about the antithesis of sin and grace in the "more or less" sphere of redemption are reciprocally related, but do not modify the feeling of absolute dependence, or God-consciousness. The latter clearly has conceptual priority, for

> The term itself [Redemption] is in this realm *merely figurative*, and signifies in general a passage from an evil condition, which is represented as a state of captivity or constraint [of the God-conscious-

---

80. See, for example, Richard Muller, "The Christological Problem as addressed by Friedrich Schleiermacher: A Dogmatic Query" in *Perspectives on Christology: Essays in Honor of Paul K. Jewett*, ed. M. Shuster & R. Muller (Grand Rapids: Zondervan, 1991); Richard R. Niebuhr, "Christ, Nature and Consciousness: Reflections on Schleiermacher in the Light of Barth's Early Criticisms" in *Barth and Schleiermacher: Beyond the Impasse?*, ed. James O. Duke & Robert F. Streetman (Philadelphia: Fortress, 1988), 11-22.

81. Maureen Junker-Kenny, "Schleiermacher's Transcendental Turn: Shifts in Argumentation between the First and Second Editions of the *Glaubenslehre*," 21-41.

82. Maureen Junker-Kenny, "Schleiermacher's Transcendental Turn: Shifts in Argumentation between the First and Second Editions of the *Glaubenslehre*," 33, emphasis added.

ness], into a better condition. . . . This certainly makes it seem as if these two conditions, that which exists before redemption and that which is to be brought about by redemption, could only be distinguished in an indefinite way, *as a more and a less.*[83]

The sphere of redemption represents the "determined" element in the pious self-consciousness, participating in the "more or less" antithesis of sin and grace. In fact, the term "Redemption" is ultimately deemed "not suitable for this new communication of a powerful God-consciousness," for the work of Christ should be regarded "as the completion, only now accomplished, of the creation of human nature."[84]

It is clear that christology does not "counterbalance" the method Schleiermacher set out in the Introduction when we think through the implications of his reduction of redemption to creation/preservation.

And we know no divine activity except that of creation, which includes preservation, or conversely, that of preservation, which includes that of creation. . . . And thus the total effective influence of Christ is only the continuation of the creative divine activity out of which the Person of Christ arose.[85]

Schleiermacher even calls the assertion of the completion of creation through Christ "an all-round test in scrutinizing Church formulae."[86] He holds on to this equation and works out its implications consistently in the *Glaubenslehre.*[87] This suggests he was aware of the impact of his method, with its "rule of equivalence," as subtended by "more or less" reciprocal relationality, on his christological statements; for this very reason, he labored to render the doctrine of redemption totally consistent with the "original expression" of the feeling of absolute dependence as determined in the pious self-consciousness, viz., the doctrine of Creation/Preservation.

Conclusion

Schleiermacher acknowledged that if any case could be found in which a real qualitative antithesis could be identified in any sphere, then the feeling of absolute dependence would be contradicted. An opposition that was more than merely "greatest and least" in a single province would imply that the poles of the antithesis are not *equivalently* absolutely dependent on God; the

83. CF, 54, emphasis added.
84. CF, 365.
85. CF, 426-27.
86. CF, 437.
87. See, for example, CF, 501, 728.

doctrine would "fall to the ground."[88] If the nature-system exists in *absolute* dependence on God, this demands that every aspect of the system be dependent equivalently (for "absoluteness" allows no gradations). Based on his methodological insistence that dogmatics must never make this fatal mistake, he consistently avoids it by formulating every Christian doctrine in terms of a "more or less," presupposing the relation of this "determined" element to the "self-identical" element in the self-consciousness. By holding together the unity of self-consciousness with a reciprocal relationality, which is more than a juxtaposition but less than a fusion, he is able to protect the feeling of absolute dependence. One could also show this regulative function in his ecclesiology, eschatology, and other doctrines. But, having examined his view of the human self, the divine attributes and redemption, we might borrow a phrase from Schleiermacher himself; "beyond these there are no difficult cases to consider."[89]

I have tried to show the constructive and regulative role of Schleiermacher's reciprocal relationality in his theology. I have argued that a failure to grasp this underlying dimension of his thought has led to much misunderstanding. This suggests a critical insight for contemporary theological method. It is important for us to render thematic our own tacit understandings of the structural relationality that constitutes the self and regulates the boundaries of knowledge for, as our analysis of Schleiermacher has shown us, this inevitably shapes epistemological assumptions and pervades doctrinal formulation.

---

88. CF, 193.
89. CF, 193.

"Reciprocal Relationality"

"Constant" element	⟷ "Variable" element
Being	⟷ Having-by-some-means-come-to-be
Abiding-in-self	⟷ Passing-beyond-self
Self-positing Element	⟷ Non-self-posited Element
Existence of Subject for itself	⟷ Co-existence of subject with an Other
Pure Receptivity	⟷ Relative Receptivity/Activity
Feeling	⟷ (Knowing) Doing
Absolute Dependence	⟷ Relative Dependence/Freedom
Highest self-consciousness (no antithesis; feeling of absolute dependence)	⟷ *Sensible* self-consciousness (antithesis of pleasant and unpleasant)
Self-identical element in pious self-consciousness (world exists in absolute dependence on God)	⟷ *Determined* element in pious self-consciousness (antithesis of sin and grace)

Chart 1

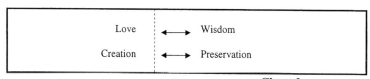

Love	⟷ Wisdom
Creation	⟷ Preservation

Chart 2

GERMAN ROMANTICISM AND FRIEDRICH SCHLEIERMACHER IN RELATION TO MARTIN BUBER'S IDEA OF JEWISH RENEWAL

Gilya Gerda Schmidt

"Wir sind auf einer Mißion;
zur Bildung[1] der Erde sind wir berufen."
(Novalis, *Blütenstaub[2]*)

During a period of dissertation research at the Buber Archives in Jerusalem in the summer of 1988, I came across a manuscript, "Die deutsche Romantik in Briefen [German Romanticism in Letters],"[3] compiled by Martin Buber (1878-1965) during the period preceding August 1905.[4]

On August 15, 1905, Buber wrote a letter to an unidentified publisher, who apparently had requested to see a sample of the manuscript he was working on.[5] He sent a sampling of thirty-three letters, "which have been chosen in such a way that you can see from them my [overall] principle of selection."[6] Twenty-six of the thirty-three letters focused on personal mat-

---

1. The two-fold meaning of *Bildung* is education, but also formation. John Wallhausser, in a paper on Schleiermacher at the Naples Conference on Romantic Dialectic (1994), "Locating the Presence and the Activity of Love in Schleiermacher's Early Ethics," understood and translated the Novalis quote in the latter sense, "We are on a mission; we are called to form the earth." (5)
2. Novalis, "Blüthenstaub," in August Wilhelm Schlegel und Friedrich Schlegel, eds., *Athenaeum. Eine Zeitschrift* I/1 (Berlin: Friedrich Vieweg dem älteren, 1798; reprint ed. Darmstadt: Wissenschaftliche Buchgesellschaft, 1983), 80.
3. Jerusalem, Jewish National and University Library, Buber Archives: Ms. Var. 350 B/1.
4. I subsequently incorporated the manuscript into my dissertation, but only recently have I arrived at a more satisfying understanding of this collection. See my dissertation 1991, chapter V.
5. Ms. Var. 350 B/1, i.
6. Ibid. For organization, see ii.
    Confessions (1-4)
    Life Plans (5-7)
    Descriptions of ecstatic experiences (8-9)
    Intimate personal experiences (10-12)
    Personal feelings (13-14)
    Love letters (15-19)
    Friendship letters (20-26)
    Personal relationship with a group (27)
    Personal relationship with nature (28-29)

ters of the heart, such as love and life, and only seven dealt with the world at large.[7] These letters, which "have never been published in a book for the general public, not even the tiniest selection," were gleaned from a total of 500 that Buber had amassed from a variety of published and unpublished sources.[8] Although Buber promised the manuscript of the Romantic letters by the end of September 1905 – six weeks hence – no publication ever took place.

Personal relationship to art (30-31)
Personal relationship to religion (32)
Personal relationship to one's own times (33).

7.   Ibid., 1.
     1. Friedrich Schlegel an seinen Bruder August Wilhelm (21.XI.1792.)
     2. Bettine Brentano an F. H. Jacobi (15.X.1808.)
     3. Clemens Brentano an Ph. O. Runge (21.I.1810.)
     4. Karoline von Fouque an Rahel Levin (1812.)
     5. Friedrich Schlegel an Novalis (2.XII.1798.)
     6. Heinrich von Kleist an Wilhelmine von Zeuge (10.X.1801.)
     7. Bettine Brentano an Karoline v. Günderode.
     8. Ludwig Tieck an Wackenroder. (12.VI.1792.)
     9. Hölderlin an Boehlendorf (2.XII.1802.)
     10. Franz von Baader an Fr. H. Jacobi (24.II.1799.)
     11. Heinrich von Kleist an seine Schwester Ulrike(1.VI.1802.)
     12. Justinus Kerner an Uhland (Mai 1809.)
     13. Hölderlin an Neuffer (10.VI.1796.)
     14. Caroline Schlegel an Goethe (26.XI.1800.)
     15. Caroline Schlegel an Schelling (März 1801.)
     16. Clemens Brentano an Karoline v. Günderode   (Frühling 1802.)
     17. Schleiermacher an Eleonore Grunow (Juni 1802.)
     18. Friedrich Creuzer an Karoline v. Günderode   (1.XI.1804.)
     19. Karoline v. Gunderode an Friedrich Creuzer   (November 1805.)
     20. Wackenroder an Tieck (Antwort of Nr. 8;15.VI.1792.)
     21. Novalis an Friedrich Schlegel (Frühling 1793.)
     22. Karoline v. Günderode an Bettine Brentano.
     23. Clemens Brentano an Karoline v. Günderode   (2.VI.1804.)
     24. Clemens Brentano an Bettine.
     25. Bettine an Tieck (3.X.1809)
     26. Clemens Brentano an Rahel Levin (1.VII.1813.)
     27. Dorothea Veit an Schleiermacher (28.XII.1799.)
     28. Joseph von Görres an seine Braut (13.IV.1800.)
     29. Achim von Arnim an die Graefin Schlitz (Juli 1802.)
     30. Henrich Steffens an Caroline Schlegel (26.VII.1799.)
     31. Tieck an Runge (24.II.1804.)
     32. Novalis an Just (26.XII.1798.)
     33. Zehn Landshuter Studenten an Görres (22.VIII.1808.)
8.   Ibid., Intro, 2.

The reason for this has been a point of fascination to me for a number of years. Why would Buber take time out of his very busy schedule to select 500 letters from "a total of many thousand,"[9] a very time-consuming task, and obviously negotiate with a publisher, only to abandon the project without another word? To my knowledge, no answer has ever been given.[10]

Here it might be useful to look at these letters in the context of Buber's overall life. Born in Vienna and raised in a tri-cultural environment, Buber was no stranger to German culture.[11] In fact, he had grown up with Schiller and Goethe as much as with Judaism in Polish Galicia. Upon graduation from the Polish *Gymnasium* in Lvov (Lemberg) in 1896, one of the first issues he became involved with was the nature of contemporary Viennese literature. The neo-Romantic whom he took to task – in Polish – for his Wertherian inwardness was Hugo von Hofmannsthal.[12] It was Buber's conviction at this time that German culture would benefit from a return to the ideals of true Romanticism. His complaint with neo-Romanticism was its decadent character – all the ills of the *fin-de-siècle* with none of the benefits of progress for humanity.

At first, Buber strove with all the fervor of a young Romantic for the reformation of German culture on the model of the original Romantics. Although he was committed to the idea of renewal, his own life took him along a two-pronged path, reminding one of Faust's two souls, which influenced his own evolution in a major way.[13]

One path led to German higher education. Between 1897 and 1904, Buber sampled offerings in philosophy, literary criticism, psychology, and art history at the universities of Vienna, Leipzig, Berlin, and Zurich.[14] This path allowed him to continue his intellectual criticism of German culture and examine the sources of earlier periods such as the Italian Renaissance as well. The studies culminated in a 1904 dissertation on the concept of individuation

---

9. Ibid., iv.
10. At this very time, Buber was also collecting "ecstatic confessions" for a book that he finally published in 1909. See Martin Buber, *Ecstatic Confessions*, ed. Paul Mendes-Flohr, trans. Esther Cameron (San Francisco: Harper & Row, 1985).
11. Avraham Shapira, "Buber's Attachment to Herder and German 'Volkism'," in *Studies in Zionism* 14/1 (Tel Aviv: Frank Cass Publishers, 1993), 1-30.
12. William M. Johnston, "Martin Buber's Literary Debut: 'On Viennese Literature' (1897)," *German Quarterly* 47 (November 1974), 556-66.
13. Shapira, "Buber's Attachment," 1. "Buber's influence must be understood against the background of the polarities which shaped his outlook: the tension that existed between his desire to strike roots in a central European milieu, on the one hand, and the search for his origins, on the other."
14. See appendix in my book, *Martin Buber's Formative Years: From German Culture to Jewish Renewal 1897-1909* (University: University of Alabama Press, 1995).

in two Christian theologians, Nicolas of Cusa (1401-1464) and Jakob Böhme (1575-1624).[15] Buber's interest in and dissatisfaction with the nature of *fin-de-siècle* individualism led him to reject the contemporary secular basis of society and directed him towards a model of humanity based in the metaphysics of the pre-Enlightenment world. Contemporary individualism would not do; modernity needed to reconnect with the Source of all life.

This was a conviction that already had been shared by the German Romantics a century earlier; they had sought out medieval Catholicism for its intensity and venerated the Virgin Mary in a new key. In fact, to Buber's mind, Friedrich Schleiermacher's (1768-1834) notion of religion epitomized the relationship between God and God's Creation,[16] despite the fact that Schleiermacher's opinion of Judaism was at best low, most notably explained with his oft-quoted statement that Judaism is "a dead religion."[17] Here one must remember that Buber's own opinion of the Jewish ritual concurred with Schleiermacher. He, too, saw the tradition as a fossil to be abolished or renewed, a position that brought him criticism and enemies. He stated:

> Ever since the destruction of the Temple, tradition has been at the center of Judaism's religious life. A fence was thrown around the law in order to keep at a distance everything alien or dangerous; but very often it kept at a distance living religiosity as well. To be sure, . . . religiosity needs forms; . . . But when, instead of uniting them for freedom in God, religion keeps men tied to an immutable law and damns their demand for freedom; . . . then religion no longer shapes but enslaves religiosity.[18]

---

15. Buber dissertation, Jerusalem, Jewish National and University Library, Buber Archives: Ms. Var. 350 A/2. This treatise was originally planned as part of a history of the concept of individuation from Aristotle to Leibniz which was, however, never written.
16. In his dissertation he wrote, "Cusa and Böhme are two of the founders of the more recent metaphysical individualism. They were authentic philosophical representatives of their [respective] epochs, whose desire for personality was described so convincingly by Wilhelm Dilthey. They were two of the first thinkers who formed the *transcendental foundation of the very personality ethics* [emphasis mine] which found its most ideally harmonious expression in Schleiermacher and its most convincing literary expression with Emerson [1803-1882]." Ms. Var. 350 A-2, 2.
17. Amy Newman, "The Death of Judaism in German Protestant Thought from Luther to Hegel," in *Journal of the American Academy of Religion* LXI/3 (Fall 1993), 455-484. See also Joseph W. Pickle, "Schleiermacher on Judaism," in *The Journal of Religion* 60 (1980), 115-137. Pickle observes that "Schleiermacher's knowledge of Judaism seems, if not limited to, at least strongly colored by the perspectives of the Haskalah-influenced community in which he moved." (137)
18. This is only one of many instances where Buber takes issue with traditional religion. "Jewish Religiosity," in *On Judaism*, ed. Nahum N. Glatzer (New York: Schocken Books Inc., 1967), 91-2.

However, Buber's hope for a renewal of the Jewish spirit and therewith the Jewish people matched that of Schleiermacher and his friends for the German spirit and the German people. It is here, I believe, that the crux of the problem lies concerning the Romantic manuscript. While Schleiermacher and the Romantic circle focused only on a revival of the German Christian spirit, Buber was interested in adapting their methods of renewal for the German Jewish spirit. This seems an illicit appropriation of German *Kulturgut*. But Buber did not think so. As a citizen of the Hapsburg Empire, he was a proud cultural German. It was also his literature and his culture that now was going to help him revive the people who had given so much to German culture and, in the process, had become strangers to themselves.

In his letter to the publisher, Buber announced his intent to spend time in Florence and Rome that Fall and Spring (1906) collecting material for a similar book on the Italian Renaissance.[19] Buber did spend the following year in Italy, but the book whose manuscript he finished in Florence is the tale of one Rabbi Nachman of Brazlav, last master of eighteenth-century Polish Hasidism. Buber dedicated *Rabbi Nachman of Brazlav* to his grandfather, Salomon Buber, a midrash scholar, whom he called "the last master of the Haskalah."[20] It is clear that Buber's change in plans is of the utmost importance. Polish Hasidism is certainly not the Italian Renaissance, nor is it German Romanticism.

Perhaps it would be helpful here to understand what Buber hoped to gain with the publication of the Romantic letters. In his letter to the publisher he stressed that "the purpose of the collection is not literary history in the usual sense."[21] He had no intention of joining those who had produced numerous philological studies on the period, such an intent was "*a priori* foreign" to his project.[22] Because there was a renewed interest in Romanticism in his time, and because he was frustrated that neo-Romanticism was taken to be the real thing, Buber wished "to present the Romantic soul in its originality,"[23] "to illustrate the uniqueness of the Romantics' personal and communal life."[24] He planned to choose only that which was "the greatest and most powerful, the most deeply personal, that which is most psychologically revealing. Needless to say, this does not coincide with the famous and

---

19. Ms. Var. 350 B/1, iv.
20. See the inside cover of Martin Buber, *Die Geschichten des Rabbi Nachman* (Frankfurt a.M.: Rütten und Löning, 1906).
21. Ms. Var. 350 B/1,, i.
22. Ibid., Intro, 1.
23. Ibid.
24. Ibid., i.

noted."[25] The famous as well as the unknown were to share the pages of his book, particularly some of the "wonderful female natures," who were not in a position to influence the public through their literature, "yet expressed beautiful and powerful words about their time to their intimate circle, wanting to be only themselves."[26] The point would be "to extract from these quiet dialogues the most important, the permanent, and to combine these simple and heartrendering confessions into a composite: German Romanticism in letters."[27] In his view, these letters truly reveal the essence of the German Romantic personalities, "with all their contradictions, iniquities, and precisely for that reason in their true humanity."[28] Hence, he would produce "a picture of the inner life of the Romantic period through their most intimate, direct, and original expressions."[29]

The book, in the form of an epistolary novel, with pictures "of the most important personalities," that are, "with few exceptions completely unknown,"[30] was to affect a broad reading public "as an essential . . . complement to the works by the Romantics and on Romanticism, and as a self-contained work." Historical and biographical material would be appended as necessary.[31]

From the introduction to the collection we may discern that Buber intended to juxtapose the total baring of the Romantic soul with the literary efforts of the Romantics in which he was not interested, because they hardly ever "exceed the fragmentary."[32] The Romantic struggle for form hindered their spontaneous expression; "only in letters were they able to express their naked humanity."[33] This humanity, "in its purity and authenticity," was their true greatness, and the letters, in turn, represented "the most beautiful and significant document of the period."[34] It is important to note that he insisted

---

25. Ibid., Intro, 1.
26. Ibid., Intro, 2.
27. Ibid.
28. Ibid., i.
29. Ibid., ii.
30. Ibid., Intro, 2.
31. Ibid., iii.
32. Ibid., Intro, 1.
33. Ibid.
34. Ibid.

on the exclusion of "all scientific apparatus,"[35] even the introduction was to merely set the scene. It is a fact that Martin Buber's relationship to German culture and to Judaism was a complicated one. He sincerely believed that, at least for him, a German-Jewish symbiosis existed.[36] Hence, he was fully German and fully Jewish. Most Germans had no problem with that. At least from 1906 on, when his books on Hasidism started to appear, Buber was as revered by Germans and Europeans in general as were other spiritual leaders of the time. This was also true of young Zionists, all over Europe, mostly students, who saw him almost as a latter-day prophet.[37] But the rabbis, in particular, found much to criticize. As a result, Buber was the man of the hour, for Gentiles and for Zionists, but not for traditional Jews.

German culture had long been Buber's treasured ideal for European Jewry. In his effort to ready his fellow Zionists for cultural autonomy as a people, Buber looked to German culture's ways and achievements. He was particularly impressed with the ways of the German Romantics: their strong

---

35. Ibid., Intro, 2. Included in the manuscript is an index of all 500 letters. Buber gave twenty-seven categories, using for his sources published works either of the individuals or by secondary authors. Thus, he used a posthumous collection of Novalis' writings; Franz von Baader's posthumous publications; Jacobi's posthumous works; Runge's posthumous writings; as well as secondary works on Friedrich Creuzer and Karoline von Günderode; Varnhagen's portrait of Rahel, written after her death; a work on Dorothea Schlegel and her sons; a biography of Hölderlin's by Litzmann; a collection of friendship letters by E.T.A. Hoffmann; correspondence of Justinus Kerner and his friends; Kleist's letters to his sister Ulrike; Kleist's letters to his fiancee; a collection of Friedrich Schlegel's letters to his brother August Wilhelm by Walzel; a collection of 300 letters by Holtei; and Schuddekopf's and Walzel's *Goethe and Romanticism*. Each source contains a list of letters with correspondent and addressee, the date of the letter, and the page number. This in spite of the fact that Buber had noted that all scientific apparatus would be avoided. One might note that he had the scientific apparatus *completed* before he even knew whether the volume would be published.
36. Shapira, "Buber's Attachment," 30. "It should be pointed out that in his deep involvement in German culture, which reached its apex in his positing a symbiosis between it and Jewish culture, Buber cannot be considered an exception. Within the milieu of self-identified German-Jewry both groups and individuals alike, including the religious, often went to great lengths to conceive of their heritage in terms of the culture of their habitat. . . . he [Buber] was untiring in his attempts to bring together the Romantic spirit and the questions and problems of his time. The entire thought and legacy of this indefatigable bridge builder bears the imprint of polar opposites and the tension between them."
37. Shapira, "Buber's Attachment," 6. "Although the room was packed with people, you entered at the head of a group of young people, especially young women, through a side entrance. The whole group sat down in the first row which apparently was reserved for you. Your black beard, your slow and serious gait, your walking in front of a group, like some *tzadik* leading his chassidim, prompted me to ask the student seated next to me – a blond Aryan – who was this person, and he replied that this Jew was a founder of a new religious sect."

personalities, their creative approaches, their originality, their uncon-
ventional ideas, their spirituality, their knack for synthesis and love of community. The proposed psychological study was to guide his fellow Zionists toward
a new personal and communal self in a land on distant shores that resembled
the Faustian vision and had been expressed in Theodor Herzl's *Altneuland*
(1902).[38] There was only one problem: for six years, since 1898, Buber had
been intensely involved in Zionist organization and ideology-shaping. Despite his love for German culture, his Jewish activities had worked on his
Jewish self, gradually transforming him. Buber was himself being renewed by
his work, without his being aware of it. He now transferred his commitment
to German cultural renewal to his own people, thereafter dedicating his
whole life to Jewish spiritual renewal instead.

We have not yet looked at the second path – Buber's extensive work in
Jewish renewal. By forming a Zionist chapter in Leipzig in 1898, Buber involved himself in organizational and publicity work for the World Zionist
Organization. He was a delegate to the annual congress from 1898 on; he
joined committees and chaired them and became active in policy matters as
well. Still a student, he traveled extensively for the cause. He also employed
his creative genius to awaken the people to a new day by writing poems,
translating short stories (primarily from Yiddish), and writing and speaking
widely on Zionism. By 1900, he was well-known in Zionist circles. Theodor
Herzl was impressed with the enthusiasm of his young colleague and, in 1901,
offered him the editorship of the Zionist newspaper *Die Welt*. Now Buber
was in a position not only to publish his own work, which he did liberally, but
also to serve as a promoter for other authors and artists as well. At the Fifth
Zionist Congress (1901), Buber organized the first art exhibit ever of Jewish
art, and truly fought like a lion of Judah for the inclusion of Zionist culture as
an intrinsic part of the Zionist platform. The Jüdische Verlag in Berlin,
founded by Buber and some friends in 1901, published journals and books on
Zionist culture that did much to spread the good news to far corners of the
world. In 1902, Buber and Chaim Weizmann,[39] later first president of the

---

38. Theodor Herzl (1860-1904), creator of modern political Zionism and first president of
the World Zionist Organization, which he founded in 1897. In 1896, he published a pamphlet, *Der Judenstaat* [The Jews' State], and in 1902, a sequel, *Altneuland* [Oldnewland],
further spelled out the romantic realization of his dream, much of which came true.

39. Chaim Weizmann (1874-1952), Russian-born leading Zionist politician and statesman. A
chemist who lived in England and helped the British in the war effort (WWI), he was instrumental in the Balfour Declaration of 1917, which promised the Jews a national home
in Palestine. He was president of the World Zionist Organization from 1920 to 1931 and
1935 to 1946.

state of Israel, together with their good friend Berthold Feiwel,[40] drew up plans for a Jewish college. Buber complained several times during these years that his efforts totally exhausted him.

It was this constituency of young Zionists, as well as the larger German-reading public in Europe, who were to be the beneficiaries of the Romantic letters, as they also comprised his readership of Chinese and Finnish folktales and Hasidic tales. In Buber's mind, the environment that produced early Zionism paralleled that of Schleiermacher and the Schlegels, Novalis and the Grimms. His friends and colleagues, with whom he had shared failures and successes over the past six years, were to receive instruction in how to renew themselves as Jews, on the model of the German Romantics.

Yet Buber's very choice of imagery also implied another connection. In 1900, Micha Josef Berdichevsky (1865-1921) had first characterized Zionist culture as *jungjüdisch*, a term difficult to translate, but perhaps best rendered as "young Judaic." It became the watchword of Zionist culture and the movement for Jewish renewal. At this time, this term was in the air in Vienna, because of the *Jung Wien* literary movement to which Hugo von Hofmannsthal (1874-1929), Hermann Bahr (1863-1934), Arthur Schnitzler (1862-1931), Peter Altenberg (1859-1919), and, a little later, also Stefan Zweig (1881-1942) belonged. *Jung Wien*, in turn, modeled itself on Heinrich Heine's *Jungdeutschland* movement, which developed as a response to decadent late Romanticism in the 1830s. Buber and his cultured Zionist friends actually shared the critical views of *Jungdeutschland* and *Jung Wien*, yet these movements were not the inspiration he sought. Their ideas would have been appropriate had he wished to reform German society, as Jung Wien hoped to reform Austria. But Buber was interested in a Jewish awakening, an authentic revival of the Jewish spirit, and his model extraordinaire was that of the German Romantics, who also had been a first after a long period of rationalism. Because of his intense involvement with the Jewish renewal movement, Buber became progressively more passionate for his people, their history, their customs, and their Bible, though not traditional religion. While he continued to admire Schleiermacher and his circle in their daring autonomy, the dilemma consisted in the inherent incompatibility of German Romantic ideals and Jewish cultural goals. It was not Schleiermacher's transcendental idealism that had lost currency, but Romantic narcissism.

In this paper, I am basically arguing that there are two types of Romanticism: the German Romanticism of Schleiermacher's time and what Buber

---

40. Berthold Feiwel (1875-1937), a German Jew, worked closely with Buber on a number of Zionist ventures, such as the Zionist newspaper, *Die Welt*, the Democratic Fraction (an opposition branch to Herzl), and the Jüdische Verlag.

called "Romantic Zionism." During his student years, Buber had studied Romanticism as well as the Italian Renaissance. He saw these movements as genuine efforts at national rebirth. Hence they belonged in the same category with Zionism, which Buber called "the conscious will of a national movement for Jewish renewal."[41] *After* I had completed this paper for the Naples conference in the summer of 1994, I happened by chance on another manuscript at the Buber Archives in Jerusalem. It was a draft of a 1918 speech entitled, "Romantic Zionism."[42] This speech analyzes two types of Romanticism: one is associated with the Italian Renaissance, the other with Zionism.

Criticizing those who disparage "Zionism as Romanticism," Buber does not deny that Zionism is Romanticism. Rather he defends Romantic Zionism as good because of its profundity.[43] In Romanticism, *Bildung* is an elevation and refinement of the personality. In Zionism, *Bildung* is much more of a construction and formation from raw material, from the bottom up. According to Buber, Jews can be proud of such basic thoughts as "Home is a garden, no matter its condition." It doesn't matter that the garden isn't perfect, what matters is having a garden at all, because "it is the basis of all true productivity."[44] Already in 1902, Buber had published an essay, "Die Schaffenden, das Volk und die [*zionistische*] Bewegung [The Productive Ones, the People, and the Zionist Movement],"[45] in which he outlined the relationship between Jewish productivity and rootedness. Comparing the Jewish people to a statue that had shattered, he asserted that only "the artist who created it" can make this statue whole.[46] For the Jewish people, this artist is "the soil of the homeland."[47] And the memory of the past, perpetuated for two thousand years, provides the vision for the future. On the example of the Italian Renaissance that reconnected "with the great *Urzeit* of the Italian people: the culture of the period, its works, its values, its life forms," Zionism also "must connect to the great *Urzeit* of our people; we too must reach for the hands of our ancestors over centuries and eons." After all, "The powers of our land created the powers of our soul, where else could we go to renew our soul?"[48] Where else indeed.

41. See "Renaissance und Bewegung," in *Die Jüdische Bewegung* (1916), 108.
42. Jerusalem, The Jewish National and University Library, Buber Archives: Ms. Var. 350 L/17.
43. Ibid., 1.
44. Ibid., 4.
45. See Die Jüdische Bewegung (1916), 68-77.
46. Ms. Var. 350 L/17, 6.
47. Ibid., 5.
48. Ibid.

But, and here comes the rub which also holds for German Romanticism, because of the two-thousand-year absence from the land, it is *not* the same type of connecting as in the Italian Renaissance. Buber asserted that "our task is more difficult, more profound." While the Italians [and the Germans] could afford to "play on the surface, we have to mine the darkest depths." While "the Italians [and the Germans] wanted to make their life greater, richer, more beautiful, we [on the other hand] want to once more have a life at all." While "the Italians [and the Germans] wanted to become stronger, we want to heal our wounds." While "the Italians [and the Germans] wanted to become freer, we want to *free ourselves* from the yoke of being the stranger."[49]

Buber concluded his dialectical juxtaposing of the two kinds of Romanticism with his favorite Faustian image: "We must *descend to the mothers*, we must descend to the powers who gave birth to values, works, and forms." For Jews, these powers can be found only in the land of Israel. But, alas, because of the long absence from the land, "we must struggle with the land in the way that Jacob struggled with God."[50] Once the land has blessed the Jews anew, they will be under its spell, hence able to draw on its powers.

The Romanticism of the Italian Renaissance and of German Romanticism provided Buber with examples of great efforts at national renewal. Buber recognized the importance of Romantic originality, spontaneity, and intensity, but he also realized that the Zionist struggle, while Romantic, was on a different level from the two models at hand. He cautioned: "Let us not make the difficult easy and dwarf that which is great."[51] It was the task of the Zionists to free themselves not only from the outer exile, but from self-alienation as a people as well.[52] Buber thought to hold up Romantic efforts as the shining example. To see why it couldn't work, we need to compare the Romantic manuscript with the Zionist reality. Overall, the manuscript provided a model for the authentic human being's struggle for survival. The focus was to be on the process – fighting adversity, coping with disappointment and disillusionment, and making an effort at a new beginning. Because the Romantics were not merely introspective, as the mystics were, the letters were particularly helpful in eavesdropping on the process. Here individuals communicated their innermost feelings to their friends. This willingness to reveal themselves, to share their life experiences, forged an authentic human bond in the form of friendship.

---

49. Ibid., 7. Emphasis is Buber's.
50. Ibid. Israel means 'one who struggled with God.'
51. Ibid.
52. Ibid., 8.

Yet immediately we run into a problem. Studying something old to create something new is traditional in literate cultures, including and especially Judaism. Buber wanted to provide his contemporaries with the opportunity to study the process of community-making from the letters. Yet study leads to reflection, not to deed. Is the deed that follows from study still spontaneous?

The very reality of the past six years had shown Buber a different way. A need to organize the enthusiasts had arisen spontaneously and many Jews, among them Buber and his friends, had accepted the challenge. Zionism had created a new community on the spur of the moment like the Romantic circle a century earlier. Would there be any point in studying the model after the fact?

The second problem that the Romantics debated had to do with the "live" nature of letters. Can dead letters replicate living dialogue? Are letters only "murky vessels for the golden wine of friendship"[53] as Friedrich Hölderlin (1770-1843), the poet of madness, complained to a friend. Is written communication one-dimensional and therefore only second-best, as Ludwig Tieck (1773-1853) lamented? Or could the importance of the words bring the "lifeless nature of the letter" to life?[54]

With the creation of worldwide Zionist chapters and the Zionist Congress, personal encounter replaced exclusive letter-writing. Meeting on a monthly basis locally, semi-annually at regional meetings, and annually at the international congress, Jews from the far corners of the world were able to establish a truly living dialogue, leaving the medium of letter-writing to those unfortunate ones who had to stay home.[55]

The Romantic concern was first and foremost with the philosophy of art. Friedrich Schlegel (1772-1829) published a fragment on universal philosophy [*Universalphilosophie*] in the literary journal *Athenaeum* (1798-1800). This

---

53. Ms. Var. 350 B/1, letter #13, June 10, 1796.
54. Ibid., letter #20, June 15, 1792 to Tieck. Wackenroder here touched on an important concern of the Romantics. German has two words for letter: *Buchstaben* are letters of the alphabet, and a *Brief* is a piece of correspondence. Hence, the implication in English is made explicit: everything to do with letters of the alphabet has the potential to be lifeless, which includes not only correspondence, but all books as well. Here it is especially revealing in connection with sacred texts, which the Zionists rejected for the spontaneous experience. Only life is a truly living work.
55. Michael Berkowitz, *Zionist Culture and West European Jewry Before the First World War* (New York: Cambridge University Press, 1993). Berkowitz writes: "In addition, the notion that all Zionists were friends, heightened in the Congress days . . . . 'We embraced and kissed each other,' reported one of the accounts of Die Welt. "We didn't know who. But then again, we already knew that we were brothers. And after we embraced and kissed each other again, we introduced ourselves. Upon saying our names, we kissed another time, as we were friends." (19)

aphorism highlighted synthesis, the most famous of romantic criteria, and became the watchword of romantic art.

Romantic poetics are progressive universalistic poetics. It is not only their function to reunite all differentiated genres of poetics, and to put poetics in touch with philosophy and rhetoric, but also to mix, even fuse poetics and prose, genius and criticism, art poetics and naive poetics, *to make poetics alive and social, and life and society poetic* [emphasis mine], to poeticize wit, and to fill and satiate art forms with substantive educational material of every kind, and to inspire them through humorous stimuli. [Romantic poetics] comprise everything poetic – from the most elaborate system of art consisting of several systems, to the sigh, the kiss, which the poeticizing child exhales in unartificed song.[56]

Romantic personal renewal resulted from the realization of the philosophical ideal through art against the odds of life. However, in reality, it was much more likely that a work of art was not completed because the artist lacked peace of mind. Dorothea Veit (1763-1839), who later became Friedrich Schlegel's wife, wrote to their friend Schleiermacher that "Now he [Schlegel] is working on the second part of *Lucinde*, as he tells me, but he isn't free and carefree as he should be. It is terrible that his worries keep him from working instead of encouraging him."[57] And detain him they did; *Lucinde* was never finished.

As we see from the example of Karoline von Günderode (1780-1806), the artist often fled from life into art, because life was so painful. Karoline dedicated herself to her poetry and sacrificed her personal happiness. Friedrich Creuzer (1771-1858) responded to her feeling "so poor in the midst of wealth." He admonished that she couldn't have it both ways. Either she could become a mother and renounce her poetry or the other way around. In

---

56. Translation Mine. The original German reads: "Die romantische Poesie . . . ist eine progressive Universalpoesie. Ihre Bestimmung ist nicht bloß, alle getrennten Gattungen der Poesie wieder zu vereinigen, und die Poesie mit der Philosophie und Rhetorik in Berührung zu setzen. Sie will, und soll auch Poesie und Prosa, Genialität und Kritik, Kunstpoesie und Naturpoesie bald mischen, bald verschmelzen, die Poesie lebendig und gesellig, und das Leben und die Gesellschaft poetisch machen, den Witz poetisieren, und die Formen der Kunst mit gediegenem Bildungsstoff jeder Art anfüllen und sättigen, und durch die Schwingungen des Humors beseelen. Sie umfaßt alles, was nur poetisch ist, vom größten wieder mehre Systeme in sich enthaltenden Systeme der Kunst, bis zu dem Seufzer, dem Kuß, den das dichtende Kind aushaucht in kunstlosen Gesang." (August Wilhelm Schlegel und Friedrich Schlegel, eds., *Athenaeum. Eine Zeitschrift* 1/2 (Berlin: Friedrich Vieweg dem älteren, 1798; reprint ed. Darmstadt: Wissenschaftliche Buchgesellschaft, 1983), 204-205.

57. Ms. Var. 350 B/1, letter #27 (October 28, 1799).

Creuzer's view, one enters the paradise of poetry "only through renunciation.
. . . Your mystical nature wants to have a heaven, wants to immerse itself into
the ocean of blessedness, wants to be fulfilled with love, wants to receive everything that you give." Yet that could not be. "The mother belongs to a
home . . . the maiden [however] glides above the clouds, eternally free and
eternally young."[58] The only way she could now consummate the relationship was through art. This sublimation of feelings sprang from the renunciation associated with Christianity, and one could say that art in fact took the
place of religion in the life of some of the Romantics.

While Romanticism proceeded from an idea, Zionism evolved from the
necessity of life. Fledgling Zionist art in the form of poems, music, etchings,
paintings, and sculpture by individuals such as Buber, Ephraim Lilien (1874-
1925), Hermann Struck (1876-1944), Alfred Nossig (1864-1943), Berthold
Feiwel, Lesser Ury (1861-1931) and others resulted from personal renewal,
not the other way around.

Narcissism seemed to poison the very air of *fin-de-siècle* culture. Heinrich Kleist's (1777-1811) essay, "Das Marionettentheater," which was written
a century earlier as a criticism of his contemporaries, inspired Buber to write
a poem, "An Narcissus,"[59] that warned his young Judaic contemporaries not
to go the way of Narcissus. Unlike Kleist's essay, which was written after the
fact, it was not a critique of an existing state. After all, Emancipation had
only just occurred (1871).

Narcissism was related to the secular nature of German culture. After
much study of *secularism*, Buber concluded that humanity needed to return to
a metaphysical foundation for life that drew on Divine bounty, not on human
bankruptcy. He complained that *Bildung* had lost its powerful influence on
the shaping of personality, and culture became confused with [utilitarian]
civilization.[60] Buber found evidence of earlier struggles in the life of the
Romantics. At a time of increasing secularization, the Romantics also tried
to turn the tide towards spiritualization, much as Buber tried to do later, yet
the form that such a turn might take was not yet clear, much less the
roadmap or "bible" for it.

Friedrich Schlegel already had recognized what Buber stressed over and
over, namely that magic had long been taken out of organized religion, of
traditional Judaism and of Christianity. Thus, many different feelers had to
be put out to see in what true religion might consist. In a letter to Novalis

---

58. Ibid., letter #18 (November 1, 1804).
59. "An Narcissus," in *Jahresbericht der Lese- und Redehalle jüdischer Hochschüler in Wien
über das Vereinsjahr 1901*, Vienna, 1901, 17.
60. "Alte und Neue Gemeinschaft," Jerusalem, Jewish National and University Library, Buber Archives: Ms. Var. 350 B/47.

dated December 2, 1798, he revealed plans for "a bible which is not a specific Bible, not like *the* Bible, but very literally and in every sense of the meaning bible, the very first work of art of this kind."[61] He thought that the Judaic and Christian Bibles imitated nature and were not an independent creation of the human spirit. But in his time, such a Bible was no longer sufficient: "My biblical project is no literary project, but a biblical one, one that is absolutely religious. . . . I am thinking of forming a new religion or rather, to herald it, for it will come and be victorious without me. . . . The new religion will be entirely magic.[62]

Both – the Romantics and Buber – were indebted to the mystical inspiration of Jakob Böhme (1575-1624). A strange, surrealistic letter from Clemens Brentano (1778-1842) to Karoline von Günderode in the Spring of 1802 provides much food for thought. Brentano actually indicated his wish to re-create himself in Karoline, or to fuse the two in such a way that his blood would flow in her veins and vice versa. He desired to both kill and re-create her.[63] Clearly afraid of his strange moods, Brentano pleaded with Karoline to "love me, if you can," and to write him "very level-headed letters": "Weep only because you are not with me in the flesh, but only in thought, for both are one, and only in the communion do we enjoy God, for all words must become flesh, this word of love as well."[64] Brentano fused secular,

---

61. Ms. Var. 350, B/1, letter #5, December 2, 1798.
62. Ibid. John Neubauer, *Novalis* (Boston: Twayne Publishers, 1980), 56. Compare section on "The Book," in which Neubauer explains that "The romantic belief in a 'book of all books' is rooted in the mystic and cabalistic traditions. . . . Novalis' encyclopedia project grew in an intimate symbiosis with Friedrich Schlegel's vision of a 'progressive Universalpoesie' that would reunite the literary genres, use philosophy and literature, and saturate the arts with "all kinds of learning." Contemplation of an encyclopedic book "led to reflections about the Bible, the archetypal book of the Judeo-Christian tradition: if the universe was to be encapsulated in a book, the Bible was the proper model." Neubauer continues: "Friedrich Schlegel and Novalis arrived independently at this conclusion, but they embarked upon quite dissimilar Bible projects. Schlegel had a literally religious project in mind, a modern Bible in service of a new religion, while he correctly observed that Novalis' project was more literary." Neubauer concludes that "Novalis came to regard the Bible as the ideal of all books while studying science and its embodiment in books, but his account makes the artistic interest evident: 'The fully developed theory of the Bible will yield the theory of writing or word-construction in general,' and this, in turn, will contain the 'symbolic, indirect doctrine of construction for the creative mind.'"
63. Ms. Var. 350, B/1, letter #16, Spring 1802. "Good night! Dear Angel! Whether you are or aren't, open the veins in your white body, so that the hot, frothing blood gushes from a thousand gorgeous fountains, this is how I want to see and drink you, until I am intoxicated and can cry over your death with madness, weep back into you all your blood and my blood through tears, until your heart once again begins to beat and you trust me because my blood beats in your pulse."
64. Ibid.

physical love with the idea of the holy communion in Catholicism, eating
Christ's body is transferred to Karoline and drinking Christ's blood likewise
– a very unchurchly, even cannibalistic, view, though not entirely in conflict
with Jakob Böhme. "Spiritual corporality" [*Geistleiblichkeit*] can indeed be
traced back to Böhme, to Novalis, and to Romantic mystics such as Franz
von Baader.[65] Brentano wanted to become Karoline's redeemer by ex-
changing her blood for his, and she, in turn, was to become his by taking on
redeemer qualities like those of Christ for the believing Christian.

Despite Schleiermacher's closeness to the Romantic circle, his appropriation of Böhme's thought differs much from that of Brentano and others.
Schleiermacher's concept of "absolute dependence," for which he has become most celebrated, would shrink from such surrealistic conceptions of
unio mystica. "Schleier," the simple, pietistic soul, communed with God in
the privacy of his heart and then proceeded to pursue his vocation. In his
famous work, *Speeches to the Cultured Despisers of Religion*, Schleiermacher
wrote: "I speak to you as a human being on the sacred mysteries of humanity
from my point of view, of that which was in me when I, in my youthful free-
thinking, searched for the unknown, and of that which is the innermost cata-
lyst of my being and which will forever remain the most important, no matter
how the tendencies of time and humanity change me."[66] Schleiermacher
tried to show his contemporaries that religion and life are not necessarily
divorced, because religion is not merely a dry system of dogmas, but a
personal concern for every human being – an ethical imperative. Religion is

---

65. Neubauer, *Novalis*, 110-2. Novalis' *Hymnen an die Nacht* also treated these images poeti-
cally. A case in point is the seventh hymn, which Neubauer translates as follows: "But
whoever has sucked from hot, beloved lips the breath of life, whose heart melted in quiv-
ering waves under holy blaze, whose eyes opened to measure the unfathomable depth of
heaven, shall eat of his body and drink of his blood eternally." He explains that in this
passage "Several traditions come together," and that it is based on John VI:54 – 'he who
eats my flesh and drinks my blood has eternal life.' But Neubauer continues that the
"eroticism [of the passage] is perhaps more indebted to the 'Song of Songs,' where the
lover is often described as delicate food. Furthermore, the sensuality of these lines relies
on the notion of 'spiritual corporality' [*Geistleiblichkeit*] found in such mystics as Jakob
Böhme, Friedrich Christoph Oetinger, and Franz von Baader." By relating spiritual and
bodily needs, in Novalis' art "conjugal union and religious communion become
metaphoric equivalents, and the physical union of two lovers becomes the image of holy
communion . . . ."

66. Friedrich Schleiermacher, *Über die Religion. Reden an die Gebildeten unter ihren
Verächtern*, in *Schriften aus der Berliner Zeit 1796-1799*, ed. Günter Meckenstock,
Kritische Gesamtausgabe I/2, ed. Hans-Joachim Birkner et al. (Berlin/New York:
Walter de Gruyter, 1984), 190-191. Hereafter cited as "KGA I/2". All translations are
mine.

"only another name for all higher feelings and aspirations; religion is the poetry of the soul."[67] For Schleiermacher, contemplation of the universe was the basis of all spiritual life, for "the universe is mirrored in humanity's inner life."[68] This theory echoed Cusa and Böhme. Having lived and studied with the Pietists in Herrnhut, Schleiermacher understood that the private communion with God must become a public celebration of the spirit, because only in this public affirmation of private feelings can human individuation occur. In his fourth speech, Schleiermacher stated categorically, "When one has religion, it is of necessity social: this is not only intrinsic to the nature of the human being, but also most assuredly in the nature of religion."[69] Private feelings, which derive from man's *unio mystica* with God, translate into "personality ethics" that coincide with God's Will. Yet the individual can only realize God's Will and thereby him/herself in activity within the human community. What lastingly attracted Buber to Schleiermacher was precisely the simple pietist who was weaned on Herrnhut humility.

It is perhaps not altogether by accident that at the time of the Romantic manuscript, Buber was already well into completing the book on Rabbi Nachman, which was published in 1906.[70] The founder of this Jewish group of pietists, Israel Baal Shem Tov, the great-grandfather of Rabbi Nachman, was born the same year as Graf Zinzendorf, 1700. Yet not until Buber's efforts on behalf of Hasidism did this mystical counterpart to Zinzendorf find appreciation in the West. Buber's own fame as a zaddik (a righteous person) by Jews and Gentiles followed from his mediation of these tales to Western readers.

Death for the Romantics was often a coveted wish because life was so difficult and painful. Kleist wrote: "Life cannot give one a more exalted gift than the opportunity to dispose of it in grand style. . . . I have no other wish than to die when I have accomplished my goal."[71] Death was perceived as a welcome escape from the wheel of time. Bettine Brentano (1785-1859) encouraged her friend, Karoline von Günderode, not to "lose faith . . . In the fi-

67. "Schleiermacher, Friedrich Daniel Ernst," *Philosophical Encyclopedia* 1967/72, Vol. 7-8, 316-9.
68. Schleiermacher, KGA I/2, 227.
69. Schleiermacher, KGA I/2, 267.
70. See letter #63 from Buber to Gustav Landauer, from Florence, dated November 9, 1905. "I have now finished the volume of tales; it will be published early in 1906 by Rütten & Löning . . . ." in *The Letters of Martin Buber, A Life of Dialogue*, ed. Nahum N. Glatzer & Paul Mendes-Flohr, trans. Richard Clara Winston & Harry Zohn (New York: Schocken Books, 1991), 108.
71. Ms. Var. 350 B/1, letter #11, May 1, 1802. The goal was "a child, a beautiful poem, and a great deed." Of the three, he achieved only the poem.

nal moment, when the light threatens to disappear, it can flare up beautifully and strongly and cleanse life from all rubbish and soot."[72] So ultimately the challenge for the Romantics was having the courage to live and to cope with the adversities.

For Jews, *life* is the most treasured of human possessions. Since it is only lent to us by God, it is not really ours to do with as we please. Rather, we are admonished to care for and return our body to God at the end of life in as good a shape as possible. Suffering is to be accepted heroically. Hence, ideas of suicide have always been frowned upon, and the severest consequences have led to exclusion from burial in the Jewish cemetery.[73]

It is possible to enjoy the beauty of creation despite suffering. Although humanity's innocence was lost, Joseph Görres (1776-1848) conceded to his bride that, at times, nature evokes memories of that childhood and mediates a momentary state of perfection.[74] Hölderlin admonished his friend Neuffer, "Oh, be happy, dear brother! Without joy the eternal beauty in us cannot blossom fully."[75] And Achim von Arnim (1781-1831) expressed his pleasure in the beauty of life, whether on a mail ship between Frankfurt and Mainz or in the choir loft of an incense-drenched church.[76] Likewise, Henrich Steffens (1773-1845) wrote to Caroline Schlegel that a recent visit to the Dresden art gallery where he viewed Raphael's *Madonna* totally captivated his senses.[77]

In the Jewish community, joyful occasions such as life cycle events and holidays engender exuberant and intense family and community celebrations, precisely because the future is so uncertain. The young Zionists dancing around the bonfire, a *Wandervogel* image transported to the Mediterranean beach, has become the classic example of simple rejoicing.

One notes with interest, that none of the Romantic examples Buber chose are of this exuberant communal nature. Rather, *depression* was rampant among the German Romantics. Heinrich Wackenroder (1773-1853), one of the pure souls, implored his friend Tieck to treasure what God gave him, his life and his health: "I did not expect . . . your progress into this most terrible depression. You cause me deepest sadness."[78] Likewise,

---

72. Ibid., letter #7. Günderode committed suicide in 1806 and Bettine Brentano subsequently wrote an epistolary biography of her life. (Bettine von Arnim, *Die Günderode*, mit einem Essay von Christa Wolf [Leipzig: Insel, 1983].)
73. Nevertheless, over time many Jews committed suicide because of their desperate circumstances. This was often seen as an act of martyrdom by the community.
74. Ms. Var. 350 B/1, letter #28 (no date, but in index dated April 13, 1800).
75. Ibid., letter #13, June 10, 1796.
76. Ibid., letter #29, July 1802.
77. Ibid., letter #30, July 26, 1799.
78. Ibid., letter #20, June 15, 1792 to Tieck. "Tieck, an angel calls to you through me: Take care of yourself, be good to yourself, make yourself happy for the sake of your friends!"

Caroline Schlegel (1763-1809), married to August Wilhelm (1767-1845), wrote to Johann Wolfgang von Goethe (1749-1832), the German national poet, expressing concern for her brother-in-law, Friedrich, who was perhaps the more brilliant of the brothers, but also the less stable emotionally.[79] Caroline pleaded with Goethe to become "Schlegel's . . . guiding star. . . . I don't know anyone else in this world who could do it. . . . Your concern, your contact has frequently been a beacon which broke through the fog that enveloped him." Caroline hoped that the human bond between the two men would serve to extract Friedrich from his dark moods.

The Romantics were primarily concerned with self-perfection, while the Jews were historically concerned with survival, civil rights, and anti-semitism. Fighting for one's life and that of one's family – perhaps having been driven from one's home by the latest edict of the Czar, or excluded from higher education because of the *numerus clausus* – puts these Romantic problems as causes for depression in perspective. Traditionally there was only one event that deserved extended grieving and at least once a year loud wailing, and that was the destruction of the Temple in Jerusalem. But now, in this new time of optimism for a life of fulfillment in the land of Israel, even such traditional outpouring of grief seemed somewhat exaggerated.

Another cause for depression was *physical separation* from family and friends. Many a Romantic poem is dedicated to the woes of the stranger or *Fremdling*. The Romantic challenge lay precisely in the effort to turn oneself around in such a situation. Hölderlin revealed to his friend Neuffer how much he suffered by being separated from him.[80] Likewise, Bettine Brentano wrote to Tieck about the great void his departure had left in her life: "I thought to have overcome all the pain which distance and separation from my friends caused, but now I am sad all over, the map of Italy hangs on the wall above the armchair, it seems so empty, you are no longer here, so why should I see the country . . . ."[81] Her brother, Clemens Brentano, lamented that he had to live abroad: "I would be happy to live near or in my fatherland, but the inflation! Everything else is almost better for me in Frankfurt, also for Sophie, who needs a social life and fun, for enjoyment is her environment."[82]

---

79. Ibid., letter #14, November 26, 1800. "He has fallen into an emotional state which would do him in even if he had no intentions of complying."
80. Ibid., letter #13, June 10, 1796. He lamented, "Dear brother, if you only were with me, that our hearts could once again rejoice with each other." Only the personal intimacy of a hug would be "the true language for me!"
81. Ibid., letter #25, October 3, 1809.
82. Ibid., letter #23, June 2, 1804.

For the Romantics, happiness, even vicarious happiness, was crucial. Kleist wrote to his fiance, Wilhelmine von Zeuge that "to make others happy is the greatest happiness in this world. But it is difficult, when we ourselves are not happy, and others hope to find their happiness in ours."[83] Wackenroder queried of Tieck: "You didn't completely forget that you were once – many years ago – happy with me? Or do you remember that you used to laugh more than once in your lifetime?" Hoping to bring about a change in Tieck's dark mood with the memory of happy times, he dramatized: "Oh dear, oh dear! I would indeed like to wrap my best, my only friend into a black cape of mourning! For my friend is – unhappy . . . ."[84] Unhappiness is very much a *Fremdling* state, a sign of being estranged from the self. Then only mediated happiness can be achieved. Friedrich wrote to August Wilhelm: "Allow me to be happy through you, since I cannot be happy myself."[85]

For centuries, Jews throughout the world had suffered separation from family and friends by being shunted from place to place at the whim of the rulers, experiencing the cruelty of Russian conscription of young sons, as well as intolerant laws and related discrimination. With the advent of the Zionist movement, physical separation was the least of the deterrents to Jewish happiness. This was a great time of rejoicing, for now a movement was underway to unite the Jewish people in body and spirit in their ancient homeland. Yet fulfillment of an ideological dream is not necessarily happiness. The reality of the *chalutzim* (pioneers) brought with it serious subsistence tasks such as draining swamps, adapting seeds and livestock to the Middle Eastern climate, laying water lines, producing electricity, developing suitable building materials for the weather conditions and terrain and designing architecture for Mediterranean life. They were not gentleman farmers, as Kleist had wanted to be, but wrested a meager crop from the barren soil.[86]

Reality and the *ideal* in life were difficult to harmonize for the Romantics. They had grand ideas and ambitions to realize those dreams, yet they did not always succeed. Friedrich Schlegel, master of philosophical synthesis, agonized over the fact that the reality and the ideal in life could not be reconciled to one's satisfaction. This duality within made living a torture. He wrote to his brother, August Wilhelm: "I feel within me perpetual dissonance, and I must admit to myself that I am not a nice person. This often leads me to the deepest despair. I lack satisfaction with myself and with oth-

83. Ibid., letter #6, October 10, 1801.
84. Ibid., letter #20, June 15, 1792, in answer to letter #8 from Tieck to Wackenroder, June 12, 1792.
85. Ibid., letter #1, November 21, 1792.
86. Ibid., letter #6, October 10, 1801.

ers, I lack gentleness and grace, which foster endearment."[87] The disparity between life and ideal caused Schlegel much anxiety. While he valiantly wrestled with the issues, he did not conquer them.

Zionism was all about realizing a dream and living an ideal. We today understand that later generations truly romanticized the Jewish pioneer experience, that life was hard and fraught with danger, but there is much evidence that the spiritual gains of Zionism's Romantic realism outweighed the hardships.

If happiness at any cost was not a Zionist goal, neither was extreme asceticism. Friedrich asked his brother August Wilhelm, why we practice deceit in our human relationships for the sake of being accepted by our family and friends? "I should especially address myself to relationships and friendships. In order to be tolerated, to be socially acceptable, to be favored, one needs to employ a great many untruths." In order to project the image others expect of us, we sell our soul to the devil, as Faust did. "It's a good thing that I feign religion before my father and respect for my family, even though I have neither."[88]

And worse yet, even the most sacred of all relationships, friendship, is not above suspicion: "If the stern hand of truth would tear the veil, you would see tiny lies even in our friendship."[89] Thus, reality was much different from fiction. In spite of his liberal philosophy, Friedrich's asceticism did not allow him to be as free a spirit in real life as were the characters in his novel *Lucinde*, because such spontaneous behavior would have been incongruent with the public image which he had to uphold. Consequently, he saw himself as the eternal sinner.[90]

This confession clashes sharply with Gershom Scholem's account of his unpleasant encounter with his father because of his Zionism. When Scholem's father found out that his son had become a Zionist, he disowned him, and threw him out of the house. Scholem's attitude resembled that of the prophet Jeremiah, who accepted the terrible truth of humanity's depravity

---

87. Ibid., letter #1, November 21, 1792.
88. Ibid.
89. Ibid.
90. Ibid. At the beginning of the letter, he thanked his brother for rebuking him "as a true sign of love" and invited him to do it again when needed. "I believe in you . . . ."

without, however, being destroyed by it.[91] In fact, in Zionist art, the figure of Jeremiah is reinterpreted as the cancer of the earth by the artist, Lesser Ury. Yet at the same time, Ury makes it quite clear that we are also God's children, who are in communion with the universe.

No matter how difficult things are, abdication of the world and renunciation of love, two important themes in German Romanticism, are not acceptable resolutions of conflict in Judaism. Kleist, a truly tragic figure, confessed in a letter to his betrothed from Paris that he had to *abdicate* the uncouth world around him. "I do not understand how a poet can sing the song of his love to such an uncouth bunch as are people."[92] Kleist considered himself too good for the world. Consequently, he retreated to an island in Switzerland: "It is good living here, I hardly ever leave the island, don't see anyone, don't read any books, newspapers, in short, I don't need anything but myself."[93] Likewise Clemens Brentano, the poet, wrote to the artist Phillip Otto Runge (1777-1810), that it was unthinkable for him to "incorporate . . . the sacred story of my psyche . . . into the loud, uninterested daily routine of the world."[94]

Love, so important for the Romantic personality, was everything but sweet. According to the examples that Buber collected, love was fraught with anguish, tension, and general unhappiness. The mood of *renunciation* that in-

91. See Gershom Scholem, *From Berlin to Jerusalem* (New York: Schocken Books, 1980), 83. "A great crisis developed between my father and myself at the beginning of the year 1917. . . . When I raised a mild objection to one of my father's assertions, he flew into a rage and said he had now had enough of the two of us [his brother Werner], that Social Democracy and Zionism were all the same, anti-German activities which he would no longer tolerate in his house, and that he never wanted to see me again. The following day I received a registered letter from him in which he demanded that I leave his house on the first of March and henceforth shift for myself." Scholem writes: "In this connection I should also say that the reason I embraced Zionism was . . . tendencies that promoted the rediscovery by the Jews of their own selves and their history as well as a possible spiritual, cultural, and, above all, social rebirth. If there was any chance of a fundamental renewal whereby the Jews would fully realize their inherent potential, this – so we believed – could happen only over there, where a Jew would encounter himself, his people, and his roots. One's attitude toward religious tradition also played a part here, and had a clear dialectical function. For from the outset the struggle between a striving for continuation and revivification of the traditional form of Judaism and a conscious rebellion against this very tradition, though within the Jewish people and not through alienation from it and abandonment of it, created an ineluctable dialectics that was central to Zionism. Watchwords like 'renewal of Judaism' or 'revivification of the heart' only verbally masked this dialectics. It was bound to break through every attempt to endow it with substance in the concrete process of building a new Jewish community, and in large measure it shaped the inner history of the Zionist movement from my youth to the present." (Ibid., 54-55.)
92. Ms. Var. 350 B/1, letter #6, October 10, 1801.
93. Ibid., letter #11, May 1, 1802.
94. Ibid., letter #3, January 21, 1810.

fluenced all of Christian love, hung heavily over Romantic love and was carried over into worldly matters of the heart as well. We see this in the correspondence between Caroline Schlegel and Friedrich Wilhelm von Schelling (1775-1854) in 1801. "If you would want to separate me from you, you would destroy my life – yet I have to flee, for fear that I upset you, and from the destructive expression of your displeasure."[95] The tension between the two seemed to be one of fatal attraction, he "thoroughly robust, stubborn, rough and noble,"[96] she conciliatory and encouraging: "accept from me that which will not subjugate your noble spirit, but calm it, console it, soothe it."[97] Her ultimate advice to him was to "take our wonderful liaison as it is, don't complain over that which cannot be. . . . You wanted a fresh, youthful happiness, youthful heart that you are."[98]

Schleiermacher likewise found an understanding heart in the wife of another. Yet the relationship was strained. "Do you know what I would like to compare you with? With a magnet that is covered with lead shavings, because it could not find a solid piece of lead [to attach itself to]."[99] He wanted to be that "solid piece of lead" for Eleonore Grunow. Yet eventually the burden of having to live out the seamy details of a divorce became too much for Eleonore. They agonized over a way to resolve their dilemma, but in the end Eleonore decided to renounce him and step out of his life.[100]

In Jewish life, Romantic love was a very recent arrival with one exception: Michal's love for David in the Bible.[101] Even the young settlers who started the first kibbutzim and moshavim in Israel oftentimes were exclusively male, not for renunciatory reasons, but for practical purposes. When material and labor were scarce, separating the sexes in men's and women's

---

95. Ibid., letter #15.
96. Ibid., letter #27, October 28, 1799.
97. Ibid., letter #15.
98. Ibid., letter #15.
99. Ibid., letter #17.
100. Wallhausser, in discussing love in Schleiermacher, writes: "One further example from the early writings shows Schleiermacher avoiding a self-absorbing narcissistic love which he sensed in Friedrich Schlegel's novel, *Lucinde*." He continues that "Schleiermacher is not wholly supportive of Schlegel's romantic love" and cites a portion from the *Confidential Letters*, translated by Blackwell: "Does not love in this book [*Lucinde*], for all the completeness of its presentation, retreat a bit too much into itself? I would have liked to see it extend also outward into the world, and there accomplish something excellent. The frivolous hero should have this much of the knight in him." Wallhausser suggests that Schleiermacher's "insistence on the active, productive character of love contains a corrective to a 'one-sided' romantic preoccupation with the affective experience of love." (5) This sort of dialectical tension between egotistical concerns and the good of the community is precisely what Buber also became sensitive to.
101. Lecture by Rabbi Joseph Telushkin in Knoxville, December 9-10, 1994.

houses made sense. While women were an important part of the community, marriage was not traditionally founded on romantic love (see "Fiddler on the Roof"). Gradually, romantic love worked itself into modern Jewish life, but fatal attractions, so common among the Romantics, could not compete with the collective worries of the settlers about subsistence matters, such as drinking water or a roof over one's head.

Friendship is the result of a successful effort at human relationships, reaping the rewards of a careful attempt at synthesis of disparate human factors. Already in Plato's time, friendship had played an important role, epitomized in the philosophical-poetic *Dialogues on Love and Friendship*. It is no coincidence that Plato played an important role for Buber as well as for Schleiermacher. Yet in order to be capable of friendship, a number of emotional and human qualities were assumed as existing: sensitivity to the needs of one's self, self-reflection, sensitivity to others, a willingness to share and to listen, a desire for profound experiences and for conversation, and the ability to care.

When the Zionist fever caught on, studying a model simply became superfluous. Ideological kinship, rather than traditional family ties, formed the basis on which individuals congregated for cultural evenings, music programs, poetry readings, lectures, and reports from the land of Israel. The sensitivity and profundity that Buber had admired in Romanticism was the very life stuff of the young Zionists.

As Romanticism in 1800, so Zionism, a century later, created for itself a spontaneous personality and community that suited the occasion. Born of two cultures, German and Jewish, cultural Zionism took from German culture much of its form, while gradually immersing itself into the Jewish spirit. Zionist building was initially at the level of rebuilding the nation in a very basic sense. Only when this task had been defined and accepted, did they turn to Jewish *Bildung*. Buber unerringly, though not always very tactfully, led those who committed themselves to the cause.

Schleiermacher himself was Buber's model of a human being who had descended to the depths of the mothers, who was not afraid to speak his mind to the cultured despisers of religion on the disparity between what was and what should be, and who took an active role in defining the personality ethics of his contemporaries. Buber saw himself as a Schleiermacher-type figure for twentieth-century Jewry, but recognized that the agenda of his people differed in essence from that of the German Romantics. Because he recognized this basic difference, he was able to extract from the Romantic regeneration movement what was useful for his own purpose, such as Schleiermacher's conception of religion, without taking offense at his overall opinion of Judaism. By and large, however, the letters Buber had chosen did not contribute to this inspiration. What Buber did take from Romanticism was the imperative that the Jew take his fate into his own hands and realize not only his own self but also his peoplehood. By 1905, when the manuscript was completed, the crucial life and death period had passed. Zionism had taken on a life of its own. Buber's *Drei Reden über das Judentum*, published in 1910, showed the intensity and maturity of his thought, and assured his place as a leader of a new Judaism indebted to German culture, but freed from any subordination to the German spirit.[102]

---

102. I am deeply grateful to Professors Terrence N. Tice, University of Michigan, and Sergio Sorrentino, University of Naples, for organizing the 1994 international conference in Naples, Italy, where I presented a shorter version of this paper. I would also like to thank Dean C. W. Minkel, Graduate School, The University of Tennessee, for funding my travel to the conference.

CONVERGENCES IN SCHLEIERMACHER AND FOUCAULT ON SUBJECTIVITY

Craig C. Stein

Introduction

In his book *The Order of Things*,[1] Michel Foucault argues that the history of knowledge is not the story of its more or less progressive accumulation. It is instead a story of epochs when the conditions for the possibility of knowing remain stable, punctuated by their periodic revolution. Foucault calls the set of conditions during such an epoch an "épistémè." Within an épistémè the same rules of formation are unconsciously employed to define the objects, form the concepts, and build the theories of a range of seemingly unrelated scholarly discourses.[2] Periodically, most recently toward the end of the eighteenth century, the conditions alter, and alter so radically that what had previously counted as knowledge no longer does, and now may even seem absurd.

Foucault illustrates just how foreign knowledge can seem when it is produced under different conditions than those of our épistémè. In the preface he writes:

This book first arose out of a passage in Borges, out of the laughter that shattered, as I read the passage, all the familiar landmarks of my thought – *our* thought, the thought that bears the stamp of our age. . . . This passage quotes a 'certain Chinese encyclopaedia' in which it is written that 'animals are divided into: (a) belonging to the Emperor, (b) embalmed, (c) tame, (d) sucking pigs, (e) sirens, (f) fabulous, (g) stray dogs, (h) included in the present classification, (i) frenzied, (j) innumerable, (k) drawn with a very fine camelhair brush, (l) *et cetera*, (m) having just broken the water pitcher, (n) that from a long way off look like flies'. In the wonderment of this taxonomy, the thing we apprehend in one great leap, the thing that, by means of the fable, is demonstrated as the exotic charm of another system of thought, is the limitation of our own, the stark impossibility of thinking *that*.[3]

---

1. Michel Foucault, *The Order of Things: An Archaeology of the Human Sciences* (Random House: New York, 1970), a translation of *Les mots et les choses*.
2. Foucault, *The Order of Things*, xi.
3. Foucault, *The Order of Things*, xv.

To elaborate on Foucault, do we not have to say that the inability to imagine thinking *"that"* has as its corollary the inability to imagine thinking *other* than we do, that is, other than according to the rules of our épistémè and within the possibilities it permits (i.e., as long as our thinking is toward knowledge)? Even our most revolutionary projections of alternative constructions of thought would have the same indispensable conditions as those that structure the most traditional or mundane thought of our age.

Schleiermacher falls within the épistémè Foucault calls Modern, which begins near the time of Schleiermacher's birth and continues into the present. So under examination, Schleiermacher's theory of human subjectivity, then, should reveal itself as having been constructed according to the rules of this, the Modern épistémè. Yet the thesis of this essay is that, as he gives it in the introduction to *The Christian Faith*, Schleiermacher's construction of human subjectivity exceeds Foucault's description, does so in ways that anticipate Foucault's critique, and offers an alternative: the formation of subjectivity through a grammar of religious affections.

Foucault's Description of the Modern Subject

The next step then is to reconstruct what are, according to Foucault, the specific conditions for the possibility of knowing in force during this épistémè. Foucault accuses Modern theories of having as their common foundation a hidden anthropology. He means by this that all that counts as truth will do so only as it forms itself to the human shape, as it refers itself back (consciously or not) to a starting point in the human subject. This human subject that Modern knowledges have as their indispensable condition did not and could not have existed before the advent of the Modern épistémè. It emerges only with the collapse of the previous épistémè (which Foucault calls the Classical) when its foundation, built on a system of representations, could no longer support it. It was no longer obvious that truth resided within an object, and that its truth was faithfully conveyed by language's representative capacity from the object to the knowing subject. In the epistemological space cleared by this collapse the Modern subject is born. The truth that had belonged to the object, the means of its communication that had belonged to language, as well as the knowing subject now all reside within the subject itself.

Knowledges in the Modern épistémè are built on the foundation of a human subject that exists in the paradoxical space maintained between the irreconcilable poles of three doublets: the empirical and the transcendental, the *cogito* and the unthought, and the retreat of the origin and its return. Before the end of the eighteenth century this space, and the subject it makes possible, did not exist. Foucault calls this subject, simply, "man."

The way modern knowledges are constructed, according to Foucault, is by looking at the Modern subject described within the paradoxical space through an "analytic of finitude." What follows next is an account of the subject described by the analytic of each of the doublets, beginning with the empirical and transcendental.

In the analytic of finitude human being is always preceded and determined by a range of material forces (e.g., life, labor, and language, the three that Foucault explicates). These demarcate man's finitude, and it is only in and by means of its finitude that man may be known.

> In one sense, man is governed by labour, life, and language: his concrete existence finds its determinations in them; it is possible to have access to him only through his words, his organism, the objects he makes. . . . Man's finitude is heralded – and imperiously so – in the positivity of knowledge.[4]

Yet it also works the other way around. Even as man is itself conditioned and determined by these forces in its taking up of them, yet they exist and are knowable only as they are taken up and given particular historical expression in man. So at one and the same time, man is known in its finitude only as the being that is determined by material forces, and yet these forces, and so the knowledges of them, depend upon their manifestation in man for their existence. The analytic of finitude explains

> how man's being finds itself determined by positivities which are exterior to it and which link it to the density of things, but how, in return, it is finite being that gives any determination the possibility of appearing in its positive truth.[5]

So, on the one hand, this subject has an empirical existence that is in principle no different from anything else in creation. It is just as much an object of scientific observation as any other empiricity. Yet man is the privileged or first born of empiricities, for it is the condition for the possibility of the very knowledges by which it is known.

> Man, in the analytic of finitude, is a strange empirico-transcendental doublet, since he is a being such that knowledge will be attained in him of what renders all knowledge possible.[6]

---

4. Foucault, *The Order of Things*, 313.
5. Foucault, *The Order of Things*, 336.
6. Foucault, *The Order of Things*, 318.

Man is both the ground of the possibility of knowledge of life, labor, and language even as man is known only through them, and concretely and historically determined by them.

We now turn to the second of the doublets, the *cogito* and the unthought. The subject that Modern knowledges are constructed upon is not simply the point of convergence of material forces, but the intentional subject who animates and knows and gives expression to these forces that are otherwise without form. Material forces and the materiality of its empirical being precede man historically, but man transcends them in the synthetic activity of its consciousness. What stands over against man, what both resists and yet anticipates the activity of the *cogito*, is finally (because its already there in Modernity's presuppositions) not a distant alterity, but man itself in its empiricity, man's own body in its mute materiality. Man is its own unthought, its own other. With the maintenance of this doublet, man in expression of its consciousness can, not only poke its nose above the waters of its own finitude, but transcend it decisively, to the point that man the transcendent consciousness is the irreconcilable counterpart, the other, of man the empirical object.

The third doublet is the retreat and return of the origin. According to Foucault, in the Modern épistémè the concern for man's origin does not take the form of a search for an actual starting point, because the épistémè includes the consciousness that one always begins in the middle of things. Instead the origin is thematized as a concern for *the original*, for the unique and never before seen configuration of the already existing elements of life, labor, and language. The present moment, then, offers itself to man as the page upon which man can write an original work (above all itself), but using elements older than memory. In this way the origin is returned to man as that which is always immanent, yet never permanent, always nearer, but never achieved.

The paradigm of the Modern subject is the author who in the creative moment of originality expresses, incarnates, and activates all the material forces – life, labor, and above all language – that both precede and outlive the author, yet have no existence apart from the author's particular, temporal, and finite creation by means of them. Yet again, because the work is original, it too is somehow eternal. Yes, the author is determined in a concrete way by these forces, yet the author also determines them, their entrance into time and space, and determines them in such a way that what is temporal, the work, ascends to the level of the transcendent. It becomes a classic work, that is, a work that transcends the particularities of its creation, and becomes the contemporary of every period. In this way the origin, the search for which was abandoned by the Modern sciences, returns to man from the direction of the future, as that which is promised to man, the completion that is to come.

Finally, Foucault foretells man's disappearance, and welcomes it: "It is comforting, however, and a source of profound relief to think that man is only a recent invention, a figure not yet two centuries old, a new wrinkle in our knowledge, and that he will disappear again as soon as that knowledge has discovered a new form." [7] The disappearance of man is, for Foucault, the return of the beginning of philosophy. The death of man is "the unfolding of a space in which it is once more possible to think."[8]

Schleiermacher's Subject: The Formation of Subjectivity
in the Grammar of Religious Affections

As described in the introduction to *The Christian Faith*, Schleiermacher's human subject has at its center neither knowing nor doing, but feeling. Schleiermacher defines feeling as a consciousness, yet distinct from knowing in that feeling is an *immediate* self-consciousness, while knowing is a consciousness mediated by self-representation.[9] This stands over against assumptions that conflate self-consciousness with self-contemplation. Feeling *is* a form of consciousness of the self, but it is direct, that is, unmediated by the intervening step of a representation of the self to the self.

Schleiermacher places feeling in a position prior to knowing and doing. While they too are constituent parts of human subjectivity, they are always determined by a prior feeling which gives them direction and to which they give expression.

Feeling is not determined by the human subject him or herself, but is determined by the influences upon the subject from outside. Human being is both constitutionally *receptive* of the influence of others, and, for its particular determination (for being what it is in any given moment), *dependent* on those influences. A subject's particular existence and history depend upon what he or she receives from others. At the heart of human subjectivity for Schleiermacher, then, stands not the restlessness of a synthetic intentionality awaiting the means of its expression, but feeling as a

---

7. Foucault, *The Order of Things*, xxiii.
8. Foucault, *The Order of Things*, 342.
9. Friedrich Schleiermacher, *The Christian Faith*, ed. H. R. Mackintosh & J.S. Stewart, (Edinburgh: T. & T. Clark, 1928), § 3.2, 6.

receptivity that responds and corresponds to those other subjects who stand
in relation to it.

The human subject experiences its receptivity as a feeling of dependence.
The feeling of dependence is the precognitive awareness that corresponds to
our reliance upon others for our determination. Its counterpart is the feeling
of freedom, which corresponds to our ability to determine others.[10] The receptivity and dependence that structure any relationship mean that human
subjectivity is not constitutionally independent of others. It must follow, then,
that human subjectivity is also not somehow constituted prior to history or
culture, but only within them in the form of its construction through
relationships with particular persons under particular conditions.

The human subject stands in a relation of reciprocal co-determination to
everything within creation.[11] This means that in relation to the whole of
creation or to any part of it, every feeling of dependence is delimited by a
feeling of freedom, and every feeling of freedom is delimited by a feeling of
dependence. As a human subject, under the conditions of time and space,
every feeling of freedom or dependence is limited and relative.[12]

So then, the feeling of *absolute* dependence as such posits neither a
subject as an individual existence, nor an object as a particular other which
stands over against the subject. This is because so long as it is as an individual
that a subject feels either free or dependent, some other, some thing or
person or world outside of the subject, is posited. To be an individual is to be
identified in distinction from, yet in relation to, an other. And when one is
related to an other the feelings of freedom and dependence are and can only
be relative and partial. The feeling of absolute dependence occurs, then, only
on the far side of the self/other, subject/object distinctions.

> The feeling of absolute dependence . . . is not the consciousness of
> ourselves as individuals of a particular description, but simply of
> ourselves as individual finite existence in general; so that we do not
> set ourselves over against any other individual being, but on the
> contrary, all antithesis between one individual and another is in this
> case done away.[13]

As feeling, the feeling of absolute dependence remains an immediate
consciousness of self, but not of the self *as a self*. The human subject feels the
feeling of absolute dependence not as a particular person, but as identified
with the whole of finite existence. This makes sense only if we infer that

---

10. Schleiermacher, *The Christian Faith*, § 4.2, 13.
11. Even in relation, Schleiermacher says, to the stars. They influence us and we them,
     however minutely. (Schleiermacher, *The Christian Faith*, § 4.2, 15.)
12. Schleiermacher, *The Christian Faith*, § 4.3, 15.
13. Schleiermacher, *The Christian Faith*, § 5.1, 19.

Schleiermacher presupposes *a distinction between being and identity*. The subject stands in immediate relation to its *Whence* as a being, and as representative of all of being, but the subject does not (yet) stand there as an individual, that is, as distinct from the rest of creation, as having an identity. Further, the subject is dependent now not on any part of creation, nor even the whole of it, but on that which determines the whole, and can be indicated, at this point, only by the gesture of the *"Whence."*

Just here Schleiermacher exceeds Foucault's critique of Modernity, and exceeds it in the direction that Foucault himself will take: Rather than the affirmation of the inimitable singularity at the heart of a particular life, rather than the guarantee of an eternal cogito that transcends the conditions of finitude, rather than the founding moment of the original identity, the feeling of absolute dependence is the cancellation of all these. What stands at the center of subjectivity then has as an effect the erasure of any transcendental identity of the self and establishes instead the temporalization of identity. We are identifiable as who we are only within the realm of distinctions, of time and space (what Schleiermacher calls the realm of antitheses). Schleiermacher's theology supports an articulation of human subjectivity where identity is established in an ongoing process of its merging and redifferentiation in relation to others, and only within time and culture.

The space cleared at the heart of human subjectivity by the cancellation of eternal identity is not created so that it can simply be filled again with some other transcendental equivalent. The two likely substitutes for the now absent transcendent identity of the subject would have been either an immediate, original knowledge of God, or the displacement of the center of the subject by the projection of transcendent intentionality onto the heavens become the presence of a God. Schleiermacher avoids both. Clearly the delimitation of the whole, and human being along with it, is not a strategy to make possible the substitution of a God who is present as the divinization of intending consciousness. This would be an attempt to shoe-horn God into creation, stuffed into the glass slipper of human consciousness.[14]

Neither is the feeling of absolute dependence a form of knowledge, because it stands only on the far side of the differences that make knowledge possible. For Schleiermacher knowledge is possible only because of the

---

14. Schleiermacher shows the limits of how far one can go in this direction: "It can be said that God is given to us in feeling in an original way; and if we speak of an original revelation of God to man or in man, the meaning will always be just this, that, along with the absolute dependence which characterizes not only man but all temporal existence, there is given to man also the immediate self-consciousness of it, which becomes the consciousness of God." (Schleiermacher, *The Christian Faith*, § 4.4, 17.)

differentiations that exist in history and culture. It is imbedded in the particularities and variations of time and space. The feeling of absolute dependence on the other hand is the immediate consciousness, the feeling, that the whole of existence comes from a source outside of it.[15]

What stands at the center of subjectivity then is nothing more than the unmediated consciousness of this dependence of the whole on a "Whence." This consciousness does not have a positive cognitive content. It is not the immediate revelation of a knowledge of God. It has instead only a *negative affective content*, that is, the feeling of the finitude of the whole.[16] The use of "Whence" is the use of a spatial metaphor for what conditions creation (including space itself). It is the gesture Schleiermacher uses to refer to what is beyond reference. This use of "Whence" is something like language's necessary attempt, which also necessarily fails, to fight its way out of the bag of referentiality.

Because the feeling of absolute dependence occurs beyond all distinctions, it never exists in its own moment as such.[17] Instead, it accompanies every moment of the sensibly determined self-consciousness, that is, every moment of temporal experience.[18] It is the "nature" of the feeling of absolute dependence "to become temporal, to manifest itself in time, by entering into relation with the sensible self-consciousness so as to constitute a moment."[19] It is as the feeling of absolute dependence enters into this relation that it becomes a determinate of specific human being (i.e., not only absolutely determinate of the whole). It determines directly neither action nor knowledge, but emotions (and then the former indirectly, through the later). While the feeling of absolute dependence remains constant, the variety of the religious emotions which disclose, express, and manifest it[20] are determined by the greater or lesser degree of its emergence into self-consciousness and the changing determination of the sensible consciousness to which it is joined.

This means then that the significations of the feeling of absolute dependence – the knowledges and activities, but above all the emotions, that represent it in time – do not inhere within it, but are instead always *attributed to it* within specific and changing contexts. Conceptually, the "most direct reflection upon it" is the idea in the term "God."[21] Yet even

---

15. Schleiermacher, *The Christian Faith*, § 4.3, 16.
16. Schleiermacher, *The Christian Faith*, § 8.2, 35.
17. Cf. Schleiermacher, *The Christian Faith*, § 4.3, 16.
18. Schleiermacher, *The Christian Faith*, § 4.3, 16.
19. Schleiermacher, *The Christian Faith*, § 5.4, 24.
20. Schleiermacher, *The Christian Faith*, § 5.3, 22.
21. Schleiermacher, *The Christian Faith*, § 4.4, 17.

designating "being in relation with God" as the equivalent of "feeling oneself absolutely dependent" only emerges through a process of development within a cultural context. "God" only *comes to be* designated this "Whence" as the feeling of absolute dependence is taken up within the differentiations of temporal life. While the idea of "God" is the most direct reflection on the feeling of absolute dependence, it is already a mediated consciousness, that is, it has already stepped into the realm of distinctions.

Affectively, the feeling of absolute dependence becomes particular religious emotions as it is related to particular moments of sensible consciousness, that is, feelings of partial freedom and dependence.[22] Because one's particular feelings are determined only in reciprocal relations with others, the emotional expressions of the feeling of absolute dependence and their development as more or less adequate expressions, also emerge only within history and culture. Far from being automatic or innate, one only *learns to feel* what it is to be in relation to God.

The intersubjective constitution of human subjectivity means that emotions are shared. They are shared as they are first expressed by one person and then imitated by another. An emotion is expressed and communicated "by means of facial expression, gesture, tones, and (indirectly) words; and so becomes to other people a revelation of the inward." Emotions are then internalized by others through "living imitation."[23]

Religions are the regular relationships and fellowships based on shared religious emotions. A church is a religious communion, "which forms an ever self-renewing circulation of the religious self-consciousness within certain definite limits, and a propagation of the religious emotions arranged and organized within the same limits."[24]

The specific identity of a religion or a church is defined by the "kindred emotions"[25] that are shared, by the set of religious affections that forms its foundation and that are identical in its members.[26] Religious communities then are not simply established on a set of religious emotions, but also cultivate, organize, and pass on these emotions. It is through the sharing of religious emotions that the community leads individuals to a clear awareness of the feeling of absolute dependence,[27] and to progress in its expression.

---

22. Schleiermacher, *The Christian Faith*, § 5.4, 22.
23. Schleiermacher, *The Christian Faith*, § 6.2, 27.
24. Schleiermacher, *The Christian Faith*, § 6.4, 29.
25. Schleiermacher, *The Christian Faith*, § 6.3, 28.
26. Schleiermacher, *The Christian Faith*, § 6.PS, 29.
27. "As regards the feeling of absolute dependence in particular, everyone will know that it was first awakened in him in the same way, by the communicative and stimulative power of expression or utterance." (Schleiermacher, *The Christian Faith*, § 6.2, 27.)

Conclusion

First, Schleiermacher does engage in a form of analytic of finitude that takes as its object the human subject. The knower is finite, and it can be argued that for Schleiermacher it is in his or her finitude that the knower makes knowledge possible. But the circle is never completed. The knowledge gained by means of the analytic of the finitude of the knower[28] does not in turn ground the original essence of the subject. Human identity is not given a foundation, does not ascend above finitude, by participating in some form of transcendental knowledge or by creating an eternal work. Instead, knowledge and activity, like the knower, are always finite and historical. The human subject as the empirical object is not one half of a paradoxical doublet whose other half is transcendental.

Unlike Modern knowledges that presume it is the nature of truth to conform to the finite conditions of human rationality in order to be knowable, for Schleiermacher that which determines the whole accommodates itself only to the finite conditions of human *affectivity*. Schleiermacher's work includes the step of an analytic of the finitude of the individual, yet this analytic concludes not with the establishing, but with the canceling of any transcendent foundation for human identity. Yet Schleiermacher goes on to take another step, through what might be called an affectics – a critical examination not with the mind but with the emotions – of the finitude of the whole, which concludes with the foundational affirmation of human being and the being of the whole. The being (not the identity) of each individual, in and by means of its finitude, along with the being of the whole, is affirmed in that each person along with the whole of creation stands in direct relation to a *Whence* who in retrospect is identified as God. In addition, the possibility of religion, the possibility of gratitude toward the infinite, is given to human being in the immediate consciousness of this relation which is the feeling of absolute dependence.

Second, particular emotions for Schleiermacher do have an existence that is comparable to life, labor, and language in Foucault's analysis of Modernity. Emotions have their particular existence at the site of the individual, yet their formation, uniqueness, and organization are at a higher level. In the case of religious emotions, their life is at the intersubjective level of human sociality that is the religious community. Yet, unlike life, labor, and language, emotions are not matter given unique form in an original creation that then serves as a transcendental foundation for the identity of the

28. A knowledge which makes possible a description of the religious emotions and a classification of the different religions.

individual. Identity is instead constructed completely within the limits of its historical and cultural contexts. And its most central element, its relation to God, is constructed within that community of shared religious emotions called the religious communion.

Contrary to Foucault's description of Modern presuppositions, what is at the heart of human subjectivity for Schleiermacher is not some unique and unrepeatable singularity, not the unthought that is waiting to be thought, not an originality that returns an origin, ever nearer but never reached. It is instead the feeling of absolute dependence and its manifestation in religious emotions that are by nature shared. We receive them from others and we pass them on to others. The heart of human subjectivity is traversed by intersubjectivity. While the particular combination of feelings, and the ease with which an individual receives some emotions but not others are unique, the constitutive elements of subjectivity, the emotions themselves, are shared.

What decenters transcendental consciousness is not the self. It is not self-negation, which cannot avoid the fundamental assertion of the self even in the negation of the self, another reinscription of a presence even, or especially, in the moment of the attempt to establish absence (a tendency in Foucault's later works). Yet neither is the self decentered by the activity of another (not even God's), which would be a kind of heteronomy. Instead, it is as finite being in relation to that which conditions it absolutely that the self is decentered as a transcendental essence, yet centered as finite being. It experiences this center only as the undifferentiated feeling that is the feeling of absolute dependence receives from the religious community the pattern of religious emotions that are the means of its expression and interpretation. Schleiermacher's subject is constitutionally dependent on others, especially as they take the form of the religious community, not only for its particular existence in any moment (its determination), but also for the entire range of affective responses to the encounter with the divine. The feeling of absolute dependence emerges into the consciousness of the individual at all only as it is evoked by means of the religious community and, after its emergence, it has no expression in particular emotions and no manifestation into history without the community. The entire patterning of piety, that is, of the religious emotions, their content, their ordering, what is and is not included within the range of emotions possible to a subject, when they emerge – in short, the *grammar of religious affections* – is a property not of the individual but of the community. The site of the expression of religious emotions is the individual, but the structure and grammar of their expression belong to the community.

SCHLEIERMACHER ON DIALECTIC AND CHRISTIAN TEACHING[1]

Georg Behrens

Friedrich Schleiermacher distinguishes two types or levels of Christian discourse. The first is the "religious speech"[2] of preaching, prayer and liturgy; for reasons that will become apparent shortly, I will call it "first-order religious discourse." The second is the discourse in which Christian teaching is articulated: I will call it "didactic discourse." Schleiermacher wants to hold that didactic discourse is generated out of and answerable to first-order religious discourse, but that it is at the same time radically different from such discourse in its nature and function. In this essay, I attempt to reconstruct his views on how didactic discourse is both derivative and different from first-order religious discourse. After rejecting an alternative account ("Formalism"), I suggest that, for Schleiermacher, the difference between religious speech and didactic discourse might be conceived as that between a "practical" and a "theoretical" discourse. The insight guiding my argument is that the key to understanding Schleiermacher's theory of Christian didactic discourse is his conception of dialectic.

As a preliminary matter, I would like to emphasize that this paper is not about Schleiermacher's theory of dogmatic theology, nor is it about his theory of doctrine, the work-product of dogmatic theology. By focussing on his account of first-order religious discourse, didactic discourse, and the relations between them, I am focussing on his account of activities that involve all adult members of the Church, not just learned theologians. These pre-dogmatic activities provide, as it were, the raw material out of which dogmatic theology fashions the system of doctrine.

I. Types of Religious Discourse.

In the second (1830) edition of *The Christian Faith*, Schleiermacher tells us that Christian "faith-sentences" [*Glaubenssätze*] can be "poetic,"

---

1. This paper was presented at the Instituto Italiano per gli Studi Filosofia in Naples, as part of the conference on "Romantic Dialectic," held in June 1994.
2. For Schleiermacher's "Theory of Religious Speech," see Friedrich Schleiermacher, *Die praktische Theologie nach den Grundsäzen der evangelischen Kirche im Zusammenhange dargestellt*, ed. Jacob Frerichs, Sämmtliche Werke I/13 (Berlin: G. Reimer, 1850), 201ff.

"rhetorical," or "didactic" in kind.[3] This classification concerns the different uses to which speakers put linguistic expressions. A sentence is poetic, if, as the result of a "heightened moment of life," it is used by a speaker to depict [*darstellen*] an aspect of self-consciousness. It is rhetorical if it is used "to move" or to influence an interlocutor, e.g., to act, to feel or to think in a certain way.[4] Preaching, as Schleiermacher explains in his *Practical Theology*, is both poetic and rhetorical: by depicting a certain form of piety, it causes a hearer's participation in that form of piety. Because in Schleiermacher's account poetic and rhetorical sentences are so similar, and because they are often treated as belonging together, e.g., in "religious speech," it is appropriate to subsume both under the term "first-order religious discourse."

Schleiermacher tells us also that faith sentences of the third variety, didactic sentences, are generated or constructed out of sentences of the first two varieties. (In this sense, then, poetic and rhetorical discourse are to be regarded as "first-order," and didactic discourse as higher order.) He invites us to imagine a state of Christian piety without teaching activity, and then to follow his account of how Christian didactic discourse might evolve out of such a state.[5]

The account begins with the generation of poetic and rhetorical faith-sentences, which together constitute the "original" linguistic expressions of pious self-consciousness. Poetic sentences are generated as soon as pious

---

3. CG 1830:16.1 All translations in this paper are my own. References to the 2nd (1830) edition of *The Christian Faith* will be according to the formula: [Der] C[hristliche] G[laube] 1830:section.subsection. References to the first (1821/2) edition will be according to the formula: CG 1821/2:section.subsection.

4. CG 1830:16.1. In the first (1821/2) edition of *The Christian Faith*, Schleiermacher sets up the contrast as being between "a picture-language aiming at affective arousal" [*eine auf Gemütserregung ausgehende Bildersprache*] and "a rhetorical language aiming at the transformation of opponents" [*eine auf Umwandlung der Gegner ausgehende rhetorische Sprache*] (CG 1821/2:2.1).

5. It should be understood that Schleiermacher does not consider the construction of Christian teaching (in the sense I am about to describe) to be the characteristic business of modern dogmatic theology. Today (as in his time) dogmatic theology finds itself in a situation, not so much of having to generate doctrine from scratch, but of critiquing and interpreting the language and formulations of traditional didactic discourse (CG 1830:16.addendum). Such formulations are given to rather than constructed by the dogmatic theologian. Schleiermacher divides his 1830 "Introduction" to *The Christian Faith* into two chapters, the first concerned with the "explanation" of dogmatic theology and its presuppositions, the second concerned with its "method." Significantly, the account of the construction of teaching within the Church is located in the first chapter (in the section entitled "Concerning the Relation of Dogmatics to Christian Piety"), while the chapter dealing with methodology opens with the claim that we need a (critical) rule for distinguishing within the "available mass" of candidate sentences between those to be admitted into the system of doctrine and those to be rejected (CG 1830:20).

self-consciousness moves beyond the level of reflex-like self-expression (in terms of gestures, mimicry, inarticulate vocalizations) and becomes the object of self-reflective thought.[6] According to Schleiermacher, "when one finds oneself in an unusually heightened state of pious self-consciousness, one will feel called to poetic representation, which proceeds most immediately from such a condition."[7] The generation of rhetorical sentences follows soon thereafter, when contextual circumstances are favorable to the performance of proclamatory acts, for the drive to communicate itself is inherent in pious self-consciousness. Didactic faith sentences, by contrast, are generated through reflection not upon pious self-consciousness itself, but upon first-order religious discourse. They arise out of "the logically ordered reflection upon the immediate linguistic expressions [*Aussagen*] of pious self-consciousness."[8] The "immediate source" for Christian teaching activity is the poetic and rhetorical discourse of the Church.[9]

The generation of Christian didactic discourse, then, occurs in two steps. The first is the transition from piety to first-order religious discourse; this transition is necessitated by pious self-consciousness itself, which intrinsically seeks to depict and to communicate itself. Indeed, depiction and communication in first-order religious discourse are the means by which alone a form of piety can be assured of continued existence. The second step is the transition from first-order religious discourse to didactic discourse. Unlike the first, this step is not necessitated by piety itself: piety can perpetuate itself

6. CG 1821/2:2.1.
7. CG 1830:16.1.
8. CG 16:addendum. Schleiermacher occasionally mentions a species of reflection which is about pious self-consciousness itself. Thus, for example, at DO 1822:296, he writes, "We find the results of reflection of religious self-consciousness wherever religion is made the object of contemplation, that is, in the form of a dogmatics [*Glaubenslehre*] . . . ." It is important to distinguish the roles, within the Church, of reflection upon first-order religious language and of reflection upon pious self-consciousness. The former occurs in the generation of didactic faith sentences: such sentences are not the products of introspection, but of reflection upon public proclamation. The latter serves as a critical check on the activity of dogmatic theology: sentences that are not verified to relate in the proper way ("expression") to Christian pious self-consciousness may for that reason be judged not to be authentic doctrines of Christianity.
9. Friedrich Schleiermacher, "Über den Gegensatz zwischen der Sabellianischen und der Athanasianischen Vorstellung von der Trinität (1822)," in Schleiermacher, *Theologisch-dogmatische Abhandlungen und Gelegenheitsschriften*, herausgegeben von Hans-Friedrich Traulsen unter Mitwirking von Martin Ohst, Kritische Gesamtausgabe I/10, ed. Hans-Joachim Birkner et al. (Berlin/New York: Walter de Gruyter, 1990), 225-306, 255.

without the addition of doctrinal discourse.[10] To account for this second step in the generation of didactic faith sentences, therefore, an appeal to a principle distinct from pious self-consciousness is necessary. The identification of this distinct principle, the force of which drives Christians to the production of didactic discourse, is the key to understanding the nature of such discourse.

Schleiermacher expresses his theory of Christian teaching activity in large part as an account of the emergence of didactic discourse from first-order religious discourse. This account provides the answers to three types of questions: (1) Why is there didactic discourse? Why does Christianity have teaching, if the needs of Christian pious self-consciousness are adequately and perfectly met by first-order religious discourse? (2) How are didactic faith sentences generated out of first-order religious discourse? (3) How do didactic faith sentences differ from the poetic and rhetorical sentences of first-order religious discourse? What features distinguish didactic faith sentences from those of "religious speech"?

Schleiermacher's short answer to these three questions reveal the focus of his account. It is the "dialectical interest"[11] operative in the Christian Church that accounts for why Christianity has didactic discourse, how it generates didactic discourse, and what features distinguish didactic discourse from its antecedents. Not surprisingly, then, the key to understanding Schleiermacher's theory of Christian teaching activity is the term "dialectical."

II. Formalism as an Account of Doctrinal Discourse.

It is sometimes assumed that Schleiermacher adopted what might be called a "formalistic" view of the relation between first-order religious discourse and didactic discourse: the view, namely, that these discourses differ from each other in certain "formal" respects unrelated to the subject-matter that they are "about," but that, in fact, they are "about" the same subject-matter in the same way.[12] Let us call those properties of a discourse by which it is related to its subject-matter its "semantic" properties. The for-

10. "Christian faith in and of itself has no need of such an apparatus, neither for the sake of its effect upon the individual soul, nor in the relations of social family life." Friedrich Schleiermacher, *Kurze Darstellung des theologischen Studiums*, ed. Heinrich Scholz (Leipzig: Deichert, 1910), 5.
11. CG 1830:16.addendum.
12. Schleiermacher himself seems to suggest this view at CG 1830:16.addendum and at CG 1830:17.2.

malistic view, then, is that there is no change in semantic properties in the transition from first-order religious discourse to didactic discourse – no semantic shift – and that didactic faith sentences stand in the same semantic relations to the same entities as do the sentences of first-order religious discourse.

How, then, does Schleiermacher conceive the semantic properties characteristic of religious speech, which, according to Formalism, are also those of doctrinal discourse? What seems clear is that the salient semantic feature of first-order religious discourse is its relation to pious self-consciousness, of which it is the "expression and presentation" [*Aeußerung und Darstellung*][13] and communication. As a sentence of religious speech, "God is gracious" (or "Jesus rose from the grave") is in the first instance "about" the religious state of the speaker,[14] though not in the sense of being an assertion about such a state. Less clear is the matter of spelling out the sense in which such a sentence is also "about" God, or "about" Jesus, the grave and other parts of the world. Schleiermacher wants to hold that the way in which first-order religious discourse is about God and the world is decidedly different from the way in which philosophical or scientific discourse is about God and the world. The semantic relation of first-order religious discourse to the world is mediated by its semantic relation to pious self-consciousness: first-order religious discourse is "about" God and the world only because it is "about" pious self-consciousness and pious self-consciousness itself in some sense "about" God and the world. By contrast, the semantic relation of philosophical discourse to God and the world is not mediated in this way: and in fact such discourse stands in no semantic relation at all to pious self-consciousness. As a sentence of speculative philosophy, "God is gracious" is "about" God, and not "about" the speaker's (or anyone else's) pious state. The term "God" refers to God, and the sentence is true just in case God is gracious. In a rough way, Schleiermacher sometimes tries to capture the important semantic difference between the two types of discourse by saying that first-order religious discourse is an articulation of "subjective" consciousness, while scientific and philosophical discourse is an articulation of "objective" consciousness.

If this account of religious speech and its semantic properties can properly be attributed to Schleiermacher, then it is easy to see why the formalistic view, which entails that didactic discourse possess the same semantic properties as religious speech, may have been an attractive option for him: it would have allowed him to satisfy what I will call his "apologetic agenda." Schleiermacher was acutely aware of the challenge posed to traditional

---

13. CG 1830:18.3.
14. Cf. *Praktische Theologie*, 85 ff.

Christian teaching by new developments in natural and historical science. Thus, while he was eager to claim that dogmatics is in some sense a "scientific" discipline, he also wanted to say that the sentences of Christian teaching cannot conflict with the sentences of speculative philosophy and science.[15] The separation of Christian theology from "the wisdom of the world" had to be guaranteed, "so that, for example, so strange a question as to whether the same sentence can be true in philosophy and false in Christian theology, or vice versa, can no longer occur, because a sentence as it is found in the one will be unable to find a place in the other."[16] Now as Schleiermacher tells us in his *Dialektik*, for two sentences to contradict each other, they must be referred in the same way to the same object;[17] they must share the same semantic properties. To ensure a "harmony" between science and Christianity, therefore, it is sufficient to claim that scientific and Christian didactic faith sentences are semantically dissimilar. If didactic faith sentences, like "religious speech" are articulations of "subjective consciousness," and scientific sentences are articulations of "objective consciousness," then indeed a disharmony is impossible.[18] If the formalistic view is right, the transition from poetic and rhetorical to didactic discourse does not involve a semantic shift. Although in some formal respects didactic faith sentences may be on the side of scientific discourse, semantically they remain on that of first-order religious discourse, being most immediately about pious self-consciousness.

In what follows (Sections III and IV), I argue that the formalistic interpretation of the term "dialectical" is anomalous when considered within the framework of Schleiermacher's own theory of dialectic. Given this framework, didactic faith sentences must be held to differ from their antecedents in first-order religious discourse by standing in a different sort of relation to non-linguistic entities which they are "about." Thus, the transition is essen-

15. See especially Friedrich Schleiermacher, "Dr. Schleiermacher über seine Glaubenslehre an Dr. Lücke," in Schleiermacher, *Theologisch-dogmatische Abhandlungen und Gelegenheitsschriften*, herausgegeben on Hans-Friedrich Traulsen unter Mitwirking von Martin Ohst, Kritische Gesamtausgabe I/10, ed. Hans-Joachim Birkner et al. (Berlin/New York: Walter de Gruyter, 1990), 337-394, 350-351.
16. CG 1830:16.addendum.
17. Friedrich Schleiermacher, *Dialektik*, ed. Rudolf Odebrecht (Leipzig: Heinrichs, 1942), 21. Further references to Odebrecht's edition of *Dialektik* will use the abbreviation D[ialektik] O[debrecht], followed by a date: 1831 for passages taken from Schleiermacher's own written "Introduction" to dialectic; 1822 for Odebrecht's reconstruction of Schleiermacher's 1822 lectures on dialectic.
18. A variant of the argument is stated explicitly at DJ 1818:59. I use the abbreviation "DJ" for Ludwig Jonas' edition of *Dialektik*, consisting of an 1814 manuscript by Schleiermacher and notes taken by students attending the lecture-series of 1818. Friedrich Schleiermacher, *Dialektik*, ed. L. Jonas (Berlin: Reimer, 1839).

tially a semantic shift of the sort that the formalistic view seeks to deny. In Section V, I offer an alternative proposal on how to conceive the semantic shift that takes place in the generation of doctrinal sentences. My proposal entails the semantic sameness of didactic faith sentences and philosophical sentences, thus raising again the question of how Schleiermacher is able to satisfy his apologetic agenda.[19] I begin, then, with an analysis of the term "dialectical" based on Schleiermacher's own reflections on the subject.[20]

III. Dialectic: The Method of Inquiry.

Schleiermacher's use of the terms "logic" and "dialectic" is dependent upon and diverges in important ways from that of Immanuel Kant.[21] Kant distinguishes between "formal" and "transcendental" logic: while the former abstracts from the relation in which a concept or judgement may stand to an object, the latter investigates the conditions under which such a relationship is alone possible. Schleiermacher uses the term "logic" to cover the area which Kant calls "formal logic." He writes, "Logic . . . can only produce such rules of proceeding in thought, which have no relation to any particular con-

---

19. On this question, I refer the reader to my article, "The Order of Nature in Pious Self-Consciousness: Schleiermacher's Apologetic Argument," in *Religious Studies* 32:1 (March 1996): 93-108.
20. One of the most important proof-texts for ascribing the formalistic view to Schleiermacher is CG 1830:30, and especially the discussion in CG 1830:30.2. This passage is about Christian doctrinal sentences, a special sub-class of Christian didactic faith-sentences. It can serve as a proof-text for the formalistic view because if the formalitstic analysis is right for doctrinal sentences, then it must be right for didactic faith-sentences, since of all Christian teaching, Church doctrine is the most developed and the farthest removed from its roots in the first-order religious discourse of the Church.
    Schleiermacher tells us that doctrinal sentences come in three "forms" distinguishable according to what they are "about." Sentences of the first form are about "human conditions of life," "human states of mind" or "inner experience" (what he has in mind here is piety); while sentences of the second and third forms are about God and the world respectively. The first, it turns out, is the "basic form" [*Grundform*], out of which the others are "developed." My claim is that these passages should always be read in relation to CG 1830:35, which gives an alternative formulation for the three "forms" of doctrinal sentences. The argument which I develop in this paper goes to show that the formalistic view cannot be ascribed to Schleiermacher, and hence that passages which have a formalistic ring should be interpreted in terms of passages which do not. Hence, it seems to me that my argument establishes the primacy of CG 1830:35 over CG 1830:30 as the key to understanding Schleiermacher's distinction between the three forms.
21. It is perhaps safe to assume that Schleiermacher's thinking on these matters was decisively influenced by his reading of Kant, which, Dilthey reports, occupied him from his 19th to his 27th year of age. Wilhelm Dilthey, *Leben Schleiermachers*, ed. Martin Redeker (Göttingen: Vandenhoeck & Ruprecht, 1970), Vol. I, 108.

242   *Georg Behrens*

tent of the same. Such [rules] can pertain only to the form."[22] What Kant
calls "transcendental logic" falls for Schleiermacher in the province of dialectic. Moreover, unlike Kant he does not discriminate between the terms
"transcendental" (for Kant an epistemological term, meaning that which is a
necessary condition of knowledge) and "transcendent" (a term of metaphysics, meaning that which cannot be an object of experience): for
Schleiermacher the transcendental conditions of knowledge are transcendent
in the sense that they cannot themselves be objects of experience. Dialectic,
he holds, encompasses both logic and metaphysics; in classical times, these
two disciplines were united, and it was only more recently (and to their mutual detriment) that they were separated.[23]

Kant, too, distinguishes between "logic," which provides a canon
(negative criterion) of knowledge, and "dialectic," which seeks to give an
organon or method for producing knowledge.[24] According to Kant, a reliable organon of knowledge is impossible, so that dialectic is always wrong-
headed, a "logic of [mere] seeming."[25] The section of *Critique of Pure Reason* entitled "Transcendental Dialectic" is conceived as a demonstration of
the confusions which result when one attempts to stretch logic beyond its
critical task to that of the "discovery and expansion" of knowledge.[26] For his
part, Schleiermacher agrees with Kant that dialectic wants to be something
more than a negative criterion of knowledge. In all but his latest writing on
the subject (variously dated between 1831 and 1833), he holds onto the notion that dialectic is a method for the production of knowledge.[27] Unlike
Kant, however, he believes that it is possible to have such a method. Dialectic, he writes, is "the organon of knowledge, that is, the seat of all formulas of
its construction."[28] It is "the technical instruction [*Kunstlehre*] for producing

---

22. DO 1831:35.
23. DO 1822:88.
24. KrV: A61/B84. Immanuel Kant, *Kritik der reinen Vernunft* (Riga: Hartknoch, 1781/1787).
    References to this work will be according to the formula KrV : standard A/B pagination.
25. KrV:A61/B84.
26. KrV:A63/B88.
27. "Logic is a merely critical discipline. One doesn't use it to compose, but to pass judg-
    ment over a given line of thought. There are rules according to which it can be known
    whether a concept possesses the proper degree of clarity, a judgment that of scope, an
    inference that of soundness; it [logic] is, as it is said, the canon of thought. For dialectic,
    which wishes to destroy all arbitrary combinations and to be the construction of knowl-
    edge itself, that [logic's critical task] is a peripheral issue" (DJ 1818:19).
28. DJ 1814:22.

real knowledge,"[29] "the theory of scientific construction,"[30] "the theory of discovery."[31]

Knowledge, the aim of inquiry, is thought [*Denken*] which corresponds in the appropriate ways to something distinct from itself [*das Gedachte*].[32] Thought becomes knowledge in virtue of "the congruence of thinking with being."[33] The criterion of knowledge, however, is intersubjective agreement among those who have followed the proper method for arriving at it. Dialectic is both this privileged method for producing intersubjective agreement among inquirers seeking to know the same object, and the methodology [*Methodenlehre*] in which this method is detailed and grounded.

Dialectic as methodology is "the explication of the technical principles for conducting dialog [*Darlegung der Grundsätze für die kunstmäßige Gesprächsführung*] in the area of pure thought."[34] Schleiermacher distinguishes three kinds of thought: "artistic" [*künstlerisch*], "business-related" [*geschäftlich*] and "pure" thought. Artistic thought is for the sake of pleasure, business-related thought for that of achieving some practical end. Pure thought is thought "for the sake of knowledge."[35] Dialog takes place when "two distinct and separate sequences of thought are alternately related to one another."[36] Each of the three kinds of thought corresponds to a distinctive form of dialog. The kind of dialog typical of thought for the sake of knowledge comes about when such thought meets with a "block" [*Hemmung*], either an individual's "hesitancy" or "uncertainty" [*Zweifel*] in choosing between two mutually exclusive theses, or a "dispute" [*Streit*] between two parties, each representing a thesis incompatible with that of the other.[37] In such a case, what results is an effort to end the dispute by deciding in favor of one or the other thesis.

Dialectic, then, tells us "how one must proceed in order to resolve dispute, whenever it arises."[38] It is the method of debate among those who share an interest in knowledge, whereby each attempts to convince the others

---

29. DJ 1818:8.
30. DJ 1814:16.
31. DO 1822:75.
32. DO 1822:127.
33. DA 1811:8.
34. DO 1831:5. For my exposition of Schleiermacher's account of dialectic, I will rely primarily upon the 1831 "introduction," both because it represents Schleiermacher's considered view on the subject, and because it belongs to the same period of productivity as the finalized version of the dogmatics (1830).
35. DO 1831:7.
36. DO 1831:5.
37. DO 1831:38.
38. DO 1831:13.

that some hypothesis regarding an object agreed upon is true. That the participants to such a debate be inquirers is a prerequisite; the point of dialectic in not to establish peace among those motivated, e.g., by a polemical desire to establish a certain party-line or orthodoxy, or by an ecumenical desire to find themselves in agreement with others. Schleiermacher thinks that the reliability of dialectic rests on the "will to know" [*Wissenwollen*] which drives its application.[39] Thus, "Dialectic is only for those who are conscious of themselves as being oriented toward knowledge or the desire to know, and it is only valid for proceeding in this direction."[40]

IV. The Dialectical Generation of Didactic Faith Sentences:
A Critique of the Formalistic View.

In the first part of this essay, I asserted that, for Schleiermacher, didactic faith sentences are generated through reflection upon first-order religious discourse, and that this generative process is driven by the "dialectical interest." I also introduced what I called the formalistic view, according to which the generation of teaching consists in recasting the poetic and rhetorical modes of expression into a mode of expression capable of satisfying certain formal canons, but leaving untouched the relation of religious discourse to its subject-matter. My aim now is to critique this formalistic view, based on the conception of dialectic elaborated above.

I would like to focus on a remark at CG 1830:16 pertaining to the motives that drive Christians to produce didactic discourse. Schleiermacher tells us that the development of the didactic mode of expression, and its differentiation from the poetic and rhetorical modes, is motivated by "the desire to resolve dispute." It is by unpacking this claim that we come to see that the generation of teaching in the Christian Church must involve a semantic shift. Both modes of first-order religious discourse are capable of falling into "apparent contradiction."[41] That is to say, it is possible to regard the sentences of first-order religious discourse in such a way as to come to the con-

---

39. DO 1831:44.
40. DO 1831:7-8.
41. CG 1830:16.3. "Most dogmatic determinations were called into being through the contradictions which rhetorical expressions had produced" (CG 1830:16.addendum). The didactic mode of expression arises "out of the task of resolving the apparent conflict between individual images and figures" used in first-order religious discourse (CG 1830:18.2). The term "apparent" [scheinbar] is of course to be understood in the sense not of "merely apparent" (i.e., appearing to obtain while in fact not obtaining), but of being evident only to one who realizes the crucial semantic shift.

clusion that some are inconsistent with others. But this way of regarding sentences presupposes the referring of such sentences to common objects, for no contradiction is possible where sentences are not so referred. Where discourse remains subjective, governed by the aim of depicting and communicating self-consciousness, the semantic relation to the objects of self-consciousness is not a reference relation. A semantic shift must take place, a reference relation must be imposed, before the contradictions between poetic and rhetorical sentences can become "apparent." This semantic shift is the essence of didactic reflection upon the language of first-order religious discourse. The contradictions latent in rhetorical or poetic discourse are evident not to the person using such discourse for its characteristic purpose, in order to depict or to communicate pious self-consciousness, but to the one reflecting upon it didactically, shifting the focus upon its mediate objects. It is the process of bringing to bear the dialectical interest that characterizes the didactic reflection upon first-order religious discourse and first raises the problem of the inconsistency of such discourse.

From these remarks, it should be evident not only that the formalistic view requires an interpretation of the term "dialectical" that is anomalous with respect to the views represented in the *Dialektik*, but also that it cannot account fully for the transition from first-order religious discourse to didactic discourse, as Schleiermacher conceives it. Rather, the following alternative interpretation would seem to be mandated. When two thoughts are referred to the same object and are found to be incompatible, the result is dispute. The dialectical method is the method for resolving dispute; the result of its application, the thought which survives the dispute, is termed knowledge. The dialectical interest driving the generation of didactic faith sentences is the interest in gaining knowledge through the dialectical resolution of dispute. The generation of didactic discourse within the Christian Church is the first step in an inquiry regarding the objects of Christian self-consciousness. It is the initial establishment of a discourse that at least pretends to make true statements about God and the world.

V. Doctrine as Theoretical Discourse.

I have said that religious speech, for Schleiermacher, is "immediately" about self-consciousness and only "mediately" about God and the world. Didactic discourse, like scientific or philosophical discourse, is about God and the world in a way "unmediated" by pious self-consciousness. The time has come now to cash in the placeholder idea of mediation, which I have in-

246

troduced into the account, in terms reflective of Schleiermacher's own conceptual framework. What I will argue in this penultimate section of my paper is that the relation of religious speech to the objects of didactic discourse,
God and the world, is "mediate" because it is determined by the practical interest of expressing and communicating pious self-consciousness. This practical interest is constitutive of a peculiar semantic relation not paralleled in
doctrinal, scientific or philosophical discourse. The difference here is that
which obtains, in general, between what Schleiermacher calls "practical" and
"scientific" thought,[42] or "conditioned" and "pure" thought.[43] Schleiermacher defines practical thought as thought or some the sake of some end extrinsic to itself: it is successful if it is conducive to the attainment of the end
in question. Scientific thought, by contrast, is for the sake of knowledge
alone. Its aim to give a true account of the way things are, an account which
corresponds in the appropriate way to reality, is not reducible to any practical
interest.[44]

Schleiermacher not only wants to say that practical thought has a different end from theoretical thought, but that it possesses different semantic
properties, and that it is able to fulfill its practical function without at the
same time corresponding to reality in the way required of theoretical
thought. Conceptions which are of no use to theory regularly find justifiable
application in practice.[45] Practical conceptions may actually prove to be
misleading when applied in a theoretical context, while from the practical
standpoint they retain a kind of special validity, so long as they "work."[46] Of
course, there is something like a correspondence relation between practical
thought and reality, in virtue of which practical thought can fulfill its function, but this relation is determined by the particular practical interest moti-
vating such thought. As Schleiermacher puts the matter, in thought conditioned by a practical interest, "I do not think the whole object, but only that
in it [an ihm] which relates to my action."[47] The objects of practical thought

---

42. DO 1822:102ff.
43. DO 1822:329ff.
44. Thus, it is possible for a theoretically significant alternative between two accounts to be
    practically indifferent. "When we regard two opposing theories in physics, e.g., concern-
    ing the calcification of metals – some claim this phenomenon is due to the metal's bind-
    ing with the oxygen, others [that it is due to] the phlogiston's escaping from the metal –
    there is a point in the interaction with the object, at which the [alternative between] the
    two theories is indifferent, namely in the practical area. Here the rightness of representa-
    tion is not the aim of [this sort of] mental activity. But in the case of natural science, this
    [alternative] is not indifferent . . . ." (DO 1822:104).
45. DO 1822:331.
46. DO 1822:104.
47. DO 1822:330.

are in effect partially constituted by our practical interests, and as such they differ from the objects of theoretical thought. Pure thought is able to constitute its object without admitting any contribution from the side of practical interest.

What I would like to suggest is that, in Schleiermacher's view, poetic and rhetorical discourse is the exteriorization of the "practical" thought of the Christian community. First-order religious discourse is for the sake of depicting and communicating piety; the speaker's practical aim is to cause her own pious state to be apprehended and replicated by members of her audience. The relation between such discourse and the objects of pious self-consciousness (God and the world) is mediated by the practical interest of depicting and communicating pious self-consciousness. Insofar as these objects are intended by first-order religious discourse, they are constituted for it by its practical interest. No semantic relation of the kind proper to theoretical discourse links first-order religious discourse to them. They are cognized only as "that in them which relates to our action." On the other hand, didactic discourse is the exteriorization of the "theoretical" thought of Christian theology. It is about the relations between God and the world, representing a theoretical level of reflection upon these objects, and is not suitable for attaining the ends of first-order religious discourse.[48]

The proposal to understand first-order religious discourse as a practical discourse, and didactic discourse as a theoretical discourse, is supported by Schleiermacher's claim that as a matter of historical and psychological fact, pure thought always arises out of practical thought,[49] and that it does so through the application of the dialectical method.[50] Subjected to theoretically motivated scrutiny (e.g., didactic reflection), practical thought appears as a mixture of error and right opinion; no matter how well it works, it contains a distortion of the object and can never qualify as knowledge. The theoretical interest takes this mixed condition as a point of departure, imposing a new semantic relation, unmediated by practical interest, between thought and its objects, so that the inconsistencies of practical thought may become "apparent." We have already seen that didactic faith sentences are generated

---

48. The distinction of the 1822 lectures between "practical" and "scientific" thought corresponds to the distinction of the 1831 "introduction" between "artistic" and "business-related" thought, on the one hand, and "pure" thought on the other. The points I make in this section do not depend on my having opted for the terminology of 1822. Just as first-order religious discourse is the linguistic exteriorization of a certain kind of practical thought, and didactic discourse that of a certain kind of scientific thought, so poetic discourse may be called the exteriorization of artistic thought, rhetorical discourse that of business-related thought, and didactic discourse that of pure thought.
49. DO 1822:332-333.
50. DO 1822:334.

through reflection upon first-order religious discourse. If such discourse is the exteriorization of a certain area of practical thought, and didactic discourse is that of a certain area of pure thought, then indeed the generation of didactic faith sentences follows a pattern not peculiar to itself but common to thought in all areas: the birth of theory out of practical thought.

VI. Recapitulation and Conclusion.

How do we explain the existence of Christian teaching? Why does Christianity come to have teaching in the first place? How is teaching generated out of first-order religious discourse? What distinguishes didactic faith sentences from the sentences of such discourse? To give an account of didactic discourse, we must, on Schleiermacher's way of looking at the matter, look to its genesis. Pious self-consciousness does not itself necessitate the generation of didactic discourse. Piety intrinsically seeks to depict itself, hence its expression in poetic discourse, and it intrinsically seeks to communicate itself, hence the rhetorical proclamation of the Church. But it does not of its own accord necessitate the addition of a third, higher-level form of discourse. To account for the necessity of this development, we must look to a separate driving principle. Schleiermacher calls this principle the "dialectical interest": it is the principle which motivates the application of the dialectical method in any appropriate context. But since dialectic is the method of inquiry, "the dialectical interest" is none other than the "interest of knowledge" which motivates all forms of inquiry. Christian teaching, we conclude with Schleiermacher, owes its existence to the interest of knowledge; and didactic faith sentences differ from the sentences of first-order religious discourse in that they possess all the properties necessary for them to serve as the vehicles for knowledge-claims. First-order religious discourse is practical, motivated by the practical interest of depicting and communicating pious self-consciousness, and its objects are constituted for it by that interest. The transition to didactic discourse consists in what I have called a "semantic shift." Didactic discourse is theoretical; as such, the semantic relation in which it stands to its objects is unmediated by any practical interest.

Why, then, is didactic discourse generated through reflection upon first-order religious discourse? If it is concerned with knowing a certain domain of objects, why does it not base itself upon a direct investigation of those objects? The answer is that there is no direct investigation of objects, if directness is taken to imply isolation from any dialogical context. Inquiry, in natural science as well as in the Church, always takes shape as the dialectical resolution of dispute. As such, every inquiry begins in a dialogical context. Christian teaching is the product of inquiry that begins in the dialogical context defined by first-order religious discourse. It is first-order religious discourse which raises the questions, blunders into the quandaries, which didactic reflection detects and seeks to resolve. In this sense, then, Christian didactic reflection differs from philosophical inquiry. The latter, though also originating and proceeding within a dialogical context, is not bound to the context of first-order religious discourse. The truth-claims competing in philosophical inquiry are not subject to such a restriction as regards their pedigree. Christian didactic reflection, by contrast, considers only those truth-claims whose pedigree leads back to pious self-consciousness itself; no speculative claims owing their existence to free, unfettered thought alone enjoy its consideration.

SOME UNIDENTIFIED TITLES FROM THE RAUSCH AUCTION CATALOGUE OF SCHLEIERMACHER'S LIBRARY AND THE MAIN CATALOGUES OF THE PUBLISHING HOUSE G. REIMER

Peter W. Foley

With the auctioning of Schleiermacher's library a catalogue of the books was printed. This has been reprinted as Günter Meckenstock, *Schleiermachers Bibliothek: Bearbeitung des faksimilierten Rauchschen Auktionskatalogs und der Hauptbucher des Verlages G. Reimer*, Schleiermacher-Archiv, Bd. 10 (Berlin/New York: De Gruyter, 1993), and it has been supplemented with an excellent scholarly edited commentary. On page 300 (Sonderliste I) 13, titles are given by the author as yet unidentified from Rauch's action catalog (=RA). A further 11 titles are given on page 335 (Sonderliste III) as titles unable to be identified from the lists of books borrowed by Schleiermacher in the main catalogues held by the publishing house G. Reimer (=HR). In relation to the entire project, this is indeed a tiny proportion. Several of these are identified here, and it is the goal of this paper to make a small addendum to this extremely useful publication. In the following, the citation as given by Meckenstock, including the number from the catalogues of Rausch and Reimer, will be cited. That will be followed in each instance by the full title as discovered by the author here.

I am grateful for the use of the Herzog August Bibliothek in Wolfenbüttel, Germany, as an invaluable resource in identifying several of these works.

2194 Blicke aus der Wissenschaft in die Geschichte des Tags, Dresden 1809   [RA 96,119]

Rüle von Lilienstern, Johann Jakob Otto August: Hieroglyphen oder Blicke aus dem Gebiete der Wissenschaft in die Geschichte des Tages, Dresden, Leipzig 1809

Publisher: Carl Gottlob Gärtner

2195 Disputatio de vi musices ad excolendum hominem, Trier 1816   [RA 80,188]

Tex, Cornelis Anne den: De vi musices ad excolendum hominem e sententia Platonis, Trier 1816 ["Disputatio inauguralis" at head of text] [No publisher given]

2196   Geschichte der neuesten Bedrückungen der evangel. Erblande des Hauses Oestreich, 1763   [RA 9,297]

Vollständige Geschichte der neuesten Bedruckungen [sic!] der Evangelischen in den Erblanden des Hauses Oesterreich mit den dazu gehörigen Urkunden und Beweisschriften

[In two parts, no author, publisher or place given] Erster Theil, 1763, 111 p. and title page. Zweiter Theil, 1764, 111 p. and title page.

2197   Geschichte über das Lutherische Gesang-Buch, Altenburg 1707   [RA 103,53]

Schmidt, Thomas: Historica et memorabilia: D. I. merckwürdige Sachen und Geschichte, so sich über das Lutherische Gesang-Buch, und dessen meisten Lieder und Versicul begeben und zugetragen, Altenburg 1707

Publisher: Johann Ludwig Richter

2199   La nourriture da l'ame ou recueil pour tous les jours de la semaine   [RA 37,1158]

Ostervald, Jean Rodolphe: La nourriture da l'ame, ou, Recueil de prieres pour tous les jours de la semaine, pour les principales fetes de l'anee, et sur differns sujets interessants: on trouvera aussi une harmonie de la Passion, qui renferme les lectures convenables pour chacun des jours de la Semaine Sainte: le tout precede d'un traite de la priere, Lusanne 1772

Publisher: J. P. Heubach

2204   Urkunden über den Anfang des 7jährigen Kriegs, Berlin
            [RA 96,124]

            Gesammelte Nachrichten und Urkunden, den im Jahr 1756 in
            Deutschland entstandenen Krieg betreffend
            5 vols [parts 1-55], 1757-1762

            [No place, author or publisher given, but clearly written using
            Prussian archival materials – which could explain Rauch's
            indication of Berlin as its place of publication]

2622   Coblenzer Adresse [HR 17.2.1818]

            [*Goerres, Josef von*:] Die Uebergabe der Adresse der Stadt
            Coblenz und der Landschaft an Se. Majestät den König in
            öffentlicher Audienz bei Sr. Durchl. dem Fürsten Staatskanzler
            am 12. Januar 1818 – Als Bericht für die Theilnehmer,
            [Koblenz] 1818

            Two editions of this work exist:
            – 48 pp. with title page and blank page. Herzog August
            Bibliothek Wolfenbüttel Gm 2527.
            – 60 pp. with title page, verse page, page for editorial note by
            author and blank page.

            Herzog August Bibliothek Wolfenbüttel Gm 2526.
            Contrary to the numbering at the HAB the 48-page edition
            must be the first edition.
            The text in the second edition is the same merely using a larger
            typeface. The editorial note to the 60-page edition indicates
            that it is now being made available to a wider audience.

EDITIONS OF SCHLEIERMACHER'S
'ÜBER DIE RELIGION' AND 'MONOLOGEN'

Terrence N. Tice

Three German texts of Schleiermacher's *Über die Religion: Reden an die Gebildeten unter ihren Verächtern*, as nearly critically edited as will ever be possible given the lack of written manuscripts, are now available for scholars wanting to settle, or at least more informedly to tackle, issues in dispute concerning both what Schleiermacher said and developments in his thinking about religion.

(1) the first edition of 1799, which has come down with but a small number of quite minor typographical errors, over a quarter of them already captured in an original index of errata, reappeared in the *Kritische Gesamtausgabe*, I/1 (Berlin & New York: Walter de Gruyter, 1984), 185-326. By my count, besides the 40 errata indicated originally, Günter Meckenstock has added 148 caught by later editors or himself and six conjectures of his own. An attentive reader would have been led astray by only a handful of these typographical errors, if that (e.g., *nur* for *nun*). Nonetheless, it is obviously of no little value to have a certified text. A remarkable, if highly complex, critical edition of all four editions, using the 1799 text as its base then proceeding to changes made successively in the three later editions, was produced by Georg Christian Bernhard Pünjer in 1879 (Braunschweig: C.A. Schwetschke und Sohn), and it appears to be virtually identical except that, as Meckenstock rightly notes, it is "difficult to read" because of all the apparatus and type font changes.

In 1899, Rudolf Otto reissued the first edition (Göttingen: Vandenhoeck & Ruprecht), dedicating it to Wilhelm Dilthey. This work reached six editions in all: 1906, 1913, 1920, 1926, in 17,800 copies total according to the publisher's records. In all, twenty-seven printings by other publishers also appeared between 1911 and 1985. In contrast, apart from the material in Pünjer's work, all but one of the other printings of these *Reden* have been from the 1831 fourth edition (for all intents and purposes identical with the third 1821 edition, as will be seen below). Of these, in the nineteenth century four were issued by the original publishing house, Georg Reimer, in 1834 (in *Sämmtliche Werke* I.1), 1843, 1859 and 1878, and six by others (1834, 1868, 1880, 1889, 1895 and 1899); in the twentieth century only two appeared using the 1821/1831 edition: 1924, introduced by Hans Leisegang (5,500 copies) and 1935 (the same, in 5,250 copies, out-of-print since 1942).[1] As a consequence, except for library users and those who could get copies of the final edition by antiquariat, the overwhelming majority of readers have used only the first edition, without benefit of Schleiermacher's extensive subsequent alterations and additions.

In English, the 1799 edition was not available, except in excerpts within editions by John Oman (1894), recently reissued by Westminster/John Knox Press, and Tice (Richmond: John Knox Press, 1969), soon to reappear in a revised edition, until Richard Crouter's translation of it (Cambridge University Press, 1988). In my own new edition, translation of the 1799 text can be constructed from the main text and footnotes; it was drawn from Pünjer's text, only proceeding backward from the 1821/1831 edition to 1806 and 1799 so that readers can see what was successively retained from 1799 and 1806 and can have all the nontypographical changes in place.

Joint editions of the *Reden* and *Monologen* in other languages also appear to be from 1799-1800: in Russian (1911), Swedish (1923), and Italian (1947). In the French (1944) edition *Discours sur la Religion* (1799) stands alone.[2]

(2) Until 1995, the only reissuings of the 1806 German edition had appeared first in Pünjer (1879), then with an introduction by Siegfried Lommatzsch in the Bibliothek theologischer Klassiker (Gotha: Perthes, 1888). In English it appeared only in excerpts within the editions of John Oman (1894) and Tice (1969). In my new edition this text appears for the first time in English, as constructed through the main text and footnotes.

In addition, Günter Meckenstock has performed yet another valuable service through the *Kritische Gesamtausgabe*, I/12 (Walter de Gruyter, 1995, lxxix, 411 S.), which offers Schleiermacher's *Über die Religion*, (2.-) 4. Auflage (1-321) and *Monologen: Ein Neujahrsgabe* (2.-) 4. Auflage (323-393). Here the main text is that of 1831. All differences in the 1806 and 1821 texts of the *Reden* are indicated in the footnotes-right down to commas, spellings and typographical changes, as with the 1799 edition. Here it is easy to see, for the first time, except through a reconstruction from the Pünjer edition, what a major work of revision had already occurred in 1806. It may be hoped that the Pünjer edition will be reprinted, for users of the excellent KGA texts alone will still not be able to see the numerous specific divergences of the 1806 text from that of 1799.

---

1. All this publishing information comes from Wichmann von Meding's painstaking chronological *Bibliographie der Schriften Schleiermachers* (Berlin & N.Y.: Walter de Gruyter, 1992). The total number of copies for all printings is not known.
2. Information about these other editions was gathered by me in the initial volume of my series of Schleiermacher bibliographies (Princeton University Press, 1966.)

(3) The 1831 text presented in *Sämmtliche Werke* and Pünjer seems to be virtually identical with that offered by Günter Meckenstock (1995). In fact, in addition to almost all of the dozen or so minor errors that are not clear changes in spelling or punctuation, another dozen or so can be correctly deciphered with ease from the 1821 text. Very often, what is listed are typographical errors in 1831. By my count, of these definite errors 9 of 13 were in the 1831 text. Only one of the changes is arguably of substantive significance (p. 80: nicht auch becomes auch nicht). Thus, the 1831 text is not so much a new edition as a reprinting of the 1821 text with a minuscule number of typographical alterations and errors. Nevertheless, Günter Meckenstock is also to be praised for certifying the exact status of these texts.

At the risk of being mistaken as overly proud, rather than as a worker happy to have fulfilled the high standards of one's craft, I have to reiterate here what I most admiringly but critically stated concerning the 1894 translation of *On Religion* by John Oman, which is still circulating. "As a first attempt," I said (1969, p. 29), "Oman's text often shows very shrewd insight. It would not have been sufficient merely to revise what he had done, however, since the whole conception was rather frequently mistaken and since his largely transcriptive technique produced a text confused, stilted, and misleading in effect."

Some displeasure has arisen concerning my 1969 translation in that it uses "perception," "perspective," or even in a couple of special instances the coined term "perspectivity," for *Anschauung* instead of the usual word "intuition" drawn particularly from translations of Kant. I do not see why the complaint need have been so pronounced, since I have fully explained my interpretation in footnotes and have very frequently indicated where *Anschauung* was the term being translated. Other translators may want to use "intuition," hopefully with similar explanations of the meanings they attach to it – and there are indeed several levels of reference in Schleiermacher's own use of the term.[3] I still think, however, that serious difficulties arise because of the connotations placed on "intuition" in both ordinary and technical usage. That is to say, often it has the bearing of a rather esoteric or even preternatural, inner insight conjured without the immediate benefit of solid sense perception [*Wahrnehmung*] and other external references or of reality testing (as in "women's intuition," often used pejoratively or as a damning with faint praise or as a mystified attribution). Or, on the other hand, it is

---

3.   See Terrence N. Tice, "Schleiermacher's Conception of Religion: 1799 to 1831," in Marco Maria Olivetti, ed., *Schleiermacher, in Archivio di Filosofia* 52, n. 1-3 (Roma, 1984), 333-356, for my detailed analysis, mostly worked out already in my 1961 dissertation at Princeton Theological Seminary.

used to stand for a particular kind of distinctly mediated thinking or synthetic outlook (as in *Weltanschauung*). For Schleiermacher, in contrast, it always means literally some type of a "looking upon," an outward-referring tendency. These types move from being a near synonym for *Wahrnehmung* to being a general outlook (including one in philosophical discourse) to being an essential component of distinctly religious experience, a view he never abandoned. When used in a pair with *Gefühl*, as is prominently done in all the editions, a pair even added in some key revised passages in 1821, it refers to a feature in what Schleiermacher otherwise spoke of as "immediate self-consciousness," meaning here a religious consciousness borne directly within and yet pointing outside oneself (as in *Anschauung des Universums*).

I focus on this particular difficulty here to typify a widespread faulty process in the reception of these texts that anyone who had gone into an adequately detailed comparison of them could detect without question. Frequently this process has centered on interpretations of *Gefühl* and *Anschauung*, sometimes almost as if he had offered nothing else of significance to the theory of religion in his five distinct, if highly integrated, discourses. This process, quite familiar in other areas of scholarship as well, goes as follows. For whatever reasons, someone purveys a quite inaccurate account of what Schleiermacher, in this case, said. For example, the word *Anschauung* is interpreted univocally and is said to be submerged from 1806 or some other "later" date in favor of *Gefühl*. (This is only in small part true, for Schleiermacher had to deal even then with misunderstandings of his various uses of the word and sometimes found some other word or phrase for it in order to speak as unmistakably as possible.) This view then sticks, for whatever perhaps additional reasons (e.g., adherence to supposed "authority," laziness, continued inattentive reading, the desire to make a preconceived point for or against Schleiermacher on independent ideological grounds, fear of being seen to differ from one's own crowd . . .). Subsequent scholars simply accept what has thus formed as the received opinion, questioning it no further. Providing all the texts, with an exact registering of all changes in place, at least deprives current serious scholars of any real excuse for purveying such error, which, wherever it appears, is both damaging to the general search for truth or understanding and is self-subverting of scholars themselves.

In summary, now available is a critical presentation of the German texts of 1799 (KGA I/1), of 1799 to 1806 to 1821/1831 (Pünjer), and of 1831 (with references to differences in 1806 and 1821) (KGA I/12). In English we have two translations of the 1799 text (by Crouter, 1988; and in the composite Edwin Mellen Press edition by Tice, 1998). (I waited to issue my 1998 edition until I could see whether any of the texts issued in the KGA differed from the critical Pünjer edition and *Sämmtliche Werke* edition that I used, and I find that they do not. I have also arranged not to have to put any of the editorial texts and notes in endnotes. A revision of my 1969 John Knox Press edition is presented as the main text with all the notes placed below. We also have the older John Oman translation of the 1831 text (with some excerpts from earlier years), still in print, and the Tice translations (with numerous additional excerpts from earlier years) of 1969, long out of print, and using the total Pünjer text in reverse order, of 1998. Both the 1806 text, as such, and the Pünjer text should be reissued to be made available in libraries and for individual use as needed. I am currently submitting a proposal to Schleiermacher: Studies and Translations series for this purpose (unless it is to be accomplished in German), to include a brief introduction indicating typical changes made in 1806 and 1821. With this complete set of texts a new era of study and interpretation should open up that is addressed to these foundation documents for the modern study of religion.

The current situation regarding *Monologen* is somewhat less complete. On the German side, we have most of what is needed: critical editions of the 1800 first edition, in KGA I/3, 1-61, edited by Günter Meckenstock (1988) and of the (2.-) 4. Auflage of (1810, 1822-) 1829. We must still go to the critical Schiele-Mulert editions of 1902 and 1914 (reprinted in 1978) to see directly what changes were made from 1800 to 1810. For the most part, the revisions from 1810 to 1829 are comparatively minor, but some are of importance. There are only twelve quite minor misspellings in comparing the actually final text of 1822 with the edition of 1829, and I find that every one of these was a typographical error in 1829. I also find that each one had already been corrected in *Sämmtliche Werke* II.1 (1846), 345-420. To this list Meckenstock adds a conjecture (p. 342) that *fühl* might be meant instead of *führ*, a plausible suggestion but one that I see no compelling reason to accept.

Wichmann von Meding reports the long, quite mixed publishing history of this work, which is similar in some respects to that of *Über die Religion*. As a single work, the 1829 edition (no doubt corrected for error) appeared again in 1834, 1836 and 1843, then in 1846, 1848, 1851, 1852, 1853, 1860, 1868 (by two publishers), 1869, 1870, 1874, 1887, 1889 and 1891. The last appearance in the nineteenth century was in 1899, using the identical 1822 text.

The turn into the twentieth century began with Friedrich Michael Schiele's critical edition in *Philosophische Bibliothek* 84 (1902) of the 1800 text with footnotes indicating the variant readings from 1810 and 1822. Schiele included a page of often substantive divergences in the much-used 1868 *Philosophische Bibliothek* 6 edition produced by Julius Hermann von Kirschmann with his introductory essay. Schiele died on August 12, 1913, aged forty-five. By the end of that year, Hermann Mulert had taken up the work Schiele had begun, adding notes to an extensive index already provided and leaving the rest of the text unaltered. For a 1914 edition, reprinted in 1978, Mulert finished Schiele's work and added a New Year's sermon from 1792, previously published in SW II.7 (1836), 135-152 (but wrongly ascribed to 1793 there). This is soon to appear in a companion volume of Schleiermacher's New Year's sermons translated by Edwina Lawler. Mulert also added a reprinting of Wilhelm Dilthey's resume and excerpts from Schleiermacher's 1792 essay *Über den Wert des Lebens*. The complete text of this previously unpublished important forerunner of the Soliloquies first appeared in KGA I/1 (1984), 391-471. This was translated, with an introduction and notes (including 43 that closely follow the course of Dilthey's influential text and show his presentation to have been "sparse and often wrong or misleading"), under the title *On What Gives Value to Life*, by Edwina Lawler and me (Edwin Mellen Press, 1995), xii, 112 p.

Other publishers also issued the 1829 text in 1922, 1923, 1924, and then again only in 1995, but all the other printings by various publishers in the twentieth century were of the 1800 text: in 1911 (three times), 1915, 1922, 1923, 1924, 1926, 1931, 1943, 1953, 1954, 1967, 1970, 1981, 1984 and 1988.

I began work on a translation of the *Soliloquies* over a decade ago but stopped to work with translative studies of all the other important preparatory works. Not all of these are yet in print, but the principal one, just mentioned, appeared in 1995. Two others of marked importance appeared earlier (both also issued by Edwin Mellen Press, all based on new texts in KGA I/1): the 1789 essay *On the Highest Good*, translated with notes and a postscript by H. Victor Froese (1992), and the 1792-93 essay *On Freedom*, translated with introduction and notes by Albert L. Blackwell (1992).

Gradually translations of his other extensive notes, essays and reviews from 1788 through 1800, all now available in critically edited German texts, are being prepared. A translation with introduction by Jeffery Hoover of the 1799 essay "Toward a Theory of Social Conduct" appeared in *New Athenaeum/Neues Athenaeum*, vol. 4 (1995), 9-39. A new, critically edited translation with accompanying study of Schleiermacher's views by Peter Foley is forthcoming. Another set of translations and introductions by the Kantian scholar Jacqueline Mariña on some early texts regarding Kant appears in the present volume. (The scholarly material from 1788 through 1800 takes up 1,246 sizable pages in KGA I/1-3. On November 21, 1800, Schleiermacher had reached his thirty-fourth birthday.)

Moreover, we now have a way to check against the Schiele-Mulert text for possible inaccuracies. My own aim has always been to provide the final

1822 text and to place all differences in the 1800 and 1810 texts in footnotes. I am also attempting to add references for the first time to the entire range of pertinent earlier works.

In closing, I want to draw special attention to the excellent editorial work of my esteemed colleague, Günter Meckenstock, now a professor of theology in the University at Kiel and successor to the late Hans-Joachim Birkner as director of the Schleiermacher-Forschungsstelle there. Perhaps only those who have attempted similarly thorough editorial work can fully appreciate the patient, reflective digging that he has done to provide not only the most accurate texts possible but also the extensive historical introductions, editorial reports, footnoted references, appendixes and indexes that he and his assistants have supplied. To indicate appreciation for the entire team working on KGA I/1-3, I mention the following persons also, as Meckenstock has: Andreas Arndt, Ulrich Barth, Hans-Joachim Birkner, Elizabeth Blumrich, Hans Dierkes, Dolly Füllgraf, Anke Hasselmann, Anke Homann, Berndt Jaeger, Martin Ohst, Hermann Patsch, Hermann Peiter, Martin Rössler, Helma Talka, Hans-Friedrich Traulsen, Wolfgang Virmond, and numerous unnamed librarians. Even these thanks are not enough, for the ongoing volumes of correspondence and of scholarly works from later years, especially including Schleiermacher's ethical writings, can also be expected to shed light on changes that Schleiermacher made to both *On Religion* and *Soliloquies* through 1821 and 1822 respectively. Even when changes were not made, these other resources enable scholars to understand their developing form and content better.

Much basic work on establishing the provenance and development of these two major works, as of finding to what thinking of others they explicitly or implicitly refer, remains to be done. All such effort affords valuable aid to those who wish to use them for their own interpretation and reflection. In the *Schleiermacher: Studies and Translations* series the latter activity is also furthered by monographic essays and notes attached to each piece.

SCHLEIERMACHER'S CORRESPONDENCE

Terrence N. Tice

The general accounting of Schleiermacher's correspondence that I included in the first *Schleiermacher Bibilography* (1966) covered eighty-eight books, collections and articles over a space of 10 pages, and several items have been added over the succeeding thirty years.[1] This part of Schleiermacher's life in itself amounts to an enormous output, and a very large proportion of what is extant is of a personal nature. This was usually the case even when Schleiermacher was transacting some sort of business, particularly with other cultured men and women. Yet, much has been lost. For example, we can now read next to nothing of any exchange with several of the most important women in his life – his mother, his cousin Frau Benike, Elenore Grunow – and almost none of the remaining correspondence is complete.

Despite all this loss, the considerable remnant bears a full, rich picture of this extraordinary person, and each portion of it is worth reading for meditative and cultural reasons, not only for purposes of scholarship. As a whole, as in various parts into which it could be organized, it amounts to a great set of cultural events at a time when human intellect and ingenuity were making bold new steps in many parts of the world. We now call these new ventures "modern," though inevitably they were also catching up and redeveloping achievements from humanity's past. They had to do with fresh graspings of perception and imagination, with reachings toward a more adequate understanding of what it takes for human beings and societies and institutions to develop morally, with how to order the process of knowing so that it will yield truly "scientific" knowledge and a genuine, critically informed comprehension of history, and finally with new and fruitful explorations of the "religious" domain. In all these areas Schleiermacher had deeply penetrating, interlocking involvement, less so with the productions of literature, trade, wealth and technology that today sometimes swamp working defini-

---

1. Besides the four volumes overseen by Ludwig Jonas and Wilhelm Dilthey, with Hildegaard Schleiermacher and Ehrenfried von Willich, the 1966 bibliography cites 22 collections (almost all containing previously unpublished letters) and 65 articles, segments or chapters (the same). Current work is done on the back of the prodigious initial efforts of Heinrich Meisner early in this century (including some foreshortened items and some errors, which now have to be checked against whatever originals have survived), and of the likes of Johannes Bauer, Otto von Boenigk, Heinrich Meisner, Ernst Müsebeck, Hermann Mulert, Karl Heinrich Sack, Walther Sattler, and Erich Schmidt.

tions of what separates off the "modern" world from its past and supposed future. Just as we must go to his sermons and to his theological and philosophical writings to observe the moral and spiritual elements that ground all the rest for him, so too does the vast correspondence of the man beckon, for these letters present a consistent record of the interpersonal, dialogical, all-pervasively spiritual and moral undergirdings of all the rest in his life. They are almost bound to strike a resonance within his later readers as well, to call us to explore our own roots and to form our own resolve – this even though we now live in rather different conditions and with a greater range of outlooks to choose among. Without "preaching," Schleiermacher, as I think, will constantly if often directly draw readers of his correspondence to these activities.

Whatever the original reasons for undertaking the painstaking chronological reconstruction of Schleiermacher's correspondence in the *Kritische Gesamtausgabe*, in my view these will be its greatest accomplishments among readers for a very long time to come. The editors now working on these volumes, Andreas Arndt and Wolfgang Virmond, are to be strongly commended for the high standards they are fulfilling in this work, as is the editorial commission that has preceded and accompanied them in their labors.

By 1995, four large volumes have appeared, and these take us through 1800, when Schleiermacher reached his thirty-second birthday, almost halfway through his life. Other volumes will take us gradually forward every few years. In addition, a volume in *Schleiermacher-Archiv* (Berlin/New York: Walter de Gruyter), edited by Arndt and Virmond, is to contain a listing of all the letters as yet known that are to be published within the series. So, now it is possible for me to begin another kind of accounting, based on this work.

Within these four volumes forty-one correspondents have been identified, though in some cases all that can be given are indications of when letters were written but no direct content. The latter information too is valuable, but it represents something of the flow of exchange, even if this must be partial, and it opens the way to later additions of newly discovered letters. In addition, much useful biographical information is likewise to be found in the editors' introduction. Ample indexes are affixed, though the one great lacuna that must eventually be filled in some way is the lack of an index of subjects and concepts. The same problem attaches to all the many volumes of the KGA issued to date. Largely drawing on information available in these volumes, in what follows I have sought to characterize the overall record of each correspondence, alphabetically arranged, with brief identifications of who Schleiermacher's epistolary companions were. In each case, I have indicated the extent of new items and newly filled-out items now available. The item numbers correspond to the succession from #187 through #274 in the 1966 bibliography, with a great many new numbers (e.g., #192nc, #259k) added in between. (Item numbers with no abc's etc. attached refer to the items initially numbered in 1966. My volume on Schleiermacher's Sermons (1997) follows a similar plan, as does the entire succession of Schleiermacher bibliographies, in which the secondary literature also has a number for each item through 1984. (After that, the items are thus far listed only year by year.) It will eventually be possible to ascertain at a glance the full extent of each correspondence. One might imagine a chronological table in which each set is represented by a bold line, in some instances reduced to a succession of dots during years in which the exchange is known to have continued but no exemplars are extant.

Eventually some means of adding new information and corrections will have to be devised, as I have done in my bibliographical listings. (Two books and four sizable up-dates have appeared, and another long up-date is scheduled for publication in 1998.) Moreover, perhaps Schleiermacher's official correspondence will need to be presented and explained in supplementary monographs as it is found. For the present, a few such items are included and a short list of addenda is being placed at the end of each KGA volume.

192n. Further (from the 1989 record of KGA V/1 in *New Athenaeum/Neues Athenaeum*): All 326 letters are accounted for in the alphabetical listing below, including the 114 letters that are only indicated, without direct content (79 from Schleiermacher and 35 to him). See the 1989 listing for 193f, 193n, 206n, 214aa, 238n, 247, 259, 265, and 274d ; also addenda in the 1997 listing for 193n, 199, 206n, 212, 228n, 244n, 247, 258n, 265 and 274n. Eight additions and corrections, but no additional letters, are pointed out in KGA V/2 (1988), S. 534; nine variant readings are listed in KGA V/3 (1992), S. 581.

192na. *Kritische Gesamtausgabe* V.2: *Briefwechsel 1796-1798 (Briefe 327-552)*, hg.v. Andreas Arndt und Wolfgang Virmond (Berlin/New York: Walter de Gruyter, 1988). lvii, 534 S. + Karte von Kreis Landsberg an der Warthe. [Note: In the 1991 bibliography initial notice was given under l86na.] These 226 letters are presented chronologically, as in the first volume. It includes 79 letters not published previously (l5 from Schleiermacher, 64 to him), plus numerous expansions of items already published. All 226 letters are listed alphabetically by correspondent below. Contents: Verzeichnis der Briefe vii-xii); Einleitung der Bandherausgeber: I. Historische Einfuhrung (xiii-xlvi), II. Editorischer Bericht (xlvi-l); Verzeichnis der einzelnen Briefwechsel (li-lvii); Briefe 327-552 (1-451); Abbildungen (455-456); Abkürzungen und editorische Zeichen (457-458); Literaturverzeichnis (459-472); Register der Namen und Werke (473-533); Ergänzungen und Korrekturen zu KGA V/1 (534). The volume also gives ten exemplars of correspondents' handwriting, a map of Gnadenfrei (1795), where Schleiermacher's sister Charlotte was then living, and an etching to which she referred in a letter.

192nb. *Kritische Gesamtausgabe* V/3: *Briefwechsel 1799-1800 (Briefe 553-849)*, hg.v. Andreas Arndt und Wolfgang Virmond (Berlin/New York: Walter de Gruyter, 1992). cxxvi, 585 S. + Karte von Berlin (1812). [Note: In the 1995 bibliography initial notice was given under #186nb.] These 306 letters (ten numbers are addenda, e.g., #551a), presented chronologically, cover Jan. 1799 to April 1800. They include 77 letters not previously published (41 from Schleiermacher, 36 to him), plus numerous expansions of items already published. All 296 letters are listed alphabetically by correspondent below; 224 of these are only indicated, without direct content. Contents: Verzeichnis der Briefe (ix-xvii); Einleitung der Bandherausgeber: I. Historische Einführung (xix-cxii); II. Editorischer Bericht (cxiii-cxvi); Verzeichnis der einzelnen Briefwechsel (cxvii-cxxvi); Briefe 553-846 (1-500); Literaturverzeichnis (505-522); Register der Namen und Werke (523-579); Ergänzungen zu KGA V/1 und KGA V/2 (581-585). This volume also gives ten exemplars of correspondents' handwriting.

192nc. *Kritische Gesamtausgabe* V/4: *Briefwechsel 1800 (Briefe 850-1004)*, hg.v. Andreas Arndt und Wolfgang Virmond (Berlin/New York: Walter de Gruyter, 1994). xciii, 481 S. These 157 letters (three letters are addenda, #994a and two under #880), presented chronologically, extend from the end of April through December 1800. They include 50 letters not previously published (18 from Schleiermacher, 32 to him), plus numerous expansions of items already published. All 157 letters are listed alphabetically by correspondent below; 47 are only indicated, without direct content. Contents: Vorwort, von Hermann Fischer im Namen der Herausgeber (v-vi); Verzeichnis der Briefe (ix-xiv); Einleitung der Bandherausgeber: I. Historische Einführung (xv-lxxxii), II. Editorischer Bericht (lxxxiii-lxxxv); Verzeichnis der einzel-

nen Briefwechsel (lxxxvii-xciii); Briefe 850-1004 (1-395); Verzeichnis
der Abbildungen (399); Abkürzungen und editorische Zeichen (401-
402); Literaturverzeichnis (403-423); Register der Namen und Werke
(425-473); Ergänzungen zu KGA V/3 (475-481). This volume also
gives nine exemplars of correspondents' handwriting, a copy of poems
from 1685 by Paul Flemming (published in 1800) and an excerpt from
a satirical cartoon on *Athenaeum* (1800).

193f. Albertini (1769-1831): The full record from KGA V/1 (1985) is as
       follows. Twelve letters from schoolmate Albertini are included, from
       26. April 1787 to 25. Dez. 1789, and indications of nine letters from
       Schleiermacher from 12. Mai 1787 to Dez. 1789, without direct con-
       tent. No correspondence is recorded in KGA V/2-4.

193n. Armendirektorium: In addition to Schleiermacher's three 1795/96 let-
       ters (26. Dez. 1795, 4. Feb. 1796, 19. Juli 1796) to the Armendirek-
       torium, Berlin, and two from it (20. Jan. 1796, 30. Juli 1796) included
       in KGA V/1 (1985), see also his letter to Oehschläger (#238n below).
       – Eight of Schleiermacher's letters are added in KGA V/2 (#395, 13.
       Juni 1797; #444, 27. Jan. 1798; #466, 10. April 1798; #506, wohl 14.
       Aug. 1798; #524, 23. Aug. 1798; #525, 24. Sept. 1798; #531, 26. Okt.
       1798; #534, 30. Okt. 1798), with nine interspersed letters from the
       Armendirektorium in 1798. All 17 letters are new. Indication of a let-
       ter from Kriegsrat Steffeck on this business is also included (#443, vor
       dem 27. Jan. 1798), as is an indication of Schleiermacher's letter to
       the Reformierte Kirchendirektorium requesting leave to visit Lands-
       berg (#505, vor dem 14. Aug 1798). – KGA V/3 (1992) includes 14
       letters, eight from Schleiermacher (12. Feb. 1800-21. Feb. 1800) –
       three with his Lutheran colleague at Charité, Johann Georg Wilhelm
       Prahmer (1770-1812), and six from the Armendirektorium (30. Jan.
       1799-18. Feb. 1800), plus indication, without direct content of another
       they sent (vor Feb. 1800). – KGA V/4 (1994) includes seven letters,
       four from Schleiermacher (22.Aug. 1800-11.Okt. 1800) and four from
       the Armendirektorium (5. Sept. 1800-1. Okt. 1800).

199.   Aulock (1764-1834): Dobschütz was mistaken as to the date of this
       letter in poetic form. It was included with a lost letter from Schleier-
       macher to his sister Charlotte kurz vor dem 31. Dez. 1796 and later
       published in KGA V/2 (1988) (#358, S. 68, 70, with photo-
       reproduction, S. 69).

201n. Of a voluminous correspondence with the Benike (Beneke) family and especially with his "Cousine" Frau Benike, with whom he had formed a very close relationship during a visit from Drossen to Landsberg an der Warthe in the Summer of 1789, nothing remains, though it is known to have extended to 1801. She was the daughter of Pastor Johann Lorenz Schumann (1719-1795), whose position Schleiermacher was to assume there in 1794-1796, and his wife Sophie Luise (1734-ca 1770), who was a sister of his uncle Stubenrauch; she was married to lawyer Gottlob Wilhelm Benike (b. ca 1754), and they had several children. In KGA V/2 (1988) 23 indications are given, without direct content, 15 of these from Schleiermacher (vor dem 24. Sept. 1796-vor dem 11. Dez. 1798); in KGA V/3 (1992) eight such indications, five of them from Schleiermacher (wohl 24. April 1799-vor dem 28. März 1800); in KGA V/4 (1994) ten, seven of these from Schleiermacher (April 1800-13. Dez. 1800).

202n. Indication, without direct content, of Schleiermacher's letter to Sara Agatha Bestvater (vor dem 7. Sept. 1792) is given in KGA V/1 (1985), S. 256. She was the youngest sister of F.C.G. Duisberg's wife (see #214aa). No further letters are known.

202t. Included in KGA V/l (1985) are four letters from Barby schoolmate Johann Jakob Beyer (vor dem 7. Sept. 1786 bis 22. Juni 1787) and indications of three letters from Schleiermacher (7. Sept. 1786, vor dem 20. Okt. 1786, vor dem 22. Juni 1787). No further letters are known.

204n. Indication, without direct content, of a letter from Pastor Georg August Wilhelm Bornemann (1749-1802) of Schlodien, near Schlobitten (wohl Aug. 1793) is given in KGA V/2 (1985), S. 310. Nothing is extant from the correspondence that appears to have succeeded this letter. Schleiermacher made a two-week visit to him at Schlodien in 1793.

206n. Brinckmann (Brinkmann) (1764-1847): In addition to an earlier (1789) letter from Schleiermacher cited in the 1966 bibliography (also in KGA V/1, which also includes three 1789 letters from Brinckmann-all of these earlier published by Meisner and Schmidt-plus one 1793 letter), of 13 letters from Schleiermacher to Brinckmann extant from the 1796-1798 period seven appear in KGA V/2 (1988) for the first time and three others completely for the first time (#363, probably Jan. 1797; #408, Sept. 1797; #445, 27. Jan. 1798; ## 447-453, ca Jan. 1798). Indications of one additional letter from Schleiermacher (#528, vor Herbst 1798) and three from Brinckmann (#446, wohl Jan. 1798; #527, vor Herbst 1798; #529, Herbst 1798) are also given. Two of Schleiermacher's letters had already been published in Briefe 4 (#448, before Feb. 1798; #453, probably the end of Jan. 1798), and three of them had been referred to in Karoline von Humboldt: Neue Briefe, hg.v. Albert Leitzmann (Halle, 1901), 142-150 (#379, Winter 1796/97; #409, probably Sept. 1797; #431, 21. Dez. 1797). – KGA V/3 (1992) includes ten letters, all previously published, five from Schleiermacher (#673, 6. Juli 1799; #758, 23. Dez. 1799 bis 4. Jan. 1800; #796, 15. Feb. 1800; #817, 22. März 1800; #847, 19. April bis 22. April 1800) and five from Brinkmann (17. Mai 1799-8. April 1800). – KGA V/4 (1994) includes six letters, only one of them new in its complete form (#869), three from Schleiermacher (#869, 17. Mai 1800...) and three from Brinckmann (27. Mai 1800-4. Juli 1800).

209n. Catel: In KGA V/1 (1985) is a correspondence of five letters from Schleiermacher and indications, without direct content, of six from his Halle schoolmate Heinrich Catel (geb. ca 1769) (26. Dez. 1790-19. Dez. 1792). Although their acquaintance continued until at least 1793/1794, in Berlin, no further correspondence is extant.

212. Die Familie von Dohna: KGA V/1 (1985) includes seven previously published letters from Schleiermacher, five to Alexander von Dohna (1771-1832) (#168, 9. Sept. 1797; #171, 16. Dez. 1791; #218, 17. Mai 1793; #271, 8. Aug. 1794; #303, 24. Nov. 1795), with indication, without direct content, of two from Alexander, and two such to Wilhelm von Dohna (1773-1845) (#281, 9. Jan. 1795; #326, wohl vor Sept. 1796), with indication, without direct content, of two from Wilhelm. – KGA V/2 (1988) includes two letters from Schleiermacher: one to Alexander (#476, 20. Juni 1798, abbreviated in Briefe 1), with a new one from Alexander (#356, 30. Dez. 1796), and one to Wilhelm (#481, 10. Juli 1798), with an indication, without direct content, of Schleiermacher's letter to him previous to that date (#480). – KGA V/3 (1992) includes only two letters from Schleiermacher; both, previously published but not in critical form, are to Wilhelm (#594, 30. März 1799; #697, 23. Sept. 1799). Also included are indications of two letters, without direct content: one from Alexander and one from

Wilhelm. It is unlikely that any personal correspondence with Alexander occurred, except for certain Gelegentheitsbriefe. Nor is any correspondence with the older brother Ludwig von Dohna (1776-1814) extant, though there are indications of two letters, without direct content, in KGA V/4 (1994): from Schleiermacher (wohl ende Okt. 1800) and from Ludwig (wohl ende Okt./Anfang Nov. 1800).

214aa. Duisberg: Further, to the nine letters in KGA V/1 (1985) listed from Schleiermacher's Halle schoolmate Friedrich Carl Gottlieb Duisberg (ca 1765-1822) in *New Athenaeum/Neues Athenaeum* (1989) (1. März 1792-6. Feb. 1796), eight published for the first time, are added indications, without direct content, of seven letters from Schleiermacher vor dem 1. März 1792-2. Mai 1795. Extant correspondence extends to 1813. Two of the letters are from both Duisberg and his new wife Anna Barbara (geb. Bestvater). The single letter from Duisberg's second youngest brother Heinrich Anton Carl Duisberg is also included, published for the first time. – KGA V/3 (1991) includes one letter from Duisberg (18. Juni 1799) and one from him and his wife Anna Barbara (geb. Bestvater) (#684, 5. Nov. 1799), both new, also an indication, without direct content, of one from Schleiermacher (9. Juli 1799).

214n. Fink: KGA V.3 (1992) presents the first ten new letters from Schleiermacher to Johann Philipp David Fink, a bookseller whom he addressed as "Faktor Fink" (19. June-31. März 1800).

214t. Friedrich Wilhelm III: KGA V/3 (1992) includes a new letter from the King Friedrich Wilhelm III (4. Feb. 1799) enabling an interim appointment at the Garnisonkirche in Potsdam.

215ag. Frölich: After Friedrich Schlegel moved to Jena, Schleiermacher was the contact person for *Athenaeum* with Heinrich Frölich (gest. 1805), a bookseller and publisher in Berlin. KGA V/3 (1992) includes only indications of two letters (wohl Anfang April 1800), while KGA V/4 (1994) presents three more from what must have been a much larger correspondence, one from Schleiermacher (6. oder 7. Aug. 1800) and two from Frölich (6. und 7. Aug. 1800).

220n. Gedike: Indications, without direct content, of two letters from Friedrich Gedike (1754-1803) (Sept. 1793), director of the Gedike

Seminar, in which Schleiermacher was later enrolled, are given in KGA V/2 (1985). No further correspondence is known.

222n. Grapow: On 6. Jan. 1799 an unknown woman, F. Grapow, wrote to Schleiermacher in his role as pastor at the Charité hospital; this letter is included in KGA V/3 (1992).

224n. Grunow: At some point after they had met in 1798, Schleiermacher and Eleonore Christian Grunow (1769 oder 1770-1837), the unhappy wife of the Lutheran pastor at the Invalidenhaus in Berlin, whom she had married on 26. Juni 1796, for a time met in her home several times a week. This relationship was no secret, certainly not within the circle of Schleiermacher's friends. Probably in the Autumn of 1799, he expressed to her the desire to marry her should she obtain a divorce, which she finally decided not to do only in the Autumn of 1805. Schleiermacher had not lived in Berlin during the last three years of their acquaintance. It appears that their correspondence was in large part destroyed by Schleiermacher's heirs, some by Dilthey. Thus, apart from a birthday greeting by her in KGA V/3 (1992) (wohl 21. Nov. 1800), only 22 letters, some of them excerpts, remain. These, all of them from Schleiermacher (21. Juni 1802-20. Aug. 1803), were previously published in *Briefe* 1.

228. Henriette Herz (1764-1847): In KGA V/2 (1988), included are six previously published letters from Schleiermacher (#435, 1. Jan. 1798); #489, 20. Juli 1798; #493, 23. Juli 1798; #516, 3. bis 6. Sept. 1798; #522, 6. Sept. bis 7. oder 8. Sept. 1798; #524, 9. Sept. 1798), with notices of one letter from Schleiermacher (#515, vor dem 3. Sept. 1798) and two from Henriette (#518, wohl 4. Sept. 1798; #523, vor dem 9. Sept. 1798). The previous publication was in *Briefe* 1 and 3 (abbreviated) and Meisner (1923). – KGA V/3 (1991) includes 37 letters from Schleiermacher (15. Feb. 1799-5. Juli 1799) and one indication of a letter from this period. It also includes 21 indications, without direct content, from Henriette Herz (21. Feb. 1799-vor dem 1. Juli 1799). – KGA V/4 (1994) has only three letters from Schleiermacher (#901, 2.-5. Juli 1800; #906, 6. Juli 1800; #909, 8. Juli 1800).

228n. Hof und Dom: In KGA V/1 (1985) indication is given of a letter from Schleiermacher to the Hof- und Dom-Ministerium (#251, Anfang 1794).

228t. Horne: A onetime roomate of Schleiermacher at Niesky, the English-
man G.W. Horne wrote Schleiermacher two letters still extant from
Gnadenfeld (19. Nov. 1784, 4. bis 16. April 1785). These were already
included in *Briefe*. Indication, without direct content, is also given of a
letter from Schleiermacher (vor dem 4. April 1785).

229. Hülsen: From the brief correspondence with the non-academic,
"free-spirited" scholar August Ludwig Hülsen (1765-1810), KGA V/3
(1992) contains four indications, without direct content, of letters
from Schleiermacher (Sept. 1799-13. April 1800) and four from
Hülsen (3. Okt. 1799-13.April 1800). The latter were already published by Meisner. – In KGA V/4 (1993) are indications of two letters from Schleiermacher (5. Juli 1800, Mai 1800) and one letter from
Hülsen (7. Mai 1800).

232n. Krasting: Schleiermacher probably met Maria Krasting (geb.
Struensee) during his 1796 visit to his sister Charlotte at Gnadenfrei.
KGA 4 (1994) has one letter from the two women (7. Juni l800) and
one from Schleiermacher (wohl Anfang Sept. 1800), neither
previously published. This seems to be the extent of their correspondence.

233n. Mahler: In KGA V/1 (1985) indication, without direct content, is
given of a letter from Schleiermacher to four-year-younger Herrn-
huter Johann Christlieb Mahler (1764-1797) (vor dem 4. Aug. 1796),
known to Schleiermacher during his school days in Barby and Niesky
and possibly later. No correspondence is known.

239n. Okely: KGA V/1 (1985) includes two letters (17. Jan. 1787, 23. März
1787) from Schleiermacher's close English friend at Barby, Samuel
Okely (1766-1787), and indication, without direct content, of one letter from Schleiermacher (vor dem 17. Jan. 1787).

244n. Reformierte Kirchendirektorium: In KGA V/2 (1988) indication is
given of a letter from Schleiermacher to the Reformierte Kirchendirektorium (#505, vor dem 14. Aug. 1798) requesting leave for a
three-day trip to Landsberg an der Warthe.

246n. Prahmer: KGA V/3 (1992) includes indication, without direct content, of a letter from Schleiermacher (vor dem 11. April 1799) to his Lutheran Charité colleague, Johann Georg Wilhelm Prahmer (1770-1812). *See also* Armendirektorium(193n).

247.   F.S.G. Sack (1738-1817):   The seven letters earlier indicated from KGA V/1 (1988) are all new (#263, #274 = 11. Okt. [not Nov.], ##288, 290, 292, 295, 307; the five others there were previously published. Indications, without direct content, of five other letters from Schleiermacher are also given (#210, vor dem 17. Feb. 1793; #219, zwischen 7. Mai und Anfang Juni 1793; #262, vor dem 6. Juli 1794; #304, vor dem 12. Dez. 1795; #306, vor dem 12. Dez. 1795). – Included in KGA V/2 (1988) are only notices of two letters from Schleiermacher (##491-492, vor dem 23. Juli 1798, 23. Juli 1798, regarding an offer to assume a pastorate in Schwedt turned down-cf. #493, Schleiermacher's report to Henriette Herz).

251.   August Wilhelm Schlegel (1767-1845): In KGA V/2 (1988), using the originals, five previously published letters by Schleiermacher from 1796-1798 are included (#437, 15. Jan. 1798, mit Zusätzen Friedrichs; #455, 17. Feb. 1798; #457, 27. Feb. 1798; #459, 6. März 1798; #535, Ende Okt. 1798) and one such from A.W. Schlegel (#440, 22. Jan. 1798), with notice of one from the latter (#458, vor dem 5. März 1798). – KGA V/3 (1992) includes five letters from Schleiermacher (5. Okt. 1799-12. April 1800), all previously published, six from A.W. Schlegel (23. Sept. 1799-12. April 1800), two of which are new and the others incompletely published in *Briefe*, and indication, without direct content, of one from Schlegel. – KGA V/4 (1994) includes 13 letters from Schleiermacher (3. Mai 1800-27. Dez. 1800), all previously published, and 15 from Schlegel (28. April 1800-22. Dez. 1800), 13 of which are new.

257n. Friedrich Schlegel (1772-1845): In KGA V/2 (1988) this item is #495. There are only indications, without direct content, of the eight letters from Schleiermacher known to be from this period. The 15 from Schlegel (see #256 above for one of them) were included in *Briefe*, mostly in abbreviated form. With some corrections in dating, these are also included, most recently, in Schlegel's *Kritische Ausgabe*, hg.v. Ernst Behler, Bd 24, hg.v. Raymond Immerwahr (München, 1985), extending from 20. Jan. 1798 to after 4. Sept. 1798. – KGA

V/3 (1992) includes only indications, without direct content, of 17 letters from Schleiermacher to Friedrich Schlegel (Anfang März 1799-wohl Anfang April 1800), sometimes also to Dorothea Veit, and seven letters from Schlegel or from him and Dorothea, several also from Dorothea alone (see #270n), in all 30 letters (1. März 1799-wohl Anfang April 1800). Of the latter two are new, 13 had been published in complete form and 15 only in incomplete form. Friedrich and Dorothea moved to Jena in Sept. 1799. – KGA V/4 (1994) includes six letters from Schleiermacher (10.-11. Juli-10. Okt. 1800), five of them in complete form for the first time, and indications, without direct content, of 11 other letters from Schleiermacher (vor dem 28. April 1800-vor dem 17. Nov. 1800) and 13 letters from Schlegel, sometimes also from Dorothea Veit (28. April 1800-8. Dez. 1800), one new and 10 in complete form for the first time, plus indication, without direct content, of one. One of Schlegel's letters (#850, vor dem 28. April 1800) has a postscript from his brother August Wilhelm.

258n. Carl Schleiermacher (geb. 1772): In KGA V/1 (1985) only one notice of a letter from Schleiermacher to his younger brother Carl is given (#237, vor dem 26. Okt. 1793) and notice of two from Carl (#226, vor dem 21. Aug. 1793; #275, vor dem 13. Okt. 1794). – In KGA V/2 (1988) only one notice of a letter from Schleiermacher is given (#412, Ende Okt. 1797) and notice of six from Carl (Anfang Nov. 1797-vor dem 8. Nov. 1798). – KGA V.3 (1992) contains only seven indications (Anfang Feb. 1799-April 1800), without direct content, of the correspondence between Schleiermacher and his brother Carl, including three letters from Schleiermacher. – Likewise, KGA V/4 (1994) has four indications, all from Carl (vor dem 15. Mai 1800-vor dem 22. Dez. 1800).

259. Charlotte Schleiermacher (1765-1831): Of the 37 items of correspondence between Schleiermacher and his older sister Charlotte, only six from him could be included from the 1796-1798 period covered in KGA V/2 (#399, 18. Aug.-24. Aug. 1797; #402, 2. Sept.-23. Nov. 1792; #424, 21. Nov.-8. Dez. 1797; #473, 23. Mai -17. Juni 1798; #496, 25. Juli-16. Aug. 1798; #530, 15. Okt.-11. Nov. 1798), and there are notices of nine others. From her 20 are extant from this period, with notices of two others. All but one of his letters-all previously published in abbreviated form in *Briefe* and with some small additions in Meisner-appear in complete form here for the first time. All 20 of

Charlotte's letters from this period are new. – KGA V/3 (1992) includes six letters from Schleiermacher to his sister Charlotte (23. März 1799-18. April 1800), two indications, without direct content, and nine new letters from her (vor dem 23. März 1799-5. Mai 1800). – KGA V/4 (1994) includes three letters from him (7. Juni 1800-29. Dez. 1800)-one (#917) a fragment published by Dilthey and two published in complete form for the first time, plus two indications without direct content, and six new letters from her.

259g. Christiane Caroline Schleyermacher (gest. 1828): KGA V/1 (1985) has an indication, without content, of one letter from Schleiermacher's step-mother Christiane Caroline Schleyermacher (#273, nach dem 20. Sept. 1794).

259k. Elizabeth Maria Schleyermacher (geb. Stubenrauch, 1736-1783): KGA V/1 (1985) includes two letters from Schleiermacher's mother Elizabeth Maria Schleyermacher (#4, 21. Jan. 1782; #11, 26. Okt. 1783). *See also* 259n.

259n. Johann Gottlieb Adolph Schleyermacher (1727-1794): KGA V/1 (1985) has 20 letters from Schleiermacher to his army chaplain father Johann Gottlieb Adolph Schleyermacher (März 1786-April/Mai 1794) and indications, without direct content, of ten more (vor dem 21. Jan. 1782-24. Okt. 1792). From his father are 25 more (21. Nov. 1781-3. Juli 1794) and such indications of three others. This is the first, most complete possible critical edition, given that almost all of the originals were destroyed and many were previously published in *Briefe* (edited mostly at the hands of Schleiermacher's daughter Hildegaard and stepson Ehrenfried von Willich) in shortened form. It is based first on the partial correspondence published by Heinrich Gelzer in 1855 (see item #448 in the 1966 bibliography), then on the Druckmanuskript for the first two volumes of *Briefe* in the Archiv des Verlages de Gruyter, which shows strikeouts and the like.

262. Schwarz (1765-1837): KGA V/4 (1994) includes two letters previously edited by Meisner from Schleiermacher's correspondence with theologian and pedagogical theorist Friedrich Heinrich Christian Schwarz, one from Schwarz (9. Nov. 1800) and one from Schleiermacher (15. Dez. 1800).

263. Spener (1749-1827): KGA V/3 (1992) has 30 letters from Schleier-
      macher (19. Feb. 1799-27. Feb. 1800), 24 of them new, and only indi-
      cations, without direct content, of eight letters from Spener (19. Feb.
      1799-vor dem 28. Dez. 1799). – KGA V/4 (1994) has six new letters
      from Schleiermacher (wohl Juni 1800-30. Okt. 1800), nothing from
      Spener.

264. Stisser: KGA V/3 (1992) has two indications, without direct content,
      of what appears to be a one-time exchange between Landsberg an der
      Warthe physician Karl Friedrich Benjamin Stisser (1770-1851) and
      Schleiermacher (vor dem 26. März 1800; vor dem 28. März 1800).

264t. David Adam Carl Stubenrauch (1774-1839): KGA V/1 (1985) has an
      indication, without content, of a letter by Schleiermacher (#296, vor
      dem 20.Aug. 1795) to Adam Carl David Stubenrauch, S.E.T. Stuben-
      rauch's only child. From their quite infrequent, occasional correspon-
      dence only one later letter is extant.

265. Samuel Ernst Timotheus Stubenrauch (1738-1807): The record from
      KGA V/1 (1985) given in *New Athenaeum/Neues Athenaeum* (1989)
      presents ten new letters from Schleiermacher's maternal uncle
      Stubenrauch. Of the 62 known to be from him during this period
      (1774-1796) all are partial and come from various sources, and only
      two come from originals (#284, 30. Jan. 1795; #317, 4.-6. Juli 1796).
      No originals from Schleiermacher within this copious early correspon-
      dence are extant. Only two snippets have come down (#43, vor dem
      25. April 1786; #242, 9. Dez. 1793), and indications are given of 23
      others, for which there is no text. In KGA V/2 (1988) the 35 letters
      from Stubenrauch during this period (Sept. 1796-1798) are all avail-
      able in full, published for the first time, whereas none of the 30 from
      Schleiermacher is extant. – KGA V/3 (1992) gives only indication,
      without direct content, of 13 letters from Schleiermacher to his uncle
      Stubenrauch (wohl Anfang Feb. 1799-vor dem 26. März 1800) and 14
      letters from his uncle (14. Jan. 1799-29. März 1800), of which 11 are
      new and three were previously published in excerpt form. – KGA
      V/4 (1994) likewise gives only indication, without direct content, of
      seven letters from Schleiermacher (vor dem 6. Juni 1800-vor dem 3.
      Dez. 1800) and 11 letters from his uncle (6. Mai 1800-28. Dez. 1800),
      of which only an excerpt from one (#990, 6. Dez. 1800) had been
      published before.

267n. Troschel: KGA V/1 (1985) includes indication, without direct content, of two letters from the Danzig publisher Ferdinand Troschel (#189, vor dem 7. Sept. 1792; #194, vor dem 18. Okt. 1792), who wished to publish "Über den Wert des Lebens," but Schleiermacher eventually declined.

270n. Dorothea (geb. Mendelssohn) Veit (1763-1839): In KGA V/2 (1988) a joint letter from Dorothea Veit with additions from Friedrich Schlegel is included (#464, 10. März 1798); this was abbreviated in *Briefe* 1, given in full in Schlegel's *Kritische Ausgabe*, hg.v. Ernst Behler, Bd 24, hg.v. Raymond Immerwahr (München, 1985), 115-117. *See also* the joint letter listed under #256 above. In addition, it has two letters from Dorothea Veit (#540, 6. Nov. 1798; #552, Ende Dez. 1798), another from Dorothea Veit and Henriette Mendelssohn (#543, 21. Nov. 1798), and indications of two further letters from Dorothea (#488, vor dem 20. Juli 1798) and Schleiermacher (#520, Anfang Sept. 1798). – In KGA V/3 (1992) only indications, without direct content, of four letters from Schleiermacher to Dorothea Veit are given, 16 letters from her alone, eight more from her and Friedrich Schlegel, plus indication of one from her. One of her letters is new (#802, wohl Ende Feb./Anfang März 1800). – KGA V/4 (1994) includes two letters from Schleiermacher (#913, 11. Juli 1800- only an excerpt published in *Briefe*; #991, 6. Dez. 1800), indications of nine more from him in this period (seven of these to both her and Friedrich Schlegel), 20 letters from her (seven of these from both her and Schlegel; three of her four brief postscripts are new), and indication of one more from her. Indication is also given of a letter from Schleiermacher to her former husband, Simon Veit (1754-1819).

271. Johann Christoph Wedeke (1755-1875): In KGA V/2 (1988) there is a letter from Johann Christoph Wedeke (#537, Anfang Nov. 1798) and an indication of one from Schleiermacher (#536, vor Nov. 1798). – Indication, without direct content, of a letter to Schleiermacher from Wedeke (#756, vor dem 20. Dez. 1799) is given in KGA V/3 (1992).

274n. Zaeslin: In KGA V/1 (1985) there are two letters from Emanuel Zaeslin (##72, 77, Barby, 3. Juni und 19. Juli 1787), also indication of a letter from Schleiermacher to his schoolmates Zaeslin and Johann Baptist von Albertini (#75, vor dem 17. Juli 1787).

SCHLEIERMACHER STUDIES IN ITALY

Sergio Sorrentino

Italian Culture Engaging Schleiermacher

Only recently (i.e., since the end of the sixties) has Schleiermacher's thought been intensively approached within Italian culture. This development displays interesting aspects that might worthwhile to point out.

There are two reasons why Italian culture has come to approach Schleiermacher's thinking and to receive it into its field of interests. These different reasons have brought about a variety of interpretive lines. I would like to throw light on these streams. They are characterized above all by one common feature, which is a basic motif among all those lines of interpretation. It is, in turn, perhaps the main concern by which Italian culture was induced to approach Schleiermacher and to take advantage of his inheritance.

It should be made evident that our culture, because of an enduring split between theological (Catholic) and secular (non-theological) thinking, contains certain objective obstacles for taking into account the work of a person like Schleiermacher, all the more so as he was a Protestant. Indeed, here in Italy theology is strongly marked by confessional and institutional features; because of these features it cannot spontaneously give any attention to Schleiermacher. On the other hand, philosophers have regarded Schleiermacher as belonging essentially to theological culture; and yet our philosophical culture holds theology suspect because of its dogmaticism and consequently its lack of scientific standards. For these reasons, there has been no interest in accepting Schleiermacher as a partner for productive dialogue or discussion. Against this background, therefore, all the streams of interpretation that have come to be concerned with Schleiermacher in Italy display this common feature: they recognize in Schleiermacher's thinking a strong impulse to freeing culture, both theological and philosophical, from ideological bonds. On the one hand, the concern is to free ourselves from all closed and absolute, totalistic thought. In this respect, this is how Schleiermacher himself considered Fichte's thought, for instance, and that is why he stood against it with all his might. On the other hand, the concern is to inveigh against dogmatic constraints that bind thinking, including, as it happens, such theological thinking in the field of Catholic theology.

All these concerns, expressed in different ways and driven by various interests, have given occasion to a rather heterogeneous set of interpretive tendencies. Here I would like to give form to four kinds of such tendencies. I will move along as through concentric circles, starting from the innermost to the outermost. It is worth noting that the latter streams recollect the exigencies and interests of former lines of interpretation.

1. The first stream of interpretation obtains historical merit in its awakening interest in Schleiermacher's thought, which previously had been nearly unknown and neglected in Italian culture. This was not concerned only with the theological field, where until now much was also yet required if knowledge of Schleiermacher's thought was to be increased, but also with the philosophical area. This stream goes back especially to his hermeneutics. Hermeneutics, indeed the interest in Schleiermacher as the founder of modern hermeneutics, was the first way through which a mainly philosophical concern with Schleiermacher's thought was awakened. Such an interest could not easily be cut off from Schleiermacher's theology. In brief, Schleiermacher's striving to attain a general hermeneutics, with all its notions of basic importance for philosophical thought such as the idea of individuality, the issue of otherness, the concept of *Verstehen* and interpretation, along with issues of their foundation in the frame of a theory of knowledge, becomes the means for achieving freedom from totalistic and binding thought. This was a necessary requirement in times when nihilism was on the rise and the destruction of metaphysics was thought to be a prerequisite to opening up new ways of doing philosophy. In the framework of Italian culture such a binding mode of thinking was essentially represented by Hegelianism, which had achieved a dominant influence in our culture along with its connected branches, such as Marxism, above all, but also certain kinds of historicism. Many deemed that such a Hegelian presence and influence, with all its branches I was hinting at, in our culture should have hindered new developments in philosophy. This interpretation is mainly linked up with Gianni Vattimo's name. See his book: *Schleiermacher filosofo dell'interpretazione* (Milano: Mursia, 1968). His philosophical work since then has been more and more qualified by the program of a "weak thinking."

2. In the second interpretive tendency there are impulses that also compel many to overcome the tradition of Hegelianism and Marxism that has dominated Italian culture. Such an interpretation sees in Schleiermacher above all the pioneer of *Liberalität* – that is, the promoter of a kind of thinking that gives rise to and develops viewpoints and arguments for a religion of *Liberalität*. In this context three points are especially evident, points that are connected with the general structure of European culture influenced

by historicism. First of all, there is the motif of a religion that is open to freedom. Then, there is that of finding an individuality that can act as the center of life interests and actual freedom. In this frame individuality is regarded as a *microcosmus*, and it is linked to a philosophical tradition coming from the Italian Renaissance and Leibniz' philosophy. Finally, the theme of historicity and historical experience also emerges, insofar as history is conceived as a vital manifestation (*Erscheinung*) of individuality. In this perspective Schleiermacher's thinking has been taken to act as a workshop wherein such motifs are melted together and handed down within European culture as inexhaustible tasks. By virtue of this thinking, which joins together freedom, individuality and historicity, piety (*Frömmingkeit*), lived religion, as it were, is freed from ecclesiastical ties, though without letting religious community (the church) recede into the background. Thereby piety (i.e., lived religion, what Schleiermacher calls *Frömmingkeit*) recovers its very nature as a creative force in history. In addition, all that signifies an increasing of secular religiosity, which in Italy is considerably present and active today, though among only a minority who reside within the intellectual class. Giovanni Moretto's research is guided by this interpretation. As examples thereof I would recall his books *Etica e storia in Schleiermacher* (Napoli: Bibliopolis, 1979) and *Ispirazione e libertà* (Napoli: Morano, 1986).

3. A third interpretive trend sees Schleiermacher as a representative of the great pietistic tradition, with its Brüdergemeinde and piety. According to this way of interpretation, Schleiermacher has concerned himself with the rights of the heart (*Herzensrechte*) and with motifs of a piety that is at the same time autonomous in its own right and compatible with modernity (i.e., the modern world). In such a perspective people render account of Schleiermacher's thought with the aim of bringing about a mediation between scientific reason (which dominates the modern world) and ecclesial piety (*Frömmigkeit*). Within such a mediation comes about a religion that is indeed present in history and society, yet this mediation does not imply that one of two poles be eliminated or soaked up by the other. On the contrary, it is meant to provide reciprocal benefits and improvements. The outstanding features of this pietistic religiosity active in Schleiermacher's thought and life are actually seen to be rooted in the foundation and formation of the modern world. Such a foundation becomes particularly visible where we are dealing with our immediate relation to God. This relation makes room for the nontransposible value of individuality. At the same time, it prepares ground or paves the way for community and "ecumenical" openness (i.e., for activity on the world) of men/women who are no longer alienated from the world or

confined to their privacy. This line of interpretation aims at taking intensively into account Schleiermacher's theological work and homiletic activity,
namely its ecclesial core. Consequently, in this framework his philosophical
activity is mainly understood as focused on a method of working at the level
of concepts and ideas. This interpretive line particularly characterizes
Roberto Osculati's perspective, as it is manifest in his large book, a sort of intellectual biography, *Schleiermacher: L'uomo, il pensatore, il cristiano*
(Brescia: Queriniana, 1979) and his introduction (pp. 5-89) to his Italian
translation of the *Kurze Darstellung, Studio della teologia: Breve presentazione*
(Brescia: Queriniana, 1978).

4. The last interpretive trend we recall here may be synthesized in the
phrase "Schleiermacher and modernity." This interpretive tendency is set
forth in three dimensions. First of all, people acknowledge a vital interconnection between philosophical and theological thinking, and because of this
link theological and philosophical interests are thought to be indissolubly
joined in their very substance. Second, a particular stress is put on the sharp
consciousness of modernity that may be derived from Schleiermacher's
thinking. Finally, in such an understanding of the area marked by modernity
much evidence is given to a strong consciousness of religious authenticity,
which also characterizes Schleiermacher's personal existence. In this frame,
Schleiermacher's thinking is seen as that of a mind striving for religious authenticity, and his philosophy is considered to hold a clear perception of how
persons may be marked by modernity. As for modernity itself, it is to be understood as that world in which thinking is entangled in antinomies. Indeed,
such a thinking, especially as presented by Schleiermacher, is able to constitute reliable sense-making at the levels of both knowledge and practice (i.e.,
through theoretical and practical reason), for the sense thus constructed is
that of a universal communication and ethical creation. Yet, this sense-
making is seen to be undermined by a situation wherein metaphysical and
ethical tenets are prone to be uncertain or obscure, so that human existence
runs the risk of being surrounded by nonsense or by an unattainable totality
(the latter either unavailable or "heteronomous"). An existence that continually runs into antinomies is an existence that makes for an experience of
nothingness; and here nothingness is understood either as nonsense looming
over existence or as a missing ground (*Abgrund*). On this argument, see my
essay *Schleiermacher e la modernità* (Torino: Claudiana, 1986). This conceptual constellation makes up the specific condition of modernity; it connotes
what we could call secularization, which sets new tasks for religious experience and theological refection. In Schleiermacher's thinking such a condition

is reflected in many ways, insofar as in it different possibilities of thinking come to be involved, like philosophy and theology, hermeneutics and dialectic, critique etc. It is to be noted that this spiritual situation marks both the perspective of Schleiermacher's thinking and the situation of our own contemporary thinking. This interpretive trend marks my own research on Schleiermacher's thinking among that of others. See my essay just cited in the volume *Schleiermacher e la modernità* (Torino: Claudiana 1986), pp. 55-87, and also *Ermeneutica e filosofia trascendentale. La filosofia di Schleiermacher come progetto di comprensione dell'altro* (Bologna: CLUEB, 1986), 359 p. Along the same line, though stressing much more the formal and epistemological aspects of Schleiermacher's philosophy, is Mario G. Lombardo's *La regola del giudizio. La deduzione trascendentale nella dialettica e nell'etica di Fr. Schleiermacher* (Milano: IPL, 1990), 414 p.

The Incidence and Influence of Schleiermacher's Works in Italy

Apart from the translation of the *Reden* and *Monologen* (in a single volume) by Gaetano Durante (Firenze: Sansoni, 1947), which received little attention and left but few tracks in the context of Italian culture, we may say that only in the last fifteen years has Schleiermacher's work found an attentive, although limited, audience. This new interest goes back to new translations of Schleiermacher's works. First of all was the translation of the *Glaubenslehre* in two volumes, issued as vol. 3/1 and 3/2 of Schleiermacher's *Opere scelte: La dottrina della fede esposta sistematicamente secondo i principi fondamentali della chiesa evangelica*, edited by Sergio Sorrentino (Brescia: Paideia, 1982-85); each volume was provided with large introductions, namely: "Fede cristiana e produttività storica nella *Glaubenslehre* di Schleiermacher" (vol. 3/1, pp. 9-124) and "Da Gesù di Nazareth alla comunità: la coscienza di Dio come principio di formazione del mondo storico" (vol. 3/2, p. 9-98). Then there is also Roberto Osculati's translation of the *Kurze Darstellung* mentioned above, a work that is difficult to read, however, because of its conciseness. Now we also have the Italian translation of some *Akademieabhandlungen*, translated by Giovanni Moretto, *Etica ed ermeneutica* (Napoli: Bibliopolis, 1984, 373 p.) and that of the Sermons for the Augustana Confessio Jubilee, translated by Roberto Osculati, *La Confessione di Augusta* (Padova: Edizioni Messaggero, 1982), 294 p. Meanwhile a new translation of the *Reden* by Salvatore Spera, *Sulla religione. Discorsi a quegli intellettuali che la disprezzano* (Brescia: Queriniana, 1989, 251 p.) has also been issued, along with the lectures on aesthetics, translated by Paolo

D'Angelo, *Estetica* (Palermo: Aestetica, 1988, 166 p.) and *Sul concetto dell'Arte* (Palermo: Centro internazionale studi di estetica, 1988, 79 p). More recently Giovanni Moretto has edited the *Weihnachtsfeier, La festa di Natale* (Brescia: Queriniana, 1994, 198 p.) and Massimo Marassi has edited *Ermeneutica* (Milano: Rusconi, 1996, 809 p.), wherein are contained in both German and Italian texts the *Hermeneutik* edited by Heinz Kimmerle, the lectures of 1832/33 edited by Friedrich Lücke (in the *Sämmtliche Werke*) and the *Allgemeine Hermeneutik* of 1809/10 in the transcript by August Twesten edited by Wolfgang Virmond (in volume two of *Internationaler Schleiermacher-Kongreß Berlin 1984*, pp. 1269-1310). There is also the translation of the *Gelegentliche Gedanken* edited by Lucio D'Alessandro, *Sull'università* (Napoli: La città del sole, 1995, 133 p.). I am also translating the Odebrecht edition of the *Dialektik* (forthcoming). Also to be edited by Moretto is a new volume (by UTET Press, Torino, forthcoming) containing among other things Schleiermacher's *Reden, Monologen* and, above all, the notes for lectures on ethics of 1812/13 (Birkner's edition of 1981).

It is not easy to indicate the extent of Schleiermacher's influence in Italian culture. I will try to do this by way of a twofold standard. First, I will show what the interest for Schleiermacher has already brought about or achieved in Italy. Then, there is the question of what it could produce, whether indeed Schleiermacher studies will continue to be pursued with the same intensity and, moreover, if more suitable conditions will arise.

In addition to numerous essays by these and other Italian authors, signs of these arising interests on the occasion of the 150th anniversary of Schleiermacher's death are two large international collections of essays produced in Italy. The first is a 618-page collection of twenty-seven essays, edited by Marco M. Olivetti in *Archivio di filosofia* 52, n. 1-3 (Padova: Cedam, 1984). The second is a 486-page volume edited by Giorgio Penzo and Marcello Farina, from a congress in Trento on April 11-15, 1985. It is entitled *F.D.E. Schleiermacher (1768-1834): Tra filosofia e teologia* (Brescia: Morcelliana, 1990). A more modest international collection comes from part of a conference held in Napoli a decade later, on June 27-29, 1994, edited by Sergio Sorrentino and Terrence N. Tice: the 187-page *La dialettica nella cultura romantica* (Roma: La Nuova Italia Scientifica, 1996).

1. If it is correct that unknowing (ignorance) brings about all kinds of prejudices, the first outcome of the Italian translations of Schleiermacher's works is that a large part of his thought, i.e., notably his theological and philosophical thought, has been potentially freed from at least the more egregious misunderstandings. As we come directly into contact with

Schleiermacher's thought in our own language, we are in the position of sweeping out all the prejudices that have previously become common opinion (*eidola fori*). In the past these prejudices often hindered a correct approach to Schleiermacher's thinking and its notional universe. Of course, that does not mean that these prejudices will be eliminated *ipso facto*; it does mean that today we may obtain a suitable criterion for overcoming these prejudices and for limiting potential misunderstandings.

2. Thereby occasion is also given to overcome the enduring and seriously hindering notion of a presumed opposition between Karl Barth and Schleiermacher. This idea has for a long time determined the interpretation of Schleiermacher among scholars in Italy, especially among theologians and philosophers of religion. We have to realize that in Italy Barth's thought has obtained a considerable and lasting influence and has brought about radical decisions (usually, either bare, sharp refusal or total, often uncritical agreement). Then we are able to understand that this opposition, explicitly formed by Barth himself, has necessarily harmed the comprehension of Schleiermacher's theology and even more of the thinking that is expressed therein. We know, however, that Barth's attitude toward Schleiermacher is more polyphonic and ambiguous than that of many Barthians, who persist in purveying such an opposition, would acknowledge. In particular, I am convinced that in this attitude, which goes back to the Barthian viewpoint and draws its interpretative trend from the putative opposition between Barth and Schleiermacher, acts as a confessional prejudice, i.e., a decision that goes back to a person's own confessional standpoint. It is, of course, not attainable through objective testing. Yet, there are in Schleiermacher's theology (cf. his *Glaubenslehre* or *Kurze Darstellung*) three factors that, in my opinion, are well fitted for overcoming this sort of prejudice and that opposition, so that both Schleiermacher's imposing theological enterprise and Barth's deep-rooted revolution in certain fields of theology may show more continuity than moments of breakthrough, even though this might essentially sound paradoxical. In any case, if we effect a closer acquaintance with Schleiermacher's theological work, we can gain an efficacious critical means of receiving Barth's theology as well without such damaging prejudices.

These three factors are the following: (a) the ecumenical openness that inspires Schleiermacher's theological discourse; (b) the kerygmatic structure or framework of religious experience – that is, the experience that occurs in the people's affects (or lived attitudes: *Gemütszuständen*), for we know that actually Schleiermacher's *Glaubenslehre* will not be but a description of these lived attitudes (*Gemütszustände*); (c) the particular, autonomous nature of theological speech and argument, which is emphasized by Schleiermacher himself in his prolegomena and is accounted for in his own demonstrations of theological argument.

A direct contact with Schleiermacher's theological works (I dare to say that in the literature there has scarcely ever been a whole reading of a work like *Christian Faith*) may deliver a suitable standard for weakening the stark alternatives that result from reading Schleiermacher's theology through Barth's spectacles, namely, the alternative between a theology based upon the primacy of the Word of God (Barth) and a theology that presumably takes its distance from such a primacy (Schleiermacher) – an alternative like that drawn up by Brunero Gherardini (Lateran University, Rome) as a result of his long, thorough study: "L'enciclopedia di Schleiermacher. Esposizione storico-critica e valutazione di *Kurze Darstellung des theologischen Studiums*" in *Lateranum* 46, 1980 (pp. 1-197; it is a monographic issue of this journal). Therein Gherardini has kept the split that Barth had set up with the theologian from Berlin. In this direction it seems me that the Italian translations of Schleiermacher's works have already brought about positive effects in two respects. They have partially eliminated discrepancies and promoted critical improvement.

3. Last, but not least, we must not forget that the *Glaubenslehre* is at the apex of Schleiermacher's activity and authorship. It is not correct to place it in contrast with other of his works such as, for instance, *On Religion* and the sermons. On the contrary, all these works, not only religious works, are to be read and understood only by starting from the *Glaubenslehre*. I dare to say that access to this main text has put us in a position to acknowledge the whole complexity of Schleiermacher's thinking, particularly of his philosophical, historical-critical, hermeneutical and related efforts. Each of them, in turn, opens up corresponding fields of research, the existence of which nobody could previously have supposed. Actually, before Schleiermacher's texts and main works had been introduced the most dominant picture of Schleiermacher was that of a sheer theologian, who had merely played a small role in Romantic circles. Inversely, the reading of his works has now accustomed us to come to terms with a much more complex figure; it shows his manifold dimensions and presents us with a universe of ideas that is far more rich and complex than we might previously have supposed. Among other aspects we may recall these: the presence of a highly interesting philosophical outlook in the prolegomena of his dogmatics; the historical and critical feature of the theological materials that he forms and that matches the structure of his doctrinal presentation; the critical and dialectical charac-

ter that constitutes an enduring tension within his theological discourse. Taking into account all that, we may argue that in Italy the now evident presence of Schleiermacher's own works consists in strongly stimulating and improving our Schleiermacher study overall.

4. There are, however, other aspects that seem to be of great importance. Some of them have not yet given rise to studies or works already published or to effects that are easy to recognize, for they are only in seed form. They go back to the influence of Schleiermacher's texts on our culture. I deem that they will bear much fruit if they are carefully and suitably improved. Maybe they are also trends that act secretly and underground. They might be effects of the recent acquaintance with Schleiermacher's work, even though they are not clearly knowable, except by an attentive observer. In this context I would recall only four possible tendencies deriving from Schleiermacher's presence in Italy.

(a) The first tendency consists of an increasing interest in a theology that is conceived as scientifically formed, namely as a knowing that is capable of making universal communication possible. Such communication will take place among faithful people, as among people of other confessions or religions and even among people without any religious faith and faithful people. In addition, Schleiermacher's theology might lead us to a scientifically supplied knowing, which gets away from the set and the status of that "private use of reason" (to use Kant's famous expression) which largely dominates our theological culture. Actually, our theology is prevalently shaped by confessional features. That is why it is prevalently unhistorical and is burdened by doctrinal authority (i.e., a doctrinal hierarchy). It is not difficult to recognize the historical causes that led thereto. Moreover, since Schleiermacher's theology sets up a connection between theological reflection and the religious experience of a community, the presence of such a theological work might promote efforts to work out a new kind of theological knowing, namely a knowing that is not the task of a separate caste (i.e., professional theologians) but also aims at purifying and renewing faith for all. These are all impulses that formerly never penetrated into Italian culture, because of the particular circumstances of such a theology, as of the historical role theology and theologians played here in Italy until Vatican II. Indeed, their work was submitted more to the hierarchy than to the people of God. That is why in Italy, within the context of Catholic culture, many scholars preferred to work on improving historical, biblical, liturgical fields, or even to do philosophical and political studies instead.

(b) In the second place, Schleiermacher's presence in Italy might assist in leading theological discussion and even a broader reflection on faith (a reflection, indeed, which is concerned with faith experience and its historical range) into the wide context of philosophical and scientific debate. Here we are dealing with the issue of inserting theology into the community of sciences and letting it share their concerns. In this respect, Schleiermacher's presence might help overcome the secular gap, or even more the break, between theology and other cultural debate. This effect would concern not only theology, wherein scientific knowing may afford much food for confronting current "world sapience" (*Weltweisheit*), but also philosophical and scientific studies, which could be enriched by theological culture. On this point, I would suggest Wolfhart Pannenberg's perspective, for example. He stresses the mutual, double contribution that can come from a confrontation between theology and anthropology: namely, both the contribution of a "critical viewpoint," which is improved by science and philosophy, and that of an "identical subject," which is formed through the history of a religious community and by its unifying force (i.e., tradition).

(c) Moreover, the results of an acquaintance with Schleiermacher's texts might incite further interest in Schleiermacher's philosophy. Actually, already a superficial insight into these texts points out that they have to be put in connection with the whole context of his thinking, without which they are not truly understandable. Within Italian Schleiermacher studies (but also elsewhere, i.e., in other contexts, as in other language areas) we may take into account the following principle: the more profound, interesting, keen our concern with Schleiermacher's theological work is, the more strongly does our interest in dealing with his philosophical work increase. So far, instead, we are scarcely taking his philosophy into account (though it is an essential part of his intellectual, cultural activity), and this normally connotes a weak, limited comprehension of his theology as well. Perhaps that is to be regretted also in other cultural, linguistic areas, including the German speaking area, where Schleiermacher's presence is much more vigorous and effective than it is in Italy thus far.

(d) Last, but not least, Schleiermacher's texts might bring about an effect that could be widely meaningful for Italian culture. Involved here is an aspect of thought that, along with many others, specially applies to our culture. Actually, Schleiermacher's dogmatics is set up in such a way that (as is widely known) it is linked up with a present ecclesial experience; indeed, this present related to a religious community (a church) depends structurally on the memory of its past and is opened both to its worldly and to its eschatological future. In fact, the figure or the outlook of a church that emerges from

Schleiermacher's *Glaubenslehre* is characterized by precisely such a dynamism or dialectical tension between church and world. It points at the future of faith, which Schleiermacher understands not only in an innerworldly sense but eschatologically as well. Hence, a linkage might take place between theological studies (set up above all to serve the tasks of dogmatics) and the streams of historical study. In Italy the latter is already characterized by a remarkable incidence of historical interests within one scholarly tradition. In this way there would be a kind of feedback, so that theology could improve its scientific craft or skill and open itself to historical consciousness. Nevertheless, until now in Italy theology has suffered from the lack of both.

BOOK NOTES AND REVIEWS

■ Gwen Griffith-Dickson, *Johann Georg Hamann's Relational Metacriticism,* Theologische Bibliothek Töpelmann, Vol. 67. Berlin/New York: Walter de Gruyter, 1995. 534 pp. ISBN 3-11-014437-9.

This impressive volume on the philosophy of Johann Georg Hamann is indeed a tour de force for a first publication on such a demanding subject. In her "Foreword," Griffith-Dickson states that it is "neither a general introduction nor a study of a particular topic of his work"; rather its purpose is "to suggest a certain way of looking at the underlying framework and tendencies of his thinking" (vii). To this end, she has included translations, commentaries, and analyses of individual works that she considers central to his thought. She has avoided giving an account of his life and times except for the biographical detail necessary for an understanding of the texts she has chosen as most important. Those texts are: *Socratic Memorabilia, Aesthetica in nuce,* "Herderschriften" (including *The Knight of the Rose-Cross* and *Philosophical Ideas and Doubts*), *Essay of a Sibyl on Marriage,* and *Metacritique of the Purism of Reason.* Only the *Essay of a Sibyl on Marriage* has been translated into English for the first time. The translations are good; the commentaries and notes are especially valuable. Griffith-Dickson has seen fit to retain Hamann's (eccentric!) emphases in the original texts in the form of boldface type. There is a select bibliography and serviceable index to the critical body of the work. The publication of this work should give a considerable impetus to further research on one of Germany's most important but neglected thinkers. However, there are some important caveats in regard to her central thesis that should be observed.

Griffith-Dickson makes frequent references to Hamann's "holism" (17, 233, 320-322 et. passim), surely not surprising, since a principal characteristic of his thought is his emphasis on "das Ganze." But her version of his concept would, if too strictly observed, tend to vitiate his equal emphasis on concreteness, on the rich and vibrant uniqueness of "every phenomenon of nature," which in turn is God's "living word," as Hamann proclaims it in such an inspirited way in *The Knight of the Rose-Cross.* This is, to be sure, by no means Griffith-Dickson's intention, for she recognizes that the Magus was a "lover and champion of the concrete" (129, cf. 16), and fortunately she departs at times from a too strict adherence to her underlying principle as, for instance, in her study of the *Socratic Memorabilia* (28-31) and the *Essay of a Sibyl on Marriage* (246-265). Her "relational" approach, however, calls to mind the current popularity of comparative studies in religion, ethics, literature, etc., which, however useful in many regards, are invariably reductive. For in order to compare different disciplines or cultures, only selected aspects of each can be treated, and thus the *totality* of each contrasted subject is, of necessity, lost. On occasion, she tends to conflate "relatedness" with "holism" (233, 234), but in the discussion of Goethe's view of Hamann's holism she makes clear "the desirability of viewing Hamann's thought as fundamentally 'relational' rather than as fundamentally 'holistic' " (321).

A difficulty with Griffith-Dickson's "principle of relationality" arises from the failure to distinguish between *two* kinds of relations that are important for a genuine understanding of Hamann's thought: (a) the relations of natural phenomena to each other and (b) the relation of relations. The former are good, because they preserve the concreteness of phenomena; the latter are bad, or at least mendacious, because they reduce natural phenomena to abstractions which are, as he wrote to F.H. Jacobi in 1787, "nothing but relations" (*"lauter Verhältnisse"*). I treated this subject thoroughly in my Chicago dissertation, but, surprisingly, she makes no reference to it in connection with her principal thesis, even though it is listed in her bibliography and in a footnote.[1] She has written me that she used the word "relational . . . in a different far less technical sense" than in my dissertation, "almost identical to the common or colloquial usage of the word" (10-14-96). However, in view of her general philosophical acumen, I find it curious that she should settle for a non-technical, "colloquial" usage of her key term.

Griffith-Dickson correctly points out that "Hamann's interpretation has moved away from the picture painted by [Rudolf] Unger and [Isaiah] Berlin, i.e., that Hamann is an irrationalist (14)." In regard to his use of reason, however, she is not comfortable with my distinction between *two* kinds of reason in relation to Hamann (19). Although she concedes that I have "given an illuminating description of how Hamann might be said to operate," she prefers not to accept my "systematic account" of the two modes of reason, but is willing to accept the idea of "two different styles of *reasoning*" (her emphasis, 117, n. 133). I find it difficult, however, to accept the idea that a physicist's or mathematician's use of reason is simply a matter of *style*, a term derived from rhetoric or literary criticism. As for my adoption of

---

1.   See James C. O'Flaherty, *Unity and Language: A Study in the Philosophy of Hamann* (Chapel Hill: University of North Caroline Press, 1952; reprinted New York: AMS Press, 1966).

Kant's term of Hamann's mode of reason, "*anschauende Vernunft*" or intuitive reason, it is understandable that some scholars are reluctant to adopt it since Hamann himself does not do so. Nevertheless, the authority of Kant is not to be lightly dismissed in the matter. Griffith-Dickson is certainly right in describing Hamann as a nominalist (19), but that fact has nothing to do with the putative "hypostatization" of reason is my interpretation of Hamann (20). For reason, being bound up with language, is neither subjective nor objective for Hamann. He would agree with Wilhelm von Humboldt's terse formulation that language is "something between the outside world and the mind, something different from both." Oswald Bayer has expressed the same idea from the standpoint of Luther's and Hamann's theology in his fruitful concept of the "center" ("*Mitte* ").[2]

In spite of Griffith-Dickson's rather thorough coverage of the prominent ideas in Hamann's metacriticism, there are significant omissions, e.g., Hamann's frequent appeal to the *coincidentia oppositorum*, which he averred to be "worth more than all Kantian criticism" (letter to Herder, 11-18-1782), and its theological correlate the *Knechtgestalt Christi*, so important for his concept of spiritual truth appearing in lowly or unexpected form.

The shortcomings of the book, as I see them, should not obscure the fact that the author has made an important contribution to Hamann studies, particularly for the English-speaking world. Griffith-Dickson provides a wealth of information in her analyses, commentaries on individual works, and explanatory notes. Further, the convenience of having translations of the works discussed under one cover will be appreciated by readers. Handsomely printed and bound, the book is expensive, but is worth the price for research libraries and serious students of Hamann, who will want to come to terms with its provocative thesis.

James C. O'Flaherty
Wake Forest University

---

2. *Autorität und Kritik: Zur Hermeneutik und Wissenschaftstheorie* (Tübingen: Mohr, 1991),
    6, 205, et. passim.

■ *Friedrich Daniel Ernst Schleiermacher. Briefwechsel 1800* (Briefe 850-1004).
Herausgegeben von Andreas Arndt und Wolfgang Virmond. (*Kritische
Gesamtausgabe*. Herausgegeben von Hermann Fischer und Gerhard Ebeling,
Heinz Kimmerle, Günter Meckenstock, Kurt-Victor Selge. Fünfte Abteilung.
Briefwechsel und biographische Dokumente Band 4). Berlin-New York: de
Gruyter 1994. XCIII + 481 Seiten. ISBN 3-11-011020-2.

Nun ist die magische Zahl von 1000 Briefen von und an Schleiermacher
überschritten, etwa ein Fünftel bis ein Sechstel des Briefwechsels (stellt man
das Drittel der nur erschlossenen Briefe in Rechnung) ist wissenschaftlich
bearbeitet und gedruckt. Das mag wohl eine festliche Bemerkung wert sein!
Der Leser ist (in den Bänden 1-3) dem Briefautor von der Jugendzeit über
Studium, Hauslehrerphase und Eintritt in den kirchlichen Dienst gefolgt, hat
lebensprägende Schritte und Freundschaftsbündnisse mitbekommen, die ersten bahnbrechenden Veröffentlichungen in ihrem Entstehen begleitet und
befindet sich nun in der Hoch-Zeit der Frühromantik. Das Geflecht der
Briefe wird dichter, das Leben Schleiermachers bekommt für den Leser im-
mer mehr Profil. Es ist etwas anderes, wenn man einen einzelnen personalen
Briefwechsel zwischen zwei Briefpartnern in einer geschlossenen, über die
Jahre zu verfolgenden Reihenfolge zu Gesicht bekommt – wie das in Einzel-
Editionen zu sein pflegt – , als wenn man ihn im Gesamt des ablaufenden
Lebensjahres liest. Das wird nun mehr und mehr möglich. Und mag auch die
Spannung steigen, weil der ungeduldige Blick des Historikers mehr als ein
Lebensjahr umfassen möchte, so sind neue Eindrücke doch nur auf diese
geduldige, um Vollständigkeit bemühte Wahrnehmung zu erlangen. Schleier-
macher hat sich am intimsten in seinen Briefen ausgesprochen, er hat als
Freund und Partner auf die vielfältig ihn erreichenden Lebensäußerungen
reagiert, sein Lebenspfad wäre ohne diese Zeugnisse nicht nachvollziehbar,
sein wissenschaftliches Werk und sein Wirken auf die Zeit blieben ohne
Kontur. Und so mag der an Schleiermacher Interessierte seufzen ob der
Tatsache, daß für den Briefwechsel nur von April bis Dezember eines Jahres
ein ganzer Band nötig wurde, so wird er doch auf den Komfort einer
wissenschaftlich kommentierten Ausgabe nicht im Ernst verzichten wollen, ja
letztlich gar nicht können.

    Die große und kleine Politik spielt auch in eine an sich zeitenthobene
wissenschaftliche Edition hinein. Das zeigt sich daran, daß als Träger der
Kritischen Gesamtausgabe nun neben die Göttinger Akademie der Wissenschaften die Berlin-Brandenburgische Akademie der Wissenschaften getreten ist. Diese hat 1994 die Berliner Schleiermacherforschungsstelle in ihre

Obhut genommen und wird über die Jahre für Kontinuität der Editionsarbeit sorgen. Die zweite Änderung hat einen traurigen Anlaß: Nach dem Tod des ersten geschäftsführenden Herausgebers Hans-Joachim Birkner ist Hermann Fischer (Hamburg) an seine Stelle getreten; Günter Meckenstock (Kiel) ist in den Kreis der Mitherausgeber gewählt worden.

Arndt und Virmond haben dem Band das gewohnte Aussehen gegeben. Die umfängliche Einleitung der Bandherausgeber beginnt mit einer Übersicht zu Leben und Werk Schleiermachers, in der neben den Briefzeugnissen auch andere zeitgenössische Quellen beigezogen werden. Was für Goethe und andere Autoren der klassisch-romantischen Zeit längst geleistet ist, wird auch hier im Laufe der Edition entstehen: eine annalistische Biographie "von Tag zu Tag". Es folgen zwei wissenschaftliche Untersuchungen, die nicht nur den Sachkommentar entlasten, sondern eigene Forschungsleistungen darstellen, dabei freilich auch das Genus "Briefedition" sprengen. Der erste Aufsatz befaßt sich mit dem Streit der neuen Generation um die "Allgemeine Literaturzeitung" in Jena, dem Bruch der Romantiker mit ihr und dem von den Brüdern Schlegel, Schelling und Fichte in verschiedener Weise betriebenen Plan der Gründung eines eigenen kritischen philosophischen Organs. Schleiermacher war, wenn auch nur als Randfigur, in diese Pläne inhaltlich und organisatorisch eingebunden und aufs höchste emotional an ihnen beteiligt. Dieser auf Schleiermachers Biographie bezogene Aspekt rechtfertigt die erneute Darstellung (zu der es bedeutende vorausgehende Untersuchungen gibt) der gescheiterten Gründung, die zugleich einen Beleg für die zerbrechende Einheit der scheinbar für die neue Zeit stehenden "Schule" abgibt. Der zweite Aufsatz erörtert Schleiermachers Besuch von Vorlesungen zur Experimental-Chemie (die Mitschriften aus dieser Vorlesung sind KGA I/3 ediert), mit vorsichtigen Schlüssen auf Schleiermachers spätere empathische, aber zurückhaltende Stellung zur Naturphilosophie.

Wie gewohnt, werden die Briefpartnerinnen und- partner Schleiermachers vorgestellt, sei es, daß die Darstellungen in den früheren Bänden fortgeschrieben werden, sei es, daß neue Persönlichkeiten genannt werden müssen. Zum Teil sind diese Briefwechsel lediglich erschlossen (Frau Benike, Ludwig Graf zu Dohna-Schlobitten, Heinrich Frölich, Eleonore Grunow, Carl Schleiermacher, Simon Veit); zum ersten Mal konnte ein Brief nur nach einem bei Dilthey zitierten Fragment abgedruckt werden (Brief 917). Erfreulicherweise sind eine Reihe, auch wichtiger, Erstdrucke zu vermelden, darunter Briefe August Wilhelm und Friedrich Schlegels, und natürlich eine Fülle von gegenüber früheren Ausgaben vervollständigten Publikationen, besonders aus dem Romantiker-Briefwechsel. Ergänzt und korrigiert ist die Darstellung August Ludwig Hülsens nach neuerer

Forschung; die Faszination Schleiermachers (und Schlegels) durch diesen Mann, aber auch der Abbruch der Beziehung wird sehr viel deutlicher als bisher. Hülsen muß Schleiermacher zu weitgehenden Äußerungen über die "Reden" veranlaßt haben (S.LXVII), so daß umso bedauerlicher wird, daß diese Briefe wahrscheinlich als verloren gelten müssen. Der wichtigste neue Korrespondent ist Friedrich Heinrich Christian Schwarz, dessen sich über Jahrzehnte hinziehende briefliche und rezensierende Beschäftigung mit Schleiermacher spannend skizziert wird, etwa mit der (bis dato unpublizierten) brieflichen Anfrage aus dem Jahr 1816, wie dieser es "im tiefsten Grund" mit dem Christentum halte (S.LXXVIII). Schwarz' Ringen mit Schleiermacher in seinen Rezensionen – niemand hat so viele und so eingehende Besprechungen über mehr als zwei Jahrzehnte hin, von den "Reden" bis zur "Glaubenslehre", geschrieben (ich darf hier noch die nicht erwähnte Rez. der Universitätsschrift in der JALZ 1809 nennen) – wäre wohl einmal eine Spezialstudie wert. Auch über eine Sammlung dieser Rezensionen könnte nachgedacht werden. – Daß Schleiermacher über eine Umbaumaßnahme in einen ärgerlichen Briefwechsel mit dem Armendirektorium geraten ist, welcher sogar zu einem behördlichen Verweis führte, wird zurecht als Fund erläutert, der die berufliche Wirklichkeit eines kleinen, abhängigen preußischen Predigers deutlicher machen kann als die private Korrespondenz.

Der Briefaustausch mit Dorothea Veit, August Wilhelm und Friedrich Schlegel – zum ersten Mal vollständig und ungekürzt publiziert – steht natürlich auch bei diesem Band im Mittelpunkt des Interesses. Aus dieser Zeit sind, auch dies zum ersten Mal, Briefe Schleiermachers an Fr. Schlegel überliefert. Der Leser verfolgt die Sammlung und den Druck des letzten Bandes der "Athenaeums" mit, den Schleiermacher besorgen muß, da die Vertreter der neuen "Schule" sich in Jena versammelt haben und der Berliner Theologe sie quasi von außen literarisch zusammenbinden muß. Gleichzeitig ist dies das Jahr des Erscheinens der Lucinde-Schrift, die nun wiederum Fr.Schlegel in Jena betreut, während die zu Anfang des Jahres herausgekommenen "Monologen" erste Echos provozieren. Das Thema "Plato" wird besonders für Schleiermacher zentral, der Schlegel regelrecht bedrängt: "Plato und Lucinde! Lucinde und Plato! ist die Losung." (Brief 953,39f) Dichterische Versuche kündigen sich an (Brief 858; 997). Und schließlich taucht hier zum ersten Mal der Plan einer "Kritik der Moral" als selbständigem Werk auf, also der "Grundlinien einer Kritik der bisherigen Sittenlehre" (1803). Ein konzeptionell wichtiges Jahr!

Die Briefe sind wie gewohnt eingehend, ja fast überreich kommentiert (wobei leider die Unsitte beibehalten ist, auch seltene Namen fast stets nur im Register zu erklären und so den Leser zum Blättern zu zwingen). Arndt und Virmond haben vielfach kleine Meisterstücke der Findigkeit und Kombinationskunst vollbracht, etwa wenn sie eine Anspielung über das Druckrecht in Dänemark aufklären (Brief 858), Falksche "Gassenlieder" gegen Kantische Philosophen auftreiben (Brief 870), eine Idylle aus A.W.Schlegels "Gedichten" (1800) auf Fr. Schlegel zurückführen (Brief 882) – dieser vollständig überzeugende Nachweis (vgl. noch Brief 903) sollte auch anderwärts angezeigt werden, damit er nicht nur in einer Anmerkung versteckt bleibt –, Brinckmanns Verhältnis zu Fr.H.Jacobi erläutern (Brief 905), eine namenlose Gedichtzeile auf Matthias Claudius zurückführen (Brief 914,204, ohne Quellenangabe) und vieles andere mehr. Sogar die Weimarer Ausgabe der Werke Goethes wird verbessert (Brief 977 S.318)! Besonders ausführlich sind die Briefe A.W.Schlegels zum Projekt der "Jahrbücher der Kunst und Wissenschaft" kommentiert, auch der Briefwechsel mit Fr.Schlegel zur Platon-Übersetzung (mit Abdruck des Schlegelschen Schemas zur Periodisierung der Werke Platos), bei der wissenschaftsgeschichtlichen Wichtigkeit der beiden Pläne durchaus mit Recht. Zu Dorothea Veits Bericht über den romantischen Physiker Johann Wilhelm Ritter ("Er ist einer Ihrer größten Liebhaber und Leser"; "er ist durchdrungen von Ihnen, und liebt Sie wahrhaft" Brief 935,18f.22) kann ich ergänzen, daß Schleiermachers "Vertraute Briefe" aus Ritters Nachlaß in der Bayerischen Staatsbibliothek München erhalten sind, mit der handschriftlichen Bemerkung "Von F.S." auf dem linken Deckblatt (was wohl angeben soll, daß Ritter das Buch von Friedrich Schlegel bekommen hat). Im Brief Dorothea Veits vom 31.10.1800 ist das "höchst rührende Gedicht" auf Auguste Böhmer, das Friedrich Schlegel mit einem verwelkten Veilchenkranz seiner Gefährtin zum Geburtstag schenkt (Brief 972,30f), ganz gewiß das Gedicht "Der welke Kranz" (F.Schlegel: *Werke*, Bd.5, S.160f, vgl. S.LXXXIII). Schon Dilthey hatte das behauptet (*Briefe* 3, S.240 Anm.), was aber die Hg. zu bezweifeln scheinen, wenn sie schreiben:"[D]as Gedicht läßt sich nicht identifizieren" (S.311, vgl. 319). Dieser Zweifel ist angesichts von Dorotheas Selbstzeugnis in ihrem Brief an Schleiermacher vom 25.Sept.1801 unnötig (*Briefe von Dorothea Schlegel an Friedrich Schleiermacher*. Mitteilungen aus dem Litteraturarchive in Berlin N.F.7, Berlin 1913, hier S.112).

Übrigens wurde die "Hebräische merkwürdigkeit", die Dorothea H.E.G.Paulus zu Weihnachten schenken will (Brief 978,31) und die zu finden Schleiermacher sich nicht getraut (Brief 991,30-33), das Buch "Sohar" (vgl. *Dorothea v.Schlegel geb. Mendelssohn und deren Söhne Johannes und Philipp*

Veit. Briefwechsel im Auftrage der Familie Veit, hg. von J.M.Raich. Briefwechsel Bd.1, Mainz: Kirchheim 1881, S.107f).
Ein Rätsel ist der Begriff "Judengott", den Schleiermacher in dem Brief
vom 10.Juli 1800 an Fr. Schlegel gebraucht im Zusammenhang einer ge-
planten, aber dann nicht durchgeführten Reise des Freundes mit Dorothea
Veit nach Dresden zur Schwester Schlegels. Tieck, der bis Ende Juni 1800 in
Jena mit den Schlegels und Schelling in einer "Kommune" (H.Timm)
gewohnt hatte, nun wieder in Berlin weilt und bald nach Weißenfels zu
Hardenberg reisen will, wird folgendermaßen referiert:"Du habest nemlich
Hardenbergen gar nicht wegen des Judengottes wirklich geschrieben und es
würde diesem eine Kleinigkeit gewesen sein es auszuwirken." (Brief 910,86-
88) Was heißt das? Die Herausgeber deuten in einer Anmerkung auf eine
Geldgabe oder einen Paß. Dafür ist der Begriff "Judengott" nach den ein-
schlägigen Lexika aber nicht gebräuchlich. Gleichzeitig ist es gänzlich aus-
geschlossen, daß Schleiermacher im Zusammenhang mit Dorothea Veit
einen antisemitischen Topos (Geld bzw. Mammon als "Gott" der Juden) –
wenn auch nur ironisch – gebraucht haben kann. Und was ("es" Neutrum!)
sollte Novalis da "auswirken"? Grimms *Deutsches Wörterbuch* (Band 1,
Leipzig 1854, S.1019) schlägt für "auswirken" die Bedeutung (a) "ausrichten,
erlangen, bewirken" (lat. conficere, perficere) vor, aber auch – in juris-
tischem Zusammenhang – (b) "entledigen" (exsolvere). Sollte Novalis das
Geld für die Reise beschaffen? (Bedeutung a) Und was hätte das mit dem
Judesein Dorotheas zu tun? Daß Juden in Sachsen einen "Leibzoll" (dies
der Fachausdruck) zu bezahlen hatten, ist bekannt – schon Dorotheas Vater
Moses Mendelssohn wurde eine Generation früher (1776) in Dresden "wie
ein polnischer Ochse" mit zwanzig Groschen verzollt (vgl. Moses
Mendelssohn *Selbstzeugnisse. Ein Plädoyer für Gewissensfreiheit und Toleranz*,
hg. v. Martin Pfeideler, Tübingen/Basel: Erdmann 1979, S.97-100), was
natürlich in der Familie bekannt war. Das läßt die Vermutung aufkommen,
daß an der fraglichen Stelle "Judenzoll" zu lesen sein könnte – sei es, daß
Schleiermacher sich verschrieben hat, oder sei es, daß die Herausgeber,
wenig wahrscheinlich, sich verlesen haben. Dieser Begriff ist als Rechts-
terminus – wie auch "Judenleibzoll" – vielfach belegt (*Deutsches Rechts-
wörterbuch. Wörterbuch der älteren deutschen Rechtssprache*. Band 6. Bearb.v.
Hans Blesken [u.a.]. Weimar: Böhlaus Nachf. 1961-1972, S.579.554). Dann
wäre der Zusammenhang möglicherweise der, daß Novalis als sächsischer
Salinen-Assessor, der sich um die Stelle eines Amtshauptmanns beworben
hat und dafür auch in absehbarer Zeit nach Dresden muß, die Schande eines
Leibzolls für Dorothea hätte abwenden sollen (Bedeutung b) und das auch
können. Wie die historischen und rechtlichen Verhältnisse für Juden in

Sachsen um 1800 waren – von einer rätselhaften "Abgabe" ist die Rede (Brief 861,60) und von der Möglichkeit, daß Hardenberg einen "neuen Paß" für Dorothea verschaffen könne (Brief 904,72) – müßte noch geklärt werden. Aber selbst bei der konjizierten Lesung bleibt das "es" weiterhin grammatisch ungeklärt. Wir stoßen hier wohl an die Grenze einer Privatsprache unter den Frühromantikern.

Die Herausgeber setzen in höchstem Maß gebildete Benutzer voraus, die Französisch (S.5), Englisch (S.207) und viel Griechisch (S.21, 192, 230, 233, 236, 350) können müssen. Hier hätte doch gelegentlich eine Übersetzung helfen sollen. Ein dummer Rezensent weiß trotz Fremdwörterbuch nicht, was "caviren" (S.156), fast auch nicht, was "Deterioration" (S.226) meint. Auch der Fremdwörtergebrauch ist geschichtlichem Wandel unterworfen; was einmal geläufig war, steht heute nicht einmal mehr in den gängigen Lexika und muß folglich erklärt werden!

Im Unterschied zu den Erstdrucken ist die Textpräsentation diplomatisch, d.h. die gelegentlich recht kühne Rechtschrift und Grammatik in den Briefen D.Veits ist bewahrt geblieben, auch natürlich Schleiermachers bewußte Orthographie. Auffällig viele Briefe haben keine Unterschrift; bei Fr. Schlegel fehlen sie fast stets, bei D.Veit oft, aber auch bei A.W.Schlegel, sogar bei Schleiermacher. Wenn dann auch noch der letzte Satz keinen Schlußpunkt hat, könnte man ein Fragment annehmen (vgl. Brief 896; 921). Um diesen Verdacht auszuschließen, schlage ich vor, unter der Rubrik *Überlieferung* die Bemerkung "ohne Unterschrift" aufzunehmen. Dort würde auch der Briefumschlag mit Adressenangabe erwähnt werden müssen, was aber bisher sichtlich noch nicht nötig war. Fehlende Punkte sollten stets durch *[.]* ergänzt werden (vgl. etwa bei Schleiermacher Brief 858,13).

Der Nachweis des Archivs, in dem das Original aufbewahrt liegt, regt mehrfach zu Überlegungen über die Überlieferungswege an. Es überrascht, daß die Briefe Schleiermachers an Fr. Schlegel im Akademie-Archiv Berlin-Mitte, also im Schleiermacher-Nachlaß, gesammelt erhalten sind. Wann sie dorthin kamen (und warum sie glücklicherweise erhalten sind, denn Dorothea Schlegel hat als Witwe den Briefnachlaß auf Wunsch ihres Mannes dezimiert, vgl. ihren Brief an Varnhagen von Ense aus dem Jahr 1833 [Heinrich Finke: *Briefe an Friedrich Schlegel*, Köln 1917, S.6f] und an A.W.Schlegel vom 18.März 1829 [*Dichter und Frauen. Abhandlungen und Mittheilungen von Ludwig Geiger*, Neue Sammlung, Berlin 1899, S.147]), wird nicht erklärt. Da der Brief A.W.Schlegels vom 27.Juli 1800 (Brief 897) als einziger nicht im Schleiermacher-Nachlaß, sondern im Schlegel-Nachlaß in Dresden erhalten ist, ist er möglicherweise nie in die Hand des Empfängers geraten, sondern in den Briefmassen des fleißigen älteren

Schlegel versunken geblieben. Es gibt auch kein direktes Echo Schleiermachers.

Der Druck ist, wie gewohnt, sehr sorgfältig. An Druckfehlern sind mir
aufgefallen: S.LVIII Anm. ("Voraussetzung"), LXI Anm. ("Einführungen"),
S.70,34 ("geworden"). Im Register der Namen sind beim Geburtsjahr Bern-
hardis zwei Zahlen vertauscht (recte: 1769) – so auch schon in KGA V/3.
Die Literaturangabe zu Ernst Behler (S.LXXII Anm.) kann im Literaturverzeichnis nicht verifiziert werden. Dort fehlt auch die bibliographische
Aufnahme des Romans von Madame de Genlis (S.161).

Der Band enthält zum Entzücken des Lesers und zur Übung seiner
Entzifferungskünste elf Faksimilia, davon sind neun Briefe und eine
Karikatur "Jahrmarkt zu Plundersweile[r]n, oder die große Buchhaendler-
Messe" aus dem "Taschenbuch für Freunde des Scherzes und der Satire" von
1800 mit einer Darstellung des kleinen verwachsenen Schleiermacher am
Arm der juno-haften Henriette Herz. (Diese Karikatur ist auch in KGA I/12
wiedergegeben.) Abkürzungs-, Literaturverzeichnis, Register der Namen und
Werke beschließen den Band. Als Ergänzungen zu V/3 enthält ein Anhang
neu entdeckte bzw. neu zugeschriebene Briefe: an Spener, an König Friedrich Wilhelm III., vom Reformierten Kirchendirektorium (Sack). Leider sind
deren Informationen nicht in die Register eingegangen.

Insgesamt wird man wie zu Band V/3 sagen können, daß mit dieser
Edition ein weiterer Meilenstein der Schleiermacher- wie Romantik-
Forschung gesetzt ist. Die internationale Forschergemeinschaft wartet auf
den Band des Jahres 1801!

Hermann Patsch
München

■ Sergio Sorrentino, *Filosofia ed esperienza religiosa*, Milano, Edizioni Guerini Studio, 1993, 227 p. ISBN 88-7802-382-5.

The title refers to the relation between philosophy and religious experience. The author offers arguments concerning the conditions of possibility of that experience and the ways in which different philosophers (like Kant, Schleiermacher, Auguste Sabatier) and theologians (like Ferdinand Christian Baur, Karl Barth, Rudolf Bultmann) have dealt with this problem. The book is divided into seven chapters, which will be briefly summarized.

The work opens with Kant, whose criticism of speculative theology together with his philosophy of religion are taken into consideration as well as his view on the relation between philosophy and religion. Among the conclusions reached by the author there are: the assessment of the transcendental structure of historico-concrete religion; the statement that not only is Kant's vision of religion placed within a secularized context, in which the autonomy of both nature and the moral world is asserted, but it is itself a factor of secularization. Religion, for Kant, no longer constitutes a part of knowledge but is rather a matter of morality. Schleiermacher's views are presented in the next two chapters. The first of these briefly examines his philosophy, which is taken to run along the lines of a transcendental philosophy. This survey helps us understand his approach to religion. Religious experience qualifies the individual. Philosophy reflects on this experience (i.e., faith) and sees in it a factor (among others) of ethical productivity; at the same time it tries to determine the relationship between faith and the whole of human experience. The following chapter looks into the concept of history and temporality in both Schleiermacher and Ferdinand Christian Baur. Historical time in Baur is internal time of consciousness, the linear time of diachronical succession in the opposition of ideal contents; history thus represents progress from one ideal quality to an opposite one. In history what comes after is superior to that which precedes. In the opposite direction, Schleiermacher conceives historical time in relation to the ethical process, in which the possibility of regression is always present. As such, it is not linear but sways between two poles: i.e., ethically positive and negative poles.

The fourth chapter deals with the "essence of Christianity" in Auguste Sabatier, a French philosopher and theologian whose analysis has drawn sparse attention; still, he studied the present topic as well. His interpretation is then compared to that of Harnack, Troeltsch and Loisy. The fifth chapter is a study on the view of history and historicity in Rudolf Bultmann. The author wishes to show how historicity in Bultmann is attained by leveling the historical element deprived of its cosmic and historifying components. Historicity is concentrated all in the event (*Geschehen*) of existential or eschatological decision. The author sees the development of this concept in Bultmann's reflections, specifically concerning three issues: whether a result of historical research can constitute the foundation of faith; what the relation is between faith and the story of Jesus; and how the relation between historicity and faith is set up. In brief, we see that for Bultmann historical temporality pertaining to human events is characterized by a lack of meaning (i.e., contingency). Thus, for him only temporality regarding faith reveals meaning and value.

The sixth chapter centers on Karl Barth, whose interpretation of "liberal theology" is criticized as being in no way justified from a historical point of view. This leads Barth to a biased, somewhat unilateral reading of the history of theology. According to the author, liberal theology that covers the post-Enlightenment period up to Barth faces a basic question concerning human beings as subject to an antinomy, i.e., the antinomy between non-sense and sense production. The author points out how liberal theology seems to be present in Barth too. Against this background three aspects emerge: the inanity of human efforts in the fields of knowledge and ethics; historicity reduced to the instant (i.e., the present time); the strictly theological origin of the act of sense giving. There is then the comparison of Barth's and Schleiermacher's theological approach; Barth's criticism is seen to be misleading with regard to Schleiermacher's thought. The author then examines several questions arising from Barth's approach and finally discusses the task of a "theological reason" (i.e., of an *intellectus fidei*).

In the concluding chapter "critical reason" faces the problem of God. Can a relationship be established between the God of faith and the God of philosophers, and if so, what kind? The author maintains that the God of philosophers is a reality that eludes the grasp of reason, i.e., the human effort to know God. Instead, "critical reason" seeks the formal and transcendental conditions of the authentic possibility of this elusion. These conditions are: the relation human being-God founded on an absolute dependence (it is the condition of an "existential otherness"); the partnership of God as an eluding, yet self-revealing reality or personal existence (this is the condition of a "dialogical otherness"); and the reality of God as providing a total, ultimate meaning (the condition of an "eschatological otherness"). The relationship thus established is that between the "figures of God" (symbols, which may be many and have to be elaborated by critical reason) and the "face of God" (which is one and is indeed revealed by God). The symbols themselves can draw us to God, and so we speak of transparent symbols. Or they turn us away from God, in which case we speak of opaque symbols. All this leads the author to conclude that the task of critical reason consists in an encounter, so to say, with the figures of humankind's religious experience. This is possible, however, even when the "face of God" is revealed, for example, to Abraham. In this way, then, the approach to religion does not assume a negative or destructive aspect. Rather, reason and religion are called to mutual understanding.

I would conclude with a few observations regarding the main thesis of the book. The comparison of two different patterns of time and history in Baur and Schleiermacher is very interesting when one considers the influence these thinkers have had on the development of theology. The brief study on Sabatier can offer a starting point for those wishing to consider an interpretation of Christianity long neglected by scholars. The chapter relating to Barth and liberal theology might arouse controversy among Barthian scholars who disagree with the author's approach. All the same, the reader will notice how the topic on religious experience gradually widens to include other problems such as those of time, history and sense-making. One might also perceive the criticism underlying Bultmann's and Barth's conceptions regarding human existence and history. The underlying argument is that if life is bound to lack any meaning outside the realm of faith, human beings are left with nothing but a decision, a leap toward faith itself. Critical reason seems rather to provide us with a bridge, open to religious experience based on what may be called the "possibility of elusion," which I spoke of above. Reason, far from treating religion as a corpse to dissect, helps it to achieve the dignity and autonomy that can make it a powerful factor of civilization and humanity and thus of history. Not faith versus history but faith in connection with historical human beings endowed with conditions allowing religious experience. In the course of history humans always have elaborated many "figures" of the only God. Thus, another task of critical reason that the author stresses is this: to evaluate the symbols created in different eras and cultures. In this way, it may form the basis for communication among the various faiths. In my opinion this result is less obvious than it may seem, given the situation in which rationality appears to be an optional item and each clan, religion or ethnic group tries to enforce its own "figure of God" on others. The question does arise, however, as to whether critical reason is the last bulwark against fundamentalism.

Luigi Di Giovanni
University of Rome

■ Karl August Varnhagen von Ense. *Werke* in fünf Bänden. Herausgegeben von Konrad Feilchenfeldt. Band 4: *Biographien, Aufsätze, Skizzen, Fragmente.* Hg.v. K.Feilchenfeldt und Ursula Wiedenmann (Bibliothek deutscher Klassiker 56). Deutscher Klassiker Verlag Frankfurt am Main 1990, 1190 S., ISBN 3-618-61580-9; Band 5: *Tageblätter.* Hg.v. K.Feilchenfeldt (Bibliothek deutscher Klassiker 112). Deutscher Klassiker Verlag Frankfurt am Main 1994, 1317 S., ISBN 3-618-61590-6.

Varnhagen lesen – das ist die Einladung, die von diesen beiden Bänden ausgeht. Bezogen sich die *Denkwürdigkeiten des eignen Lebens* (*Werke* Bd.1-3, siehe *New Athenaeum/Neues Athenaeum* II, 1991, 178-181) auf die Biographie des Autors (1785-1858) und spiegelten auf höchst informative Art die preußisch-deutsche Welt in ganz persönlicher Weise bis 1834, also die Zeitgrenze, die durch den Tod Goethes, Hegels und Schleiermachers gekennzeichnet werden kann, so bieten die beiden abschließenden Bände der *Werke* eine neue, nicht weniger wichtige Perspektive: Band 4 stellt den Schriftsteller und Historiker Varnhagen vor, Band 5 den akribischen Beobachter des Tagesgeschehens, der sein Tagebuch bis zum Morgen seines Todestages ungeschminkt und gezielt für die Nachwelt führt. Beide Aspekte waren nur noch Spezialisten geläufig, eine Wiederentdeckung war an der Zeit.

Der Band *Biographien, Aufsätze, Skizzen, Fragmente* enthält acht Biographien, zwölf Porträts, 16 Aufsätze, drei Flugschriften, 16 Korrespondenz-Nachrichten, fünf Denkschriften sowie – unter dem sehr offenen Titel "Skizzen und Fragmente" – eine Fülle unterschiedlicher kürzerer Texte zwischen einem Satz und mehreren Druckseiten. Der Kommentarteil nimmt, samt Personenregister, ein gutes Drittel des Bandes ein; wie in den *Denkwürdigkeiten* folgt der Textkommentar dem Schema Textüberlieferung (meist wird der Erstdruck wiedergegeben, sonst die dritte Auflage der *Vermischten Schriften* von 1875/76) – Entstehung – Selbstaussagen des Autors zum Werk – Wirkung – Stellenkommentar. Diese Anordnung ist leserfreundlich, vielleicht von der Tatsache abgesehen, daß Namen grundsätzlich nur im Personenregister erklärt werden. Bei der Kommentierung kann man sich auf die Kompetenz der Herausgeber verlassen, die eine Unmenge von Bezügen und Anspielungen aufschlüsseln und den Leser zum Zeitgenossen der Texte zu machen sich bemühen. Je nach Bedürfnis wird man sich manchmal noch mehr ins einzelne gehende Kommentierung wünschen oder manche Erklärung für überflüssig halten – hier kann ein Editor es nicht allen Benutzern rechtmachen. Grundsätzlich wird man sagen müssen, daß Texte wie die Varnhagens ohne möglichst eingehenden Kommentar dem heutigen Leser nur halb verständlich bleiben würden, daß also Herausgeber (und Verlag!) für die Bereitstellung eines solchen ungewöhnlichen Erläuterungsumfangs uneingeschränktes Lob verdienen.

Die Auswahl – leider fehlen Literaturkritiken – zeigt die Vielseitigkeit Varnhagens, der sich als Chronist seiner Zeit sah und ein ungeheures Material ansammelte, das – seit dem Krieg bekanntlich in Krakau liegend – in seiner Masse bis heute nur teilweise ausgewertet ist. Die Herausgeber haben die Krakauer Materialien beigezogen, ohne allerdings den Ehrgeiz zu haben, aus dem Nachlaß zu edieren. Gern hätte der Benutzer neben dem Verzeichnis der Hilfsmittel eine Varnhagen-Bibliographie erhalten, die ja im Laufe der Arbeitsjahre entstanden sein muß und ein Desiderat darstellt.

Varnhagen ist ein großartiger Stilist gerade in seinen historischen Biographien und Porträts. Dabei arbeitet er auch bei den zeitgenössischen Themen durchaus mit den Mitteln des Historikers, d.h. er bezieht sich keineswegs nur auf eigene Erfahrungen und Aufzeichnungen, die er subjektiv bearbeitet, sondern er zieht Quellen aller Art bei, wie etwa die inzwischen gedruckten Briefwechsel, z.B. den zwischen Goethe und Schiller, Memoiren, ihm zugängliche persönliche Notizen und Briefe, Zeitungsberichte und anderes. Das gibt diesen Arbeiten, über das historistische Interesse hinaus, eine bleibende Bedeutung. Man mag das etwa an den Arbeiten über den Prinzen Louis Ferdinand von Preußen, Friedrich von Gentz, Wilhelm von Humboldt, Karoline von Fouqué, Ludwig Robert, Alexander von der Marwitz, Adam Müller, Clemens Brentano und Ludwig Tieck sehen. Hier spielt als Quellengrund auch immer der Nachlaß seiner Frau Rahel eine wichtige Rolle. Bei aller Kenntnis intimer Verhältnisse bleibt der Autor aber stets dezent; er denunziert nie, vor allem nicht bei der Bezugnahme auf noch lebende Personen. So deutet er die Liebe Marwitzens zu Henriette Schleiermacher ohne Namensgebung nur an (S.329f – im Kommentar nicht angegeben). Diese lebte bei Erscheinen des Aufsatzes (1836) ja noch! Auf "Mad. Schleiermacher" sollte, wie Varnhagen auch für Rahels Nachlaß bestimmte, ebenso wie auf die "Hofräthin Herz" zu Lebzeiten Rücksicht genommen werden (vgl. Ursula Isselstein: *Studien zu Rahel Levin Varnhagen.* Torino: Stampatori 1993, S.204). Das gilt auch für die nicht genannte "Geliebte" des Prinzen Louis Ferdinand (S.107), nämlich Pauline Wiesel, die Freundin Rahels (die an der gleichen Stelle als "die Kleine" erwähnt, im Kommentar und im Register aber nicht entschlüsselt wird). Den Essay über W. von Humboldt von 1838 führt Varnhagen ganz auf Rahels Einsicht und Urteil zurück, ohne zu verraten, daß diese es war, die Humboldt in ihren Briefen "Mephistopheles" nannte (S.191). Auch für diese feinsinnige Darstellung gilt, daß zu Lebzeiten des Bruders Alexander von Humboldt manches nur für Eingeweihte angedeutet werden konnte (S.852) – zu denen sich dank des Kommentars nun auch der moderne Leser zählen darf. Für das rücksichtsvolle Porträt Achim von Arnims erntete der Verfasser von Bettine nur Hohn (S.882). Offener konnte er sich in einem – zu Lebzeiten wohl unveröffentlichten – Porträt Caroline von Fouqués äußern. Das gilt vor allem von seiner Charakteristik Brentanos (etwa 1838), wo er die Grenze zum Klatsch durchaus überschritt – freilich in einem zurückgehaltenen Text, den erst seine Nichte Ludmilla von Assing veröffentlichte. Leider sehr kurz ist der Nachruf auf Ludwig Tieck, in dem Varnhagen diesen als Repräsentanten einer nun, nach 1853, abgeschlossenen Epoche bezeichnete: "Durch die Bekanntschaft mit den Brüdern Schlegel und Friedrich von Hardenberg nahm seine Poesie einen höheren Schwung, und er wurde mit ihnen Stifter der sogenannten romantischen Schule, die mit schweren Kämpfen unter Verachtung und Hohn, sich zur glänzenden Herrschaft in fast ganz Europa emporarbeitete, und deren Erlöschen er allein von den Stiftern noch erlebte!" (S.363) Hier nimmt Varnhagen Rudolf Hayms "Die romantische Schule" von 1870 mit historischem Blick vorweg.

Die Sammlung der "Aufsätze" beginnt mit einem frühen Essay von 1804 "Über den literarischen Geist des Zeitalters", der seit seinem Erscheinen hier zum ersten Mal wiedergedruckt ist. Varnhagen – der mit dem Titel übrigens August Wilhelm Schlegels seinerzeit (1802) "ein paarmal" gehörte Berliner Vorlesungen (vgl. *Denkwürdigkeiten* I, S.222) nachahmt, die unter dem Titel "Ueber Literatur, Kunst und Geist des Zeitalters" 1803 in Band II, Heft 1 der von Friedrich Schlegel herausgegebenen Zeitschrift "Europa" veröffentlicht wurden – erweist sich hier als Anhänger der Frühromantik, der klar und unmißverständlich die Bedeutung der beiden Schlegels verkündet. Er spricht bereits von einer "Schlegelschen Schule" (S.369) und möchte das Schimpfwort "Schlegelianer" zum Ehrennamen machen. Die folgenden überwiegend politischen Aufsätze stammen aus der Zeit der Befreiungskriege und der Neuordnung Europas in den Jahren danach. Eine hübsche, kulturgeschichtlich interessante Ausnahme von dieser Thematik macht der besonders sorgfältig kommentierte Beitrag "Vom Ausschneiden" über die Papierschneidekunst, in der Varnhagen ein Meister war (wie der Abdruck einer Silhouette S.832 dem Leser sehr schön beweist). Wichtige zeitgenössische Urteile zur Rezeption des Saint-Simonismus in Deutschland stellen die Aufsätze "Über den Saint-Simonismus" und "Im Sinne der Wanderer" von 1832 dar, wobei in dem zweiten Goethe in die Nähe von Saint-Simon gerückt wird. (Die Diskussion ging noch weiter, wie man den bei Werner Greiling abgedruckten Texten entnehmen kann: Karl August Varnhagen von Ense: *Kommentare zum Zeitgeschehen. Publizistik – Briefe – Dokumente 1813-1858*, Leipzig: Reclam 1984, S.89-98).

Die unter dem Titel "Flugschriften" versammelten Schriften Varnhagens, sämtlich anonym, die beiden ersten seit dem Erscheinen zum ersten Mal wieder gedruckt, zeigen den Verfasser in einer anderen publizistischen Gattung, und zwar – wie das Echo zeigt – durchaus Aufsehen erregend. Varnhagen erklärt 1814 einen Bund freier Hansestädte als Kern eines demokratischen Deutschlands und äußert eine "Deutsche Ansicht der Vereinigung Sachsens mit Preußen", in der er die Sachsen in ein durch den Geist der Liberalität geprägtes neues Preußen zu "gemeinsamer Deutschheit" (S.529) einlädt. Der Leser reibt sich die Augen und fragt sich, ob der Verfasser geträumt oder ironisch übertrieben hat. Aber hier liegt eine gleich nach seinem Eintritt in preußische Staatsdienste in Wien von Hardenberg und Stein geforderte Auftragsarbeit vor, mit der er seine Anstellung rechtfertigen mußte (vgl. *Denkwürdigkeiten* II, S.579f), und vielleicht hat Hardenberg vor dem Neuling taktisch klug so liberal geredet. Der Wiener Kongreß entschied anders, und wenn Varnhagen wenige Wochen nach dem Druck seine eigene Schrift – gleichfalls anonym – in einer Rezension als sophistisch und aus ministerieller Schule stammend zerreißt und preußisch mit jakobinisch gleichsetzt (S.1001f), so ist das weniger befremdlich als vielmehr ein Hinweis darauf, daß der neue Diplomat erkannt hatte, welches Spiel man mit seiner schmeichelhaft gerühmten Feder getrieben hat. Das Preußen, das er den Sachsen versprochen hatte, gab es nicht und wird es nicht geben. Man kann dieses Wissen zwischen den Zeilen aus Varnhagens Briefen an Hardenberg aus diesen Tagen lesen (bei Greiling S.10-12). Die gleiche Hoffnung und Skepsis, die kritische Liebe zu Preußen beweist sich noch eine Generation später, wenn Varnhagen sich mit einem "Schlichte(n) Vortrag an die Deutschen über die Aufgabe des Tages" in die Debatten von 1848 einmischt und bei aller vorsichtigen Zurückhaltung Deutschlands Einheit auf Preußen und auf der Führerschaft des preußischen Königs beruhen sieht, sofern dieser Staat "fortan einer der freiesten Staaten in Deutschland sein wird" (S.539). Sein wird, keineswegs schon ist! Das protestantisch-romantische Programm – auch Schleiermacher sah es so ähnlich – verrät sich in der abschließenden Berufung auf den "prophetischen Dichter" (S.541) Novalis mit dessen Weissagung einer Vereinigung von Monarchie und Republik von 1798. Die Schrift entsprang – wie Varnhagen an den Verleger Reimer schrieb – "einer Art Gewissensdrang", was ja immer Hinweis auf einen längeren inneren Prozeß ist (*Aus dem Archiv des Verlages Walter de Gruyter. Briefe Urkunden Dokumente.* Bearbeitet von Doris Fouquet-Plümacher und Michael Wolter. Berlin/New York: de Gruyter 1980, S.71).

Unter dem Titel "Korrespondenz-Nachrichten" sind journalistische Ar-
beiten Varnhagens gesammelt, frech formulierte des jungen Autors über
Berlin, kritische aus der Zeit als Offizier und Diplomat, schließlich wieder
über Berlin und seine Schriftsteller und Schriftstellerinnen – Bettina von
Arnim wird 1848 "ewig junge Genialität" bescheinigt (S.598) – aus der
Spätzeit. In der gleichen temporalen Reihenfolge sind "Skizzen und Fragmente" gesammelt. Hier sind zwei glänzende – erst 1930 veröffentlichte –
Seiten über "Die Brüder Schlegel" zu nennen, in denen die gesamte Schule
der Frühromantik bis zu ihrer Spaltung skizziert ist. Die Brüder werden als
"echte Revolutionsmänner" gekennzeichnet, die mit denen, die sich ihnen
anschlossen, eine wahre Umwälzung bewirkt hätten. "Wer es nicht erlebt
hat, wird sich kaum vorstellen können, welche Gärung damals in Berlin war,
wie alle Begriffe, Ansichten und Urteile schwankten." (S.612f) Fragmente
über Bonaparte, W. von Humboldt, Metternich, Talleyrand sind ebenso von
historischem Interesse wie ein Essay über "Voß und Stolberg". Varnhagen
stimmt in dieser Darstellung Voß und seiner Schrift *"Wie ward Friz Stolberg
ein Unfreier?"* (1819) von Herzen zu. Ob dieser Beitrag zu Varnhagens
Lebzeiten gedruckt wurde, muß offenbleiben. (Der im Kommentar S.1077
aus einem Brief zitierte "Abdruck" ist sichtlich die Schrift von Voß selbst. In
dem gleichen Brief wird eine hübsche Anekdote über einen Disput Rahels
mit Schleiermacher erzählt. Schleiermacher – der Stolbergs Gegenschrift
besaß, s. Günter Meckenstock: *Schleiermachers Bibliothek.* Schleiermacher-
Archiv Bd. 10, Berlin/New York: de Gruyter 1993, S.331 – hatte Voß wohl
den Vorwurf des Geklatsches gemacht, worauf Rahel replizierte: "[...] wenn
solche Mittheilungen diesen Namen verdienen, so giebt es keine Geschichts-
forschung mehr, und selbst das jüngste Gericht [...] verliert allen Stoff.") Von
besonderem Interesse ist der leider nur kurze Aufsatz "Schleiermacher und
Friedrich Schlegel" von 1836, in dem Varnhagen mit biographischem
Insiderwissen auf das Leben der ehemaligen Freunde zurückblickt und
Schleiermacher gegen Schlegels spätere Feindschaft verteidigt. Zum ersten
Mal kommt hier in der Öffentlichkeit zur Sprache, daß Schlegel den früheren
Genossen bei der Sammlung seiner Gedichte auch poetisch aus der früh-
romantischen Schule getilgt hatte (vgl. dazu auch H.Patsch: *Die Sphinx der
Religion. Friedrich Schlegels Sonett 'Die Reden über die Religion'.* In:
Festschrift Tice – erscheint hoffentlich 1996). "Friedrich Schlegel [...] war in
Hinsicht des Charakters seines alten Freundes im größten Irrtum, und
tadelte an ihm gerade das, was er im eignen Gemüt am reichsten finden
konnte!" (S.673) – nämlich Haß und Verfolgungssucht. Leider bleibt Varnhagen aber im Biographischen und Anekdotischen stecken, ohne die
denkerische Entwicklung er beiden Männer zu vergleichen. (Im Stellen-

kommentar auf S.1084 – wiederholt S.1119 – ist bedauerlicherweise ein Fehler unterlaufen: Schleiermacher ist keineswegs der Autor der anonymen Schrift "Drey Briefe an ein humanes Berliner Freudenmädchen über die Lucinde von Schlegel" von 1800! Der Irrtum rührt daher, daß in dem von den Kommentatoren benutzten Ausstellungskatalog *Friedrich Schleiermacher zum 150. Geburtstag. Handschriften und Drucke.* Bearbeitet von Andreas Arndt und Wolfgang Virmond, Berlin/New York: de Gruyter 1984, S.54f dieses Pamphlet und Schleiermachers gleichfalls anonyme "Vertraute Briefe über Friedrich Schlegels Lucinde" nebeneinander im Titelblatt faksimiliert sind.) Von den weiteren Schriften sei ein Bericht erwähnt, in dem Achim von Arnim als Antisemit erscheint, und eine umfängliche, leider Fragment gebliebene Darstellung des Jahres 1848.

Den Schluß des Bandes bilden "Denkschriften", die sämtlich zu Lebzeiten Varnhagens in den Akten begraben blieben und erst von der Varnhagen-Forschung entdeckt und veröffentlicht wurden. Neben dem Vorschlag zu einem "weimarischen Lexikon" und zur Gründung einer Goethe-Gesellschaft ist besonders wichtig die "Denkschrift über das Junge Deutschland", die der Autor 1836 auf Wunsch Metternichs ausarbeitete. Hier legt Varnhagen ein gutes Wort für die "jungen Talente" ein und bekennt sich dazu, daß das jetzige "alte Deutschland" auch einmal jung und oppositionell gewesen sei: "Wenn ich bedenke, daß ich den Verfasser der Lucinde [Friedrich Schlegel] später mit dem päpstlichen Christusorden geziert gesehen, und Schleiermacher, der diese Lucinde mit philosophischem Ernst angepriesen und im Athenäum die Ehe mit bitterm Hohn angegriffen hat, als Gottesgelehrten und Prediger hier im höchsten Ansehen vor Augen gehabt habe, so kann ich auch für den Verfasser der Wally [Karl Ferdinand Gutzkow] noch jede Geschickswendung für möglich halten, ja noch mehr, ich möchte sie bestimmt voraussagen!" (S.771)

Die Textgestaltung ist makellos. Der Band enthält vier Abbildungen in Schwarzweiß (was bei dem Ölgemälde von Jacob van Ruisdael nicht ganz sachgemäß erscheint). An Kleinigkeiten in der Kommentierung sind mir aufgefallen: Der Abt Montesquieu von S.441 kann nicht der im Register S.1154 genannte Philosoph scin. Die "Denkschrift" Benjamin Constants S.459 kann schwerlich 1779 entstanden sein, da dieser damals erst zwölf Jahre alt war (S.982; hier ist auch als siebenjähriger Reisender Constant mit Varnhagen verwechselt). Der genaue Titel des S.77 erwähnten Buches von August Hermann Niemeyer lautet: *Beobachtungen und Reisen in und außer Deutschland. Nebst Erinnerungen an denkwürdige Lebenserfahrungen und Zeitgenossen in den letzten fünfzig Jahren.* Vieten Bandes Zweite Hälfte.

Beobachtungen auf einer Deportationsreise nach Frankreich im Jahr 1807.
Halle 1826 (zu S.809f). Das nicht nachgewiesene Schleiermacher-Zitat über
die Konvertiten, "daß sie nur in zwei verschiedenen Formen ihre religiöse
Unfähigkeit an den Tag zu legen bestimmt waren" (S.172), stammt aus den
"Anmerkungen zur Nachrede", die Schleiermacher der dritten (und vierten)
Auflage seines Werkes "Ueber die Religion. Reden an die Gebildeten unter
ihren Verächtern" 1821 (bzw. 1831) hinzugefügt hatte (Friedrich Schleiermacher. Kritische Gesamtausgabe I.Abteilung Band 12: *Über die Religion (2.-
)4. Auflage, Monologen (2.-)4. Auflage.* Herausgegeben von Günter Meckenstock, Berlin/New York: de Gruyter 1995, S.321). Ein schönes Beispiel dafür,
wie Varnhagen auch die späteren Auflagen der berühmten Jugendwerke
seines Lehrers gründlich studiert und in sein Gedächtnis aufgenommen
hatte!

Varnhagens "Tageblätter" – der Hg. bevorzugt mit Recht diese vom
Autor (statt "Tagebücher") gebrauchte Bezeichnung – umfassen die Jahre
1819, d.h. seit Varnhagens Abberufung aus Karlsruhe und seiner Kaltstellung
in Berlin, bis 1858 und geben einen eigentümlichen, zugleich subjektiv ge-
brochenen wie um objektive Dokumentation bemühten Spiegel der Epoche.
Der Tagebuchschreiber begründet "das genaue Aufzeichnen einzelner Züge
und Tagesbemerkungen" unter Berufung auf Goethe und erwartet mit
diesem, daß "das Wesentliche der Geschichte" im Geringfügigen der
Gegenwart enthalten sein könne. (S.43: 19.März 1822) Diese Hoffnung hat
ihn fast siebentausend Blätter beschreiben lassen (S.854), von denen seine
Nichte Ludmilla Assing nach seinem Tod etwa 40% hat drucken lassen. Der
Hg. mußte für seine Edition aus insgesamt 19 Bänden auswählen, d.h. er
lieferte – ohne Rückgriff auf den Nachlaß – in jedem Fall nur eine Auswahl
der Auswahl. Diese aber ist durchaus großzügig ausgefallen: den etwa 850
Seiten "Tageblättern" ist ein über 300 Seiten umfassender Stellenkommentar
beigefügt, der überwiegend gleichfalls aus übrigen Tageblättern besteht, so-
daß insgesamt ein Umfang von 1200 Seiten angesetzt werden kann. Die
Dokumentation der einzelnen Jahre ist sehr unterschiedlich; sie steigert sich
– analog zu Assing – in der Menge besonders stark nach 1848 und macht
damit zugleich die verheerende Wirkungsgeschichte der Aufzeichnungen
(S.867-880) verständlich. (Die bei Assing noch vorhandenen Verschlüsselun-
gen der Namen sind unter Rückgriff auf den Register-Band von H.H.
Houben, 1905, aufgelöst.)

Der Inhalt der "Tageblätter" läßt sich natürlich nicht referieren. Der
Leser unterliegt durchaus einem gewissen Sog in seiner Lektüre, kann aber
unmöglich auf alles seine Aufmerksamkeit richten. Die Auswahl der Edition
will sich aus dem Versuch erklären lassen, "ohne Rücksicht auf die liter-

arische Bedeutung der einzelnen Aufzeichnungen deren Vielseitigkeit ebenso wie deren gelegentliche Belanglosigkeit zu dokumentieren" (S.895). So erscheint es sachgemäß, wenn der Benutzer sich die ihn interessierenden Gebiete über das Register der Namen erschließen wird. Das soll an dieser Stelle über Schleiermacher und sein Personenumfeld geschehen.

Sehr eindrücklich bekommt man in den Aufzeichnungen das allgemeine Klima der Verfolgungssucht nach der Ermordung Kotzebues mit. Die Entlassung de Wettes beschäftigt Varnhagen immer wieder, auch die möglichen Konsequenzen für Schleiermacher, der als "Verführer der Jugend" gilt (S.19f: 17.März 1820). Hier kann der Kommentar ergänzt werden: Das Schreiben Schleiermachers im Namen der Fakultät (S.19: 9.März 1820) steht bei Max Lenz: *Zur Entlassung de Wettes*, in: *Philotesia. Paul Kleinert zum LXX.Geburtstag dargebracht* von Adolf Harnack (u.a.), Berlin:Trowitzsch 1907, S.339-388 (wo im übrigen auch Varnhagens "Tageblätter" angeführt werden). Zur "gesetzlosen Gesellschaft" (S.21, 28), deren Mitbegründer Schleiermacher war, vgl. meine Monographie *Alle Menschen sind Künstler* (Schleiermacher-Archiv 2), Berlin/New York:de Gruyter 1986, S.166f. Eine Notiz belegt Schleiermachers Mitgliedschaft in der "spanischen Gesellschaft", der gleichfalls "gefährliche(r) Geist" verbürgt wird (S.78f: 31. Dezember 1823). Man erfährt, daß Schleiermacher bei Prinz August von Preußen zu Mittag aß (S.171: 28.Dezember 1827), also durchaus Hofkontakte pflegte. Die Nachricht vom Tod Friedrich Schlegels soll Adam Müller so erschüttert haben, daß er selbst an einem Nervenschlag verschied (S.190: 26.Januar 1829). Der langjährige Streit um die vom preußischen König Friedrich Wilhelm III. favorisierte neue Liturgie wird als durch Schleiermacher angenommen und damit beendet erklärt (S.197: 12.März 1829). Den Briefen Henriette Schleiermachers an Rahel Varnhagen werden 1833 "bedeutende Lebenszüge" beigemessen (S.229). (Sie sind inzwischen gedruckt worden.) Schleiermachers Tod wird nicht kommentiert.

Einigermaßen sensationell ist die Nachricht, daß Henriette Herz bereits 1836 die Briefe Schleiermachers an sie der Witwe für eine Druckauswahl hat zur Verfügung stellen sollen, sich aber noch ziert (S.240f: 26. Februar 1836). H.Herz hat bekanntlich lediglich eine gekürzte, also zensierte, Abschrift dieses Briefwechsels hergestellt und die Originale vernichtet. Nach dem, was Varnhagen nicht ohne Sarkasmus berichtet, muß man wohl doch mit größeren Eingriffen der Hofrätin rechnen! Als die Briefe Jahrzehnte später gedruckt sind (*Aus Schleiermacher's Leben. In Briefen.* Berlin: Reimer 1858 – also die erste Auflage von Band 1 und 2), ist Varnhagen der vielleicht einzige kompetente und sehr kritische Leser: "[A]lles ist lückenhaft, verstümmelt, das ganze hier gegebne Bild ist ein falsches [...]. Frau Hofrätin Herz erscheint hier schwächlich, empfindsam, urteillos, wie sie es in der Tat war; die für sie schmeichelhaften Äußerungen hat sie doch stehen lassen, ihre Versicherung lautete, grade wegen solcher Äußerungen habe sie die besten Briefe verbrannt, um nicht der Eitelkeit beschuldigt zu werden, – diese Eitelkeit steht nun im hellsten Lichte!" (S.837: 12.August 1858, vgl. S.838f: 17.August 1858) (Weitere kritische Äußerungen aus den *Tagebüchern* Band XIV, Hamburg 1870 anläßlich der Briefausgabe, z.b. zu Schleiermachers "pfäffischer Eitelkeit und Hoffahrt" [S.347], hat der Hg. nicht abgedruckt.) Überhaupt sind die Äußerungen der letzten Lebensjahre Varnhagens zu Schleiermacher von höchstem Wert, da sie aus einer Warte erfolgen, die dem Theologen bei aller lebensgeschichtlichen Kenntnis zurückhaltend bis skeptisch gesinnt ist, also ein anderes Bild gibt, als es die Familie in ihrer Sammlung der Briefe beabsichtigt hat. Das Urteil über den Gaß-Briefwechsel (*Fr.Schleiermacher's Briefwechsel mit J.Chr.Gaß. Mit einer biographischen Vorrede* hg.v. Dr.W.Gaß. Berlin:Reimer 1852) ist von sachkundiger Ablehnung geprägt, mit der – vielleicht doch nur legendarischen – Ergänzung, Schleiermacher habe sich wegen der gescheiterten Liebe zu Eleonore Grunow "tothungern" wollen (S.616: 3.September 1852). (Das hat Varnhagen auch für die Zeit um 1812/1813 behauptet, als Henriette Schleiermacher sich in Alexander von der Marwitz verliebte und die Ehe ernsthaft in Gefahr kam. Vgl. die – sonst nicht gedruckte – Notiz bei: *Auf frischen kleinen abstrakten Wegen. Unbekanntes und Unveröffentlichtes aus Rahels Freundeskreis.* Ausgewählt und erläutert von Friedhelm Kemp. Nachrichten aus dem Kösel-Verlag, München, Dezember 1967, S.7) Die zeitweilig recht schwierigen Eheverhältnisse werden immer wieder beschworen als Beleg dafür, daß die Sammlungen ein insgesamt geschöntes Bild ergäben. Der Abschluß der Lektüre ist um ein abwägendes Urteil bemüht: "Und wie hat Schleiermacher gearbeitet, mit welcher Pflichttreue, mit welcher Unverdrossenheit! In Summa, er bleibt einer der Besten seiner Zeit, und all der Tadel, den ich sonst ausgesprochen, hebt dies nicht auf!" (S.841f: 1.September 1858)

Abschließend bleibt zu sagen, daß die "Tageblätter" natürlich nicht hinreichend gewürdigt sind, wenn sie lediglich nach Schleiermacher abgeklopft werden. Das kann nur in einer Zeitschrift für Schleiermacher-Forschung von Interesse sein. Andere Leser werden andere Bezüge suchen. Die umfänglichen Notizen über das Revolutionsjahr 1848 sind – in Ablehnung wie Zustimmung – schon immer als besondere Quellen angesehen worden. Auch anschließend hat ihr Verfasser kein Blatt vor den Mund genommen, so daß man einen lebendigen Eindruck von Preußen und – auf den zahlreichen

Reisen – von den andren deutschen Staaten erhält. Ein verknüpfendes Band bilden all die Jahre die Würdigungen Goethes und – natürlich – Rahels.
Der Band enthält zu Beginn des Kommentarteils eine erhellende wissenschaftliche Darstellung der Bedeutung Varnhagens als Tagebuch-Schriftsteller, von Druck und Wirkung der Ausgabe, nebst vier Abbildungen und einer Zeittafel. Das umfängliche Personenregister hat verständlicherweise die Fülle der Namen nicht durchweg mit Daten versehen können. Der Spezialist wird hier im Gebrauchsfalle weiterkommen. Der Druck ist vorzüglich und spiegelt so auf schöne Weise die Editionsleistung!

Hermann Patsch
München

IN MEMORIAM

ERNST BEHLER (1928-1997)

I write to celebrate the life of Professor Ernst Behler, who, for many of us, has summed up the best in our calling: absolutely tireless in a deeply felt and rigorously pursued scholarship, devoted and gracious in his teaching, perspicacious and inventive in his administration, committed to his family – always welcoming – always eager to encourage. By way of reflecting on his approach to life, I think it fitting to appeal to Friedrich Schlegel, the thinker who occupied so much of Ernst Behler's time and whose life and thought he made accessible to the world. In an *Athenaeum* aphorism, Schlegel explores the English word "Liberal," which, according to the Oxford English Dictionary, meant at once "pertaining to a free man," "directed to general intellectual enlargement and refinement; not narrowly restricted," and, finally, "free in bestowing; bountiful, generous, open-hearted." For those of us who worked with Prof. Behler, it is easy to see how he could be described in these terms. As always, however, such terms by themselves tend to limit rather than expand our vision. As was his penchant, Schlegel cast this term within a more dynamic meaning.

> "Liberal" means being almost unaware of being free in all directions and from all sides; means living one's whole humanity; means holding sacred whatever acts, is, and develops, according to the measure of one's power; means taking part in all aspects of life and not letting oneself be seduced by limited opinions into a hatred or contempt for life.

In his efforts to wrestle with the intellectual issues of our generation, Ernst Behler practiced this freedom in a way that both employed and called into question disciplinary rigor. While avoiding a slavish dedication to narrow academic concerns, he committed his formidable energies and intellect to scholarly and critical pursuits. This took shape not only in many thousands of pages of meticulous and insightful scholarship but also in the practical outworking of that scholarship in the students who studied with him and in those institutional forms that reflected his desire for a critically informed and dynamic inquiry. Of greatest importance to me personally, was the intellectual work he did that offered a way both to consider a topic closely while still avoiding the seductions of limited opinions and circumscribed methodologies, which, as Schlegel wrote, lead to "a hatred or contempt for life." For me, the core of this work was Behler's celebration of Schlegel's irony – that form of serious play that allows us mortals to speak as well as remain honest and, in so doing, check the drift toward nihilism. Perhaps it is here that I, one student among thousands, am most thankful for his life and work. By remaining free and tolerant, by living his whole humanity and holding sacred the various elements of his life, Ernst Behler made it possible for me to understand and appreciate the wisdom in Schlegel's final written reflection on irony.

Genuine irony is the irony of love. It arises from the feeling of finiteness and of one's own limitations and the apparent contradiction of these feelings with the concept of infinity inherent in all genuine love.

So, in conclusion, Ernst Behler's life and spirit still resonates both in his work – the ideas that he developed, taught, and rethought – and in the memory of his humanity as cherished by his family, friends, and students. His life was a fine wreath of interwoven thought, scholarship, and moral response to his world. I write from only one corner of that bountiful life, touched no doubt by the sum of it, but only able to reflect on few single threads of the whole. Nevertheless, I wish to celebrate a life richly, graciously, and generously lived. For this reason I offer up these few words in tribute.

James Clowes
Director, Comparative History of Ideas
University of Washington